Accolades for th[illegible]ion

"A well-researched, attractive collection of recipes from bed and breakfast inns across our land. A gem of a book."
— ***The Toronto Star***

"Bed-and-breakfasts are truly 'inn.' *Rise & Dine Canada* offers easy and mouthwatering recipes for breakfast, brunch, and tea."
— ***Canadian Press Newswire***

"If cooking and travel are a passion for someone you know, give them *Rise & Dine Canada.*"
— ***The Readers Showcase***

"This delicious quick bread — Trinity Bay Tea Loaf — is featured in the B&B cookbook *Rise & Dine Canada.*"
— ***Chatelaine***

"More than just a cookbook, *Rise & Dine Canada* whets your appetite for Canadian adventure. Marcy Claman has written another sure-to-be best-seller."
— ***The Suburban***

"*Rise & Dine Canada* is a welcome addition to the bed and breakfast cookbook library. Many of the recipes are regional in nature."
— ***Yellow Brick Road, The Bed & Breakfast Newsletter***

"If you enjoy leisurely Sunday breakfast and brunches, *Rise & Dine Canada* is a plethora of new ideas for you."
— ***Good Cheer***

"Recipes include mouth-watering treats like Ginger Scones or Gooseberry-Orange Marmalade."
— ***The Montreal Gazette***

"There's nothing like traveling to eat fine cuisine at a B&B inn. A very delicious travel guide, *Rise & Dine Canada* brings together the best of both worlds."
— ***Book Banter***

"*Rise & Dine Canada* is a collection of recipes from selected Canadian B&Bs, offering varied regional flavors."
— ***Bed & Breakfast***

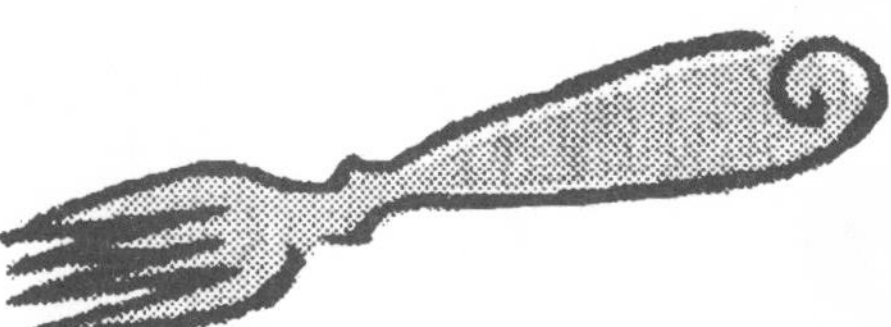

Recipes featured on *Canada AM* and in *Chatelaine*

Dedicated to my parents,
Lorraine and Perry,
who always encouraged me to put
as much syrup on my French toast as I wanted.

SECOND EDITION

Rise & Dine

CANADA

Savory Secrets from Canada's Bed & Breakfast Inns

MARCY CLAMAN

Callawind Publications Inc.

MONTREAL, CANADA

Rise & Dine Canada: Savory Secrets from Canada's Bed & Breakfast Inns

Cataloguing in Publication Data
Claman, Marcy, 1963–
Rise & dine Canada : savory secrets from Canada's bed & breakfast inns

2nd ed.
Includes index.
ISBN 1-896511-11-2

1. Breakfasts. 2. Brunches. 3. Cookery, Canadian. 4. Bed and breakfast accommodations—Canada. I. Title. II. Title: Rise and dine Canada.

TX733.C53 1999 641.5'2 C98-901178-X

Copyediting: Sarah Weber Cover illustration and design: Shari Blaukopf Indexing: Christine Jacobs

10 9 8 7 6 5 4 3 2 1

Printed in Canada

Callawind Publications Inc.
3383 Sources Boulevard, Suite 205, Dollard-des-Ormeaux, Quebec, Canada H9B 1Z8
2083 Hempstead Turnpike, Suite 355, East Meadow, New York, USA 11554-1730
E-mail: info@callawind.com http://www.callawind.com

Distributed in North America by Firefly Books Ltd.
3680 Victoria Park Avenue, Willowdale, Ontario, Canada M2H 3K1

Contents

Acknowledgments

A heartfelt thank-you goes out to the innkeepers of all the bed & breakfast inns appearing in this book for allowing me to publish your recipes, and especially for your continued enthusiasm.

The *Rise & Dine* cookbook series wouldn't be as mouthwatering without Shari Blaukopf's beautiful cover design.

Many thanks to Sarah Weber for your careful tending to the words that make up the sentences that make up the paragraphs that make up the chapters that make up the book!

My family and friends have been a constant source of inspiration from the beginning. I thank you all for helping me test recipes and giving me the feedback I needed to make this book the best it could be.

Thank you to Lenny — my breakfast partner in crime — for tolerating my morning meal obsession! You'll always be the champion French toast maker in my books.

Introduction

What's a bed & breakfast (B&B) inn? It's a charming home-away-from-home characterized by heavenly breakfasts, a warm ambiance, hospitable innkeepers, and the interesting company of other guests. When was the last time you enjoyed such comforts at the average hotel or motel?

I'm a true breakfast lover, and, while driving in the countryside on our honeymoon, my husband Lenny and I came upon an oh-so-quaint and inviting B&B. The promise of a memory-making breakfast was too good to pass up. We weren't disappointed (even today I remember those wonderful apricot pancakes!). And so began our exploration of the charm and culinary delights of B&B travel.

Some years later, winding our way home from yet another B&B stay (the taste of an unforgettable homemade apple strudel was still lingering in my mouth), the idea for a combination B&B cookbook and travel guide came to me. The result was the best-selling *Rise & Dine: Savory Secrets from America's Bed & Breakfast Inns* (currently in its second edition and entitled *Rise & Dine America).* Soon after, *Rise & Dine Canada* — the best-selling Canadian sequel — followed.

I was delighted at the success of the Canadian edition, and I'm so pleased to be able to bring out this new edition of it. It features totally updated and expanded B&B travel information, a convenient lay-flat binding, and, of course, even more delectable and easy guest-tested recipes than ever.

The choice of B&Bs included in this book depended on a variety of sources: my own personal experience, recommendations from family and friends, and recommendations from various publications and travel guides devoted to B&B travel. The B&Bs selected were asked to share their secrets for breakfast, brunch, and afternoon tea — recipes that hit the spot with their guests day in and day out.

If this book whets your appetite for exploring Canada's B&Bs, use it as a guide to your travels whether you're interested in cozying up to a roaring fire at a restored 19th-century Victorian mansion, staying at a hand-crafted log cabin, or enjoying a nautical adventure on a floating houseboat. Since B&Bs are like people (no two are alike!), I've tried to represent as many different B&Bs as possible — from rustic to ultimate luxury.

Whatever your taste in culinary adventures or your budget, you're bound to find a B&B or two in this book that suit you perfectly. Each recipe is accompanied by a description of the contributing B&B and a guide to the cost for double occupancy per night (excluding taxes) in Canadian dollars. Please note that rates are current as of this book's printing and are subject to change without notice.

$ = under $50 $$ = $50 – $89 $$$ = $90 – $120 $$$$ = over $120

Here's to many memorable B&B meals and travel adventures — right from your kitchen table!

— Marcy Claman

Index of B&Bs

Manitoba

Ontario

Ontario (continued)

Québec

New Brunswick

(continued on next page)

Prince Edward Island

Alberton — *Cold Comfort Farm* 86

Bay Fortune — *The Inn at Bay Fortune* 32, 262

Bideford — *Hilltop Acres Bed & Breakfast* 55, 62, 318

Charlottetown — *Dundee Arms Inn* 35, 119

Charlottetown — *The Shipwright Inn* 80, 100, 177, 316

Little Sands — *Bayberry Cliff Inn* 182, 286

Summerside — *Silver Fox Inn* 49, 102

Nova Scotia — Mainland

Annapolis Royal — *Bread and Roses Country Inn* 78, 125, 142, 149

Chester — *Mecklenburgh Inn* 47, 101, 194, 241

Dartmouth — *Riverdell Estate* 60, 206

East Lawrencetown — *Seaboard Bed & Breakfast* 205, 321

Halifax — *Fresh Start Bed & Breakfast* 66, 170

Middleton — *Fairfield Farm Inn* 155, 184, 288

Port Williams — *The Old Rectory Bed & Breakfast* 156, 191

Nova Scotia — Cape Breton Island

Port Hood — *Haus Treuburg* 157

Newfoundland

Lewisporte — *Northgate B&B* 18, 326

Little Rapids — *Humber Gallery Hospitality Home* 26, 143, 276

Robert's Arm — *Lake Crescent Inn* 135, 220, 298, 317, 327

Sunnyside — *Brookside Hospitality Home* 59, 117, 176

Trinity — *Campbell House* 93

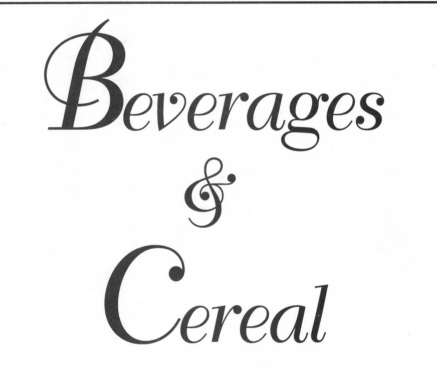

Beverages & Cereal

Apple-Cranberry Juice

2 quarts chilled apple juice
2 cups chilled cranberry juice (recipe follows)
2 teaspoons lemon juice

Combine the apple, cranberry, and lemon juice, and refrigerate. ***Variation:*** For a refreshing punch, add 4 cups ginger ale before serving. ***Yield: 10 cups.***

Cranberry juice:
1 quart fresh cranberries
2 quarts boiling water
2 – 3 cinnamon sticks
Juice of 2 lemons
Juice of 2 oranges
Honey

Pour the cranberries into the boiling water. Add the cinnamon sticks, and bring the mixture to a boil. Simmer 20 – 30 minutes until the berries are very soft. Mash the berries, and cool the berry mixture to lukewarm. Remove the cinnamon sticks. Strain the juice, and press the berry pulp to get out all the juice. Add the lemon and orange juice and honey to taste. Chill. ***Yield: 3 quarts.***

Bay View Farm / La Ferme Bay View

Helen and Garnett Sawyer
PO Box 21,
337 New Carlisle West, Route 132
New Carlisle, Québec G0C 1Z0
Tel: (418) 752-2725/6718
$

ABOUT THE B&B

Situated between New Carlisle and Bonaventure, Bay View Farm offers country hospitality in a beautiful seaside environment on the rugged Baie des Chaleurs coastline of Québec's Gaspé Peninsula. Seaside accommodations include five comfortable guest rooms and a fully equipped cottage. At breakfast, enjoy Bay View's farm-fresh eggs, meat, homemade muffins, scones, jams, jellies, and beverages, as well as fresh fruits and vegetables in season from the farm's garden and orchards. Additional meals are available on request at reasonable rates. Handicrafts are on display throughout the house. Enjoy the breathtaking panoramic seascapes, participate in the Bay View Folk Festival (second weekend of August) with folk music and dancing, or visit Percé Rock and the archaeological caves of Saint-Elzéar.

SEASON

May – November

ACCOMMODATIONS

5 rooms with shared baths;
1 private cottage with private bath

Elgin Manor B&B

Penny and Dave Grimshaw
RR #2
Port Sandfield, Ontario P0B 1J0
Tel: (705) 765-5325
$$ – $$$$

ABOUT THE B&B

Nestled on a quiet bay of picturesque Lake Joseph is the unique and heartwarming Elgin Manor B&B, a 1920s Tudor home surrounded by English gardens and a water's edge fireplace. As you relax in a wooden Muskoka chair, you're sure to see some antique wooden launches, for which the Muskoka Lakes are famous, or perhaps the old steamship Segwun *pass by. The manor is decorated with antiques throughout and handmade quilts grace each guest room. Launch excursions and old-fashioned picnic lunches packed in wicker baskets can be arranged. Elgin Manor B&B is situated in the heart of Muskoka cottage country (two hours north of Toronto), an area that offers year-round activities — from summer nature walks, fishing, swimming, canoeing, and midnight strolls under a million glistening stars to tours of local artisans' studios, ice skating, and snowshoeing and cross-country skiing in the panoramic countryside.*

SEASON

all year

ACCOMMODATIONS

3 rooms with private baths;
1 honeymoon cabin with private bath

Bedtime Tea

"When pouring yourself a cup of this soothing tea, be sure to use your favorite antique teapot, cup, and saucer. You're sure to dream pleasant dreams! At Elgin Manor, we pick the herbs fresh from our garden." — Penny Grimshaw

8 cups hot water
Handful of fresh or ½ handful of dried chamomile leaves
Handful of fresh or ½ handful of dried mint leaves

Combine the water, chamomile leaves, and mint leaves in a teapot, and let steep until the tea has reached the strength you prefer. ***Yield: 8 cups.***

Beyond-the-Pale Oatmeal

3 cups water
1⅔ cups large-flake rolled oats
2 eggs, lightly beaten
⅔ cup raisins
½ cup maple syrup
¼ cup brown sugar
¼ cup chopped nuts (walnuts, pecans, or almonds)
¼ cup dark molasses
½ teaspoon ground cinnamon
½ teaspoon ground ginger
¼ teaspoon freshly ground nutmeg

Ground cinnamon
Milk or half-and-half

Preheat the oven to 350°F. Heat the water to boiling in a saucepan. Reduce the heat to medium-low. Add the oats, and cook, stirring, 5 minutes. Add the eggs, raisins, maple syrup, brown sugar, nuts, molasses, cinnamon, ginger, and nutmeg, stir, and pour into an oven-proof dish. Bake 60 minutes (or microwave on medium-low 60 minutes). Sprinkle the edges of open soup bowls with cinnamon, then spoon in the oatmeal. Serve with milk or half-and-half. ***Tip:*** Omit the raisins, and serve with brandy- or Grand Marnier-soaked raisins or currants. ***Yield: 4 – 6 servings.***

Lakewinds

Jane and Stephen Locke
PO Box 1483, 328 Queen Street
Niagara-on-the-Lake, Ontario
L0S 1J0
Tel: (905) 468-1888
Fax: (905) 468-1061
E-mail: lakewind@niagara.com
www.lakewinds.niagara.com

$$$$

ABOUT THE B&B

A special experience awaits you at Lakewinds, a circa-1881, restored Victorian manor operated by Jane and Stephen Locke. Situated on an acre of quiet trees and gardens, Lakewinds offers unparalleled views of the Niagara-on-the-Lake Golf Club and Lake Ontario. The guest rooms, elegantly appointed with antiques, have been designed for comfort and privacy and feature private baths. Guests are invited to the games room for billiards or cards and, in summer, can enjoy refreshing dips in the heated pool or simply relax in rocking chairs on the veranda. Sumptuous breakfasts feature fruits, vegetables, and herbs from Jane's garden. Only one-and-a-half hours south of Toronto, Niagara-on-the-Lake is a charming town offering world-class theater, shops, fine restaurants, and beautiful parks — all with a turn-of-the-century ambiance. The many estate wineries in the area offer tours and tastings, while golf courses, tennis courts, and countless hiking and biking trails await the active visitor.

SEASON

all year

ACCOMMODATIONS

6 rooms with private baths

Chaplin's Country B&B

Kathy and Ron Chaplin
RR #5, Box 43
Saskatoon, Saskatchewan S7K 3J8
Tel/Fax: (306) 931-3353
E-mail: chaplinr@duke.usask.ca
www.dbs2.com/chaplins
$

ABOUT THE B&B

Experience the wide open spaces and blue sky of Canada's prairies at Chaplin's Country B&B, a working farm with Jersey cows, pigs, sheep, goats, and chickens. Enjoy a rest on the veranda and view awesome sunsets, or stroll through the barnyard and watch the evening milking. This gracious country home has a handmade spiral staircase, knotty pine paneling, and prairie antiques. For privacy, the guest bedrooms, TV lounge, and bathroom are all on the second floor. Chaplin's country breakfast, including French toast with homemade syrups, sausage, fresh fruit in season, and beverages, is a real eye-opener, while an evening snack of apple cake and hot cider always hits the spot. Saskatoon, only 15 minutes away, offers many fine restaurants, shops, and attractions. Other area diversions include the Western Development Museum, Wanuskewin Heritage Park, University of Saskatchewan, and numerous provincial parks and golf courses. Kathy and Ron pride themselves on their prairie hospitality and comfortable facilities.

SEASON

all year

ACCOMMODATIONS

3 rooms with shared bath

Breakfast Punch

2 quarts ginger ale (8½ cups)
2 quarts lemon-lime flavored carbonated drink (8½ cups)
12-ounce can frozen orange juice, thawed
1 teaspoon banana extract
1 teaspoon vanilla

Mix the ginger ale, carbonated drink, orange juice, banana extract, and vanilla together gently. Place the punch in a large plastic container that has a tight fitting screw lid to preserve the fizz. ***Yield: About 4½ quarts.***

Brücher Muesli

"One of our first B&B guests, an older man from Sweden, gave me this recipe. It was developed by a Swedish doctor in the 1950s to help Swedes eat more fiber and bring down cholesterol. Dr. Brücher's original recipe calls for grated apples, but I found they turned brown before guests arrived at the table, so I use berries instead. This is perfect on a hot summer morning." — Glenda Carter

3 cups large-flake rolled oats (do not use quick-cooking rolled oats)
Blueberries
Strawberries, sliced
Toasted almonds
Maple syrup
1% milk or half-and-half

Soak the oats overnight in enough water to cover. In the morning, drain the oats well. Divide the oats among 4 bowls. Top with blueberries, strawberries, almonds, maple syrup, and milk. ***Yield: 4 servings.***

Wyndswept Bed & Breakfast

Glenda and Bob Carter
Box 2683
Hinton, Alberta T7V 1Y2
Tel: (780) 866-3950
Fax: (780) 866-3951
E-mail: wyndswep@agt.net
$$ – $$$

ABOUT THE B&B

The Jasper area's first four-star B&B, Wyndswept Bed & Breakfast is built on the side of a hill in the Folding Mountain Range. From this vantage point, guests marvel at the 180-degree panoramic view of the Rocky Mountains, a nearby valley, and the spectacular sunrises and sunsets. Some 38 different wildflowers thrive on the hill. Wildlife such as bears, deer, elk, and bighorn sheep can be seen right outside the window while guests enjoy a five-course heart-healthy breakfast. The decor of each guest suite has a different theme, and all suites have private baths and luxurious bedding. At night, you can rest on hand-hewn benches by the cozy fire pit and watch the stars or listen to the howl of wolves and coyotes. Wyndswept is located in a quiet mountain village at the eastern edge of Jasper National Park. Your hosts are long-time residents who know the area well and can suggest points of interest. Glenda is retired after working for 30 years as a mental health therapist, while Bob is a quality control auditor and the resident star gazer.

SEASON

all year

ACCOMMODATIONS

2 suites with private baths

Sproule Heritage Place B&B

Vera and Winston Sproule
PO Box 43, Site 14, RR #1
Strathmore, Alberta T1P 1J6
Tel: (403) 934-3219
$$

ABOUT THE B&B

While Sproule Heritage Place B&B has been featured by both Hallmark USA and Alberta Government Telephone in their television commercials, this farm actually had less high-profile beginnings. In 1909, the site was little more than a well-trodden buffalo trail when the Scheer family settled on the open prairie east of Calgary. Years later, the stately house and barn became a landmark to travelers on a road that today is the Trans-Canada Highway. Vera and Winston Sproule purchased the farm in 1985 and began extensive renovations to restore its 1920s elegance. As a result, the site has been declared an Alberta Registered Historic Resource. Artisans and designers of furniture and quilts, Vera and Winston (a country pastor for four years in Yukon and 24 years in Alberta) assure you a comfortable bed in one of three charming bedrooms and an interesting breakfast.

SEASON

all year

ACCOMMODATIONS

1 room with private bath;
2 rooms with shared bath

Fruit Smoothie

2 cups orange juice
½ cup thawed frozen sweetened strawberries
½ cup thawed frozen unsweetened raspberries
1 banana
1 teaspoon honey

Combine the orange juice, strawberries, raspberries, banana, and honey in a blender until smooth. ***Yield: About 4 cups.***

Healthy Porridge

"Very healthful, high in fiber, and scrumptious!" — June Leschied

1 cup large-flake rolled oats
2 – 3 dried apricots, cut into pieces
2 – 3 prunes, cut into pieces
2 tablespoons lemon juice
½ green apple, peeled, cored, and chopped
Raisins

Milk or half-and-half

Place the oats, apricots, prunes, lemon juice, apple, and raisins in a saucepan, and add enough water just to cover. Let stand overnight. In the morning, bring the oat mixture to a gentle boil and stir. Serve with milk or half-and-half (no sugar is needed!). ***Yield: 3 servings.***

Northgate B&B

June and Carl Leschied
106 Main Street
Lewisporte, Newfoundland
A0G 3A0
Tel: (709) 535-2258
$$

ABOUT THE B&B

Experience true Newfoundland hospitality at Northgate B&B, a large and beautifully restored country-style home overlooking Lewisporte harbor. Upon arrival, enjoy afternoon tea in one of the sitting rooms with fireplace and hardwood floors. The four charming guest rooms have either private or shared bath. Wholesome full breakfast of Northgate's own fresh brown eggs, homemade bread, cereals, and wild berry jams is served in the large dining room, a smoke-free environment. Northgate is located near craft shops, a museum, laundromat, provincial parks and swimming areas, scenic villages, strawberry "U-picks," and salmon rivers. Explore the beautiful islands of Notre Dame Bay on your hosts' 40-foot tour boat, or enjoy lunch beside an iceberg or a cook-out in a former island settlement. Trips can be arranged to Beothuk Indian haunts or to a remote island cabin for a one- or two-night stay.

SEASON

May 1 – October 31

ACCOMMODATIONS

2 rooms with private baths;
2 rooms with shared bath

Elgin Manor B&B

Penny and Dave Grimshaw
RR #2
Port Sandfield, Ontario P0B 1J0
Tel: (705) 765-5325
$$ – $$$$

ABOUT THE B&B

Nestled on a quiet bay of picturesque Lake Joseph is the unique and heartwarming Elgin Manor B&B, a 1920s Tudor home surrounded by English gardens and a water's edge fireplace. As you relax in a wooden Muskoka chair, you're sure to see some antique wooden launches, for which the Muskoka Lakes are famous, or perhaps the old steamship Segwun *pass by. The manor is decorated with antiques throughout and handmade quilts grace each guest room. Launch excursions and old-fashioned picnic lunches packed in wicker baskets can be arranged. Elgin Manor B&B is situated in the heart of Muskoka cottage country (two hours north of Toronto), an area that offers year-round activities — from summer nature walks, fishing, swimming, canoeing, and midnight strolls under a million glistening stars to tours of local artisans' studios, ice skating, and snowshoeing and cross-country skiing in the panoramic countryside.*

SEASON

all year

ACCOMMODATIONS

3 rooms with private baths;
1 honeymoon cabin with private bath

Old-fashioned Iced Tea

"Best served dockside on summer afternoons while you relax in a Muskoka chair and watch antique wooden boats pass by."
— Penny Grimshaw

2 flavored tea bags (lemon recommended)
Sugar

Fresh mint leaves
Lemon slices

Put the tea bags in a 1-quart antique Mason jar, fill it with cold water, and place the jar in a sunny window for about 2 – 3 weeks. Turn the jar upside down periodically to mix the tea and water. Once the mixture looks the color of tea, strain it and add sugar to taste. Serve chilled in a tall glass. Top with fresh mint leaves and a slice of lemon. ***Yield: 4 cups.***

Orange Juice Spritzer

"Some people can't function in the morning until they've had their coffee. With me, it's orange juice!" — Bonnie Evans

6-ounce can frozen orange juice, thawed
1 cup cold water
1 tablespoon lemon juice
1½ cups lemon-lime flavored carbonated drink

Orange slices

In a large pitcher, combine the orange juice, water, and lemon juice. Just before serving, slowly add the carbonated drink; stir gently to blend. Serve over ice and garnish with orange slices. ***Yield: 4 cups.***

Cornelius White House Bed & Breakfast

Bonnie and Frank Evans
8 Wellington Street
Bloomfield, Ontario K0K 1G0
Tel/Fax: (613) 393-2282
$ – $$

ABOUT THE B&B

Located on the historic Loyalist Parkway at the west end of a farming community in picturesque Prince Edward County, the Cornelius White House is named for its original owner, a Dutch settler who built this charming red-brick house in 1862. Today, a sense of history and design combine with European furnishings and accents to create a unique B&B. Three guest rooms on the second floor open onto the sitting room below, which has a cathedral ceiling. There is also a suite on the main floor. The house is air conditioned and is a smoke-free environment. A full breakfast of fruit, a hot main course, and fresh baked goods is served in the Dutch Treat Tea Room. Outstanding restaurants are nearby, as well as antique and craft shops, galleries, studios, and museums. Cornelius White House is just 10 minutes from Sandbanks and Outlet Beach Provincial Parks, famous for the largest freshwater sand dunes in the world. Prince Edward County, with its panoramic views and gentle rolling hills, is a cyclist's dream come true.

SEASON

all year

ACCOMMODATIONS

2 rooms with private baths;
2 rooms with shared bath

Karriage House (1908) Bed & Breakfast

Sue and Tom Chamberlain
5215-47 Street
Wetaskiwin, Alberta T9A 1E1
Tel: (888)/(403) 352-5996
$$

ABOUT THE B&B

Built in 1908 in Alberta's oldest city, Karriage House still retains its original architecture, with arches, alcoves, curved walls, and fine woodwork. Surrounded by hedges, big spruce trees, and tall fences, Karriage House is a perfect hideaway for that special weekend. Experience the charm of the cozy second-floor bedrooms with shared bath or the intimacy of the summer guest cottage. Savor an evening by the fire in the living room or browse in the Curio Shop, featuring antiques, collectibles, dried flowers, and original artwork. A wholesome breakfast is served in the dining room or on the deck. Tom is a great cook and loves skiing and restoring old cars. Sue enjoys gardening, decorating, art, and eating Tom's cooking! In summer, Tom manages the original Reynolds Museum, founding place of the Reynolds-Alberta Museum of Transportation. Forty-five minutes from Edmonton, Karriage House is within walking distance of year-round recreation facilities and the historic downtown. Your hosts can arrange biplane and antique aircraft flights.

SEASON

all year

ACCOMMODATIONS

2 rooms with shared bath;
1 summer cottage with private bath

Tom's Oatmeal

2 cups water
¼ cup raisins
¾ cup large-flake rolled oats
¼ cup triticale flakes*
1 apple, peeled, cored, and cut into chunks
½ teaspoon ground cinnamon

Half-and-half
Maple syrup or brown sugar

**Note: Similar in appearance to rolled oats, this product is made from the kernels of a plant that is a cross between wheat and rye.*

In a saucepan, bring the water and raisins to a boil. Add the oats and triticale flakes. Cover, reduce the heat to a simmer, and cook about 10 – 12 minutes. Stir only occasionally (the flakes should be separate, and not mushy). Add the apple and cinnamon, and cook about 3 minutes (the apples should be cooked but firm). Serve hot with half-and-half and maple syrup or brown sugar. ***Yield: 3 – 4 servings.***

Weston Lake Granola

"While we have made adaptations to the originals over time, we gratefully acknowledge that many of our best ideas have come from our guests! This granola is great as a cereal with fruit and milk or yogurt, or as a snack." — Susan Evans

5 cups large-flake rolled oats
1 cup flaked unsweetened coconut
1 cup powdered non-instant skim milk
1 cup soy flour*
1 cup sunflower seeds
1 cup whole raw hazelnuts, almonds, or pecans
¾ cup sesame seeds
1 cup honey
1 cup vegetable oil

**Note: Available at health food stores.*

Preheat the oven to 300°F. Combine the oats, coconut, powdered milk, soy flour, sunflower seeds, nuts, and sesame seeds. In a microwave, heat the honey gently to liquefy it, then combine with the oil. Add the honey mixture to the oats mixture, combine, and spread on 2 baking sheets. Bake 27 – 30 minutes, stirring at 10-minute intervals, until golden brown. Cool and store in a large, airtight plastic bag in the refrigerator.
Yield: 10 cups.

Weston Lake Inn Bed & Breakfast

Susan Evans and Ted Harrison
813 Beaver Point Road
Salt Spring Island, British Columbia
V8K 1X9
Tel: (250) 653-4311
$$$

ABOUT THE B&B

Perched on a knoll of well-tended flowering trees and shrubs overlooking Weston Lake, the inn is a serene and comfortable adult getaway on the rural south end of Salt Spring Island. The three tastefully decorated guest bedrooms have private baths, down duvets, and fresh flower bouquets. Original Canadian art and beautiful petit point (done by host Ted) grace the rooms. Guests have the exclusive use of a cozy fireside lounge with library, TV, and VCR, and an outdoor hot tub overlooking the lake. Creative breakfasts feature fresh eggs from the inn's chickens and produce from the large organic garden, such as berries, herbs, and asparagus in season. Near Victoria, Salt Spring Island offers a mild climate, exceptional beauty, a thriving community of artists and craftspeople, and an abundance of outdoor activities. Since opening Weston Lake Inn in 1986, hosts Susan and Ted have been fine-tuning their B&B craft, restoring the house, landscaping, and enjoying their 10-acre paradise with guests. Susan loves gardening, while Ted loves sailing and offers charters aboard their 36-foot sloop.

SEASON

all year

ACCOMMODATIONS

3 rooms with private baths

Appetizers & Side Dishes

Baked Beans

2 cups dried Boston beans (also called navy or pea beans)
2 cups diced salt pork
½ cup brown sugar
¼ cup molasses
½ tablespoon powdered mustard
1 teaspoon salt
Pepper
1 onion, chopped

Soak the beans for a few hours in enough water to cover. Simmer gently for 1½ hours, then drain. Put the beans in an ovenproof dish or bean crock with the salt pork, brown sugar, molasses, mustard, salt, and some pepper. Stir well. Add enough water to cover the beans. Add the onion, and mix. Bake in a preheated slow oven (300°F) for 6 – 8 hours, covered. Add boiling water when needed to keep the beans moist. The dish may be left uncovered to brown for the last hour, if desired. Adjust the seasonings. ***Yield: 8 servings.***

Bay View Farm / La Ferme Bay View

Helen and Garnett Sawyer
PO Box 21,
337 New Carlisle West, Route 132
New Carlisle, Québec G0C 1Z0
Tel: (418) 752-2725/6718

$

ABOUT THE B&B

Situated between New Carlisle and Bonaventure, Bay View Farm offers country hospitality in a beautiful seaside environment on the rugged Baie des Chaleurs coastline of Québec's Gaspé Peninsula. Seaside accommodations include five comfortable guest rooms and a fully equipped cottage. At breakfast, enjoy Bay View's farm-fresh eggs, meat, homemade muffins, scones, jams, jellies, and beverages, as well as fresh fruits and vegetables in season from the farm's garden and orchards. Additional meals are available on request at reasonable rates. Handicrafts are on display throughout the house. Enjoy the breathtaking panoramic seascapes, participate in the Bay View Folk Festival (second weekend of August) with folk music and dancing, or visit Percé Rock and the archaeological caves of Saint-Elzéar.

SEASON

May – November

ACCOMMODATIONS

5 rooms with shared baths;
1 private cottage with private bath

Montréal Oasis

Lena Blondel
3000 Breslay Road
Montréal, Québec H3Y 2G7
Tel: (514) 935-2312
$$

ABOUT THE B&B

In pilgrim days, the evergreen tree was a sign of shelter, good food, and warm hospitality. It's fitting, then, that two towering evergreens frame the door to Montréal Oasis. This charming B&B with original leaded windows and slanted ceilings is located in downtown Montréal's west end, close to the Fine Arts Museum, chic Crescent Street and Greene Avenue shopping and restaurants, and the "main drag," St. Catherine Street. The beautiful and safe neighborhood with its spacious Elizabethan-style houses and pretty gardens is locally referred to as the Priest Farm district — once a holiday resort for priests. Originally from Sweden, your world-traveled hostess Lena has lived in many countries around the globe, which is evident from the African, Asian, and Swedish art that graces the B&B. The three guest rooms feature Scandinavian and Québecois furniture. Lena loves good food, and serves three-course gourmet breakfasts featuring delicious, fresh ingredients. A friendly Siamese cat resides on the main floor.

SEASON

all year

ACCOMMODATIONS

3 rooms with shared baths

Berry Soup

"A starter course on a hot summer day." — Lena Blondel

3 cups water
¾ cup concentrated raspberry or strawberry juice (not cocktail)
1 tablespoon potato flour
Fresh fruits such as ½ cup chopped gooseberries and 1 cup red currants, or ½ cup raspberries and 1 cup blueberries
Confectioners' sugar

Whole berries
Mint leaves

Bring the water, juice, and potato flour to a boil, stirring constantly. Let cool. Add the fruits, and sweeten with confectioners' sugar. Serve the soup in chilled fruit cups decorated generously with whole berries and a mint leaf or two. ***Yield: 5 servings.***

Bloody Mary Soup

1 medium onion, chopped
3 celery stalks, diced
2 tablespoons butter
2 tablespoons tomato purée or paste
1 tablespoon sugar
5 cups tomato juice
1 tablespoon lemon juice
1 tablespoon salt
2 teaspoons Worcestershire sauce
¼ teaspoon pepper
4 ounces vodka

Snipped chives or chopped parsley

In a large pot, sauté the onion and celery in the butter until the onion is light brown. Add the tomato purée and sugar. Sauté 1 minute. Add the tomato juice, and simmer 8 – 10 minutes. Add the lemon juice, salt, Worcestershire sauce, and pepper, and mix. Strain the soup. Add the vodka just before serving. Serve either hot or chilled, sprinkled with chives or parsley. ***Yield: 6 servings.***

Humber Gallery Hospitality Home

Edna and Eldon Swyer
26 Roberts Drive
Little Rapids, Newfoundland
A2H 6C3
Mailing address: PO Box 15
Corner Brook, Newfoundland
A2H 6C3
Tel: (709) 634-2660
E-mail: eldonswyer@thezone.net
$$

ABOUT THE B&B

A popular stop for the British royal family, Little Rapids (near Corner Brook) is home to Humber Gallery, an impressive cedar abode with cathedral ceilings, fireplace, wraparound sun deck, two guest rooms with double beds, one guest room with twin beds, and one guest room with a queen bed. A nutritious breakfast is served, and other meals and use of the barbecue and picnic area can be arranged. An excellent spot for an overnight stay when going or coming from Gros Morne National Park, this B&B is in the heart of the Humber Valley Reserve near Marble Mountain Ski Resort, mini-golf facilities, "U-pick" strawberry farms, Bay of Islands tourist attractions, South Brook and Pasadena beaches on Deer Lake, and the Humber River. Edna and Eldon can provide maps, tourist literature, a licensed salmon fishing guide, and insider tips on area attractions.

SEASON

June – September;
February – March

ACCOMMODATIONS

1 room with private bath;
3 rooms with shared baths

Montréal Oasis

Lena Blondel
3000 Breslay Road
Montréal, Québec H3Y 2G7
Tel: (514) 935-2312
$$

ABOUT THE B&B

In pilgrim days, the evergreen tree was a sign of shelter, good food, and warm hospitality. It's fitting, then, that two towering evergreens frame the door to Montréal Oasis. This charming B&B with original leaded windows and slanted ceilings is located in downtown Montréal's west end, close to the Fine Arts Museum, chic Crescent Street and Greene Avenue shopping and restaurants, and the "main drag," St. Catherine Street. The beautiful and safe neighborhood with its spacious Elizabethan-style houses and pretty gardens is locally referred to as the Priest Farm district — once a holiday resort for priests. Originally from Sweden, your world-traveled hostess Lena has lived in many countries around the globe, which is evident from the African, Asian, and Swedish art that graces the B&B. The three guest rooms feature Scandinavian and Québecois furniture. Lena loves good food, and serves three-course gourmet breakfasts featuring delicious, fresh ingredients. A friendly Siamese cat resides on the main floor.

SEASON

all year

ACCOMMODATIONS

3 rooms with shared baths

Broiled Grapefruit

"On cold winter days, I like to serve this grapefruit as an appetizer." — Lena Blondel

2 grapefruits, halved
Brown sugar
4 grapes or strawberries

Loosen sections from each grapefruit half, and remove the seeds. Sprinkle some brown sugar over each grapefruit half, and broil in the oven just until the edges turn brown. Top with a grape or a strawberry. ***Yield: 4 servings.***

Crunchy Brunchy Vegetable Salad

"This is a great brunch salad to serve with quiche."
— Karen Gauthier

2 cups broccoli florets
1 cup cauliflower florets
1 medium red onion
1 cup grated cheddar cheese
1 cup raisins
1 cup roasted unsalted sunflower seeds
5 – 6 slices bacon, cooked and chopped
1 cup mayonnaise
3 tablespoons sugar
1 tablespoon vinegar
Pepper
Salt

Chop the broccoli, cauliflower, and onion (a food processor works well). Combine the vegetables with the cheese, raisins, and sunflower seeds. Stir in the bacon. In a separate bowl, whisk together the mayonnaise, sugar, and vinegar, and season with pepper and salt. Pour the dressing over the vegetable mixture. Mix well and serve immediately. ***Tip:*** Make the salad the evening before by mixing together all the ingredients except the cheese, sunflower seeds, and bacon, which can be added right before serving. ***Yield: 8 servings.***

The Carriage House Bed & Breakfast

Karen and Gary Gauthier
PO Box 1424, 94 Kenyon Street West
Alexandria, Ontario K0C 1A0
Tel: (613) 525-0321
E-mail: carriage@glen-net.ca
$$

ABOUT THE B&B

Located in the heart of Glengarry County — an area settled by Scots — The Carriage House is named for the world-renowned Munro and McIntosh Carriage Works, which once operated in Alexandria. The spacious home, built around a 150-year-old log cabin, combines the charms of the past with the modern conveniences of the present. In winter, guests can relax in front of the fireplace, and in summer, enjoy a relaxing view of the lake from the wraparound veranda. A hearty, three-course breakfast is a great beginning for the day's activities. Golf enthusiasts can play a round on the town's 18-hole course. For those who prefer shopping, there are numerous antique stores, art and craft stores, and a Rob McIntosh china outlet. The Carriage House is located an hour's drive from two of Canada's most vibrant cities: Montréal and Ottawa.

SEASON

all year

ACCOMMODATIONS

3 rooms with shared bath

Dilled Potato Puff

"My mother, Beth Prior, has an art of making a leftover meal taste like a gourmet delight. This is one of her secret recipes." — Jo Mader

4 cups cooked potatoes (if leftovers, reheat for easy handling)
½ teaspoon dried dill weed
½ teaspoon salt
¼ teaspoon garlic salt
¼ teaspoon pepper
½ cup sour cream
Grated or sliced cheddar cheese

Gravy and hot meat, or cold cuts

Mash the potatoes with the dill weed, salt, garlic salt, and pepper. Beat the sour cream into the potato mixture, and place in a casserole dish. Sprinkle the top with cheese. Cover, and place in the microwave on medium power or in the oven at 350°F until heated through and the cheese melts. Delicious with gravy and hot meat, or with cold cuts. ***Yield: 4 – 6 servings.***

Bluenose Country Vacation Farm

Jo and Kenneth Mader
PO Box 173
Qu'Appelle, Saskatchewan S0G 4A0
Tel: (306) 699-7192
$$

ABOUT THE B&B

For an old-fashioned welcome where Mother Nature wraps you in her arms, there's no place like Bluenose Country Vacation Farm. Step back in history as you admire the English-style split fieldstone home — a striking landmark on the prairie landscape since 1904. Stroll through the farmyard, pet the farm animals, see the large farm machinery new and old, and spend some time in the Agriculture Education Center, with hands-on displays and model farm machinery for children to play with. After a refreshing swim in the indoor heated pool, try your hand at mini-golf while the children frolic in the playground. In early morning, the call of a meadowlark breaks the stillness and you're eventually coaxed to the breakfast table by the smells of homemade bread and sizzling bacon. Country high tea is served from May to September, and lunch and dinner meals can also be arranged. Bluenose is a short drive from picturesque Qu'Appelle Valley with its sparkling lakes and sandy beaches, and a few minutes from the town's stores and attractions.

SEASON

all year

ACCOMMODATIONS

6 rooms with private baths

Granola Parfait

"This is a healthy, attractive dish to be made just before serving so the granola won't go soggy from the yogurt." — Yvonne Parker

4 tablespoons plus 1 teaspoon granola (recipe follows)
French vanilla yogurt
Strawberry jam
Cashew nut

Place 4 tablespoons granola in a small parfait dish. Place a layer of French vanilla yogurt over the granola. Top with a teaspoon of strawberry jam. Sprinkle the remaining granola over the jam, and top with a cashew nut. ***Yield: 1 serving.***

Granola:
¾ cup honey
¾ cup vegetable oil
⅓ cup water
1½ tablespoons vanilla
½ tablespoon salt
8 cups quick-cooking rolled oats
1 cup flaked unsweetened coconut
1 cup nuts (combination of chopped peanuts, almonds, sunflower seeds, sesame seeds, etc.)
1 cup wheat germ
¾ cup brown sugar

(continued on next page)

Orchard Lane Bed & Breakfast

Yvonne Parker
13324 Middle Bench Road
Oyama, British Columbia V4V 2B4
Tel: (250) 548-3809
$$

ABOUT THE B&B

Smack dab between Kelowna and Vernon is Orchard Lane, a newly built Victorian B&B nestled in a private orchard. From the sprawling veranda is a panoramic view of the beautiful central Okanagan Valley, while nearby Kalamalka and Wood Lakes reflect the hills and distant mountains. Inside, a welcoming foyer and spiral staircase lead to romantic and comfortable bedrooms. Visitors lounge in the formal living room with fireplace, stroll through the flower gardens or nearby orchard, admire the terraced landscaping framed by giant trees, or take a refreshing dip in the outdoor hot tub. Your hostess, Yvonne, serves a full gourmet breakfast — made from produce grown in her garden — in the formal dining room or on the veranda. You'll quickly discover that one of her favorite hobbies is making crafts, which are displayed throughout the house. Alpine skiing, fishing, biking, hiking, and other recreational choices await you and there are golf courses and beaches aplenty to explore. This area is truly a corner of paradise.

SEASON

all year

ACCOMMODATIONS

2 rooms with shared bath;
1 room with private bath

Preheat the oven to 300°F. Whip together the honey, oil, water, vanilla, and salt until well mixed. In a large bowl, combine the oats, coconut, nuts, wheat germ, and brown sugar. Pour the honey mixture over the oats mixture, and mix well. Spread the granola ½" deep in shallow, ungreased baking pans. Bake 30 minutes, then stir. Continue baking, stirring every 15 minutes, until golden brown — about 1½ hours. Store in an airtight container until ready to use. ***Tip:*** This granola freezes well. ***Yield: About 10 cups.***

Island Blue Mussel and Sweet Potato Chowder with Spicy Butter

(Recipe from Open Kitchen: A Chef's Day at The Inn at Bay Fortune *by Michael Smith, Callawind Publications)*

5 pounds island blue mussels
4 tablespoons water
1 large onion, chopped (about 2 cups)
4 tablespoons butter
4 cloves garlic, chopped
2 medium carrots, grated
2 medium sweet potatoes, grated
2 cups milk
1 cup heavy cream
1 teaspoon Bay Fortune seasoning*
1 teaspoon salt
1 teaspoon Tabasco

Spicy butter:
2 tablespoons butter
2 tablespoons heavy cream
2 tablespoons molasses
½ tablespoon Tabasco
¼ teaspoon ground allspice
¼ teaspoon ground cloves

**Note: To make Bay Fortune seasoning, combine equal parts, by weight, of whole dried bay leaf, coriander seed, and fennel seed. Grind them together in a spice grinder. Use 2 bay leaves as a substitute, but remember to remove them before puréeing the soup.*

(continued on next page)

The Inn at Bay Fortune

David Wilmer and Michael Smith
Bay Fortune
Prince Edward Island C0A 2B0
Tel: (902) 687-3745
Fax: (902) 687-3540
$$$ – $$$$

ABOUT THE B&B

Built in 1910 as the summer home of Broadway playwright Elmer Harris, this inn has enjoyed a place in the Bay Fortune artists' community ever since. In 1989, innkeeper David Wilmer restored the home to its former splendor, taking full advantage of its location overlooking Bay Fortune and the Northumberland Strait beyond. Uniquely decorated with a combination of island antiques and pieces created by local craftspeople, the 17 guest suites all have private baths and a view of the sea, and most have a fireplace in the sitting area. The dining room is the highest rated in Atlantic Canada by Where to Eat in Canada. *Chef Michael Smith has earned an international reputation for his focus on fresh island ingredients, and his contemporary cuisine is recognized for its lively combinations and detailed methods. The Inn at Bay Fortune is close to top-flight golf courses and deep-sea fishing, and less than an hour from Charlottetown, with its active nightlife and some of Canada's best theater.*

SEASON

May – October

ACCOMMODATIONS

17 suites with private baths

Place the mussels and water in a pot with a tight fitting lid. Place the pot over high heat, and steam the mussels 10 – 12 minutes until the shells open. Discard any mussels that don't open. Remove the meat from the shells and set the meat aside, and reserve some shells to use in the presentation. Strain and reserve the remaining liquid.

In a large pot, sauté the onion in the butter over high heat for about 10 minutes. Stir frequently, and turn the heat down slightly every few minutes to prevent burning. Add the garlic and continue cooking until the onion is golden brown. Add the carrot, sweet potato, milk, cream, Bay Fortune seasoning, salt, Tabasco, and 1 cup of the mussel broth. Bring the mixture to a boil, reduce the heat to low, cover the pot, and let it simmer gently for 30 minutes, until the vegetables are soft. Stir frequently to prevent scorching on the bottom of the pot. After 30 minutes, check the vegetables for doneness. If they are soft, remove the pot from the heat. If they are slightly al dente, simmer a few minutes longer or until done. Purée the soup thoroughly in a blender, and strain through a fine mesh strainer. If necessary, adjust the consistency of the soup with the remaining mussel liquid. The soup should be pleasantly thick but not goopy.

For the spicy butter, put the butter, cream, molasses, Tabasco, allspice, and cloves in a small saucepan, and bring the mixture to a simmer, stirring frequently. Remove from the heat, and allow the mixture to cool to room temperature.

To serve, return the soup to the pot and heat it, stirring frequently, until it is almost at serving temperature. Add the reserved mussel meat, and heat, stirring, for a few minutes until heated through. Ladle the soup into warmed bowls. Drizzle the spicy butter around the surface of the soup. Gently shake each bowl to swirl the butter slightly. You may also pull a toothpick through the butter to create patterns. Use a few of the mussel shells to garnish the soup, or tuck them in between the bowl and its underliner. ***Yield: 4 – 6 servings.***

Oven-Baked Pepper Bacon

1½ pounds lean bacon, sliced
2½ teaspoons coarsely ground black pepper

Preheat the oven to 400°F. Arrange the bacon in 2 jelly roll or roasting pans. If all the slices don't fit into 2 pans, you can save space by slightly overlapping the lean edge of each slice with the fat edge of the next. Sprinkle the black pepper evenly over the bacon. Bake 25 – 30 minutes. The bacon should be chewy-crispy but not dry. Drain the bacon on paper towels, and serve immediately. ***Tip:*** Line the jelly roll pans with foil to aid in cleanup. ***Yield: 8 servings.***

The Carriage House Bed & Breakfast

Karen and Gary Gauthier
PO Box 1424, 94 Kenyon Street West
Alexandria, Ontario K0C 1A0
Tel: (613) 525-0321
E-mail: carriage@glen-net.ca
$$

ABOUT THE B&B

Located in the heart of Glengarry County — an area settled by Scots — The Carriage House is named for the world-renowned Munro and McIntosh Carriage Works, which once operated in Alexandria. The spacious home, built around a 150-year-old log cabin, combines the charms of the past with the modern conveniences of the present. In winter, guests can relax in front of the fireplace, and in summer, enjoy a relaxing view of the lake from the wraparound veranda. A hearty, three-course breakfast is a great beginning for the day's activities. Golf enthusiasts can play a round on the town's 18-hole course. For those who prefer shopping, there are numerous antique stores, art and craft stores, and a Rob McIntosh china outlet. The Carriage House is located an hour's drive from two of Canada's most vibrant cities: Montréal and Ottawa.

SEASON

all year

ACCOMMODATIONS

3 rooms with shared bath

Dundee Arms Inn

Pat Sands
200 Pownal Street
Charlottetown,
Prince Edward Island C1A 3W8
Tel: (902) 892-2496
Fax: (902) 368-8532
E-mail: dundee@dundeearms.com
$$$$

ABOUT THE B&B

Dundee Arms Inn, with its copper sconces, antique clock, and china cabinets, exemplifies Victorian country charm in the heart of the city. Built in 1903 for Parker Carvell, this gracious mansion is a fine example of the Queen Anne revival style. The house was a private residence until 1956 when the building was converted into a guest house. It became an inn in 1972. While extensive renovations have been made to satisfy the needs of today's guests, the original character and charm of the house remain. Eight guest rooms are furnished with period antiques and contain such modern conveniences as a telephone, color TV, and AM/FM radio. Over the years, the Dundee has welcomed thousands of guests to The Griffon Room, its internationally acclaimed restaurant, which has received accolades from En Route *and* Gourmet *magazines. The inn is a five-minute walk from downtown Charlottetown.*

SEASON

all year

ACCOMMODATIONS

8 rooms with private baths

Pan Seared Sea Scallops with Pesto and Shallot Butter

1 pound fresh sea scallops
2 tablespoons olive oil
6 tablespoons butter
2 tablespoons chopped shallots
1½ tablespoons pesto
1 tablespoon lemon juice
Pepper
Salt

Lemon slices
Snipped dill

Sear the scallops in the olive oil until they are starting to become opaque. Add the butter, shallots, and pesto. Turn the scallops, and sear 1 minute. Add the lemon juice and a pinch of pepper and salt, and turn off the heat. Divide the scallops between 4 small, warm plates, and garnish with lemon slices and dill. ***Yield: 4 servings.***

Polenta

"We serve this especially to guests who have allergies to gluten and other wheat products." — Anne-Marie and Irving Bansfield

3 cups water or milk
¼ teaspoon salt
1 cup cornmeal
¼ cup grated Parmesan cheese or a combination of other grated cheeses
1 tablespoon butter
¼ teaspoon ground nutmeg (optional)
Butter

Combine the water and salt, and bring to a boil. Just at the boiling point, add the cornmeal in a steady stream, and beat without stopping until the polenta is thick and separates from the sides of the pot (about 5 minutes). Remove the pot from the heat, and stir in the cheese, butter, and optional nutmeg. Place the polenta in a serving dish, and press it to the sides and smooth out the top. Butter the surface and serve. ***Tips:*** The polenta can also be flattened into a greased casserole or pie plate, topped with grated mozzarella cheese, thinly sliced tomato, or pieces of bacon or ham, and baked in a preheated 375°F oven for 15 – 20 minutes. Polenta makes a tasty reheated leftover. ***Yield: 6 servings.***

Le Gîte Park Avenue B&B

Anne-Marie and Irving Bansfield
54 Park Avenue
Ottawa, Ontario K2P 1B2
Tel: (613) 230-9131
$$

ABOUT THE B&B

A bright, airy ambiance and artistic decor await you at Park Avenue B&B, an elegant, brick 1906 home located in a charming residential area of downtown Ottawa, Canada's capital. In addition to high-quality beds done up in classic cotton and linen sheets and duvets, each guest room is furnished with a desk and swivel chair, a rocking chair, bookshelves, excellent lighting, and attractive works of art. Ideal for families, the third-floor suite has two bedrooms and a private bath. The mood throughout the house is one of relaxation and warmth. Park Avenue B&B is close to the Parliament Buildings, art galleries, and museums, and is only three minutes (by foot) from the Rideau Canal, which freezes into the world's longest skating rink. Ottawa has a number of exciting festivals and activities, including Winterlude, a winter carnival held each February. Anne-Marie and Irving make it a point to know what's going on when in Ottawa so they can advise their guests on what to see and do.

SEASON

all year

ACCOMMODATIONS

1 suite with private bath;
2 rooms with shared bath

Bay View Farm / La Ferme Bay View

Helen and Garnett Sawyer
PO Box 21,
337 New Carlisle West, Route 132
New Carlisle, Québec G0C 1Z0
Tel: (418) 752-2725/6718
$

ABOUT THE B&B

Situated between New Carlisle and Bonaventure, Bay View Farm offers country hospitality in a beautiful seaside environment on the rugged Baie des Chaleurs coastline of Québec's Gaspé Peninsula. Seaside accommodations include five comfortable guest rooms and a fully equipped cottage. At breakfast, enjoy Bay View's farm-fresh eggs, meat, homemade muffins, scones, jams, jellies, and beverages, as well as fresh fruits and vegetables in season from the farm's garden and orchards. Additional meals are available on request at reasonable rates. Handicrafts are on display throughout the house. Enjoy the breathtaking panoramic seascapes, participate in the Bay View Folk Festival (second weekend of August) with folk music and dancing, or visit Percé Rock and the archaeological caves of Saint-Elzéar.

SEASON

May – November

ACCOMMODATIONS

5 rooms with shared baths;
1 private cottage with private bath

Smoked Mackerel Pâté

½ pound cream cheese, softened
½ pound smoked mackerel, skinned and boned
2 tablespoons lemon juice
2 tablespoons minced onion
1 tablespoon butter
½ teaspoon fennel seed
¼ teaspoon black pepper
½ cup finely diced green pepper

Blend the cream cheese, mackerel, lemon juice, onion, butter, fennel seed, and pepper in a food processor. Remove the cheese mixture from the processor, then mix in the green pepper. Press the cheese mixture into a bowl, and refrigerate, covered, for at least 3 hours. ***Tip:*** Smoked herring may be substituted for the smoked mackerel, but be careful to take out all small bones before processing. This pâté is great spread on pumpernickel bread, whole wheat crackers, or French bread. ***Yield: 2½ cups.***

Muffins

Boston Muffins

"This recipe, which is at least 75 years old, is from the recipe files of Grandma Avery who lived in the Ottawa valley."
— Anne MacWhirter

1 cup brown sugar
¾ cup shortening
1½ cups milk
1 egg
½ cup molasses
1 teaspoon baking soda
3 cups all-purpose flour
½ teaspoon ground cinnamon
½ teaspoon ground cloves
Chopped walnuts (optional)
Raisins (optional)

Preheat the oven to 350°F. Mix together the brown sugar and shortening. Add the milk, egg, molasses, and baking soda, and combine. Mix together the flour, cinnamon, and cloves, and add to the milk mixture. Add optional walnuts and/or raisins, and mix. Place the batter in greased muffin cups, and bake 30 minutes. ***Yield: 24 muffins.***

Gîte à la ferme MACDALE Bed and Breakfast

Anne and Gordon MacWhirter
365 Route 132, Hope, PO Box 803
Paspébiac, Québec G0C 2K0
Tel: (418) 752-5270
$

ABOUT THE B&B

For a relaxing holiday, visit the Gaspé Peninsula and MACDALE Bed and Breakfast. Situated overlooking Baie des Chaleurs on a beef farm that has been active for five generations, this spacious three-story home offers two family rooms and a variety of guest accommodations. The aroma of fresh coffee and assorted muffins and pastries will awaken you and whet your appetite for an old-fashioned home-baked breakfast that includes farm-fresh eggs. Thanks to MACDALE's central location, tourist attractions such as world-famous Percé Rock and Forillon Park are well within day-trip driving distance. A seawater therapy resort is just minutes away, as are many museums, points of historical interest, and sports facilities. Anne is a first grade teacher while Gordon has recently retired from teaching junior high school mathematics.

SEASON

all year

ACCOMMODATIONS

1 loft with private bath;
4 rooms with shared baths

Company House Bed & Breakfast

Jill and Jerry Whiting
PO Box 1159, 172 Company Avenue
Fort Qu'Appelle, Saskatchewan
S0G 1S0
Tel: (306) 332-6333
$$

ABOUT THE B&B

Company House is located in the beautiful Qu'Appelle Valley, northeast of Regina, Saskatchewan, in the resort town of Fort Qu'Appelle. The house, built in the early 1900s, has an ornately decorated tin ceiling, bright chandeliers, beveled glass windows, maple floors, and ceramic tile fireplaces with cherrywood mantles, all of which contribute to a restful atmosphere. Guests can relax in front of the fireplace or in the private lounge complete with television and library. There are two large guest rooms with comfortable double beds. Enjoy a continental or hearty home-cooked breakfast in the quiet dining room. Company House is within walking distance of beaches and places to go fishing, canoeing, birdwatching, hiking, and shopping (including local pottery and Native craft galleries). Close by are golf courses, tennis courts, ski hills, cross-country and skidoo trails, and many historical sites.

SEASON

all year

ACCOMMODATIONS

2 rooms with shared bath

Buttermilk–Saskatoon Berry Muffins

"Saskatoon berries are a favorite to most Saskatchewanites — on a hot July day, families go berry picking in nearby Saskatoon bushes. A breakfast at Company House is not complete without these muffins." — Jill Whiting

2 cups all-purpose flour
½ cup sugar
2½ teaspoons baking powder
1 teaspoon lemon zest
½ teaspoon baking soda
½ teaspoon salt
1 cup buttermilk
1 egg
⅓ cup vegetable oil
1 cup fresh or thawed and drained frozen Saskatoon berries or blueberries
Sugar

Preheat the oven to 400°F. Grease a 12-cup muffin pan. Combine the flour, ½ cup sugar, baking powder, lemon zest, baking soda, and salt in a large mixing bowl. Stir until well blended. Beat the buttermilk, egg, and oil together in a separate bowl until well mixed. Make a well in the center of the flour mixture, and pour in the buttermilk mixture. Stir just until the dry ingredients are moistened (the mixture should be somewhat lumpy). Fold in the berries. Fill the muffin cups two-thirds full, and sprinkle the top of the muffins with sugar. Bake 20 – 25 minutes. Remove them from the pan, and serve piping hot. ***Yield: 12 muffins.***

Carrot Muffins

"Tasty, with a bit of crunch!" — Karen Gauthier

1 cup all-purpose flour
2 teaspoons baking powder
1 teaspoon baking soda
½ teaspoon ground cinnamon
½ teaspoon salt
1 cup bran (use only natural bran)
¾ cup brown sugar
¼ cup wheat germ
¾ cup grated carrot
¼ cup chopped almonds
¼ cup chopped dried apricots
2 tablespoons sesame seeds
1 tablespoon dried orange peel or grated zest of 1 orange
1 egg
1 cup buttermilk
¼ cup vegetable oil

Preheat the oven to 400°F. Sift together the flour, baking powder, baking soda, cinnamon, and salt. Stir in the bran, brown sugar, and wheat germ. Stir in the carrot, almonds, apricots, sesame seeds, and orange peel. In a separate bowl, beat the egg, add the buttermilk and oil, and mix thoroughly. Add the egg mixture to the flour mixture, and stir just enough to moisten the dry ingredients. Divide the batter between 12 greased muffin cups, and bake 20 minutes or until a toothpick inserted in the center comes out clean. ***Yield: 12 muffins.***

The Carriage House Bed & Breakfast

Karen and Gary Gauthier
PO Box 1424, 94 Kenyon Street West
Alexandria, Ontario K0C 1A0
Tel: (613) 525-0321
E-mail: carriage@glen-net.ca
$$

ABOUT THE B&B

Located in the heart of Glengarry County — an area settled by Scots — The Carriage House is named for the world-renowned Munro and McIntosh Carriage Works, which once operated in Alexandria. The spacious home, built around a 150-year-old log cabin, combines the charms of the past with the modern conveniences of the present. In winter, guests can relax in front of the fireplace, and in summer, enjoy a relaxing view of the lake from the wraparound veranda. A hearty, three-course breakfast is a great beginning for the day's activities. Golf enthusiasts can play a round on the town's 18-hole course. For those who prefer shopping, there are numerous antique stores, art and craft stores, and a Rob McIntosh china outlet. The Carriage House is located an hour's drive from two of Canada's most vibrant cities: Montréal and Ottawa.

SEASON

all year

ACCOMMODATIONS

3 rooms with shared bath

Wooded Acres Bed & Breakfast

Elva and Skip Kennedy
4907 Rocky Point Road
Victoria, British Columbia V9C 4G2
Tel: (250) 478-8172 or
(250) 474-8959
$$$

ABOUT THE B&B

Elva and Skip's country house truly is a labor of love, made from scratch with logs from their property. The emptiness that settled in once their children had "grown and flown" inspired Elva and Skip to turn their dream home into an old-fashioned B&B. Secluded in three acres of forest, Wooded Acres invites you to relax in your own sheltered hot tub amid relics of bygone times. Enjoy a full breakfast of fresh-daily house specialties (including scones and biscuits) served at your convenience. Bedrooms are decorated with antiques, queen beds, and cozy down-filled duvets, while candlelight and lace add a special touch throughout the B&B. Nearby Victoria, British Columbia's capital, is known for its breathtaking scenery, beaches, and wilderness parks. The area offers a wealth of walking trails, golf courses, fishing and birdwatching areas, and numerous venues for the work of local artisans. Wooded Acres is located conveniently close to all amenities in Victoria (30 minutes away) and the rural splendor of Sooke (20 minutes away).

SEASON

all year

ACCOMMODATIONS

2 suites with private baths

Chocolate Chip–Banana Muffins

2 cups all-purpose flour
2 teaspoons baking powder
½ teaspoon salt
Cream of tartar
½ cup butter
¾ cup granulated sugar
2 eggs
½ cup milk
1 teaspoon vanilla
1 banana, mashed
½ cup small chocolate chips
1 teaspoon brown sugar
1 teaspoon ground cinnamon

Preheat the oven to 375°F. Mix the flour, baking powder, salt, and a pinch of cream of tartar in a bowl. In a separate bowl, cream the butter and granulated sugar, and beat in the eggs one at a time. Add the milk and vanilla, and mix. Add the banana and chocolate chips, and mix. Make a well in the center of the flour mixture, and add the banana mixture. Stir just enough to moisten the dry ingredients. Place the batter in greased muffin cups. Combine the brown sugar and cinnamon, and sprinkle on the tops of the muffins. Bake 20 – 25 minutes. ***Tip:*** Place water in any unused muffin cups to keep the muffins moist. ***Yield: 10 muffins.***

Chocolate-Zucchini Muffins

¾ cup butter
2 cups sugar
3 eggs
½ cup milk
2 teaspoons almond extract
2 cups grated zucchini
2½ cups all-purpose flour
½ cup cocoa powder
2½ teaspoons baking powder
2 teaspoons ground cinnamon
1½ teaspoons baking soda
½ teaspoon salt
Sliced almonds

Preheat the oven to 375°F. Cream the butter with the sugar. Beat in the eggs one at a time. Add the milk and almond extract, and mix. Add the grated zucchini, and mix. Sift together the flour, cocoa powder, baking powder, cinnamon, baking soda, and salt. Add to the egg mixture, and stir just until the dry ingredients are moistened. Place the batter in greased muffin cups, and top with a few sliced almonds. Bake 20 – 25 minutes. ***Tip:*** These muffins freeze well. ***Yield: 24 muffins.***

Wooded Acres Bed & Breakfast

Elva and Skip Kennedy
4907 Rocky Point Road
Victoria, British Columbia V9C 4G2
Tel: (250) 478-8172 or
(250) 474-8959
$$$

ABOUT THE B&B

Elva and Skip's country house truly is a labor of love, made from scratch with logs from their property. The emptiness that settled in once their children had "grown and flown" inspired Elva and Skip to turn their dream home into an old-fashioned B&B. Secluded in three acres of forest, Wooded Acres invites you to relax in your own sheltered hot tub amid relics of bygone times. Enjoy a full breakfast of fresh-daily house specialties (including scones and biscuits) served at your convenience. Bedrooms are decorated with antiques, queen beds, and cozy down-filled duvets, while candlelight and lace add a special touch throughout the B&B. Nearby Victoria, British Columbia's capital, is known for its breathtaking scenery, beaches, and wilderness parks. The area offers a wealth of walking trails, golf courses, fishing and birdwatching areas, and numerous venues for the work of local artisans. Wooded Acres is located conveniently close to all amenities in Victoria (30 minutes away) and the rural splendor of Sooke (20 minutes away).

SEASON

all year

ACCOMMODATIONS

2 suites with private baths

Willow House B&B / La Maison des Saules

Pat Le Baron and Allan Watson
30 Western Avenue, PO Box 906
Sutton, Québec J0E 2K0
Tel: (514) 538-0035
$$

ABOUT THE B&B

A lovely 96-year-old Loyalist-style home with views of a running brook and a pond, Willow House is situated in the hub of an artisans community with many local arts and crafts shops nearby. Pat's claim to fame is home baking, and her specialties include ginger-lemon, blueberry, poppy seed, and carrot-bran muffins, and squash, oatmeal, and granola breads. (Suppers or lunches can be arranged on request.) Other Willow House niceties include a private garden where you can watch many species of birds come and go, and a cozy lounge where you can while away the hours listening to classical music (with Pat's miniature collie, Chloe, to keep you quiet company). Situated in the Eastern Townships, Sutton is a popular getaway for cycling, hiking, walking, golf, boating, skiing, antique and outlet shopping, and admiring spectacular fall foliage. About one-and-three-quarter hours from Montréal and a half hour from the Vermont border, Willow House welcomes both children and pets and permits smoking in some areas of the B&B.

SEASON

all year

ACCOMMODATIONS

4 rooms with shared baths

Cranberry-Orange Muffins

2 cups all-purpose flour
1 cup sugar
1½ teaspoons baking powder
1 teaspoon salt
½ teaspoon baking soda
¾ cup orange juice
2 tablespoons vegetable oil
1 egg, well beaten
Zest of 1 orange
1 cup chopped cranberries

Preheat the oven to 400°F. Sift the flour, sugar, baking powder, salt, and baking soda together in a large bowl. In a separate bowl, combine the orange juice, oil, egg, and orange zest. Add the flour mixture to the juice mixture, and mix just until the dry ingredients are moistened. Gently fold in the cranberries. Spray the muffin cups with non-stick cooking spray, and fill them three-quarters full with the batter. Bake 20 minutes. These muffins are best served warm. ***Tip:*** You can also freeze fresh cranberries in season and, when ready to use, thaw them slightly and chop. ***Yield: 12 muffins.***

Doughnut Muffins

1¾ cups all-purpose flour
¾ cup sugar
1½ teaspoons baking powder
½ teaspoon ground nutmeg
½ teaspoon salt
¼ teaspoon ground cinnamon
¾ cup milk
⅓ cup vegetable oil
1 egg

Coating:
¾ cup sugar
1 teaspoon ground cinnamon
Melted butter

Preheat the oven to 350°F. Combine the flour, sugar, baking powder, nutmeg, salt, and cinnamon. Mix the milk, oil, and egg, add to the flour mixture, and stir just until combined. Place the batter in greased muffin cups, and bake 20 – 25 minutes. Remove immediately from the muffin pan. For the coating, combine the sugar and cinnamon in a small bowl. Dip each muffin first in the melted butter, then in the cinnamon mixture. Serve warm or at room temperature. ***Yield: 12 muffins.***

Gîte à la ferme MACDALE Bed and Breakfast

Anne and Gordon MacWhirter
365 Route 132, Hope, PO Box 803
Paspébiac, Québec G0C 2K0
Tel: (418) 752-5270
$

ABOUT THE B&B

For a relaxing holiday, visit the Gaspé Peninsula and MACDALE Bed and Breakfast. Situated overlooking Baie des Chaleurs on a beef farm that has been active for five generations, this spacious three-story home offers two family rooms and a variety of guest accommodations. The aroma of fresh coffee and assorted muffins and pastries will awaken you and whet your appetite for an old-fashioned home-baked breakfast that includes farm-fresh eggs. Thanks to MACDALE's central location, tourist attractions such as world-famous Percé Rock and Forillon Park are well within day-trip driving distance. A seawater therapy resort is just minutes away, as are many museums, points of historical interest, and sports facilities. Anne is a first grade teacher while Gordon has recently retired from teaching junior high school mathematics.

SEASON

all year

ACCOMMODATIONS

1 loft with private bath;
4 rooms with shared baths

Mecklenburgh Inn

Suzi Fraser
78 Queen Street
Chester, Nova Scotia B0J 1J0
Tel/Fax: (902) 275-4638
www.destination-ns.com/
lighthouse/mecklenburgh
$$

ABOUT THE B&B

Constructed by shipwrights in 1890, Mecklenburgh Inn is located in the heart of seaside Chester, which has catered to summer visitors and sailing enthusiasts for over 150 years. Sleep in the spacious and comfortably appointed bedrooms filled with period furniture and other interesting objects Suzi has collected over the years, then enjoy a delicious breakfast while you plan the day ahead. You might wander the historic village streets, stopping to watch the yacht races on Mahone Bay, or browse through craft shops and boutiques. Or, maybe a sailboat ride, bicycle ride, or game of golf or tennis would be more your style. Later, relax on the balcony while the sun sets over the western shore of the bay and village activity lulls. You might consider an evening meal at one of the excellent restaurants in the area or catch a play at the Chester Playhouse. At the end of the day, the living room is the perfect place to wind down chatting by the fire or perusing travel books and magazines.

SEASON

May 24 – November 7

ACCOMMODATIONS

4 rooms with shared baths

Fruity Yogurt Muffins

2 cups all-purpose flour
⅓ cup sugar
1 teaspoon baking powder
1 teaspoon baking soda
½ teaspoon salt
1½ cups finely diced fruit (such as strawberries)
1¼ cups plain yogurt
¼ cup melted butter
1 tablespoon lemon juice

Preheat the oven to 350°F. Mix together the flour, sugar, baking powder, baking soda, and salt in a large bowl. Toss the fruit in the flour mixture briefly. Mix together the yogurt, butter, and lemon juice in a separate bowl, then add to the flour mixture. Pour the batter into a greased 12-cup muffin pan, and bake 20 minutes. *Tip:* Place water in any unused muffin cups to keep the muffins moist. ***Yield: 10 muffins.***

Hot Cereal Muffins

½ cup multigrain hot cereal mix
¾ cup milk
1 egg, beaten
3 tablespoons vegetable oil
1½ cups all-purpose flour
⅔ cup sugar
1½ tablespoons baking powder
½ cup chopped dried apricots
½ cup raisins

Preheat the oven to 375°F. Soak the cereal in the milk for 15 minutes. Add the egg and oil to the cereal mixture, and mix well. In a separate bowl, combine the flour, sugar, and baking powder. Stir the flour mixture into the cereal mixture. Stir in the apricots and raisins. Divide the batter among 12 greased muffin cups. Bake 15 – 20 minutes until a toothpick inserted in the center comes out clean. ***Yield: 12 muffins.***

Water's Edge B&B

Mary Ellen and Ed Ironside
Box 635, 331 Park Street
Tofino, British Columbia V0R 2Z0
Tel: (250) 725-1218
Fax (250) 725- 1219
$$ - $$$

ABOUT THE B&B

Water's Edge B&B, a contemporary cedar house, is set amid towering rainforest that frames views of small islands in Clayoquot Sound and the open Pacific Ocean. Stairs lead from the cliff-top location to rocky tidal pools directly below. Two beautiful beaches are reached by a short scramble along the rocks or by a five-minute stroll along a boardwalk to Tonquin Park. The home's builder was a boat carpenter, fisher, beachcomber, and sawmill operator, and his love of nature is evident in the design. The large windows and high wood ceilings frame the magnificent views. Tofino is a scenic fishing village, minutes from Pacific Rim National Park and Long Beach with its 13 miles of sandy beach. In the area you can walk the beach or hike in the rainforest, go fishing, diving, kayaking, or cycling, and play tennis or golf. Whale watching is a favorite pastime. Hosts Mary Ellen and Ed, who have lived in different parts of Canada and abroad, love traveling, reading, photography, gardening, and meeting people.

SEASON

all year

ACCOMMODATIONS

1 room with private bath;
2 rooms with shared bath

Silver Fox Inn

The Zambonin Family
(Mario, Susan, Jessica, Matthew)
61 Granville Street
Summerside, Prince Edward Island
C1N 2Z3
Tel: (902) 436-4033
E-mail: silver.fox.inn@pei.sympatico.ca
www3.pei.sympatico.ca/peinns/silv-fox.htm
$$

ABOUT THE B&B

The name of this inn recalls the fascinating story of two poor trappers who went from rags to riches developing the silver fox industry in Prince Edward Island from 1880 to 1914. Built in 1892 as a private residence, Silver Fox Inn was designed by the famed architect William Critchlow Harris (1854 – 1913), whose brother Robert Harris gained world recognition as a portrait artist (his painting entitled "The Fathers of Confederation" is known to every Canadian). The Silver Fox has been carefully preserved and retains the original beauty of its spacious rooms with fireplaces and fine woodwork. Six bedrooms, each with private bath, feature period furnishings. Breakfast includes freshly baked muffins and biscuits and homemade preserves. The quiet location is central to Summerside's business and shopping district. Annual area events include the Lobster Carnival, Hydroplane Regatta, and Highland Gathering.

SEASON

all year

ACCOMMODATIONS

6 rooms with private baths

Maple-Bran Muffins

1 cup all-purpose flour
¼ cup sugar
3 teaspoons baking powder
½ teaspoon salt
1 cup bran (use only natural bran)
½ cup milk
5 tablespoons melted butter
3 tablespoons maple syrup
1 egg, beaten
½ teaspoon vanilla

Preheat the oven to 400°F. Mix together the flour, sugar, baking powder, and salt. Mix in the bran. Combine the milk, butter, maple syrup, egg, and vanilla in a separate bowl. Make a well in the flour mixture, add the milk mixture, and mix briefly. Place the batter in greased muffin cups, and bake 20 minutes. ***Tip:*** Place water in any unused muffin cups to keep the muffins moist. ***Yield: 8 muffins.***

Miracle Date and Pecan Muffins

"If you like your muffins with crunch, don't leave out the pecans!"
— Doloris Paquin

1 cup boiling water
1½ cups chopped dates
2 teaspoons baking soda
1 cup Miracle Whip salad dressing or mayonnaise
¾ cup brown sugar
½ cup bran
1½ cups all-purpose flour
½ teaspoon ground cinnamon
½ teaspoon ground nutmeg
¼ cup chopped pecans

Preheat the oven to 375°F. In a large bowl, pour the boiling water over the dates and baking soda. Mix and allow to cool. Add the Miracle Whip and brown sugar, and mix well. Add the bran, and mix well. Sift in the flour, cinnamon, and nutmeg, and stir to blend. Place the batter in a greased 12-cup muffin pan, and top each muffin with pecans. Bake 20 minutes. ***Yield: 12 muffins.***

The Green Door Bed & Breakfast

Doloris Paquin
PO Box 335, 376 Berford Street
Wiarton, Ontario N0H 2T0
Tel: (519) 534-4710
$ – $$

ABOUT THE B&B

"Completely comfortable, wonderfully welcoming," is how one recent guest described The Green Door. Built at the turn of the century, this red-brick, stately, restored Victorian house is situated on Wiarton's main street and is within a few minutes' walk of shops and restaurants. The main floor has a dining room and a charming and spacious living room with bay windows. Up the wooden staircase are three guest bedrooms, two with double beds and one with two single beds, as well as a large guest bathroom. The high ceilings and spacious rooms lend an airy feeling to this B&B with all the comforts and coziness of home. Outside, enjoy the large garden, maple-shaded deck, and barbecue facilities.

SEASON

all year

ACCOMMODATIONS

1 room with private bath;
2 rooms with shared bath

Twin Pillars Bed & Breakfast

Bev Suek and Joe Taylor
235 Oakwood Avenue
Winnipeg, Manitoba R3L 1E5
Tel: (204) 284-7590 or
(204) 452-4925
Fax: (204) 452-4925
E-mail: tls@escape.ca
www.escape.ca/~tls/twin.htm

$ – $$

ABOUT THE B&B

Enjoy turn-of-the-century hospitality and ambiance at Twin Pillars, aptly named for the two stately white pillars out front. Beautiful antique-filled rooms and lively conversation with congenial hosts Bev and Joe give this B&B a friendly, homey atmosphere. Twin Pillars welcomes children and dog lovers (there's a resident dog in the hosts' part of the house). Group catering, baby-sitting, free laundry facilities, and designated smoking rooms are also offered. The house specialty is a breakfast of home-baked croissants and homemade jams. Situated in a quiet residential area, Twin Pillars is across from a beautiful park, and down the street from a vintage movie house, restaurants, and a bus route. Assiniboine Park and Zoo is 20 minutes by car, while downtown and the Forks National Park and Market are each 10 minutes by car.

SEASON

all year

ACCOMMODATIONS

4 rooms (including 1 suite) with shared baths

Oat Bran–Raisin Muffins

1 cup all-purpose flour
¾ cup brown sugar
¼ cup vegetable oil
2 teaspoons baking powder
¼ teaspoon salt
1 cup buttermilk
1 egg
1 cup oat bran
⅔ cup raisins
1 teaspoon baking soda

Preheat the oven to 400°F. Whisk together the flour, brown sugar, oil, baking powder, and salt. Gently add the buttermilk, egg, oat bran, raisins, and baking soda. Fill paper-lined muffin cups three-quarters full with batter. Bake about 20 minutes. ***Tip:*** Place water in any unused muffin cups to keep the muffins moist. ***Yield: 18 muffins.***

Overnight Bran-Raisin Muffins

"A weaving trick of mine is to count out loud, which I suggest you try when adding the separate cups of ingredients for this recipe. This way, if you're interrupted, you're more likely to remember where you were!" — Ann Fleischer

6 eggs
2 cups sugar
1 cup vegetable oil
1 tablespoon molasses
2 teaspoons baking powder
1 teaspoon baking soda
1 teaspoon salt
3 cups milk
3 cups all-purpose flour
5 cups bran
½ cup raisins

Mix together the eggs, sugar, oil, molasses, baking powder, baking soda, and salt. Add the milk, and mix. Add the flour, 1 cup at a time, and mix after each addition. Add the bran, 1 cup at a time, and mix after each addition. Add the raisins, and let the mixture stand overnight in the refrigerator — that's the secret. In the morning, remove from the refrigerator about 45 minutes before baking. Preheat the oven to 400°F. Pour the batter into greased muffin cups, and bake 20 minutes. ***Yield: 48 muffins.***

Cedar Gables

Ann and Don Fleischer
4080 Magog Road
North Hatley, Québec J0B 2C0
Tel: (819) 842-4120
$$ – $$$

ABOUT THE B&B

Established in 1985 as North Hatley's premier B&B, Cedar Gables is a large circa-1890 house located on beautiful Lake Massawippi in the heart of Québec's magnificent Eastern Townships (30 minutes from the US border and one-and-a-half hours from Montréal). The house is exquisitely decorated with many antique Oriental carpets and a few surprises. Bright and colorful guest rooms offer lake or garden views, coordinated bed and bath linens, Yardley soaps, terry robes, and oh-so-comfy beds with spreads by innkeeper Ann herself — an expert weaver and spinner. Breakfasts are hearty and memorable. While enjoying your custom-blended coffee, you'll be able to count no less than 30 fresh fruits in your fruit cup and sample up to 26 different homemade jams (banana daiquiri is a favorite!). In winter, cozy up to one of the three fireplaces and play games, read, or listen to music. In summer, lounge on the lakeside sun deck, swim, canoe, or fish. The unique village of North Hatley, where some of the finest dining in North America is available — is a five-minute walk away.

SEASON

all year

ACCOMMODATIONS

5 rooms (including 1 suite) with private baths

Morrison Manor

Nancy and Jerry Morrison
RR #1
Morpeth, Ontario N0P 1X0
Tel: (519) 674-3431
$$

ABOUT THE B&B

Built in 1989 especially as a B&B, Morrison Manor is a warm and charming three-story hand-crafted log home just a few minutes from the natural environment of Rondeau Provincial Park. On the first floor of the manor is a cozy living room with a fireplace. A full country breakfast is served in the large dining room where fresh herbs hang overhead. Six guest bedrooms are on the second floor, and two large private suites that overlook fields, a pond, and the full length of Rondeau Bay are on the third floor. Each room has a different country style, and a door that opens onto a large porch. Besides the park, which is a bird-watcher's paradise, the area features a winery, buffalo farm, art gallery, cultural center, antique shops, car races, seasonal festivals, and much more. Nancy, a secondary school teacher, and Jerry, a quality-control technician, enjoy cooking, gardening, traveling, theatergoing, birdwatching, walking, decorating, and playing shuffleboard.

SEASON

all year

ACCOMMODATIONS

2 suites with private baths;
6 rooms with shared baths

Poppy Seed Muffins

1¼ cups sugar
1¼ cups vegetable oil
1 cup evaporated skim milk
3 eggs
2½ cups all-purpose flour
2¼ teaspoons baking powder
⅛ teaspoon salt
¼ cup poppy seeds
1¼ teaspoons vanilla

Preheat the oven to 350°F. Combine the sugar, oil, evaporated milk, and eggs with an electric mixer until well blended. In a separate bowl, sift the flour, baking powder, and salt together. Add the flour mixture to the egg mixture, and beat on low. Add the poppy seeds and vanilla, and beat until smooth. Pour the batter into a greased 12-cup muffin pan, and bake 20 minutes. ***Yield: 12 muffins.***

Pumpkin-Pecan Muffins

2 eggs, beaten
1½ cups sugar
1 cup cooked mashed pumpkin
½ cup soya oil
⅓ cup water
1⅔ cups all-purpose flour
1 teaspoon baking soda
1 teaspoon ground cinnamon
½ teaspoon baking powder
½ teaspoon salt
1 cup chopped pecans

Preheat the oven to 350°F. In a large bowl, mix the eggs, sugar, pumpkin, oil, and water. In a separate bowl, combine the flour, baking soda, cinnamon, baking powder, and salt. Add the flour mixture to the pumpkin mixture, and mix well. Fold in the pecans. Fill paper-lined muffin cups three-quarters full with the batter. Bake 20 – 25 minutes or until a toothpick inserted in the center comes out clean (do not over-bake). Cool on a wire rack. ***Yield: 12 muffins.***

The Catalpa Tree

Connie Ellis
2217 London Line
Sarnia, Ontario N7T 7H2
Tel: (800) 276-5135 or
(519) 542-5008
Fax: (519) 541-0297
$

ABOUT THE B&B

Built in 1894 by the host's great-grandfather, William Beatty, this family home displays true Victorian fashion, complete with gingerbread trim. The house, which is situated on a 100-acre crop farm, has been lovingly maintained in its original form. The B&B's decor complements the design of the house but also incorporates modern conveniences such as gas fireplaces and central air conditioning. Furnishings are a warm mix of contemporary and traditional pieces. A full gourmet breakfast is served in the parlor. The original dining room is now a lounge where guests can visit, relax with a good book, watch a favorite television program, enjoy a video, or play a game. A golf course is located at the end of the lane. In the area are many historical points of interest, a community theater, a water amusement park, a harness racing track, and places to go fishing, swimming, and boating. Picnic lunches or dinner are available by advance request.

SEASON

all year

ACCOMMODATIONS

3 rooms with shared bath

Hilltop Acres Bed & Breakfast

Janice and Wayne Trowsdale
Route 166
Bideford, Prince Edward Island
Mailing address: PO Box 3011
Ellerslie, Prince Edward Island
C0B 1J0
Tel/Fax: (902) 831-2817
$ – $$

ABOUT THE B&B

Enjoy the quiet of the country in this renovated 1930s residence in historic Bideford — where Anne of Green Gables *author Lucy Maud Montgomery first taught school from 1894 to 1895. Relax on the second-story balcony overlooking scenic Malpeque Bay or in the large living room. Stroll about the spacious lawn, play croquet, or bike or walk around the 75-acre property. Bedrooms have a queen pillowtop bed, a double bed, or two single beds. A four-piece shared bath with a whirlpool tub is for guests only. Hilltop Acres specializes in homemade muffins and preserves served in the guest breakfast room. Just minutes from the village of Tyne Valley, Green Provincial Park, and the Shipbuilding Museum, Hilltop Acres is also a half hour from golf courses and shopping centers, and one hour from Confederation Bridge. Your hosts are non-smokers and enjoy sharing the history and culture of the area. Janice is an office clerk and Wayne is a school bus driver, carpenter, and handyman.*

SEASON

June – October
(off-season by reservation)

ACCOMMODATIONS

3 rooms with shared bath

Quick Banana Muffins

"I have had many requests from my guests to share this recipe. The wheat-oat flour gives extra flavor and my guests like the hint of cinnamon on top." — Janice Trowsdale

⅓ cup corn or olive oil
1 cup sugar
1 egg
4 teaspoons milk
½ teaspoon vanilla
2 ripe bananas, mashed
1½ cups wheat-oat flour
1 teaspoon baking soda
½ teaspoon salt
Cinnamon sugar

Preheat the oven to 350°F. Cream the oil and sugar. Add the egg, milk, vanilla, and banana, and mix. Add the flour, baking soda, and salt, and mix until moistened. Pour the batter into a greased 12-cup muffin pan. Sprinkle the tops of the muffins with cinnamon sugar, and bake 20 – 25 minutes. ***Yield: 12 muffins.***

Rhubarb-Oat Muffins

¼ cup vegetable oil
¾ cup brown sugar
1 cup all-purpose flour
2 teaspoons baking powder
1 teaspoon baking soda
¼ teaspoon salt
1 cup buttermilk
1 egg
⅓ cup large-flake rolled oats
⅓ cup oat bran
⅓ cup wheat germ
1¼ cups chopped rhubarb

Preheat the oven to 400°F. Combine the oil, brown sugar, flour, baking powder, baking soda, and salt. Add the buttermilk, egg, rolled oats, oat bran, and wheat germ. Mix gently, then fold in the rhubarb. Fill paper-lined muffin cups three-quarters full with batter. Bake about 20 minutes.
Tip: Place water in any unused muffin cups to keep the muffins moist.
Yield: About 14 muffins.

Twin Pillars Bed & Breakfast

Bev Suek and Joe Taylor
235 Oakwood Avenue
Winnipeg, Manitoba R3L 1E5
Tel: (204) 284-7590 or
(204) 452-4925
Fax: (204) 452-4925
E-mail: tls@escape.ca
www.escape.ca/~tls/twin.htm
$ – $$

ABOUT THE B&B

Enjoy turn-of-the-century hospitality and ambiance at Twin Pillars, aptly named for the two stately white pillars out front. Beautiful antique-filled rooms and lively conversation with congenial hosts Bev and Joe give this B&B a friendly, homey atmosphere. Twin Pillars welcomes children and dog lovers (there's a resident dog in the hosts' part of the house). Group catering, baby-sitting, free laundry facilities, and designated smoking rooms are also offered. The house specialty is a breakfast of home-baked croissants and homemade jams. Situated in a quiet residential area, Twin Pillars is across from a beautiful park, and down the street from a vintage movie house, restaurants, and a bus route. Assiniboine Park and Zoo is 20 minutes by car, while downtown and the Forks National Park and Market are each 10 minutes by car.

SEASON

all year

ACCOMMODATIONS

4 rooms (including 1 suite)
with shared baths

The Lookout at Schooner Cove

Marj and Herb Wilkie
3381 Dolphin Drive
Nanoose Bay, British Columbia
V9P 9H7
Tel/Fax: (250) 468-9796
www.pixsell.bc.ca/bb/1169.htm
$$

ABOUT THE B&B

Situated halfway between Victoria and Tofino on unspoiled Vancouver Island, this West Coast contemporary cedar home stands in a woodsy setting of rocks and tall evergreens. The wrap-around deck affords a 180-degree view of the Strait of Georgia and the majestic mountains beyond. Relax and savor this "little bit of heaven" or hike, golf, kayak, sail, fish, or sightsee. Take a day trip to the wild western shore of the island and Pacific Rim National Park or head south to charming Victoria. The vacation suite will accommodate four people and, with its private entrance and deck and fully equipped kitchen, makes a popular headquarters for an island stay. Hearty breakfasts are served in the dining room overlooking the ocean. After running a store in New York's Catskill Mountains for 17 years, Marj (from Australia) and Herb (from the US) established The Lookout in 1988 and enjoy helping their guests have a memorable stay.

SEASON

May – October
(or by arrangement)

ACCOMMODATIONS

1 vacation suite with private bath;
1 room with private bath;
1 room with shared bath

Rhubarb-Pecan Muffins

"Voted the best muffins ever by hundreds of enthusiastic guests!"
— Marj Wilkie

2 cups all-purpose flour
¾ cup sugar
1½ teaspoons baking powder
1 teaspoon salt
½ teaspoon baking soda
¾ cup chopped pecans
¾ cup orange juice
¼ cup vegetable oil
1 egg, beaten
1¼ cups chopped rhubarb
2 teaspoons orange zest
Halved pecans

Preheat the oven to 350°F. In a large bowl, mix together the flour, sugar, baking powder, salt, baking soda, and pecans. In a smaller bowl, beat together the orange juice, oil, and egg. Mix in the rhubarb and orange zest. Add the orange juice mixture to the flour mixture, and mix quickly. Spoon the batter into a greased 12-cup muffin pan, decorate each muffin with a half pecan, and bake 25 – 30 minutes. *Tip:* Fresh rhubarb works best in this recipe. ***Yield: 12 muffins.***

Sourdough Blueberry Muffins

4 cups sourdough sponge batter*
1½ cups whole wheat flour
½ cup sugar
¼ cup powdered non-fat milk
1 teaspoon salt
½ cup melted butter
1 egg
¾ cup blueberries
1 teaspoon baking soda
1 tablespoon water

**Note: In the evening (or at least 12 hours before using), make the sponge batter (see pages 88 – 89).*

Preheat the oven to 375°F. Reserve 1 cup of the sponge batter, and return it to your sourdough starter container. Sift the flour, sugar, powdered milk, and salt into a bowl. Make a well in the center. Mix the butter and egg thoroughly with the remaining sponge, and add the sponge mixture to the well in the flour mixture. Stir only enough to moisten the dry ingredients. Add the blueberries. Dissolve the baking soda in the water, and add to the batter just before filling greased muffin cups three-quarters full. Bake 30 – 35 minutes. ***Tip:*** Place water in any unused muffin cups to keep the muffins moist. ***Yield: 20 mini or 12 regular-sized muffins.***

Hawkins House Bed & Breakfast

Carla Pitzel and Garry Umbrich
303 Hawkins Street
Whitehorse, Yukon Y1A 1X5
Tel: (867) 668-7638
Fax: (867) 668-7632
$$$$

ABOUT THE B&B

To stay at the Hawkins House Bed & Breakfast is to share a once-in-a-lifetime Yukon experience with your hosts Carla, Garry, and their two sons. Each guest room in this custom-built, luxury Victorian B&B highlights a different Yukon theme and features private bath and balcony, oak floor, bar sink, refrigerator, cable TV, and VCR. Guests can take a Jacuzzi soak in the Fleur de Lys Room, watch videos about Native peoples in the First Nations Room, step back into gold rush days in the Victorian Tea Rose Room, or admire the splendid view of the SS Klondike *paddlewheeler and Canyon Mountain from the balcony of the Fireweed Room. Especially geared to the business traveler, Hawkins House provides the convenience of a private telephone line and answering machine, fax service, and a work table with a light and computer jack. Breakfast is a homemade feast of northern and international delights — from the home-smoked salmon pâté and moose sausage to jams, syrups, and sourdough pastries.*

SEASON

all year

ACCOMMODATIONS

4 rooms with private baths

Brookside Hospitality Home

Pearl and Lloyd Hiscock
PO Box 104
Sunnyside, Newfoundland A0B 3J0
Tel: (709) 472-4515
$

ABOUT THE B&B

You'll be welcomed like family at Brookside Hospitality Home, a well-maintained ranch-style dwelling in the rural community of Sunnyside. Pearl and Lloyd have lived in Sunnyside practically all their lives and know what Newfoundland hospitality is all about. Get to know them over a cup of tea or coffee, which is provided along with a bedtime snack. In the morning, make your way to the breakfast nook, which overlooks the water, where homemade bread and jam, cereals, and juices await you. Radio, cable TV, laundry facilities, and ample parking are also available. Let your well-informed hosts direct you to the best sights in the province. Lloyd is a boat enthusiast and you may want to look in on his latest boat building project in the shed. Pearl keeps busy with her household responsibilities. Brookside is about one-and-a-half hours' drive from the Argentia Ferry to North Sydney, Nova Scotia, and one hour's drive from St. John's, capital of Newfoundland.

SEASON

all year

ACCOMMODATIONS

2 rooms with shared bath

Spiced Apple Muffins

1½ cups all-purpose flour
1 cup sugar
2 teaspoons baking powder
2 teaspoons ground cinnamon
1 teaspoon baking soda
1 cup peeled, cored, and chopped apple
½ cup raisins or walnuts
2 eggs
½ cup buttermilk or ½ cup milk mixed with 1½ teaspoons lemon juice
½ cup melted butter

Preheat the oven to 400°F. In a large bowl, mix the flour, sugar, baking powder, cinnamon, and baking soda. Add the apple and raisins, and toss to coat them with the flour mixture. In a small bowl, beat the eggs. Add the buttermilk and butter, and beat. Add the egg mixture to the flour mixture, and stir just until blended. Fill greased muffin cups two-thirds full. Bake 15 – 20 minutes. ***Yield: 12 muffins.***

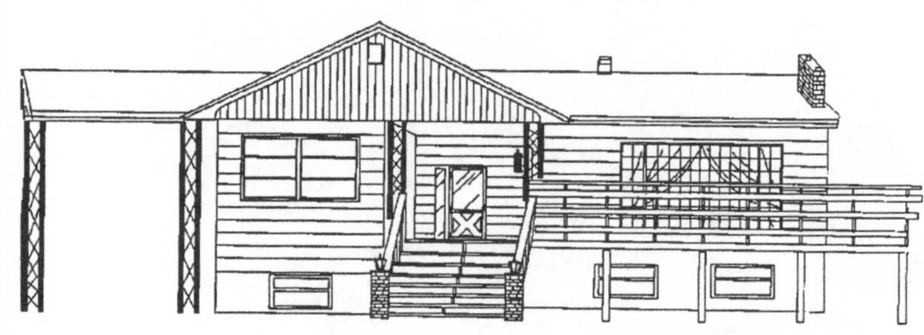

Strawberry-Oatmeal Muffins

"A great snack anytime!" — Isabel Christie

1½ cups all-purpose flour
¾ cup quick-cooking rolled oats
1 tablespoon baking powder
½ teaspoon ground cinnamon
½ teaspoon salt
¼ cup butter or margarine
½ cup sugar
1 egg, beaten
1 cup milk
½ teaspoon almond extract
1 cup diced fresh strawberries or thawed, well-drained, diced frozen strawberries
Melted butter
Ground nutmeg

Preheat the oven to 400°F. Mix together the flour, oats, baking powder, cinnamon, and salt. Cream together the butter, sugar, and egg. Stir the flour mixture into the butter mixture alternately with the milk. Add the almond extract. Fold in the strawberries. Spoon into a greased 12-cup muffin pan. Bake 25 minutes or until golden brown. Brush with melted butter, and sprinkle with nutmeg. ***Yield: 12 muffins.***

Riverdell Estate

Clare and Isabel Christie
68 Ross Road
Dartmouth, Nova Scotia B2Z 1B4
Tel/Fax: (902) 434-7880
$$ – $$$

ABOUT THE B&B

Nestled among the trees beside a babbling brook, Riverdell offers modern luxury with good, old-fashioned hospitality. Antiques, collectibles, and handmade quilts adorn this charming Cape Cod home. The large rooms with private or shared baths include two "special occasion" suites — both with a double whirlpool and one with a fireplace. There's lots of space to read, relax, or birdwatch from the sunny Florida Room where your homemade breakfast is served. All this is within minutes of the ocean beach, golf course, and Dartmouth and Halifax — two cities full of adventure. Whatever your leisure interests may be, your knowledgeable hosts Clare and Isabel will ensure you get the most out of your stay.

SEASON

all year

ACCOMMODATIONS

4 rooms with private baths;
2 rooms with shared baths

Au Fil des Saisons

Odile Côté and David Leslie
324, 21e Rue
Québec City, Québec G1L 1Y7
Tel: (418) 648-8168
$$

ABOUT THE B&B

A warm, friendly, and healthy stay awaits you at Au Fil des Saisons. Just a five-minute drive from historic and charming Old Québec, this two-story brick house is on a quiet, tree-lined residential street with ample parking. The owners have created an ecologically healthy environment with natural products and materials, such as cotton sheets, wool comforters, hardwood floors, and antique furniture, and, needless to say, this is a smoke-free B&B. Two inviting bedrooms on the second floor share a common bathroom. In warm weather, take pleasure in rocking on the deck near the garden or contemplating the good life by the pond. When the winds blow cold, warm up in the living room and sip some tea in front of a fire. In the morning, follow your nose down to a feast of organically grown and home-made foods, and chat with your hosts to a background of classical music. Odile and David will provide you with tourist guides and maps and take the time to ensure you make the most of your visit to picturesque Québec City and the surrounding region.

SEASON

all year

ACCOMMODATIONS

2 rooms with shared bath

Whole Wheat–Fruit Muffins

"The original recipe came from a friend who made these muffins for us at Christmas. It has evolved over time and this is the way we like them the best. We use organic ingredients for this recipe wherever possible." — David Leslie

2 cups whole wheat pastry flour (soft, finely milled, low-gluten flour)
1 teaspoon alum-free baking powder*
2 eggs
½ cup maple syrup or honey
½ cup milk
1 teaspoon vanilla
1½ cups berries or chopped fruit (such as blueberries, raspberries, strawberries, bananas, or apples)
¼ cup melted butter

**Note: Available at health food stores.*

Preheat the oven to 350°F. Mix together the flour and baking powder. In a second bowl, mix the eggs, maple syrup, milk, and vanilla. Pour the egg mixture into the flour mixture. Add the berries and butter, and mix. Pour the batter into a greased 12-cup muffin pan. Bake 25 minutes. ***Yield: 12 muffins.***

Wild Blueberry-Buttermilk Muffins

"These muffins are especially good when the wild blueberries are in season, but are equally good using frozen ones. Simply fold them in quickly and don't overwork the batter." — Janice Trowsdale

2 cups all-purpose flour
2½ teaspoons baking powder
½ teaspoon salt
6 tablespoons butter
½ cup brown sugar
½ cup granulated sugar
2 eggs
¾ cup buttermilk
2 cups wild blueberries

Topping (optional):
¼ cup ground walnuts
4 teaspoons granulated sugar
½ teaspoon ground cinnamon

Preheat the oven to 400°F. In a bowl, combine the flour, baking powder, and salt. In another bowl, cream the butter, brown sugar, and granulated sugar; beat in the eggs, add the buttermilk, and mix until well blended. Pour the egg mixture over the flour mixture, and stir just until the dry ingredients are moistened. Fold in the blueberries, and place the batter in a greased 12-cup muffin pan. For the optional topping, mix together the walnuts, granulated sugar, and cinnamon, and sprinkle over the muffins just before baking them. Bake 20 – 25 minutes. ***Yield: 12 muffins.***

Hilltop Acres Bed & Breakfast

Janice and Wayne Trowsdale
Route 166
Bideford, Prince Edward Island
Mailing address: PO Box 3011
Ellerslie, Prince Edward Island
C0B 1J0
Tel/Fax: (902) 831-2817
$ – $$

ABOUT THE B&B

Enjoy the quiet of the country in this renovated 1930s residence in historic Bideford — where Anne of Green Gables *author Lucy Maud Montgomery first taught school from 1894 to 1895. Relax on the second-story balcony overlooking scenic Malpeque Bay or in the large living room. Stroll about the spacious lawn, play croquet, or bike or walk around the 75-acre property. Bedrooms have a queen pillowtop bed, a double bed, or two single beds. A four-piece shared bath with a whirlpool tub is for guests only. Hilltop Acres specializes in homemade muffins and preserves served in the guest breakfast room. Just minutes from the village of Tyne Valley, Green Provincial Park, and the Shipbuilding Museum, Hilltop Acres is also a half hour from golf courses and shopping centers, and one hour from Confederation Bridge. Your hosts are non-smokers and enjoy sharing the history and culture of the area. Janice is an office clerk and Wayne is a school bus driver, carpenter, and handyman.*

SEASON

June – October
(off-season by reservation)

ACCOMMODATIONS

3 rooms with shared bath

Quick & Yeast Breads

Bannock Bake

"A popular activity at The Fieldstone Inn is baking bannock on a stick over an open fire. Our bannock recipe has been sent all over the world. One of our guests from Japan faxed to request the recipe for a barbecue party they were hosting in Tokyo!" — Carrie Brennan

5 cups all-purpose flour
2 tablespoons baking powder
1 teaspoon ground cinnamon
1 teaspoon salt
½ cup margarine
2 cups water
Jam or cheese spread

Combine the flour, baking powder, cinnamon, and salt. Add the margarine, and mix with a fork until the margarine is finely blended. Stir in the water. Roll the dough into balls (bigger than a golf ball and smaller than a baseball). Squeeze a ball onto the end of a small stick or branch from a tree. Bake the bannock over an open fire, and turn frequently. When nicely browned (about 15 minutes), remove the bannock from the stick and fill the bread with your favorite jam or cheese. ***Yield: 20 – 25 bannocks.***

The Fieldstone Inn

Carrie and Kelly Brennan
PO Box 26038
Regina, Saskatchewan S4R 8R7
Tel: (306) 731-2377
Fax: (306) 731-2369
E-mail: fieldstone.inn@
sk.sympatico.ca
$$

ABOUT THE B&B

Winner of the 1998 Tourism Saskatchewan Award of Excellence for "Rookie of the Year," The Fieldstone Inn is nestled on the southern slopes of the Qu'Appelle Valley. The inn was built in 1903 by Helen Pomphrey Lauder, who immigrated to Canada from Scotland in search of her youngest son, John, who had run away with the local barmaid. Over the next 76 years, five generations of Lauders lived and prospered in their fieldstone home. In 1995, the Brennans purchased the property and began restoring the house to its original elegance. The house features stone walls two feet thick, wood floors, arched stained glass windows, a cozy parlor with a fireplace, and a formal dining room, library, and living room. After a hearty country breakfast, guests can take a walk around the farm, go exploring in the Hidden Valley Nature Refuge adjacent to the B&B, or go canoeing. Other area attractions include St. Nicolas Historic Church, Qu'Appelle Valley Market Gardens, Regina Beach, Buffalo Jump, and the Last Mountain Bird Sanctuary.

SEASON

all year

ACCOMMODATIONS

3 rooms with shared bath

Cedar Gables

Ann and Don Fleischer
4080 Magog Road
North Hatley, Québec J0B 2C0
Tel: (819) 842-4120
$$ – $$$

ABOUT THE B&B

Established in 1985 as North Hatley's premier B&B, Cedar Gables is a large circa-1890 house located on beautiful Lake Massawippi in the heart of Québec's magnificent Eastern Townships (30 minutes from the US border and one-and-a-half hours from Montréal). The house is exquisitely decorated with many antique Oriental carpets and a few surprises. Bright and colorful guest rooms offer lake or garden views, coordinated bed and bath linens, Yardley soaps, terry robes, and oh-so-comfy beds with spreads by innkeeper Ann herself — an expert weaver and spinner. Breakfasts are hearty and memorable. While enjoying your custom-blended coffee, you'll be able to count no less than 30 fresh fruits in your fruit cup and sample up to 26 different homemade jams (banana daiquiri is a favorite!). In winter, cozy up to one of the three fireplaces and play games, read, or listen to music. In summer, lounge on the lakeside sun deck, swim, canoe, or fish. The unique village of North Hatley, where some of the finest dining in North America is available — is a five-minute walk away.

SEASON

all year

ACCOMMODATIONS

5 rooms (including 1 suite) with private baths

Butter Rolls

½ cup sugar
1 tablespoon salt
2 cups boiling water
1 cup margarine
2 packages active dry yeast (2 tablespoons)
2 eggs, beaten
7 cups all-purpose flour

Dissolve the sugar and salt in the boiling water. Add the margarine, and dissolve. When cooled to lukewarm, add the yeast and wait 5 – 10 minutes until dissolved. Add the eggs and 2 cups of the flour, and stir until smooth. Add the remaining flour, and stir until well blended. Cover well, and refrigerate overnight or until doubled in size. In the morning, punch down the dough, turn it out on a lightly floured surface, and knead 2 – 3 minutes. Let the dough stand for 10 minutes covered with the bowl (this will help the dough to warm up). Divide the dough into 3 parts. Roll each part into a circle a little less than ½" thick. Cut into equal-sized triangles, and roll up each piece beginning at the wide end. Place on a lightly greased cookie sheet, and let rise until doubled in size. Preheat the oven to 425°F, and bake 5 minutes until lightly golden. Remove the rolls from the pan and cool. ***Yield: 48 rolls.***

Cape Breton Breakfast Bread

"Molasses, buttermilk, and oatmeal were staples in many Nova Scotia homes. This bread, which we often serve at Fresh Start, was a childhood treat. It's wonderful with a dish of applesauce."
— Innis and Sheila MacDonald

2 cups buttermilk
¾ cup molasses
2 teaspoons baking soda
1 teaspoon salt
1 cup all-purpose flour
1 cup whole wheat flour
1 cup large-flake rolled oats
½ cup raisins

Preheat the oven to 400°F. Grease a 9 x 5 x 3" loaf pan. Combine the buttermilk, molasses, baking soda, and salt. In a separate bowl, combine the all-purpose flour, whole wheat flour, and oats. Make a well in the center of the flour mixture, and blend in the buttermilk mixture. Fold in the raisins. Place the batter in the prepared loaf pan. Reduce the oven temperature to 350°F, and bake the loaf 60 minutes. ***Tip:*** This bread is great for toasting when it's a couple of days old. ***Yield: 1 loaf.***

Fresh Start Bed & Breakfast

Innis and Sheila MacDonald
2720 Gottingen Street
Halifax, Nova Scotia B3K 3C7
Tel: (902) 453-6616
$ – $$

ABOUT THE B&B

Fresh Start Bed & Breakfast is an 1895 Victorian mansion, one of the few North End houses to escape destruction by the Halifax Explosion of 1917. It's located in an interesting area populated by families, artists, craftspeople, and students. Citadel Hill, historic properties, and the uniquely designed Hydrostone District are within walking distance. Halifax is a friendly city with many restaurants, live theater, wonderful crafts, and a lively nightlife. In July, visitors come for the International Tattoo Festival and, in August, for the International Buskers Festival. Conveniently located on a bus route, informal Fresh Start lets guests decide when to check in and check out. Laundry service and off-street parking are available, and breakfast tastes great! Guests enjoy relaxing in solitary quiet, visiting with the hosts and other guests, reading in the library, or watching TV. The two owners are sisters and nurses. They are also enthusiastic grandmothers and travelers! Innis likes gardening, crafts, and social activism, while Sheila likes cooking and reading.

SEASON

all year

ACCOMMODATIONS

2 rooms with private baths;
6 rooms with shared baths

DeWitt's Bed and Breakfast

Irene DeWitt and Wendy Kelly
RR #1
Airdrie, Alberta T4B 2A3
Tel: (403) 948-5356
Fax: (403) 912-0788
E-mail: dewitbnb@cadvision.com
$$

ABOUT THE B&B

A relaxing stay in the country awaits you at DeWitt's Bed and Breakfast. Enjoy a hearty, home-cooked breakfast either on the flower filled patio or in the dining room, from which the Rocky Mountains can be seen. The three bedrooms are simple yet elegant: The Evergreen Room has a huge picture window, twin beds, and a private bathroom; The Knotty Pine Room has a double bed and a shared bathroom; and The Whispering Spruce Room has a queen bed and a shared bathroom. DeWitt's B&B is located a short distance west of Airdrie and within 20 minutes of Calgary and the international airport. It's an hour's drive to the scenic Kananaskis country, on the way to Canmore and Banff National Park. Nearby attractions include the Calgary Stampede, Calgary Zoo, and Glenbow Museum.

SEASON

all year

ACCOMMODATIONS

1 room with private bath;
2 rooms with shared baths

Cinnamon Loaf

"A favorite with our guests." — Wendy Kelly

¼ cup butter or shortening
1 cup granulated sugar
2 eggs, well beaten
1½ cups all-purpose flour
1½ teaspoons baking powder
1 teaspoon baking soda
¼ teaspoon salt
1 cup sour cream
½ cup flaked unsweetened coconut
¼ cup brown sugar
½ tablespoon ground cinnamon

Preheat the oven to 350°F. Grease a standard loaf pan. Cream the butter and granulated sugar. Add the eggs, and combine thoroughly. In a separate bowl, sift together the flour, baking powder, baking soda, and salt. Add the flour mixture to the butter mixture alternately with the sour cream; set aside. In another bowl, combine the coconut, brown sugar, and cinnamon. Place one-third of the coconut mixture in the prepared pan, followed by half the batter, one-third of the coconut mixture, and the remaining batter. Twirl a knife through the batter to spread the coconut mixture through it (for a marbled effect). Sprinkle the remaining coconut mixture over the top of the batter, and bake 45 minutes. Reduce the oven temperature to 300°F, and bake for another 30 minutes. ***Yield: 1 loaf.***

Cinnamon Twist Bread

"Our main goal is to serve a well-prepared, delicious breakfast geared to our guests' preferences." — Simon Vermegen

2 teaspoons active dry yeast
¼ cup honey
3 cups all-purpose flour
⅔ cup lukewarm milk
1 egg yolk
Salt

Cinnamon mix:
⅔ cup butter or margarine (or mix half butter and half margarine)
1 cup brown sugar
3 tablespoons ground cinnamon
3 tablespoons ground ginger
2 medium apples, peeled, cored, and diced
¾ cup raisins

Mix the yeast with some honey and 4 tablespoons of the flour. Add ¼ cup of the lukewarm milk, and mix well. Let stand until the yeast becomes active and bubbly (this is called a sponge). Place the remaining honey and flour, the egg yolk, and a pinch of salt in a mixing bowl. Add the sponge and three-quarters of the remaining milk (don't add all the milk, as different flours in different seasons can react differently — the dough should have a soft and dry feel to it).

(continued on next page)

Cobble House Bed & Breakfast

Ingrid and Simon Vermegen
3105 Cameron-Taggart Road, RR #1
Cobble Hill, British Columbia
V0R 1L0
Tel/Fax: (250) 743-2672
E-mail: stay@cobble-house.com
www.cobble-house.com
$$

ABOUT THE B&B

Cobble House Bed & Breakfast is located on southeastern Vancouver Island, in a rural area with wineries and many recreational opportunities. Victoria and the world-famous Butchart Gardens are about an hour away, as is ferry access from Washington State and mainland British Columbia. The new home, which was designed and built by the hosts, is in a private 40-acre forest with a creek. The atmosphere is warm, welcoming, and relaxing. The very spacious and colorful Hummingbird, Jay, and Heron rooms are decorated with wicker and antiques. Your host Simon is a former executive chef and can prepare dinners for guests by prior arrangement. The family, which includes two beloved dogs, has lots of hobbies and interests — antique car restoration, miniature train collecting, reading, crafts, decorative painting, antique collecting — but never enough time to enjoy them all!

SEASON

all year

ACCOMMODATIONS

3 rooms with private baths

Mix with a mixer for about 5 minutes (this is to develop the gluten in the dough). Cover with a clean tea towel or clean plastic wrap, and let the dough stand in a warm, draft-free place until it doubles in size.

While the dough is rising, mix the butter, brown sugar, cinnamon, and ginger well. Line a greased 12 x 3½ x 2½" baking pan with half of the butter mixture.

When the dough has doubled, punch it down. Place the dough on a floured surface. Mix in the apples and raisins, and split the dough in 3 equal portions. Roll the portions into rolls the length of the baking pan. Braid these rolls together, place in the baking pan, and spread the remaining butter mixture over the top. Cover with a towel or plastic wrap, and let the dough stand in a warm, draft-free place until it has doubled in size. Preheat the oven to 350°F – 375°F and bake about 25 – 30 minutes. ***Yield: 1 loaf.***

Note: Since every oven is different, temperature and placement in the oven may affect baking time. Therefore, keep close watch over the baking process when baking this bread for the first time.

Country White Bread

2 tablespoons sugar
5 cups lukewarm water
2 packages active dry yeast (2 tablespoons)
4 tablespoons canola oil
2 tablespoons salt
14 – 16 cups all-purpose flour

Dissolve the sugar in 1 cup of the lukewarm water. Add the yeast, and let stand 3 – 5 minutes until dissolved and bubbly; stir. In a separate bowl, stir the remaining lukewarm water, the oil, and the salt together. Combine the yeast mixture with the oil mixture. Gradually add about 11 – 12 cups of the flour, and keep adding flour just until the dough can be picked up from the bowl. Cover with a cloth, and let rise in a warm place until doubled in size. Punch down. Knead, incorporating more flour, until a soft dough forms. Shape into 4 loaves, and place in lightly greased loaf pans. Cover and let the loaves rise again until doubled in size. Preheat the oven to 350°F and bake about 30 minutes. ***Yield: 4 loaves.***

Sanford House Bed & Breakfast

Elizabeth and Charlie Le Ber
PO Box 1825, 20 Platt Street
Brighton, Ontario K0K 1H0
Tel/Fax: (613) 475-3930
$$

ABOUT THE B&B

Sitting majestically on the crest of a hill, Sanford House Bed & Breakfast is a red-brick Victorian home close to Main Street in the friendly town of Brighton. This century-old home with turret and covered veranda has offstreet parking, a separate guest entrance, and three large, bright, and comfortable air conditioned bedrooms. Guests can choose to relax in the round turret room; in the lounge with television, VCR, videos, board games, and books; in the spacious, bright Victorian parlor; or on the veranda. Delicious home-baked breakfasts, often spotlighting apples grown in nearby orchards, are served in the guest dining room. It's a short drive to beautiful Presqu'ile Provincial Park's sandy beaches, nature trails, fine birdwatching areas, and marsh boardwalk. If antique hunting is a passion, there are numerous antique shops right in Brighton and in the surrounding area. Applefest, a celebration of the harvest in September, is a particularly lovely time to visit the area. When not entertaining their B&B guests, Elizabeth and Charlie enjoy cycling and nature walks.

SEASON

all year

ACCOMMODATIONS

3 rooms with shared bath

Orchard Lane Bed & Breakfast

Yvonne Parker
13324 Middle Bench Road
Oyama, British Columbia V4V 2B4
Tel: (250) 548-3809
$$

ABOUT THE B&B

Smack dab between Kelowna and Vernon is Orchard Lane, a newly built Victorian B&B nestled in a private orchard. From the sprawling veranda is a panoramic view of the beautiful central Okanagan Valley, while nearby Kalamalka and Wood Lakes reflect the hills and distant mountains. Inside, a welcoming foyer and spiral staircase lead to romantic and comfortable bedrooms. Visitors lounge in the formal living room with fireplace, stroll through the flower gardens or nearby orchard, admire the terraced landscaping framed by giant trees, or take a refreshing dip in the outdoor hot tub. Your hostess, Yvonne, serves a full gourmet breakfast — made from produce grown in her garden — in the formal dining room or on the veranda. You'll quickly discover that one of her favorite hobbies is making crafts, which are displayed throughout the house. Alpine skiing, fishing, biking, hiking, and other recreational choices await you and there are golf courses and beaches aplenty to explore. This area is truly a corner of paradise.

SEASON

all year

ACCOMMODATIONS

2 rooms with shared bath;
1 room with private bath

Date Bread

1 teaspoon baking soda
¾ cup boiling water
1 cup chopped dried dates
¾ cup sugar
1 tablespoon butter
1 egg
1 teaspoon vanilla
1¾ cups all-purpose flour
½ cup chopped walnuts

Preheat the oven to 350°F. Add the baking soda to the boiling water, and pour over the dates. In a separate bowl, cream the sugar and butter. Add the egg and vanilla, and mix well. Mix the flour with the walnuts, and add alternately with the date mixture to the butter mixture. Bake in a greased loaf pan about 60 minutes. ***Yield: 1 loaf.***

David's Sweet Sourdough Bread

"My cousin's husband, Ken, is a bread-making expert and he's the one who taught me how to bake bread. I now have a sourdough starter and have since taken his basic recipe and made it my own. We use organic ingredients for this recipe wherever possible."— David Leslie

Starter:

2 cups whole wheat bread flour (a commercial flour that can be bought from your local bakery)
2 cups lukewarm water

In a ceramic or glass bowl, mix the flour with the water. Cover and leave at room temperature. Stir with a wooden spoon each morning and evening for 4 days. At that point, the starter should have a fermented smell similar to beer. Put the starter in a glass container in your refrigerator — this is the sourdough "mother," which should be used every week to remain vibrant. (If you don't have an abundance of yeast spores in your kitchen from past bread making, add 1 package active dry yeast and 2 teaspoons honey to the starter).

(continued on next page)

Au Fil des Saisons

Odile Côté and David Leslie
324, 21e Rue
Québec City, Québec G1L 1Y7
Tel: (418) 648-8168
$$

ABOUT THE B&B

A warm, friendly, and healthy stay awaits you at Au Fil des Saisons. Just a five-minute drive from historic and charming Old Québec, this two-story brick house is on a quiet, tree-lined residential street with ample parking. The owners have created an ecologically healthy environment with natural products and materials, such as cotton sheets, wool comforters, hardwood floors, and antique furniture, and, needless to say, this B&B is smoke-free. Two inviting bedrooms on the second floor share a common bathroom. In warm weather, take pleasure in rocking on the deck near the garden or contemplating the good life by the pond. When the winds blow cold, warm up in the living room and sip some tea in front of a fire. In the morning, follow your nose down to a feast of organically grown and home-made foods, and chat with your hosts to a background of classical music. Odile and David will provide you with tourist guides and maps and take the time to ensure you make the most of your visit to picturesque Québec City and the surrounding region.

SEASON

all year

ACCOMMODATIONS

2 rooms with shared bath

Step 1:
2 cups bread flour
1½ cups water
1 cup sourdough starter

Two evenings before the morning you want to bake your bread, prepare the sourdough sponge batter. Mix together the flour, water, and sourdough starter. Cover and let stand overnight at room temperature. The mixture will form bubbles.

Step 2:
1 cup sourdough sponge batter
2½ cups bread flour
⅓ cup maple syrup or honey
1 teaspoon salt
1 cup raisins (optional)

The next morning, prepare the dough. Take out 1 cup of the sponge. Mix the remaining sponge back into the refrigerated sourdough "mother," and refrigerate. Add the flour, maple syrup, salt, and optional raisins to the sponge. Mix and then knead on a lightly floured surface for 5 minutes. Place in a lightly greased bowl, cover, and let rise during the day at room temperature.

Step 3:
Butter

That evening, punch the dough down, and knead it for 5 minutes. Shape the dough into a loaf, and butter the surface. Place the dough in a buttered 8 x 4" glass baking dish. Cover and let rise in a warm spot overnight.

Step 4:
The next morning, preheat the oven to 325°F. Bake 60 minutes. ***Yield:* *1 loaf.***

Dill Bread

1 package fast-rising instant yeast (1 tablespoon)
2½ cups all-purpose flour
¼ cup lukewarm water
1 cup creamed cottage cheese, at room temperature
2 tablespoons sugar
1 tablespoon dried onion
1 tablespoon butter
2 teaspoons dill seed
1 teaspoon salt
¼ teaspoon baking soda
1 egg
Melted butter
Salt

Add the yeast to the flour, and set aside. Place the water in a food processor, and add, one at a time, the cottage cheese, sugar, onion, butter, dill seed, salt, baking soda, egg, and the flour mixture, beating well after each addition. Lightly grease an 8" round casserole, and place the dough inside. Cover with a towel, and keep in a warm place until the dough has doubled in size. Preheat the oven to 350°F, and bake 40 – 50 minutes. After removing from the oven, brush the top of the bread with melted butter and sprinkle with salt. ***Yield: 1 loaf.***

Gwenmar Guest Home

Joy and Keith Smith
PO Box 59, RR #3
Brandon, Manitoba R7A 5Y3
Tel: (204) 728-7339
Fax: (204) 728-7336
E-mail: smithj@docker.com
$

ABOUT THE B&B

Space, privacy, and quiet is what you'll find at Gwenmar. This 1914 heritage home was the summer retreat of Manitoba's former Lieutenant Governor (from 1929 to 1934), J.D. McGregor, who named the estate after his daughter Gwen. Since 1980, Joy and Keith Smith have welcomed B&B guests to this relaxing countryside escape. Gwenmar breakfasts are memorable, particularly the home-baked bread and jams and jellies made from Gwenmar's wild berries. Joy, a home economist, is an avid gardener and a major contributor to Canada's heritage seed program, while Keith is a retired agrologist involved in overseas projects. In the summer, you can visit with them on the big, shaded veranda or go for walks on the beautiful grounds or in the valley. In the winter, sit by the fire or go cross-country skiing. Gwenmar is also a short drive from downtown Brandon, with shopping, restaurants, a water-slide, an air museum, golf courses, and the childhood home of Stone Angel *author Margaret Laurence.*

SEASON

all year

ACCOMMODATIONS

2 rooms with private baths;
2 rooms with shared bath

Company House Bed & Breakfast

Jill and Jerry Whiting
PO Box 1159, 172 Company Avenue
Fort Qu'Appelle, Saskatchewan
S0G 1S0
Tel: (306) 332-6333
$$

ABOUT THE B&B

Company House is located in the beautiful Qu'Appelle Valley, northeast of Regina, Saskatchewan, in the resort town of Fort Qu'Appelle. The house, built in the early 1900s, has an ornately decorated tin ceiling, bright chandeliers, beveled glass windows, maple floors, and ceramic tile fireplaces with cherrywood mantles, all of which contribute to a restful atmosphere. Guests can relax in front of the fireplace or in the private lounge complete with television and library. There are two large guest rooms with comfortable double beds. Enjoy a continental or hearty home-cooked breakfast in the quiet dining room. Company House is within walking distance of beaches and places to go fishing, canoeing, birdwatching, hiking, and shopping (including local pottery and Native craft galleries). Close by are golf courses, tennis courts, ski hills, cross-country and skidoo trails, and many historical sites.

SEASON

all year

ACCOMMODATIONS

2 rooms with shared bath

Multigrain Bread

Step 1:
⅓ cup barley flakes*
⅓ cup cracked wheat
⅓ cup flax seed
⅓ cup large-flake rolled oats*
⅓ cup millet
⅓ cup rye flakes*
⅓ cup sesame seeds
⅓ cup wheat flakes*
4 cups boiling water

**Note: You can use 1⅓ cups of any combination of these cereals.*

Add the barley flakes, cracked wheat, flax seed, rolled oats, millet, rye flakes, sesame seeds, and wheat flakes to the boiling water. Let cool, or leave overnight.

Step 2:
2 cups warm water
⅔ cup evaporated milk
⅓ cup vegetable oil
⅓ cup molasses

Combine the water, milk, oil, and molasses with the cereal mixture.

(continued on next page)

Step 3:
1 – 2 teaspoons sugar or honey
2 cups lukewarm water
3 packages active dry yeast (3 tablespoons)

Dissolve the sugar in the water. Add the yeast. Leave for 10 minutes until frothy. Stir well.

Step 4:
3 – 4 cups all-purpose flour
3 – 4 cups whole wheat flour

Put the cereal mixture and the yeast mixture in a large bowl, and beat in the flours (using a hand mixer if available). Transfer to a lightly greased bowl, cover, and leave in a warm place for about 90 minutes (or until spongy and the surface cracks).

Step 5:
3 tablespoons salt
4 cups (approximately) all-purpose flour
4 cups (approximately) whole wheat flour

Punch the dough down, and add the salt. Work the flours in by hand, alternating cups of all-purpose and whole wheat flour (don't make the dough too hard and dry). Knead well for about 5 – 10 minutes. Let the dough rise, covered with a damp cloth, until doubled in size.

Step 6:
Sesame seeds

Punch the dough down. Divide it into 6 loaves, and place them in greased loaf pans. Sprinkle sesame seeds on each loaf. Let the loaves rise until doubled in size.

Step 7:
Preheat the oven to 450°F, then turn down to 375°F. Bake the loaves 40 – 50 minutes or until they sound hollow when tapped underneath.
Yield: 6 loaves.

No-Fail Banana Bread

"This recipe, which my daughter-in-law gave me, makes a no-fail, moist loaf."— Anna Doorenbos

½ cup butter or margarine
1 cup sugar
2 eggs
1 cup mashed very ripe banana (about 3 medium)
1¾ cups all-purpose flour
1 teaspoon baking soda
½ teaspoon baking powder
½ teaspoon salt

Preheat the oven to 350°F. Cream the butter and sugar together. Beat in the eggs one at a time. Add the banana, and blend. In a second bowl, stir the flour with the baking soda, baking powder, and salt. Add the flour mixture to the banana mixture, stirring only to moisten the dry ingredients. Place in a greased loaf pan, and bake about 60 minutes. ***Yield: 1 loaf.***

Anna's Bed and Breakfast

Anna and Robert Doorenbos
204 Wolf Street
Thompson, Manitoba R8N 1J7
Tel: (204) 677-5075
$ – $$

ABOUT THE B&B

Visit Anna's Bed and Breakfast to experience what Canadian Dutch hospitality is all about. This adult-oriented and smoke-free B&B offers a private guest suite with its own entrance and parking space, two single beds, private bath, kitchenette, and den with TV and telephone. Anna enjoys cooking and will get your day off to a delicious start with a full breakfast served in the main dining room. Oriental meals are another specialty and, along with traditional meals, are available for an additional charge. The greenhouse, which is connected to the cozy and informal living room, opens onto the deck and lends a summer atmosphere to the home — even in the dead of winter! Thompson is the home base of travelers to fly-in fishing lodges and Churchill (Manitoba) and other northern communities. It also boasts the longest alpine ski season in Manitoba. Guest pick-up can be arranged as well as scenic touring by car. Your hosts Anna and Robert moved to Canada from Holland and have lived in Thompson since 1971. Robert, an award-winning visual artist, comes from Egypt and Anna from Indonesia.

SEASON

all year

ACCOMMODATIONS

1 suite with private bath

Nova Scotia Brown Bread

"Copies of this recipe are always on hand to give to our guests, so now there are variations being made from Alabama to Zimbabwe!"
— Monica Cobb

8 cups hot water
4 cups quick-cooking rolled oats
1 cup molasses
½ cup cornmeal
¼ cup softened lard or vegetable shortening
1 tablespoon salt
1 cup lukewarm water
3 packages active dry yeast (3 tablespoons)
1 tablespoon sugar
16 cups (approximately) all-purpose flour

In a large bowl, combine the hot water, oats, molasses, cornmeal, lard, and salt. In a separate bowl, combine the lukewarm water, yeast, and sugar, and let stand until the yeast has dissolved. Add the yeast mixture to the oats mixture, and combine.

(continued on next page)

Bread and Roses Country Inn

Monica and Richard Cobb
PO Box 177, 82 Victoria Street
Annapolis Royal, Nova Scotia
B0S 1A0
Tel: (902) 532-5727
$$

ABOUT THE B&B

Bread and Roses Country Inn is a rare Nova Scotia example of a brick Queen Anne revival house. Built circa 1882, this smoke-free inn has many fine design details, such as a large entrance hall with sweeping staircase, intricate woodwork, and etched glass windows. The nine guest rooms on three floors are all distinctively decorated with antiques. The owners' eclectic art collection, which includes whimsical Nova Scotia folk art, contemporary Canadian paintings, and Inuit sculpture, is displayed throughout the house. Breakfast includes Monica's brown bread and granola, local preserves, yogurt, juice, and tea or coffee. Guests enjoy gathering in the parlor each evening for tea and sweets and to share stories of their Nova Scotian adventures. Nearby are historic sites, museums, artists' studios, golf courses, walking trails, and excellent restaurants. Port-Royal, Canada's oldest permanent European settlement (1605) is a short drive away. Having traveled extensively throughout the Maritime provinces, Monica and Richard can provide touring tips tailored to your interests.

SEASON

March 1 – October 30

ACCOMMODATIONS

9 rooms with private baths

Gradually add the flour to the oats mixture. Keep adding flour until the dough is firm enough to knead. Turn out onto a lightly floured surface, and knead for about 10 minutes. ***Variation:*** You can use any type of flour — all-purpose, whole wheat, wheat, oat, or any combination — but a heavier flour requires more yeast.

Place the dough in a lightly greased bowl, and cover it with a tea towel, which will stop the dough from drying out. Let the dough rise in a warm place until doubled in size. Punch the dough down, remove it from the bowl, and cut the dough into 6 pieces. Form them into loaves, and put them in lightly greased pans. Let the dough rise once more, covered with a tea towel, until doubled in size. Preheat the oven to 350°F, and bake 45 minutes. When ready, the loaves should sound hollow when tapped. Let cool on wire racks. ***Tip:*** This bread freezes well. ***Yield: 6 loaves.***

Overnight Rolls

"Nothing can beat the smell of bread baking in the morning, especially if you don't have to get up at the crack of dawn to make the necessary preparations!" — Judy Hill

1 package active dry yeast (1 tablespoon)
2½ cups lukewarm water
½ cup plus 1 teaspoon sugar
3 eggs, well beaten
½ cup vegetable oil
2½ teaspoons salt
6½ cups all-purpose flour

Rhubarb and apple compote (see recipe on page 177)

At around 5 pm, combine the yeast, ½ cup of the water, and 1 teaspoon of the sugar in a large bowl. Let stand for 10 minutes. Grease 3 (12-cup) muffin pans. To the yeast mixture, add the remaining water and sugar and the eggs, oil, salt, and flour, and knead well (about 5 – 10 minutes). Place in a lightly greased bowl, cover, and let rise in a warm spot until doubled in size. Punch down at 60-minute intervals 4 times, then form into clover rolls (3 small rounds placed in each muffin cup). Cover and leave to rise overnight. In the morning, bake 15 minutes in a preheated 350°F oven. Serve with rhubarb and apple compote. ***Tip:*** These rolls freeze well. ***Yield: 36 rolls.***

The Shipwright Inn

Judy and Jordan Hill
51 Fitzroy Street
Charlottetown,
Prince Edward Island C1A 1R4
Tel: (902) 368-1905
Fax: (902) 628-1905
E-mail: shipwright@isn.net
www.isn.net/ShipwrightInn
$$$ – $$$$

ABOUT THE B&B

The Shipwright Inn is an elegant Victorian home built in the 1860s by the accomplished Charlottetown shipbuilder James Douse. This award-winning heritage inn is located in Olde Charlottetown, one block east of Queen Street and within a three-minute walk of the historic waterfront area, dining, and shopping. In keeping with its shipbuilding heritage, The Shipwright Inn's decor has a nautical theme. While savoring breakfast beneath the dining room chandelier, you might imagine the rope-insignia china (circa 1810) in use at the captain's table of a clipper ship. Your hosts Judy and Jordan Hill have carefully collected period antiques, art work, Victorian memorabilia, family quilts, and old books and artifacts related to the sea for your enjoyment. The seven guest rooms have polished pine floors, some of which were previously ship's planking that was reused by the home's builder. Each bedroom features a private bath, goose down duvets, a TV and telephone, a ceiling fan, and air conditioning. All rooms are smoke free.

SEASON

all year

ACCOMMODATIONS

7 rooms with private baths

River Park Farm

Margaret Whetter
PO Box 310
Hartney, Manitoba R0M 0X0
Tel/Fax: (204) 858-2407
$$

ABOUT THE B&B

River Park Farm is a Victorian guest home built in 1910 on 10 acres of lawn and garden on the banks of the Souris River. Recently restored and redecorated, the heritage farmstead has a cozy and casual charm that often sparks memories of childhood visits to a grandma's home in the country. Guests can glimpse deer, raccoons, woodchucks, and many birds while breakfasting on the veranda or in the sun room. Grain elevators in the distance are silhouetted against beautiful prairie sunrises and sunsets. There are walking trails along the river, a nearby golf course and swimming pool, and canoes available either for professionally led or self-guided trips. Margaret Whetter, the owner and hostess, is a home economist who considers cooking an art form and an act of love. She finds the opportunity to share the stories of her guests' lives a great privilege.

SEASON

all year

ACCOMMODATIONS

4 rooms with shared baths;
7-bed attic room with private bath

Pineapple-Coconut Braid

"This is my basic bread dough recipe — with a tasty variation. It's quick, requires no hands-on kneading, and is foolproof! You do, however, need a fairly heavy-duty mixer with a dough hook." — Margaret Whetter

Dough:
3 cups very hot water
⅓ cup sugar
⅓ cup vegetable oil
2 eggs
1 teaspoon lemon zest
¼ teaspoon ground mace
7 – 8 cups all-purpose flour
2 packages fast-rising instant yeast (2 tablespoons)
1 tablespoon salt

Pineapple mixture:
1½ cups crushed pineapple and juice
½ cup sugar
1½ tablespoons cornstarch
3 teaspoons lemon juice

Toasted flaked coconut

(continued on next page)

In the large mixing bowl with regular beaters, combine the water, sugar, oil, eggs, lemon zest, and mace. Beat until frothy. In a separate bowl, combine the flour and yeast. Add 4 cups of the flour mixture to the water mixture, and beat well. Remove the beaters, and replace them with a dough hook. Add 3 – 4 more cups of the flour mixture and the salt, and mix thoroughly until a soft dough forms. Let stand 15 minutes (still in the mixing bowl with the dough hook in). Turn on the mixer for about 1 minute. Let stand another 15 minutes. Turn the mixer on again for about 1 minute to stir down the risen dough. It's now ready to form into braided loaves.

While the bread is rising in the mixer, cook the pineapple and juice, sugar, and cornstarch in a saucepan until thick. Add the lemon juice. Cool the pineapple mixture. When the dough is ready, divide it in half. Divide each half into 3 pieces and roll each piece into a 13 x 6" rectangle. Spread the pineapple mixture over each (saving some for the glaze), and roll up from the long side (as for cinnamon buns). Seal the edges. On each of 2 greased cookie sheets, place 3 rolls seam side down, 1" apart. Braid, then pinch the ends together. Let rise until doubled in size. Preheat the oven to 375°F, and bake about 20 minutes. While hot, glaze with the leftover pineapple mixture and sprinkle with toasted coconut. ***Tip:*** To make basic bread, simply omit the lemon zest, mace, and pineapple mixture, then braid or shape into loaves or rolls. ***Yield: 2 braided loaves.***

Hummingbird Hill B&B

Marianne and Gary Persia
254 Edmond Road
Astorville, Ontario P0H 1B0
Tel: (800) 661-4976 or
(705) 752-4547
Fax: (705) 752-5150
E-mail: mabb@vianet.on.ca
www.on-biz.com/hummingbirdhill
$$

ABOUT THE B&B

This secluded B&B close to North Bay is set on six acres and is surrounded by extensive gardens. The unique cedar home comprises two geodesic domes with an open concept living room, 26-foot cathedral ceiling, and skylights. Two spiral staircases lead to three guest rooms, which are decorated with antiques and have a TV and duvet-covered beds. Guests can relax in the solarium among tropical plants, sit in the living room in front of a cozy wood fire, or, in winter, watch the deer feed outside. Have a sauna, enjoy a glass of homemade wine in the hot tub, or, in summer, observe nature while you dine in the screened cedar gazebo. A full breakfast is provided, and gourmet meals are available with all-inclusive weekends. Marianne has done the landscaping, while Gary is a construction foreman. North Bay offers cross-country and downhill skiing, ice fishing, snowmobiling, swimming, and boating. Close by are artisans' studios, the Dionne quintuplets' home and museum, and Algonquin Park.

SEASON

all year

ACCOMMODATIONS

2 rooms with private bath;
1 room with shared bath

Pulla Bread

"Pulla, a Finnish bread, makes a great afternoon sweet. It's also great for French toast. I make this bread at least once and sometimes twice a day! You'll need a bread machine for this recipe." — Marianne Persia

1 egg
Milk
2 tablespoons butter or margarine
½ cup sugar
⅓ teaspoon salt
3⅛ cups all-purpose flour
1⅛ teaspoons yeast for bread machines
1½ teaspoons finely ground cardamom

Place the egg in a measuring cup, and add enough milk to equal 1¼ cups. Add the egg mixture to the bread maker, followed by the butter, sugar, salt, flour, yeast, and cardamom. Set the bread machine to the "sweet" setting, and proceed according to the manufacturer's directions. ***Yield: 1 small loaf.***

Pumpkin and Plum Loaf

1 cup butter
1 cup sugar
1 teaspoon orange zest
3 eggs
1 cup chopped orange sections and pitted sliced plums, marinated 15 minutes in their juices
¾ cup cold mashed pumpkin*, cooked fresh or canned
¼ cup orange juice
2 cups all-purpose flour
1 teaspoon baking powder
⅓ cup milk

**Note: Use ordinary pumpkin (not butternut) and don't add butter and milk when mashing it.*

Preheat the oven to 350°F – 375°F. Cream the butter, sugar, and orange zest together until light and fluffy. Add the eggs one at a time, beating well after each addition. Stir in the marinated oranges and plums, the pumpkin, and the orange juice. Combine the flour and baking powder, and sift into the egg mixture alternately with enough milk to give the batter a soft consistency. Spread in a greased, deep loaf pan and bake 60 – 75 minutes. Let stand 5 minutes, then turn onto a wire rack to cool. ***Yield: 1 loaf.***

Australis Guest House

Carol and Brian Waters
35 Marlborough Avenue
Ottawa, Ontario K1N 8E6
Tel/Fax: (613) 235-8461
E-mail: waters@intranet.ca
www.bbcanada.com/1463.html
$$

ABOUT THE B&B

The first established and longest operating B&B in the Ottawa area, Australis is a multiple winner of the Ottawa Hospitality Award and has been recommended by Newsweek. *Located downtown on a quiet, tree-lined street, one block from the Rideau River (with its ducks and swans) and Strathcona Park, Australis is but a 20-minute walk from the Canadian Parliament Buildings. This stately, 60-year-old house has leaded windows, fireplaces, oak floors, and eight-foot high stained glass windows overlooking the hall. Three spacious guest rooms, including one room with private bath and one suite, display many of the hosts' collectibles gathered while living in different parts of the world. Hearty and delicious breakfasts, featuring award-winning home-baked breads and pastries, ensure you'll start the day just right. Off-street parking and free pick-up and delivery to and from the bus and train stations are available. Your hosts' Australian and English heritages combined with their time in Canada create a truly international and relaxed B&B experience.*

SEASON

all year

ACCOMMODATIONS

1 room with private bath;
2 rooms (including 1 suite) with shared bath

Latimer on Oxford

Pat and Bill Latimer
37 Oxford Street West
Moose Jaw, Saskatchewan S6H 2N2
Tel: (306) 692-5481
$ – $$

ABOUT THE B&B

Built in 1911, this faithfully restored foursquare neo-Greek revival home greets you with Corinthian columns decorated with cherubs, which support the front balcony. The solid oak front door with acanthus leaf appliqué and beveled oval glass encourages you to come inside. Interior oak picture frame floors, leaded glass windows, pocket doors, and plate rails recall an era when quality craft, natural materials, and functional design ruled the day. Choose either the Oriental, Western, or Victorian guest rooms with shared bath, or the elegant Violet guest room with private bath. Also on the site is a little red coach house with exposed beams and a hay loft. Plan your visit to coincide with the Moose Jaw Minuet breakfast and your morning is begun with a cheer. A specialty produced by the heartland oven are golden brown rusks. Temple Gardens Thermo Mineral Spa, the museum and public library, City Hall, shops, and restaurants are a 10-minute walk downtown. Your hosts' interests include art, literature, and music.

SEASON

all year

ACCOMMODATIONS

1 room with private bath;
3 rooms with shared bath

Rusks

"This recipe was a favorite at the Kilsyth Agricultural Fair of 1917 in Ontario. It comes from a newspaper clipping."
— Pat and Bill Latimer

4 tablespoons butter
4 tablespoons sugar
1 teaspoon salt
2 cups scalded milk
1 package active dry yeast (1 tablespoon)
¼ cup lukewarm water
6 cups (approximately) all-purpose flour
2 eggs, well beaten

Dissolve the butter, sugar, and salt in the milk. Dissolve the yeast in the water. When the butter mixture has cooled to lukewarm, add the yeast mixture and 3 cups of the flour. Cover tightly, and set in a warm place to form a sponge (wait at least 2 hours for the sponge to be covered with large air bubbles). Add the eggs and enough flour to the sponge to make a stiff batter. Knead until smooth and elastic (about 10 minutes). Place in a lightly greased bowl, cover, and allow to rise until doubled in size. Punch down. Divide the dough in half, and shape each half into a rectangular roll. Place each roll on a lightly greased baking sheet. Cover loosely, and let rise until doubled in size. Preheat the oven to 375°F. Bake 15 minutes. Reduce the temperature to 350°F, and bake an additional 10 – 15 minutes or until the tops are brown. Let cool. Slice the bread about ½" thick, and place the slices, flat side down, on a baking sheet. Bake in a preheated 250°F oven for about 60 minutes or until the slices are light brown and completely crisp. ***Yield: About 36 small rusks.***

Scottish Baps

"These soft and chewy rolls are the breakfast roll of choice in Scotland." — Marilyn Wells

¾ cup milk
¾ cup water
¼ cup lard
2 teaspoons sugar
1½ teaspoons salt
1 package active dry yeast (1 tablespoon)
5 cups all-purpose flour

Mix the milk and water in a saucepan, and heat to lukewarm. Add the lard, sugar, and ½ teaspoon of the salt. Stir until dissolved. Dissolve the yeast in about ½ cup of the milk mixture. Sift the flour and remaining salt into a large, warmed bowl. Make a well in the center of the dry ingredients, and pour in the yeast mixture. Work the yeast into the flour by hand, adding enough of the milk mixture to make a soft but manageable dough (depending on the quality of the flour, you may need up to 4 tablespoons more or less liquid). Knead the dough vigorously until shiny and pliable. Roll into a ball. Place the dough in a bowl, cover it with a damp cloth, and let stand in a warm place until the dough has doubled in size.

Preheat the oven to 475°F. Punch down the dough; knead it lightly and divide it into 12 evenly sized balls. Arrange them well apart on 2 – 3 baking sheets. Flour your palms generously, and flatten the balls into discs, then press a hole in the center of each with your thumb (this is a characteristic feature of a Scottish bap). Cover them, and leave the baps to rise again until puffy (about 20 minutes). Bake about 10 minutes, until the baps are just golden under their floury coating. Serve very fresh. ***Yield: 12 baps.***

Cold Comfort Farm

Marilyn and Kennedy Wells
PO Box 105
Alberton, Prince Edward Island
C0B 1B0
Tel: (902) 853-2803
$

ABOUT THE B&B

Cold Comfort Farm takes its name from an English comic novel and is not a description of the hospitality offered! Situated on Matthews Road off route 12 near the town of Alberton, the house was built during Prince Edward Island's silver fox ranching boom early in the century, and is surrounded by gardens and farmland on the coast of an ocean inlet. Rooms are furnished with a mix of traditional Prince Edward Island and European furniture, reflecting the owners' long residence abroad. There is an extensive library, and conversation or solitude are equally available. Breakfast features home baking, fresh fruit, and Cold Comfort's own granola. An excellent golf course, beautiful red and white sand beaches, and a number of good restaurants are nearby.

SEASON

mid-June – mid-September

ACCOMMODATIONS

3 rooms with shared bath

Gwenmar Guest Home

Joy and Keith Smith
PO Box 59, RR #3
Brandon, Manitoba R7A 5Y3
Tel: (204) 728-7339
Fax: (204) 728-7336
E-mail: smithj@docker.com
$

ABOUT THE B&B

Space, privacy, and quiet is what you'll find at Gwenmar. This 1914 heritage home was the summer retreat of Manitoba's former Lieutenant Governor (from 1929 to 1934), J.D. McGregor, who named the estate after his daughter Gwen. Since 1980, Joy and Keith Smith have welcomed B&B guests to this relaxing countryside escape. Gwenmar breakfasts are memorable, particularly the home-baked bread and jams and jellies made from Gwenmar's wild berries. Joy, a home economist, is an avid gardener and a major contributor to Canada's heritage seed program, while Keith is a retired agrologist involved in overseas projects. In the summer, you can visit with them on the big, shaded veranda or go for walks on the beautiful grounds or in the valley. In the winter, sit by the fire or go cross-country skiing. Gwenmar is also a short drive from downtown Brandon, with shopping, restaurants, a water-slide, an air museum, golf courses, and the childhood home of Stone Angel *author Margaret Laurence.*

SEASON

all year

ACCOMMODATIONS

2 rooms with private baths;
2 rooms with shared bath

Sesame Crisp Bread (Norwegian Flat Bread)

Dough:
1½ cups all-purpose flour
1 cup whole wheat flour
½ teaspoon salt
1 cup warm water

Topping:
1 egg, beaten
Dried dill weed
Garlic powder
Sesame seeds
Other seasonings, such as red pepper flakes, sautéed onion and bacon, poppy seeds, grated Parmesan cheese, and seasoning salt (optional)

Combine the all-purpose flour, whole wheat flour, and salt in a mixing bowl. Stir well to blend. Add the water, and stir with a wooden spoon until the mixture forms a soft dough. Turn out onto a floured surface, and knead well for 10 minutes. Place in a lightly greased bowl for 2 hours to relax the gluten and allow the dough to be rolled very thin. Divide the dough into 4 parts. Roll each piece into a very thin oval (about 12" long). Preheat the oven to 425°F. Place the pieces on lightly greased baking sheets, and brush with the beaten egg. Sprinkle with dill weed, garlic powder, and sesame seeds, and optional seasonings. Prick the dough well with a fork (or the bread will puff badly). Bake 10 – 15 minutes. Serve whole, breaking off pieces as desired. ***Yield: 4 flat breads.***

Sourdough Starter

"I'm notorious for forgetting to save my starter. I get talking to guests as I cook and I don't take any out, so I end up making new starter every month! Good thing my starter didn't come over the Chilkoot Pass during the gold rush as some have. Sourdough isn't for a beginner cook, but it's a fun challenge for an experienced one."
— Carla Pitzel

2 cups all-purpose flour
2 cups lukewarm water
3 tablespoons sugar
1 package active dry yeast (1 tablespoon)

Place the flour, water, sugar, and yeast in a 1-gallon crock. Stir the mixture until it is a smooth, thin paste. Cover and let stand in a warm place to sour. Stir the mixture several times a day. In 2 or 3 days, your sourdough starter will be ready. It if smells like stinky socks, throw it away! If it has a yeasty-alcohol smell, it's fine.

If you want to use this starter, prepare the sponge batter (recipe follows) at least 12 hours before you plan to make your sourdough recipe. If you don't need to use your starter right away, store it as described on the following page.

(continued on next page)

Hawkins House Bed & Breakfast

Carla Pitzel and Garry Umbrich
303 Hawkins Street
Whitehorse, Yukon Y1A 1X5
Tel: (867) 668-7638
Fax: (867) 668-7632
$$$$

ABOUT THE B&B

To stay at the Hawkins House Bed & Breakfast is to share a once-in-a-lifetime Yukon experience with your hosts Carla, Garry, and their two sons. Each guest room in this custom-built, luxury Victorian B&B highlights a different Yukon theme and features private bath and balcony, oak floor, bar sink, refrigerator, cable TV, and VCR. Guests can take a Jacuzzi soak in the Fleur de Lys Room, watch videos about Native peoples in the First Nations Room, step back into gold rush days in the Victorian Tea Rose Room, or admire the splendid view of the SS Klondike *paddlewheeler and Canyon Mountain from the balcony of the Fireweed Room. Especially geared to the business traveler, Hawkins House provides the convenience of a private telephone line and answering machine, fax service, and a work table with a light and computer jack. Breakfast is a homemade feast of northern and international delights — from the home-smoked salmon pâté and moose sausage to jams, syrups, and sourdough pastries.*

SEASON

all year

ACCOMMODATIONS

4 rooms with private baths

Storing your starter
Your starter will keep indefinitely in a clean, covered glass container in the refrigerator. Never use a metal container or leave a metal spoon in the starter or sponge. If your starter hasn't been used for several weeks, it may need to sit out an extra night at warm room temperature before being using.

Sponge batter
The sponge batter is what gives sourdough its characteristic flavor. It must be prepared at least 12 hours before adding additional ingredients.

1 cup sourdough starter
2 cups lukewarm water
2 cups all-purpose flour

Place 1 cup starter in a warmed earthenware bowl. Slowly stir in the lukewarm water. Stir in the flour, and mix until the batter is smooth. Cover tightly, and let stand in a warm place, free from drafts, to develop at least 12 hours or overnight. In the morning, the sponge will have doubled and will be covered with air bubbles. It will have a pleasant, yeasty odor.

This recipe makes 4 cups sponge batter. Return 1 cup of this batter to your refrigerated starter (this "feeds" your starter by replenishing the amount used to make the sponge batter). You're now left with 3 cups sponge batter for your sourdough recipe. If this will not be enough, increase the sponge batter recipe by one-half or double it.

Note: Using yeast in this recipe makes up for the lack of yeast spores in the air of your kitchen. If you want to make a real starter (i.e., you have an abundance of yeast spores in the air from past bread making), omit the yeast and add 4 tablespoons sugar to the starter — it will sour just the same, but will take about 5 days. If you make it this way, you will need freshly ground organic flour and pure water (which hasn't been chlorinated or treated), otherwise it may not work.

Spicy Cheese Corn Bread

(Recipe from Joan Peggs Eggs, *written and published by Joan Peggs)*

1 cup milk
¾ cup cornmeal
½ cup all-purpose flour
½ cup whole wheat flour
¼ cup sugar
4 teaspoons baking powder
½ teaspoon cayenne
½ cup grated medium cheddar cheese
1 egg
⅓ cup vegetable oil

Béchamel sauce (see recipe on page 234)

Preheat the oven to 400°F. Lightly grease a 9" square pan. Mix together the milk and cornmeal in a medium bowl. Allow to stand 5 minutes. In a large mixing bowl, sift together the all-purpose flour, whole wheat flour, sugar, baking powder, and cayenne. Stir in the cheese. Place the egg and oil in a blender, and blend for 10 seconds. Add the egg mixture to the cornmeal mixture. Stir well. Add the cornmeal mixture to the flour mixture. Combine, using a fork, just until the dry ingredients are moistened. Pour the batter into the prepared pan. Bake about 25 minutes. Serve hot with 1 tablespoon béchamel sauce per serving. ***Tip:*** To make basic corn bread, omit the cheese and cayenne. ***Yield: 1 (9 x 9") corn bread.***

The Inn on St. Andrews

Joan Peggs
231 St. Andrews Street
Victoria, British Columbia V8V 2N1
Tel: (800) 668-5993 or (604) 384-8613
Fax: (604) 384-6063
E-mail: joan_peggs@bc.sympatico.ca.
www.bctravel.com/andrews.html
$$

ABOUT THE B&B

The Inn on St. Andrews is as lovely today as when it was built in 1913 by Edith Carr, eldest sister of the famous Canadian artist and author Emily Carr. This Tudor-style heritage property features elegant woodwork, stained and beveled glass, and large bright bedrooms. After a wholesome breakfast in the formal dining room, you can congregate in the sunroom overlooking the east garden or on the sun deck overlooking the west garden, in the cozy TV room, or in the larger drawing room. The inn is ideally located in James Bay, close to Victoria's inner harbor with ferry and seaplane terminals, the Parliament buildings, the Royal British Columbia Museum, famed Empress Hotel, and downtown shops. A short walk brings you to Beacon Hill Park and the oceanfront. Your host Joan Peggs believes in modern comfort and old-fashioned hospitality, and provides guests with her own map highlighting walking and driving destinations and recommended restaurants.

SEASON

all year

ACCOMMODATIONS

1 room with private bath;
2 rooms with shared bath

Gwenmar Guest Home

Joy and Keith Smith
PO Box 59, RR #3
Brandon, Manitoba R7A 5Y3
Tel: (204) 728-7339
Fax: (204) 728-7336
E-mail: smithj@docker.com
$

ABOUT THE B&B

Space, privacy, and quiet is what you'll find at Gwenmar. This 1914 heritage home was the summer retreat of Manitoba's former Lieutenant Governor (from 1929 to 1934), J.D. McGregor, who named the estate after his daughter Gwen. Since 1980, Joy and Keith Smith have welcomed B&B guests to this relaxing countryside escape. Gwenmar breakfasts are memorable, particularly the home-baked bread and jams and jellies made from Gwenmar's wild berries. Joy, a home economist, is an avid gardener and a major contributor to Canada's heritage seed program, while Keith is a retired agrologist involved in overseas projects. In the summer, you can visit with them on the big, shaded veranda or go for walks on the beautiful grounds or in the valley. In the winter, sit by the fire or go cross-country skiing. Gwenmar is also a short drive from downtown Brandon, with shopping, restaurants, a water-slide, an air museum, golf courses, and the childhood home of Stone Angel *author Margaret Laurence.*

SEASON

all year

ACCOMMODATIONS

2 rooms with private baths;
2 rooms with shared bath

Sun-dried Tomato Bread

"I adapted this from an olive bread recipe. It can also be adapted to include such ingredients as smoked salmon, black olives, and green olives." — Joy Smith

7 cups all-purpose flour
⅔ cup chopped sun-dried tomatoes
3 tablespoons olive oil
2 packages fast rising instant yeast (2 tablespoons)
½ tablespoon salt
2 cups lukewarm water

Mix together the flour, tomatoes, oil, yeast, salt, and water to form a soft dough (you may not need to add all the water). Knead for 10 minutes until the dough is smooth and elastic. Place the dough in a lightly greased bowl, cover with a towel, and let rise in a warm place until the dough has doubled in size. Punch the dough down, divide it in half, shape each piece into a round loaf, and place on a greased pan. Cover and let rise again until doubled in size. Preheat the oven to 375°F, and bake 30 minutes. ***Yield: 2 large loaves.***

Traditional Lemon Loaf

1 cup sugar
½ cup margarine
2 eggs
1½ cups all-purpose flour
1 teaspoon baking powder
1 teaspoon salt
½ cup milk
1 teaspoon vanilla
Zest of 1 lemon

Glaze:
⅓ cup sugar
Juice of 1 lemon

Preheat the oven to 325°F. Mix the sugar and margarine in a food processor. Add the eggs one at a time. Sift together the flour, baking powder, and salt, and add to the egg mixture alternately with the milk. Add the vanilla and lemon zest. Mix until well blended. Pour the batter into a greased and floured loaf pan, and bake 60 minutes. For the glaze, combine the sugar and lemon juice, and pour over the warm cake.
Yield: 1 loaf.

Bruce Gables B&B

Elsie and Jorn Christensen
PO Box 448, 410 Berford Street
Wiarton, Ontario N0H 2T0
Tel: (519) 534-0429
Fax: (519) 534-0779
$$

ABOUT THE B&B

Whether in French, German, Spanish, Danish, or English, Elsie and Jorn bid you "welcome" to Bruce Gables, their spacious turn-of-the-century home. Relax in the large living room, which has been restored to its Victorian splendor and furnished with period furniture and antiques. Two of the three large bedrooms have bay windows that overlook the town of Wiarton and the clear blue waters of Colpoy's Bay. A hearty breakfast, served in the elegant dining room, is your choice of crêpes, pancakes, waffles, French toast, eggs Benedict or Florentine, omelets, or any other style of eggs. In the garden, picnic tables and a gas barbecue are available for the guests to use. Known as the "gateway to the Bruce," the town of Wiarton makes a perfect headquarters for exploring the Bruce Peninsula. With Georgian Bay to the east and Lake Huron to the west, the Bruce offers abundant water recreation, not to mention some of the most breathtaking scenery in Ontario from its high limestone bluffs. In addition, the area's provincial parks are natural habitats for many varieties of birds and animals.

SEASON

May – October

ACCOMMODATIONS

3 rooms with shared baths

Campbell House

Tineke Gow and Family
Trinity, Newfoundland
Tel: (877) 464-7700 or
(709) 464-3377
Fax: (709) 464-3377
E-mail: tgow@nf.sympatico.ca
www.newcomm.net/campbell
$$ – $$$$

ABOUT THE B&B

This heritage home was built around 1840 for an Irish navigation teacher, James Campbell, considered to be the foremost nautical teacher in Newfoundland at a time when Trinity was a thriving commercial center with a bustling harbor. A 1993 Southcott Award-winner for excellence in restoration, Campbell House is furnished with period antiques and offers a magnificent view of the ocean from every room. Throughout June and July, you might even spot an iceberg or two from your bedroom window! Members of the host family are ardent gardeners and musicians, and may treat you to an impromptu concert of traditional fiddle music. Nearby easy walking trails take you through myriad Atlantic wildflowers and breathtaking land and seascape vistas. Local boat tours leave Trinity several times daily to bring you close to marine wildlife, such as puffins, murres, bald eagles, and whales.

SEASON

May – October

ACCOMMODATIONS

4 rooms with private baths;
2-bedroom vacation home

Trinity Bay Tea Loaf

2 cups hot strong tea
1 cup raisins
2½ cups all-purpose flour
1 cup sugar
2 teaspoons baking soda
2 teaspoons ground cinnamon
2 teaspoons ground nutmeg
1 teaspoon salt
¼ teaspoon ground cloves
½ cup shortening

Preheat the oven to 350°F. Pour the tea over the raisins, and let cool (this can be done anytime). Sift together the flour, sugar, baking soda, cinnamon, nutmeg, salt, and cloves. Cut in the shortening. Add the tea mixture, and stir until the dry ingredients are moistened. Bake 50 – 60 minutes in a greased loaf pan. ***Yield: 1 loaf.***

Vortbread

"This is a Swedish bread I only make in winter. It's dark in color, tasty, and goes well with cold weather, sharp cheddar, and scrambled eggs seasoned with nutmeg and garnished with fresh parsley."
— Lena Blondel

3 cups rye flour
1 cup all-purpose flour (plus a little extra, if needed)
5 teaspoons active dry yeast
1 tablespoon sea salt
3 tablespoons butter or margarine
2 cups porter ale
⅓ cup dark maple syrup
½ tablespoon orange zest
1 teaspoon freshly ground ginger or ½ tablespoon pounded anise seeds and ½ tablespoon pounded fennel seeds

Mix together the rye flour, all-purpose flour, yeast, and salt; set aside. Melt the butter, and add the porter, maple syrup, orange zest, and ginger. Heat the porter mixture to lukewarm, and add it to the flour mixture. Knead well, adding more all-purpose flour until the dough is smooth and elastic. Place in a lightly greased bowl, cover with a towel, and let rise in a warm place until the dough has doubled in size. Punch it down. Work the dough on a whole wheat-floured surface until smooth. Shape the dough into 2 loaves, and place them in lightly greased baking pans. Let the dough rise again until doubled in size. Bake in a preheated oven at 400°F for 40 minutes. ***Yield: 2 loaves.***

Montréal Oasis

Lena Blondel
3000 Breslay Road
Montréal, Québec H3Y 2G7
Tel: (514) 935-2312
$$

ABOUT THE B&B

In pilgrim days, the evergreen tree was a sign of shelter, good food, and warm hospitality. It's fitting, then, that two towering evergreens frame the door to Montréal Oasis. This charming B&B with original leaded windows and slanted ceilings is located in downtown Montréal's west end, close to the Fine Arts Museum, chic Crescent Street and Greene Avenue shopping and restaurants, and the "main drag," St. Catherine Street. The beautiful and safe neighborhood with its spacious Elizabethan-style houses and pretty gardens is locally referred to as the Priest Farm district — once a holiday resort for priests. Originally from Sweden, your world-traveled hostess Lena has lived in many countries around the globe, which is evident from the African, Asian, and Swedish art that graces the B&B. The three guest rooms feature Scandinavian and Québecois furniture. Lena loves good food, and serves three-course gourmet breakfasts featuring delicious, fresh ingredients. A friendly Siamese cat resides on the main floor.

SEASON

all year

ACCOMMODATIONS

3 rooms with shared baths

Park View Bed & Breakfast

Gladys and Carson Langille
254 Cameron Street
Moncton, New Brunswick E1C 5Z3
Tel: (506) 382-4504
$$

ABOUT THE B&B

This art deco home was built in 1940 as a residence for Mrs. Inez Robinson, owner of Moncton's first business college. The architectural plans came from the 1939 New York World's Fair, and this was the first art deco home in Moncton. The curved living room windows look out on beautiful Victoria Park in the city's center. Opened as a B&B in 1989, this charming home has three guest rooms with cable TV, telephones, and exquisite shared bath, spacious living room with fireplace, elegant dining room, and cozy kitchen. Your hosts provide a warm welcome, a hearty, home-cooked breakfast of your choice, and a wealth of information about the area. Gladys is a part-time school teacher, while Carson enjoys playing bridge and painting landscapes. A collection of works by local artists graces their walls. Nearby is superb dining, shopping, beaches, parks, museums, galleries, theater, a must-see tidal bore (where the tide goes up and down very quickly), and the famous Magnetic Hill (you'll never believe this phenomenon unless you experience it yourself!).

SEASON

all year

ACCOMMODATIONS

3 rooms with shared bath

Wheat Germ Bread

½ cup butter
½ cup sugar
2 eggs
1 teaspoon vanilla
½ cup all-purpose flour
½ cup whole wheat flour
3½ teaspoons baking powder
¼ teaspoon salt
1 cup milk
1 cup wheat germ

Preheat the oven to 350°F. Cream together the butter and sugar. Add the eggs and vanilla, stirring to blend. Combine the all-purpose flour, whole wheat flour, baking powder, and salt, and add alternately with the milk to the egg mixture. Fold in the wheat germ. Place the batter in a greased 8 x 4 x 3" loaf pan (or double the recipe and place in a greased tube pan). Bake 40 minutes. ***Yield: 1 loaf.***

Zucchini Loaf

"One of our sons spent a summer working for a neighboring Hereford beef farm. The proprietor, 'Tewkie' Reford (her family name is Tewksbury), shared this recipe with him. Tewkie's 'zukes' are monstrous and tasty. I make a dozen loaves in the summer and freeze them for special occasions." — Ken Fisher

3 cups all-purpose flour
1¾ cups sugar
1¼ cups wheat germ
1 cup chopped nuts
3 teaspoons baking soda
1 teaspoon ground cinnamon
1 teaspoon salt
4 cups grated zucchini
2 eggs
2 teaspoons vanilla
⅔ cup canola or vegetable oil

Preheat the oven to 350°F. Combine the flour, sugar, wheat germ, nuts, baking soda, cinnamon, and salt. In a separate bowl, mix the zucchini, eggs, vanilla, and oil. Add the zucchini mixture to the flour mixture, and combine thoroughly. Grease 2 loaf pans, and divide the dough between the pans. Bake 45 minutes or until the tops of the loaves are browned and a toothpick inserted in the center comes out clean. ***Yield: 2 loaves.***

Wanaki-on-the-Ottawa

Ken Fisher
133 avenue des Plages
Pontiac (Luskville), Québec J0X 2G0
Tel: (819) 455-9295
Fax: (819) 455-9213
E-mail: kfisher@magi.com
$$

ABOUT THE B&B

The Algonquin word wanaki *means "a serene state of being," which is an apt description of a stay at Wanaki-on-the-Ottawa. Located at the end of a rural wooded cul-de-sac, Wanaki offers quiet seclusion in a new, large home. Wanaki's decks, porches, and three guest rooms overlook a private sandy beach and offer a panoramic view of the Ottawa River and dramatic sunsets. In winter, guests can skate, snowshoe, snowmobile, cross-country ski, or relax in front of the fireplace. In summer, guests can swim, sail, canoe, fish, or enjoy an evening around the campfire. Year round, guests can keep in shape right on the premises — at Wanaki's indoor swim spa and exercise room. Nearby attractions include Luskville Falls and Gatineau Park. Breakfasts are sumptuous, include fresh fruit, and are catered to all tastes. The house is wood-heated in winter and air conditioned in summer. Wanaki — only 30 minutes from downtown Ottawa in scenic Pontiac County, Québec — is an ideal setting for retreats, parties, and family reunions.*

SEASON

all year

ACCOMMODATIONS

3 rooms with shared baths

Cakes & Pies

Almond-Banana-Raspberry Breakfast Cake

¾ cup sugar
½ cup margarine
3 eggs
1 banana, mashed
¼ cup milk
¼ cup sour cream
1 teaspoon almond extract
2 cups all-purpose flour
1½ teaspoons baking powder
1½ cups fresh raspberries

Frosting:
1 cup confectioners' sugar
¼ cup softened margarine
1 – 2 teaspoons lemon juice

Preheat the oven to 350°F. Lightly butter a 9" square pan. In a large bowl, combine the sugar, margarine, eggs, and banana. Beat until light and fluffy. Beat in the milk, sour cream, and almond extract. Add the flour and baking powder. Stir just until the dry ingredients are moistened. Pour half the batter into the pan, and top with the berries. Pour the remaining batter over the berries. Bake 50 – 55 minutes. Remove the cake from the oven, and let cool. In the meantime, prepare the frosting. In a small bowl, beat together the confectioners' sugar and margarine. Add enough lemon juice to obtain a spreadable consistency. Spread the frosting over the warm cake. ***Yield: 9 servings.***

Fraser House

Sheila and Dennis Derksen
PO Box 211, 33 1st Street East
Letellier, Manitoba R0G 1C0
Tel: (204) 737-2284
$

ABOUT THE B&B

Memories are made at this elegant and romantic 1916 home. Hardwood floors, area rugs, and antique furniture enhance the home's Victorian decor. Spacious rooms combined with great hospitality make your stay most enjoyable. Relax with a beverage and home-baked goodies in the parlor or on the veranda or patio. Breakfast may consist of a puffy egg pancake or freshly baked croissants and muffins, along with the season's fresh fruit, served in the formal dining room. Fraser House is located just a few minutes north of the US border in the heart of Manitoba's bustling agricultural area, and is near places to golf, fish, shop, and ski. Sheila enjoys craft projects and holds painting classes during the winter months, while Dennis enjoys carpentry and is employed as a fertilizer dealer.

SEASON

all year

ACCOMMODATIONS

2 rooms with shared bath

Spring Valley Guest Ranch

Jim Saville
PO Box 10
Ravenscrag, Saskatchewan S0N 0T0
Tel: (306) 295-4124
$$

ABOUT THE B&B

Come enjoy an afternoon visit or an overnight stay at Spring Valley Guest Ranch. This three-story, 1913 home is nestled in a tall grove of cottonwood poplars near a spring-fed stream in a pleasant wooded valley with many varieties of flora and fauna. There are more than a thousand acres of hills and valleys to explore, either on foot or on horseback. You are invited to dine, choosing from a unique menu, in the licensed Country Tea Room, which houses over 200 duck replicas. Poultry, sheep, horses, and a donkey can be visited in the barnyard. The craft shop in the log cabin is filled with treasures of leather, wood, and pottery and with knitted and beaded crafts — all made by local artists. An excellent area for naturalists, photographers, and hikers, Ravenscrag is only 20 minutes from Cypress Hills Provincial Park, on the Alberta border.

SEASON

all year

ACCOMMODATIONS

4 rooms with shared baths;
1 log cabin with shared bath

Angel Food Cake

"If you raise chickens and get lots of extra 'cackleberries,' you can use the egg whites for this recipe and leftover egg yolks for my jelly roll (see recipe on page 164), both great for afternoon or after-dinner treats." — Jim Saville

1 cup cake flour
1½ cups sugar
1¼ cups egg whites (about 10 egg whites)
1¼ teaspoons cream of tartar
¼ teaspoon salt
1 teaspoon vanilla

Fresh berries or fruit

Preheat the oven to 350°F. Sift the flour and ½ cup of the sugar together 4 times; set aside. Beat the egg whites until soft peaks form, then gradually add the remaining sugar, the cream of tartar, and the salt, and beat until stiff (but not dry) peaks form. Add the vanilla. Fold the flour mixture gently into the egg mixture. Pour the batter into an ungreased angel food cake pan, and bake 45 minutes. Serve topped with fresh berries or fruit. ***Yield: 12 servings.***

Apple Streusel Coffee Cake

2¼ cups all-purpose flour
¾ cup sugar
¾ cup butter or margarine
½ teaspoon baking powder
½ teaspoon baking soda
¾ cup buttermilk or sour milk
1 egg, beaten
19-ounce can apple pie filling
⅓ cup currants
½ teaspoon ground cinnamon

Island clotted cream topping (see recipe on page 316)

Preheat the oven to 375°F. Combine the flour and sugar in a large bowl. Cut in the butter until the mixture is crumbly; set aside ½ cup of this crumb mixture. To the remainder, add the baking powder and baking soda. In a separate bowl, combine the buttermilk and egg. Add the egg mixture to the larger quantity of the crumb mixture, and stir just until the crumb mixture is moistened. Spread two-thirds of the batter over the bottom and part way up the sides of a greased 9" springform pan. Combine the pie filling, currants, and cinnamon, and spoon over the batter. Drop spoonfuls of the remaining batter over the filling. Sprinkle with the reserved crumb mixture. Bake about 60 minutes. Cool 10 minutes before serving. Serve with island clotted cream topping. ***Tip:*** This cake freezes well. ***Variation:*** Instead of using apple pie filling, currants, and cinnamon, try cherry pie filling with ½ teaspoon almond extract mixed in and slivered almonds sprinkled on top with the reserved crumb mixture. ***Yield: 12 servings.***

The Shipwright Inn

Judy and Jordan Hill
51 Fitzroy Street
Charlottetown,
Prince Edward Island C1A 1R4
Tel: (902) 368-1905
Fax: (902) 628-1905
E-mail: shipwright@isn.net
www.isn.net/ShipwrightInn
$$$ – $$$$

ABOUT THE B&B

The Shipwright Inn is an elegant Victorian home built in the 1860s by the accomplished Charlottetown shipbuilder James Douse. This award-winning heritage inn is located in Olde Charlottetown, one block east of Queen Street and within a three-minute walk of the historic waterfront area, dining, and shopping. In keeping with its shipbuilding heritage, The Shipwright Inn's decor has a nautical theme. While savoring breakfast beneath the dining room chandelier, you might imagine the rope-insignia china (circa 1810) in use at the captain's table of a clipper ship. Your hosts Judy and Jordan Hill have carefully collected period antiques, art work, Victorian memorabilia, family quilts, and old books and artifacts related to the sea for your enjoyment. The seven guest rooms have polished pine floors, some of which were previously ship's planking that was reused by the home's builder. Each bedroom features a private bath, goose down duvets, a TV and telephone, a ceiling fan, and air conditioning. All rooms are smoke free.

SEASON

all year

ACCOMMODATIONS

7 rooms with private baths

Mecklenburgh Inn

Suzi Fraser
78 Queen Street
Chester, Nova Scotia B0J 1J0
Tel/Fax: (902) 275-4638
www.destination-ns.com/
lighthouse/mecklenburgh
$$

ABOUT THE B&B

Constructed by shipwrights in 1890, Mecklenburgh Inn is located in the heart of seaside Chester, which has catered to summer visitors and sailing enthusiasts for over 150 years. Sleep in the spacious and comfortably appointed bedrooms filled with period furniture and other interesting objects Suzi has collected over the years, then enjoy a delicious breakfast while you plan the day ahead. You might wander the historic village streets, stopping to watch the yacht races on Mahone Bay, or browse through craft shops and boutiques. Or, maybe a sailboat ride, bicycle ride, or game of golf or tennis would be more your style. Later, relax on the balcony while the sun sets over the western shore of the bay and village activity lulls. You might consider an evening meal at one of the excellent restaurants in the area or catch a play at the Chester Playhouse. At the end of the day, the living room is the perfect place to wind down chatting by the fire or perusing travel books and magazines.

SEASON

May 24 – November 7

ACCOMMODATIONS

4 rooms with shared baths

Apple Tart

Crust:
1¼ cups all-purpose flour
⅓ cup sugar
¼ teaspoon ground nutmeg
½ teaspoon baking powder
½ teaspoon salt
½ cup cold unsalted butter
1 whole egg
1 tablespoon milk

Filling:
8-ounce package cream cheese, softened
¼ cup sugar
2 egg yolks
½ teaspoon vanilla

Topping:
3 apples, peeled, cored, and thinly sliced
⅓ cup sugar
½ teaspoon cornstarch
½ teaspoon ground cinnamon

Preheat the oven to 350°F. Grease a 10" tart pan. Combine the flour, sugar, nutmeg, baking powder, and salt in a food processor. Add the butter, and process briefly until the mixture is crumbly. Beat the egg and milk in a separate bowl, then add to the flour mixture. Process just until the dough forms a ball. Pat the dough into the prepared pan. For the filling, blend the cream cheese and sugar in the food processor, then add the egg yolks and vanilla and blend until smooth. Spread the filling evenly over the crust. Arrange the apples on top of the filling. Combine the sugar, cornstarch, and cinnamon, and sprinkle over the apples. Bake 30 minutes. Reduce the temperature to 300°F, and bake an additional 10 minutes. ***Yield: 6 – 8 servings.***

Blueberry Coffee Cake

1 cup sugar
¼ cup softened shortening
1 egg
½ cup milk
2 cups all-purpose flour
2 teaspoons baking powder
½ teaspoon salt
1 teaspoon vanilla
2 cups blueberries, washed and well drained

Crumb topping:
½ cup sugar
⅓ cup all-purpose flour
½ teaspoon ground cinnamon
¼ cup softened butter

Preheat the oven to 375°F. Mix together the sugar, shortening, and egg. Stir in the milk. Sift together the flour, baking powder, and salt, and stir into the batter along with the vanilla. Blend in the blueberries. Pour the batter into a greased 9" square pan. For the topping, combine the sugar, flour, and cinnamon, blend in the butter until the topping is crumbly, and sprinkle on top of the batter. Bake 45 – 50 minutes. ***Yield: 12 servings.***

Silver Fox Inn

The Zambonin Family
(Mario, Susan, Jessica, Matthew)
61 Granville Street
Summerside, Prince Edward Island
C1N 2Z3
Tel: (902) 436-4033
E-mail: silver.fox.inn@pei.sympatico.ca
www3.pei.sympatico.ca/peinns/silv-fox.htm
$$

ABOUT THE B&B

The name of this inn recalls the fascinating story of two poor trappers who went from rags to riches developing the silver fox industry in Prince Edward Island from 1880 to 1914. Built in 1892 as a private residence, Silver Fox Inn was designed by the famed architect William Critchlow Harris (1854 – 1913), whose brother Robert Harris gained world recognition as a portrait artist (his painting entitled "The Fathers of Confederation" is known to every Canadian). The Silver Fox has been carefully preserved and retains the original beauty of its spacious rooms with fireplaces and fine woodwork. Six bedrooms, each with private bath, feature period furnishings. Breakfast includes freshly baked muffins and biscuits and homemade preserves. The quiet location is central to Summerside's business and shopping district. Annual area events include the Lobster Carnival, Hydroplane Regatta, and Highland Gathering.

SEASON

all year

ACCOMMODATIONS

6 rooms with private baths

Chocolate Chip Streusel Coffee Cake

DeWitt's Bed and Breakfast

Irene DeWitt and Wendy Kelly
RR #1
Airdrie, Alberta T4B 2A3
Tel: (403) 948-5356
Fax: (403) 912-0788
E-mail: dewitbnb@cadvision.com
$$

ABOUT THE B&B

A relaxing stay in the country awaits you at DeWitt's Bed and Breakfast. Enjoy a hearty, home-cooked breakfast either on the flower filled patio or in the dining room, from which the Rocky Mountains can be seen. The three bedrooms are simple yet elegant: The Evergreen Room has a huge picture window, twin beds, and a private bathroom; The Knotty Pine Room has a double bed and a shared bathroom; and The Whispering Spruce Room has a queen bed and a shared bathroom. DeWitt's B&B is located a short distance west of Airdrie and within 20 minutes of Calgary and the international airport. It's an hour's drive to the scenic Kananaskis country, on the way to Canmore and Banff National Park. Nearby attractions include the Calgary Stampede, Calgary Zoo, and Glenbow Museum.

SEASON

all year

ACCOMMODATIONS

1 room with private bath;
2 rooms with shared baths

Streusel topping:
½ cup all-purpose flour
½ cup brown sugar
¼ cup margarine
1 cup chocolate chips
¼ cup chopped walnuts

Batter:
8-ounce package cream cheese
1½ cups granulated sugar
¾ cup margarine
3 eggs
¾ teaspoon vanilla
2½ cups all-purpose flour
1½ teaspoons baking powder
¾ teaspoon baking soda
¼ teaspoon salt
¾ cup milk

For the topping, combine the flour and brown sugar. Cut in the margarine until the mixture resembles coarse crumbs. Stir in the chocolate chips and walnuts; set aside. For the cake batter, grease and flour a 13 x 9" baking pan. Combine the cream cheese, granulated sugar, and margarine, and mix until well blended. Blend in the eggs and vanilla. In a separate bowl, combine the flour, baking powder, baking soda, and salt. Add the flour mixture alternately with the milk to the cream cheese mixture, stirring well after each addition. Spoon the batter into the prepared pan, and sprinkle with the streusel. Bake about 40 minutes. Cool on a wire rack. ***Yield: 12 servings.***

Chocolate Soufflé Torte

"This is a chocolate lovers' dessert." — *Marianne Persia*

1 cup whole toasted almonds, cooled
⅓ cup plus 3 tablespoons granulated sugar
¾ cup butter
1 pound bittersweet chocolate
½ cup heavy cream
2 tablespoons vegetable oil
6 eggs, separated

Confectioners' sugar
½ cup toasted sliced almonds
Almond whipped cream (recipe follows)

Preheat the oven to 350°F. Grease and flour the bottom and sides of a 9" springform pan (or line the bottom and sides with parchment paper, then grease with butter). In a food processor, process the whole almonds and 3 tablespoons of the granulated sugar until the nuts are finely ground. In a heavy saucepan or double boiler, melt the butter over medium-low heat. Add the chocolate, cream, and oil, and whisk until smooth. Stir in the almond mixture, and cool the mixture slightly.

(continued on next page)

Hummingbird Hill B&B

Marianne and Gary Persia
254 Edmond Road
Astorville, Ontario P0H 1B0
Tel: (800) 661-4976 or
(705) 752-4547
Fax: (705) 752-5150
E-mail: mabb@vianet.on.ca
www.on-biz.com/hummingbirdhill
$$

ABOUT THE B&B

This secluded B&B close to North Bay is set on six acres and is surrounded by extensive gardens. The unique cedar home comprises two geodesic domes with an open concept living room, 26-foot cathedral ceiling, and skylights. Two spiral staircases lead to three guest rooms, which are decorated with antiques and have a TV and duvet-covered beds. Guests can relax in the solarium among tropical plants, sit in the living room in front of a cozy wood fire, or, in winter, watch the deer feed outside. Have a sauna, enjoy a glass of homemade wine in the hot tub, or, in summer, observe nature while you dine in the screened cedar gazebo. A full breakfast is provided, and gourmet meals are available with all-inclusive weekends. Marianne has done the landscaping, while Gary is a construction foreman. North Bay offers cross-country and downhill skiing, ice fishing, snowmobiling, swimming, and boating. Close by are artisans' studios, the Dionne quintuplets' home and museum, and Algonquin Park.

SEASON

all year

ACCOMMODATIONS

2 rooms with private bath;
1 room with shared bath

With an electric mixer, beat the egg whites on high speed until they stand in soft peaks. Gradually add ⅓ cup granulated sugar, and beat until the eggs stand in stiff peaks. In a separate bowl, beat the egg yolks with a whisk until they thicken and are pale yellow, about 5 minutes (or use an electric beater on low speed). Gradually beat the chocolate mixture into the egg yolks. Fold in the egg whites. Pour the batter into the prepared pan. Bake 35 minutes or until the sides crack and puff (a cake tester inserted in the center will come out moist with batter). Cool the cake on a rack, cover with plastic wrap, and refrigerate overnight. Loosen the cake from the sides of the pan with a knife, and remove the cake from the pan. Dust the cake with confectioners' sugar, and sprinkle with the toasted almonds. Serve chilled or at room temperature with almond whipped cream. ***Yield: 12 – 14 servings.***

Almond whipped cream:
1 cup chilled heavy cream
1 teaspoon almond extract
2 tablespoons granulated sugar

Beat together the cream, almond extract, and granulated sugar. Refrigerate the almond whipped cream until the cake is ready to serve.

Coffee-Walnut Coffee Cake

2 eggs
½ cup soft margarine
½ cup sugar
⅓ cup chopped walnuts
1 tablespoon coffee extract
1 cup all-purpose flour
1 tablespoon baking powder
Salt

Filling:
⅓ cup soft margarine
1 cup confectioners' sugar
2 teaspoons coffee extract
2 teaspoons milk
Walnut halves

Preheat the oven to 325°F. Butter 2 (7") straight-sided layer cake pans, and line the bottom with buttered wax paper. Put the eggs, margarine, sugar, walnuts, and coffee extract in a bowl. Sift in the flour with the baking powder and a pinch of salt. Beat with a wooden spoon for 2 or 3 minutes until well combined. Divide the batter between the prepared pans, level the surface, and bake 35 – 40 minutes (until the cake tops are spongy to the touch). Turn the cakes out on a wire rack to cool before removing the lining paper.

Make the filling while the cakes are baking. Beat the margarine, confectioners' sugar, coffee extract, and milk in a bowl until smooth. Sandwich the cakes together with two-thirds of the filling between them. Top with the remaining filling. Mark the filling with the prongs of a fork in a decorative pattern. Place walnut halves on top of the cake. ***Yield:* *12 – 14 servings.***

Barbara Ann's Bed 'n Breakfast Vacation Farm

Barbara Ann and Ted Witzaney
PO Box 156
Denzil, Saskatchewan S0L 0S0
Tel: (306) 358-4814
$

ABOUT THE B&B

Specially geared for families, Barbara Ann's B&B is located on the Witzaney farm, where they've been raising crops and hogs since 1911. The petting zoo includes traditional farm animals and more exotic ones, including a llama and Muscovy ducks. Barbara Ann's breakfast (and other meals served on request) feature farm-fresh milk, eggs, cheese, and vegetables; home-baked goods, such as buns, pies, and cookies; homemade jams, jellies, relishes, and pickles; and pork raised on the farm. Homemade sausages are the specialty of the house. Picnic and barbecue facilities, a sandbox and swing set, a horseshoe pit, lawn bowling and badminton equipment, and an 18-hole miniature golf course are all on the property. When not tending to guests, Barbara Ann enjoys sewing and craft making, while Ted enjoys woodworking. Both like to spend time with their 10 grandchildren. Denzil is about a half-hour drive west of Unity, Saskatchewan, and a 45-minute drive east of Provost, Alberta.

SEASON

all year

ACCOMMODATIONS

2 rooms with shared bath

Cornelius White House Bed & Breakfast

Bonnie and Frank Evans
8 Wellington Street
Bloomfield, Ontario K0K 1G0
Tel/Fax: (613) 393-2282
$ – $$

ABOUT THE B&B

Located on the historic Loyalist Parkway at the west end of a farming community in picturesque Prince Edward County, the Cornelius White House is named for its original owner, a Dutch settler who built this charming red-brick house in 1862. Today, a sense of history and design combine with European furnishings and accents to create a unique B&B. Three guest rooms on the second floor open onto the sitting room below, which has a cathedral ceiling. There is also a suite on the main floor. The house is air conditioned and is a smoke-free environment. A full breakfast of fruit, a hot main course, and fresh baked goods is served in the Dutch Treat Tea Room. Outstanding restaurants are nearby, as well as antique and craft shops, galleries, studios, and museums. Cornelius White House is just 10 minutes from Sandbanks and Outlet Beach Provincial Parks, famous for the largest freshwater sand dunes in the world. Prince Edward County, with its panoramic views and gentle rolling hills, is a cyclist's dream come true.

SEASON

all year

ACCOMMODATIONS

2 rooms with private baths;
2 rooms with shared bath

Cornelius White House Cake

"Our boys don't especially enjoy cake with icing, so we have this sponge-type cake on hand just about all the time. It's very moist and can stay fresh for days (that is, if it's not all gobbled up right away!)."
— Bonnie Evans

4 eggs
1 large vanilla instant pudding mix
1 yellow cake mix (Duncan Hines recommended)
¾ cup sweet sherry
¾ cup vegetable oil
1 tablespoon ground nutmeg

Confectioners' sugar
Fresh fruit (optional)
Whipped cream (optional)

Preheat the oven to 350°F. Mix together the eggs, pudding mix, cake mix, sherry, oil, and nutmeg. Beat about 5 minutes. Pour the batter into a greased angel food pan. Bake about 60 minutes, checking after 45 minutes. Turn out onto a cake rack, cool, and sprinkle with confectioners' sugar. Serve topped with optional fruit and whipped cream. ***Yield: 10 – 12 servings.***

Country Apple Cake

4 eggs
2 cups plus 2 tablespoons sugar
1 cup vegetable oil
3 cups all-purpose flour
3 teaspoons baking powder
½ teaspoon salt
4 apples, peeled, cored, and sliced (McIntosh recommended)
2 tablespoons ground cinnamon
½ cup orange juice
2 teaspoons vanilla
Poppy seeds

Frosting:
1 cup confectioners' sugar
4 teaspoons lemon juice

Preheat the oven to 350°F. In a large bowl, beat together the eggs, 2 cups of the sugar, and the oil. In a second bowl, combine the flour, baking powder, and salt. In a third bowl, combine the apples, cinnamon, and remaining sugar. Add the flour mixture to the egg mixture, and combine. Stir in the orange juice and vanilla. Pour ½ cup of the batter into a greased and floured tube pan, then add half of the apple mixture. Add the rest of the batter, then the remaining apple mixture. Sprinkle with poppy seeds. Bake 75 minutes. For the frosting, mix the confectioners' sugar with the lemon juice, then drip the lemon mixture over the warm cake. ***Yield: 12 – 16 servings.***

Chaplin's Country B&B

Kathy and Ron Chaplin
RR #5, Box 43
Saskatoon, Saskatchewan S7K 3J8
Tel/Fax: (306) 931-3353
E-mail: chaplinr@duke.usask.ca
www.dbs2.com/chaplins
$

ABOUT THE B&B

Experience the wide open spaces and blue sky of Canada's prairies at Chaplin's Country B&B, a working farm with Jersey cows, pigs, sheep, goats, and chickens. Enjoy a rest on the veranda and view awesome sunsets, or stroll through the barnyard and watch the evening milking. This gracious country home has a handmade spiral staircase, knotty pine paneling, and prairie antiques. For privacy, the guest bedrooms, TV lounge, and bathroom are all on the second floor. Chaplin's country breakfast, including French toast with homemade syrups, sausage, fresh fruit in season, and beverages, is a real eye-opener, while an evening snack of apple cake and hot cider always hits the spot. Saskatoon, only 15 minutes away, offers many fine restaurants, shops, and attractions. Other area diversions include the Western Development Museum, Wanuskewin Heritage Park, University of Saskatchewan, and numerous provincial parks and golf courses. Kathy and Ron pride themselves on their prairie hospitality and comfortable facilities.

SEASON

all year

ACCOMMODATIONS

3 rooms with shared bath

Cranblue Coffee Cake

*"This cake is so popular with my guests that I had to put it on the computer so I could just print off copies when they request the recipe."
— Connie Ellis*

2⅓ cups all-purpose flour
½ cup granulated sugar
3 teaspoons baking powder
½ teaspoon salt
2 eggs
¾ cup milk
¼ cup vegetable oil
½ cup fresh or frozen cranberries
½ cup fresh or frozen blueberries
⅓ cup packed brown sugar
¼ cup margarine or butter
¼ cup chopped walnuts
1 teaspoon ground cinnamon

Preheat the oven to 350°F. Mix together 2 cups of the flour, and the granulated sugar, baking powder, and salt in a large bowl. In a separate bowl, beat the eggs until frothy. Mix in the milk and oil. Pour the egg mixture into the flour mixture, and mix. Fold in the cranberries and blueberries. Place the batter in a lightly greased 9" tube or bundt pan. Mix together the remaining flour and the brown sugar, margarine, walnuts, and cinnamon. Sprinkle the brown sugar mixture over the top of the batter. Bake 45 – 50 minutes or until a toothpick inserted in the center comes out clean. Cool the cake in the pan for at least 10 minutes. Serve the cake right (topping) side up. ***Tip:*** If using frozen berries, you do not need to thaw them before folding into the batter. ***Yield: 12 servings.***

The Catalpa Tree

Connie Ellis
2217 London Line
Sarnia, Ontario N7T 7H2
Tel: (800) 276-5135 or
(519) 542-5008
Fax: (519) 541-0297
$

ABOUT THE B&B

Built in 1894 by the host's great-grandfather, William Beatty, this family home displays true Victorian fashion, complete with gingerbread trim. The house, which is situated on a 100-acre crop farm, has been lovingly maintained in its original form. The B&B's decor complements the design of the house but also incorporates modern conveniences such as gas fireplaces and central air conditioning. Furnishings are a warm mix of contemporary and traditional pieces. A full gourmet breakfast is served in the parlor. The original dining room is now a lounge where guests can visit, relax with a good book, watch a favorite television program, enjoy a video, or play a game. A golf course is located at the end of the lane. In the area are many historical points of interest, a community theater, a water amusement park, a harness racing track, and places to go fishing, swimming, and boating. Picnic lunches or dinner are available by advance request.

SEASON

all year

ACCOMMODATIONS

3 rooms with shared bath

Flan Breton

"This recipe comes from my Breton-Canadian roots. It's called 'Fars Foun' in Breton." — Anne-Marie Bansfield

1 cup pitted prunes, raisins, or fresh cherries
¾ cup all-purpose flour
½ cup sugar
3 eggs
2 cups whole milk, at room temperature
2 tablespoons melted butter
1 tablespoon vanilla
Salt

Preheat the oven to 350°F. Butter a deep pie plate or large glass casserole. Cover the bottom of the dish with either prunes, raisins, or cherries. In a bowl, combine the flour and sugar. Add the eggs and mix, then add the milk little by little. Stir in the butter, vanilla, and a pinch of salt. Pour the batter over the fruit in the pie plate. Bake 40 – 50 minutes until a knife inserted in the flan's center comes out clean. The top should be golden and firm to the touch. ***Yield: 6 servings.***

Le Gîte Park Avenue B&B

Anne-Marie and Irving Bansfield
54 Park Avenue
Ottawa, Ontario K2P 1B2
Tel: (613) 230-9131
$$

ABOUT THE B&B

A bright, airy ambiance and artistic decor await you at Park Avenue B&B, an elegant, brick 1906 home located in a charming residential area of downtown Ottawa, Canada's capital. In addition to high-quality beds done up in classic cotton and linen sheets and duvets, each guest room is furnished with a desk and swivel chair, a rocking chair, bookshelves, excellent lighting, and attractive works of art. Ideal for families, the third-floor suite has two bedrooms and a private bath. The mood throughout the house is one of relaxation and warmth. Park Avenue B&B is close to the Parliament Buildings, art galleries, and museums, and is only three minutes (by foot) from the Rideau Canal, which freezes into the world's longest skating rink. Ottawa has a number of exciting festivals and activities, including Winterlude, a winter carnival held each February. Anne-Marie and Irving make it a point to know what's going on when in Ottawa so they can advise their guests on what to see and do.

SEASON

all year

ACCOMMODATIONS

1 suite with private bath;
2 rooms with shared bath

Hawkins House Bed & Breakfast

Carla Pitzel and Garry Umbrich
303 Hawkins Street
Whitehorse, Yukon Y1A 1X5
Tel: (867) 668-7638
Fax: (867) 668-7632
$$$$

ABOUT THE B&B

To stay at the Hawkins House Bed & Breakfast is to share a once-in-a-lifetime Yukon experience with your hosts Carla, Garry, and their two sons. Each guest room in this custom-built, luxury Victorian B&B highlights a different Yukon theme and features private bath and balcony, oak floor, bar sink, refrigerator, cable TV, and VCR. Guests can take a Jacuzzi soak in the Fleur de Lys Room, watch videos about Native peoples in the First Nations Room, step back into gold rush days in the Victorian Tea Rose Room, or admire the splendid view of the SS Klondike *paddlewheeler and Canyon Mountain from the balcony of the Fireweed Room. Especially geared to the business traveler, Hawkins House provides the convenience of a private telephone line and answering machine, fax service, and a work table with a light and computer jack. Breakfast is a homemade feast of northern and international delights — from the home-smoked salmon pâté and moose sausage to jams, syrups, and sourdough pastries.*

SEASON

all year

ACCOMMODATIONS

4 rooms with private baths

Hawkins House Shortcake

"This recipe is my all-time favorite and the only three-ingredient cake I know. It's really quick to prepare for those unexpected guests who just drop in. We serve it with Yukon wild berries and whipped cream." — Carla Pitzel

Dough:
4 eggs, separated
4 tablespoons vanilla sugar*
4 tablespoons all-purpose flour

Topping:
1 large banana
Fresh berries

Sweetened whipped cream:
1 cup heavy cream
1 – 3 tablespoons confectioners' sugar
½ teaspoon vanilla

**Note: Vanilla sugar is found in German specialty stores or delicatessens. If not available, use regular sugar and add ½ teaspoon vanilla to the beaten egg yolks.*

(continued on next page)

Preheat the oven to 400°F. Butter a shortcake or flan pan. Beat the egg whites in a small bowl until they stand in soft peaks. Transfer them to a large bowl. Beat the egg yolks in a small bowl with the vanilla sugar until thick and pale yellow. Pour the yolk mixture over the egg whites, and blend, making sure all the egg whites are mixed in (there should be no lumps of meringue). Fold in the flour. Spoon the batter into the pan. Bake 10 minutes, reduce the temperature to 350°F, and bake another 20 minutes. When the cake has cooled, remove it from the pan. Cut the banana lengthwise into 4 slices. Curve the banana slices along the inside rim of the cake. Cover the top of the cake with fresh berries. Beat together the heavy cream, confectioners' sugar, and vanilla, and spread over the fruit. ***Yield: 10 servings.***

Barbara Ann's Bed 'n Breakfast Vacation Farm

Barbara Ann and Ted Witzaney
PO Box 156
Denzil, Saskatchewan S0L 0S0
Tel: (306) 358-4814
$

ABOUT THE B&B

Specially geared for families, Barbara Ann's B&B is located on the Witzaney farm, where they've been raising crops and hogs since 1911. The petting zoo includes traditional farm animals and more exotic ones, including a llama and Muscovy ducks. Barbara Ann's breakfast (and other meals served on request) feature farm-fresh milk, eggs, cheese, and vegetables; home-baked goods, such as buns, pies, and cookies; homemade jams, jellies, relishes, and pickles; and pork raised on the farm. Homemade sausages are the specialty of the house. Picnic and barbecue facilities, a sandbox and swing set, a horseshoe pit, lawn bowling and badminton equipment, and an 18-hole miniature golf course are all on the property. When not tending to guests, Barbara Ann enjoys sewing and craft making, while Ted enjoys woodworking. Both like to spend time with their 10 grandchildren. Denzil is about a half-hour drive west of Unity, Saskatchewan, and a 45-minute drive east of Provost, Alberta.

SEASON

all year

ACCOMMODATIONS

2 rooms with shared bath

Hazelnut Coffee Cake

1 cup all-purpose flour
1 cup whole wheat flour
¾ cup brown sugar
1 teaspoon baking powder
1 teaspoon baking soda
1 teaspoon ground cinnamon
1 teaspoon ground nutmeg
½ teaspoon salt
1 egg
⅔ cup milk
¼ cup honey
½ cup ground hazelnuts

Topping:
1 cup sifted confectioners' sugar
1 – 2 tablespoons hot milk
½ cup whole hazelnuts

Preheat the oven to 350°F. Mix together the all-purpose flour, whole wheat flour, brown sugar, baking powder, baking soda, cinnamon, nutmeg, and salt. Combine the egg, milk, and honey, add to the flour mixture, and blend well. Fold in the ground hazelnuts. Pour the batter into a greased 9" square baking pan, and bake about 60 minutes. Cool slightly, then remove from the pan. For the topping, combine the confectioners' sugar and hot milk, and beat until smooth. Drizzle the topping carefully over the top of the cooled cake in a lattice or cross-hatch design. Place whole hazelnuts in the squares formed by the lattice design. ***Yield: 12 servings.***

Heart-Healthy Applesauce Cake

"A favorite with guests, this applesauce cake has no eggs."
— Anna Doorenbos

½ cup margarine or butter
1 cup brown sugar
1 cup unsweetened applesauce
2 cups all-purpose flour
1 teaspoon baking soda
1 teaspoon ground cinnamon
½ teaspoon ground cloves
½ teaspoon salt
½ cup raisins
½ cup slivered almonds

Preheat the oven to 350°F. Cream the margarine and brown sugar. Gradually add the applesauce. Sift together the flour, baking soda, cinnamon, cloves, and salt, and add to the butter mixture. Add the raisins and almonds. Spread the batter in a greased loaf pan, and bake about 60 minutes. ***Yield: 12 servings.***

Anna's Bed and Breakfast

Anna and Robert Doorenbos
204 Wolf Street
Thompson, Manitoba R8N 1J7
Tel: (204) 677-5075

$ – $$

ABOUT THE B&B

Visit Anna's Bed and Breakfast to experience what Canadian Dutch hospitality is all about. This adult-oriented and smoke-free B&B offers a private guest suite with its own entrance and parking space, two single beds, private bath, kitchenette, and den with TV and telephone. Anna enjoys cooking and will get your day off to a delicious start with a full breakfast served in the main dining room. Oriental meals are another specialty and, along with traditional meals, are available for an additional charge. The greenhouse, which is connected to the cozy and informal living room, opens onto the deck and lends a summer atmosphere to the home — even in the dead of winter! Thompson is the home base of travelers to fly-in fishing lodges and Churchill (Manitoba) and other northern communities. It also boasts the longest alpine ski season in Manitoba. Guest pick-up can be arranged as well as scenic touring by car. Your hosts Anna and Robert moved to Canada from Holland and have lived in Thompson since 1971. Robert, an award-winning visual artist, comes from Egypt and Anna from Indonesia.

SEASON

all year

ACCOMMODATIONS

1 suite with private bath

Elgin Manor B&B

Penny and Dave Grims
RR #2
Port Sandfield, Onta
Tel: (705) 765-5
$$ – $$$$

ABOUT THE B&

Nestled on a quiet bay of picturesque Lake Joseph is the unique and heartwarming Elgin Manor B&B, a 1920s Tudor home surrounded by English gardens and a water's edge fireplace. As you relax in a wooden Muskoka chair, you're sure to see some antique wooden launches, for which the Muskoka Lakes are famous, or perhaps the old steamship Segwun *pass by. The manor is decorated with antiques throughout and handmade quilts grace each guest room. Launch excursions and old-fashioned picnic lunches packed in wicker baskets can be arranged. Elgin Manor B&B is situated in the heart of Muskoka cottage country (two hours north of Toronto), an area that offers year-round activities — from summer nature walks, fishing, swimming, canoeing, and midnight strolls under a million glistening stars to tours of local artisans' studios, ice skating, and snowshoeing and cross-country skiing in the panoramic countryside.*

SEASON

all year

ACCOMMODATIONS

3 rooms with private baths;
1 honeymoon cabin
with private bath

…mingbird Cake

…een throughout Muskoka from May to … ake with afternoon tea on the deck near the … feeders (which may have 8 to 10 visiting … can enjoy the birds' beautiful colors and … their wings buzzing."

2…
1 t…
1 tea…
1 teas…
3 eggs
1½ cups …
2 teaspoon…
8-ounce can…
2 cups mashe…

Icing:
8-ounce package c…am cheese
½ cup butter
1 teaspoon vanilla
3 – 4 cups confectioners' sugar

Fresh edible flowers
Fresh fruit

(continued on next page)

Preheat the oven to 350°F. In a mixing bowl, combine the flour, sugar, baking soda, salt, and cinnamon. In a small bowl, beat the eggs, then add the oil and vanilla, and mix again. Add the egg mixture to the flour mixture, and combine. Stir in the pineapple and banana. Spoon the batter into 3 greased 8" layer pans. Bake about 25 minutes. Turn the pans upside down onto cooling racks. For the icing, blend the cream cheese and butter. Stir in the vanilla. Gradually add the confectioners' sugar, and mix until smooth. When the layers are cool, frost the top of each layer with icing. Stack the iced layers, and frost the sides of the cake. Decorate with fresh edible flowers and fruit to resemble a hummingbird (use the fruit as the body and the flower petals as the wings). This cake can be refrigerated. ***Yield: 10 – 12 servings.***

Brookside Hospitality Home

Pearl and Lloyd Hiscock
PO Box 104
Sunnyside, Newfoundland A0B 3J0
Tel: (709) 472-4515
$

ABOUT THE B&B

You'll be welcomed like family at Brookside Hospitality Home, a well-maintained ranch-style dwelling in the rural community of Sunnyside. Pearl and Lloyd have lived in Sunnyside practically all their lives and know what Newfoundland hospitality is all about. Get to know them over a cup of tea or coffee, which is provided along with a bedtime snack. In the morning, make your way to the breakfast nook, which overlooks the water, where homemade bread and jam, cereals, and juices await you. Radio, cable TV, laundry facilities, and ample parking are also available. Let your well-informed hosts direct you to the best sights in the province. Lloyd is a boat enthusiast and you may want to look in on his latest boat building project in the shed. Pearl keeps busy with her household responsibilities. Brookside is about one-and-a-half hours' drive from the Argentia Ferry to North Sydney, Nova Scotia, and one hour's drive from St. John's, capital of Newfoundland.

SEASON

all year

ACCOMMODATIONS

2 rooms with shared bath

Impossible Pie

"After this has baked, you have a definite bottom crust, a lovely custard filling, and a rich butter-coconut topping."
— Pearl Hiscock

4 eggs
2 cups milk
1 cup flaked unsweetened coconut
1 cup sugar
½ cup all-purpose flour
¼ cup melted butter
1 teaspoon vanilla
½ teaspoon baking powder
¼ teaspoon salt

Preheat the oven to 350°F. Mix together the eggs, milk, coconut, sugar, flour, butter, vanilla, baking powder, and salt. Pour the batter into a buttered 10" glass pie plate, and bake 60 minutes. ***Yield: 6 servings.***

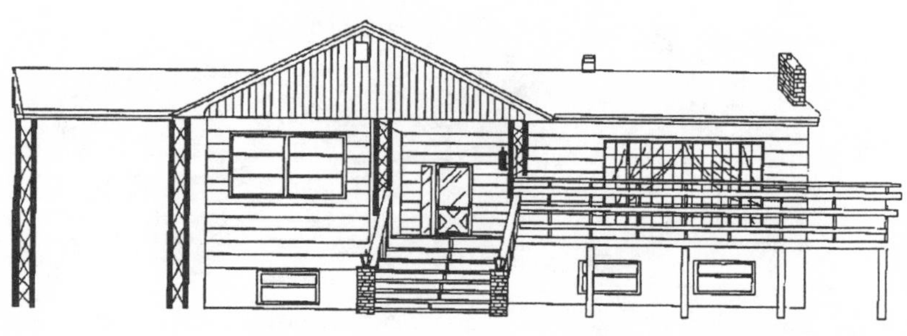

Mandarin Orange Coffee Cake

2 cups all-purpose flour
1 cup sugar
2½ teaspoons baking powder
1 teaspoon salt
½ teaspoon ground nutmeg
½ cup margarine
¾ cup milk
1 egg
1 teaspoon vanilla
11-ounce can mandarin oranges, drained

Preheat the oven to 350°F. Combine the flour, sugar, baking powder, salt, and nutmeg. Cut in the margarine until fine crumbs form. Reserve ½ cup of the crumbs for the topping. To the remainder, add the milk, egg, and vanilla. Spread the batter in a greased 8" square pan. Spread the oranges on top, and cover with the remaining crumbs. Bake 40 – 45 minutes. *Yield: 9 – 12 servings.*

Park View Bed & Breakfast

Gladys and Carson Langille
254 Cameron Street
Moncton, New Brunswick E1C 5Z3
Tel: (506) 382-4504
$$

ABOUT THE B&B

This art deco home was built in 1940 as a residence for Mrs. Inez Robinson, owner of Moncton's first business college. The architectural plans came from the 1939 New York World's Fair, and this was the first art deco home in Moncton. The curved living room windows look out on beautiful Victoria Park in the city's center. Opened as a B&B in 1989, this charming home has three guest rooms with cable TV, telephones, and exquisite shared bath, spacious living room with fireplace, elegant dining room, and cozy kitchen. Your hosts provide a warm welcome, a hearty, home-cooked breakfast of your choice, and a wealth of information about the area. Gladys is a part-time school teacher, while Carson enjoys playing bridge and painting landscapes. A collection of works by local artists graces their walls. Nearby is superb dining, shopping, beaches, parks, museums, galleries, theater, a must-see tidal bore (where the tide goes up and down very quickly), and the famous Magnetic Hill (you'll never believe this phenomenon unless you experience it yourself!).

SEASON

all year

ACCOMMODATIONS

3 rooms with shared bath

Maple Butter Tarts

Dundee Arms Inn

Pat Sands
200 Pownal Street
Charlottetown,
Prince Edward Island C1A 3W8
Tel: (902) 892-2496
Fax: (902) 368-8532
E-mail: dundee@dundeearms.com
$$$$

ABOUT THE B&B

Dundee Arms Inn, with its copper sconces, antique clock, and china cabinets, exemplifies Victorian country charm in the heart of the city. Built in 1903 for Parker Carvell, this gracious mansion is a fine example of the Queen Anne revival style. The house was a private residence until 1956 when the building was converted into a guest house. It became an inn in 1972. While extensive renovations have been made to satisfy the needs of today's guests, the original character and charm of the house remain. Eight guest rooms are furnished with period antiques and contain such modern conveniences as a telephone, color TV, and AM/FM radio. Over the years, the Dundee has welcomed thousands of guests to The Griffon Room, its internationally acclaimed restaurant, which has received accolades from En Route *and* Gourmet *magazines. The inn is a five-minute walk from downtown Charlottetown.*

SEASON

all year

ACCOMMODATIONS

8 rooms with private baths

Tart shell:
2 cups cake flour
¾ teaspoon salt
¾ cup shortening
4 – 5 tablespoons water

Filling:
⅔ cup melted butter
2 cups brown sugar
4 eggs
¾ cup maple syrup
1 teaspoon vanilla
Salt

Whipped cream

Preheat the oven to 375°F. Mix together the flour and salt. Cut in the shortening with a pastry blender until the mixture resembles coarse oatmeal. Add the water 1 tablespoon at a time until the dough sticks together. On a floured surface, roll the dough until it is very thin. Using a large frozen juice can with the ends removed, cut the dough into circles. Grease 24 muffin cups, and pat the circles of dough into the bottom and sides of the muffin cups. For the filling, blend the butter with the brown sugar. Add the eggs, maple syrup, vanilla, and a pinch of salt. Fill each muffin cup three-quarters full with the filling. Bake 15 minutes or until a toothpick inserted in the center comes out clean. Serve with whipped cream. ***Yield: 24 tarts.***

Melt-in-Your-Mouth Shortbread Tarts

"These are wonderful to serve with a nice cup of tea or coffee when our guests arrive." — Dwyla Beglaw

Tart shell:
1 cup butter or margarine
½ cup confectioners' sugar
1½ cups all-purpose flour
1 tablespoon cornstarch

Coffee cream filling:
1¼ cups milk
¼ cup cornstarch
⅔ cup sugar
1 tablespoon instant coffee powder
1 cup plus 2 tablespoons butter, at room temperature

Preheat the oven to 325°F. Grease 24 tart or mini muffin cups. Cream the butter and sugar with an electric mixer. Add the flour and cornstarch, and mix. Divide the dough among the tart cups, and pat it with your fingers to line each tart cup. Prick the bottom of each tart shell with a fork, and bake 20 minutes. Watch carefully — the shells should not brown — and prick them with a fork if they puff up.

(continued on next page)

Tall Cedars Bed & Breakfast

Dwyla and Ed Beglaw
720 Robinson Street
Coquitlam, British Columbia
V3J 4G1
Tel/Fax: (604) 936-6016
E-mail: tallcedars_bnb@bc.sympatico.ca
www/bbcanada.com/2490.html
$$

ABOUT THE B&B

For Dwyla and Ed Beglaw, operating a B&B is not just a business, it's an adventure! Seasoned B&B innkeepers, for over 11 years they have welcomed guests from all over the world to their gracious family home located 20 minutes from Vancouver. Tall fir and cedar trees surround the house, and, in summer, the walkway is bordered with beautiful flower beds. Guest rooms have queen or twin beds, ceiling fans, and comfy eiderdowns. Guests can choose from a full or continental breakfast. Tall Cedars is close to Simon Fraser University and Burrard Inlet and is minutes from serene Como Lake — ideal for strolling, jogging, and fishing — Rocky Point Park — a great spot for rollerblading, cycling, and boating — shops, movie theaters, and a restaurant that serves the best fish and chips this side of England. At the end of the day, guests can wind down on the lit, covered flower garden balcony (where smoking is permitted) and enjoy refreshments.

SEASON

all year

ACCOMMODATIONS

1 room with private bath;
2 rooms with shared bath

For the coffee cream, combine ⅓ cup of the milk and the cornstarch in a small bowl; set aside. In a small saucepan, bring the remaining milk, sugar, and coffee to a boil. Stir the coffee mixture into the reserved milk mixture. Return the milk mixture to the saucepan, and bring to a boil, stirring constantly until the milk mixture is smooth and has thickened. Remove it from the heat, cover with plastic wrap, and cool completely. In a large bowl, beat the butter until light and fluffy. Gradually add the milk mixture to the butter, beating well after each addition. Using a pastry bag with a large tip, pipe the coffee cream into the tart shells. Keep the tarts refrigerated, but allow them to reach room temperature before serving. ***Tips:*** The tart shells and the coffee cream both freeze well. The tarts are also delicious when filled with lemon curd or your favorite jam. ***Yield: 24 tarts.***

Open-Faced Wild Blueberry Cake

"My friend gave me this recipe 30 years ago while she was living in the southern province of Limburg in Holland. I'm still using it today because it uses a minimal amount of fat and eggs. I pick wild muskeg blueberries in the bushes at the back of our house and keep them in the freezer for whenever I make this cake."— Anna Doorenbos

¼ cup butter or margarine
¼ cup sugar
1 egg
1 teaspoon vanilla
1 cup all-purpose flour
½ teaspoon baking powder
½ teaspoon baking soda
½ cup skim milk or 1% milk
Wild blueberry filling (recipe follows)
Package of powdered glaze for fresh fruit

Vanilla ice cream or whipped cream

(continued on next page)

Anna's Bed and Breakfast

Anna and Robert Doorenbos
204 Wolf Street
Thompson, Manitoba R8N 1J7
Tel: (204) 677-5075
$ – $$

ABOUT THE B&B

Visit Anna's Bed and Breakfast to experience what Canadian Dutch hospitality is all about. This adult-oriented and smoke-free B&B offers a private guest suite with its own entrance and parking space, two single beds, private bath, kitchenette, and den with TV and telephone. Anna enjoys cooking and will get your day off to a delicious start with a full breakfast served in the main dining room. Oriental meals are another specialty and, along with traditional meals, are available for an additional charge. The greenhouse, which is connected to the cozy and informal living room, opens onto the deck and lends a summer atmosphere to the home — even in the dead of winter! Thompson is the home base of travelers to fly-in fishing lodges and Churchill (Manitoba) and other northern communities. It also boasts the longest alpine ski season in Manitoba. Guest pick-up can be arranged as well as scenic touring by car. Your hosts Anna and Robert moved to Canada from Holland and have lived in Thompson since 1971. Robert, an award-winning visual artist, comes from Egypt and Anna from Indonesia.

SEASON

all year

ACCOMMODATIONS

1 suite with private bath

Preheat the oven to 350°F. Cream the butter with the sugar. Add the egg and vanilla, and beat well. In a separate bowl, combine the flour, baking powder, and baking soda. Stir the flour mixture and milk alternately into the butter mixture until the batter is smooth. Grease a 9" flan form, and pour the batter into it. Bake 25 – 30 minutes. Turn the cake out of the form onto a plate.

Pour the wild blueberry filling on top of the cake. Prepare the powdered glaze according to the package directions. Brush the glaze onto the fruit filling. Serve with vanilla ice cream or whipped cream. ***Variation:*** You can substitute any fresh fruit for the blueberries, or you can use canned fruit. If using canned fruit, prepare a glaze by mixing the juice from the canned fruit with a thickener (such as cornstarch or tapioca). ***Yield: 8 – 12 servings.***

Wild blueberry filling:
1½ cups washed wild blueberries
½ cup water
¼ – ½ cup sugar
Juice of ½ lemon
Ground cinnamon
Cornstarch

Bring the blueberries, water, sugar, lemon juice, and a pinch of ground cinnamon to a boil, and simmer 5 minutes. Thicken with cornstarch, and remove from the heat.

Orange Cake

"Of all my recipes, this has been the one most requested by my guests." — Monique Sanders

2 cups all-purpose flour
½ cup sugar
2½ teaspoons baking powder
½ teaspoon salt
Zest of 1 orange, grated
1 egg, lightly beaten
½ cup milk
½ cup orange juice
⅓ cup vegetable oil

Streusel topping:
¼ cup all-purpose flour
¼ cup sugar
2 tablespoons butter or margarine
2 tablespoons grated orange zest

Thin curls of orange zest

Preheat the oven to 350°F. Sift together the flour, sugar, baking powder, and salt. Stir in the orange zest. Make a well in the center of the flour mixture, add the egg, milk, orange juice, and oil, and stir just enough to moisten the dry ingredients (the batter should be lumpy). Pour the batter into a greased 9" springform pan or an angel food pan. For the streusel, blend together the flour, sugar, butter, and orange zest until the mixture is crumbly. Sprinkle the topping over the batter. Bake 30 minutes or until golden. Garnish with curls of orange zest. ***Yield: 12 servings.***

Limestone & Lilacs

Monique and John Sanders
1775 Highway #38
Kingston, Ontario K7P 2Y7
Tel: (613) 545-0222
E-mail: john.sanders@sympatico.ca
$$

ABOUT THE B&B

Limestone & Lilacs rests on 27 picturesque acres on the northwest outskirts of Kingston. The romantic 1820s limestone farmhouse has been elegantly restored and stands out among the many limestone homes for which Kingston is known. The house has high ceilings, and the interior limestone walls are the perfect backdrop for graceful furnishings and Canadiana. A full gourmet breakfast is served in the elegant dining room. Kingston's waterfront area is only 12 minutes away, and from there you can cruise the famous Thousand Islands. Visit Kingston's 17 museums and Fort Henry — built during the War of 1812 — or shop in various boutiques. Monique and John, who speak English and French, opened their B&B in 1995 after working for corporations in Montréal, Toronto, and Pennsylvania.

SEASON

all year

ACCOMMODATIONS

3 rooms with shared baths

Orange Peel–Sherry Cake

2 cups candied orange peel
⅔ cup sweet sherry
1 cup margarine
1½ cups sugar
4 eggs
2½ cups all-purpose flour
1 teaspoon baking powder

Soak the candied peel in ⅓ cup of the sherry overnight (cover with plastic wrap). Preheat the oven to 350°F. Cream the margarine and sugar until fluffy. Add the eggs one at a time, mixing well after each addition. Combine the flour and baking powder, then add to the margarine mixture, mixing just until the dry ingredients are moistened. Fold in the sherry-soaked orange peel. Spread the mixture into a greased and floured bundt pan. Bake 65 – 75 minutes. Cool 20 minutes in the pan, then invert to remove the cake. Wrap the cake in cheesecloth. Soak the cheesecloth with the remaining ⅓ cup sherry. Cover the wrapped cake in aluminum foil, and refrigerate for 4 days. ***Tips:*** When serving, cut small pieces (this cake is quite filling!). Wrap any leftovers back in the cheesecloth and foil, and refrigerate. This cake will keep for about 2 weeks. ***Yield: 24 servings.***

Bread and Roses Country Inn

Monica and Richard Cobb
PO Box 177, 82 Victoria Street
Annapolis Royal, Nova Scotia
B0S 1A0
Tel: (902) 532-5727

$$

ABOUT THE B&B

Bread and Roses Country Inn is a rare Nova Scotia example of a brick Queen Anne revival house. Built circa 1882, this smoke-free inn has many fine design details, such as a large entrance hall with sweeping staircase, intricate woodwork, and etched glass windows. The nine guest rooms on three floors are all distinctively decorated with antiques. The owners' eclectic art collection, which includes whimsical Nova Scotia folk art, contemporary Canadian paintings, and Inuit sculpture, is displayed throughout the house. Breakfast includes Monica's brown bread and granola, local preserves, yogurt, juice, and tea or coffee. Guests enjoy gathering in the parlor each evening for tea and sweets and to share stories of their Nova Scotian adventures. Nearby are historic sites, museums, artists' studios, golf courses, walking trails, and excellent restaurants. Port-Royal, Canada's oldest permanent European settlement (1605) is a short drive away. Having traveled extensively throughout the Maritime provinces, Monica and Richard can provide touring tips tailored to your interests.

SEASON

March 1 – October 30

ACCOMMODATIONS

9 rooms with private baths

Pear Coffee Cake

"Pears were always a special treat when I was growing up in Kansas, and this recipe originates with my mother. My sister loved the fruit so much that her childhood nickname was (you guessed it) 'Pear.'"
— Diana Habkirk

3 tablespoons brown sugar
2 cups plus 2 tablespoons all-purpose flour
¼ teaspoon ground nutmeg
6 tablespoons butter
1 teaspoon baking powder
½ teaspoon baking soda
½ teaspoon ground cinnamon
½ teaspoon salt
⅛ teaspoon ground cloves
¾ cup granulated sugar
1 egg
1½ teaspoons orange zest
⅓ cup orange juice
1 cup bran flake cereal
1 pear, peeled, cored, and chopped
⅔ cup chopped walnuts

Preheat the oven to 350°F. In a bowl, combine the brown sugar, the 2 tablespoons flour, and the nutmeg. Cut in 1 tablespoon of the butter. In another bowl, combine the 2 cups flour, baking powder, baking soda, cinnamon, salt, and cloves. In a third (large) bowl, combine the remaining butter and the granulated sugar. Beat until fluffy. Add the egg and orange zest, and beat well. Add the flour mixture to the egg mixture, alternating with the orange juice. Stir in the cereal, pear, and walnuts, and mix well. Spread the batter into a greased 9 x 5 x 2" pan. Sprinkle with the brown sugar mixture. Bake 30 minutes. ***Yield: 12 servings.***

Brio Haus

Diana and Les Habkirk
3005 Brio Entrance
Whistler, British Columbia V0N 1B3
Tel: (800) 331-BRIO (2746)
or (604) 932-3313
E-mail: briohaus@whistler.net
$$ – $$$

ABOUT THE B&B

Brio Haus is an intimate B&B located in Canada's premier ski resort area. Enjoy charming rooms, fitted with cozy goose down duvets, in a European-style alpine home, and awake to a full home-baked breakfast, often featuring one of the pear specialties of the house. After skiing, hiking, canoeing, or horseback riding, you can prepare your own snacks and dinners in the guest kitchen loaded with amenities. After that, warm yourself by the evening fire in the guest lounge and watch a variety of complimentary movies. Or, ease sore muscles after an active day with a soak in the Jacuzzi moon tub and sauna. Brio Haus is centrally located, an easy walk to Whistler Village and ski lifts via the Valley Trail, and right across the street from the golf course. Diana and Les spent many years as a bus tour guide team in the Canadian Rockies before opening their lodge in 1989. Les now runs the local transit system and Diana works full time seeing to the needs of her B&B guests.

SEASON

all year

ACCOMMODATIONS

3 rooms with shared bath

Sanford House Bed & Breakfast

Elizabeth and Charlie Le Ber
PO Box 1825, 20 Platt Street
Brighton, Ontario K0K 1H0
Tel/Fax: (613) 475-3930
$$

ABOUT THE B&B

Sitting majestically on the crest of a hill, Sanford House Bed & Breakfast is a red-brick Victorian home close to Main Street in the friendly town of Brighton. This century-old home with turret and covered veranda has offstreet parking, a separate guest entrance, and three large, bright, and comfortable air conditioned bedrooms. Guests can choose to relax in the round turret room; in the lounge with television, VCR, videos, board games, and books; in the spacious, bright Victorian parlor; or on the veranda. Delicious home-baked breakfasts, often spotlighting apples grown in nearby orchards, are served in the guest dining room. It's a short drive to beautiful Presqu'ile Provincial Park's sandy beaches, nature trails, fine birdwatching areas, and marsh boardwalk. If antique hunting is a passion, there are numerous antique shops right in Brighton and in the surrounding area. Applefest, a celebration of the harvest in September, is a particularly lovely time to visit the area. When not entertaining their B&B guests, Elizabeth and Charlie enjoy cycling and nature walks.

SEASON

all year

ACCOMMODATIONS

3 rooms with shared bath

Pecan–Sour Cream Coffee Cake

Topping:
¾ cup dark brown sugar
1 tablespoon all-purpose flour
1 teaspoon ground cinnamon
¼ cup butter
1 cup chopped pecans

Batter:
1½ cups unbleached or all-purpose flour
1 teaspoon baking powder
½ teaspoon baking soda
2 eggs
¾ cup sour cream
¼ cup maple syrup
1 teaspoon vanilla

Preheat the oven to 375°F. Prepare the topping by mixing together the brown sugar, flour, and cinnamon. Cut in the butter with a fork or pastry blender. Add the pecans, toss to make the mixture crumbly, then set aside. To make the batter, sift together the flour, baking powder, and baking soda. In a separate bowl, beat the eggs until thickened. Add the sour cream, maple syrup, and vanilla to the eggs, and beat well. Gently combine the egg mixture with the flour mixture. Add 1 cup of the topping mixture, and stir gently. Pour the batter into a buttered 8" square baking pan. Sprinkle with the remaining topping mixture. Bake 35 minutes. Serve warm. ***Yield: 9 servings.***

Prairie Treat Pie

"When we have out-of-province visitors, we make sure to serve them Saskatoon berries, 'the pride of the prairies,' in some form. This pie is our all-time favorite." — Charlene Siemens

4 cups Saskatoon berries or blueberries
2 tablespoons water
1 tablespoon lemon juice
1 cup sugar
1 tablespoon cornstarch
Pastry for 1 double-crust pie (9")
1 tablespoon butter
Milk (optional)
Sugar (optional)

Preheat the oven to 425°F. Simmer the berries, water, and lemon juice for 10 minutes, covered. Mix the sugar and cornstarch, and add to the berry mixture. Bring to a boil, then cool slightly. Place the filling in the lower pastry crust, and dot with the butter. Cover with the other crust, seal the edges, and cut vents in the top crust. If desired, brush the pie top lightly with milk and sprinkle with sugar. Bake 15 minutes. Reduce the temperature to 350°F, and bake 30 minutes longer. ***Yield: 6 – 8 servings.***

Longview Bed & Breakfast

Charlene and Bob Siemens
PO Box 53
Fiske, Saskatchewan S0L 1C0
Tel: (306) 377-4786
$

ABOUT THE B&B

Peaceful surroundings, nature walks, farm-fresh meals, and barnyard animals are what you can expect at Longview, a working prairie farm southwest of Saskatoon. While listening to the howl of the coyote, fall asleep in your private guest cottage with its own bath and deck, then wake up to the crow of the rooster. Join hosts Charlene and Bob in their home for a hearty breakfast (and other meals if requested) — all of which take advantage of the produce, eggs, and meat from the farm. For those who want to really get away from it all, Longview offers a rustic cottage surrounded by a grove of trees and a choir of birds. A short drive away, you can find ancient petroglyphs and teepee rings. Your hosts especially welcome families, and enjoy visiting with their guests and sharing their love of the land.

SEASON

May – September

ACCOMMODATIONS

1 private cottage (3 rooms with shared bath);
1 rustic cabin

Sproule Heritage Place B&B

Vera and Winston Sproule
PO Box 43, Site 14, RR #1
Strathmore, Alberta T1P 1J6
Tel: (403) 934-3219
$$

ABOUT THE B&B

While Sproule Heritage Place B&B has been featured by both Hallmark USA and Alberta Government Telephone in their television commercials, this farm actually had less high-profile beginnings. In 1909, the site was little more than a well-trodden buffalo trail when the Scheer family settled on the open prairie east of Calgary. Years later, the stately house and barn became a landmark to travelers on a road that today is the Trans-Canada Highway. Vera and Winston Sproule purchased the farm in 1985 and began extensive renovations to restore its 1920s elegance. As a result, the site has been declared an Alberta Registered Historic Resource. Artisans and designers of furniture and quilts, Vera and Winston (a country pastor for four years in Yukon and 24 years in Alberta) assure you a comfortable bed in one of three charming bedrooms and an interesting breakfast.

SEASON

all year

ACCOMMODATIONS

1 room with private bath;
2 rooms with shared bath

Quick Coffee Cake

"My neighbor Joan Tiede shared this delicious recipe with me and I, in turn, have passed it along to many of our guests." — Vera Sproule

1 cup sour cream
1 teaspoon baking soda
½ cup soft butter
1 cup sugar
2 eggs
1¾ cups all-purpose flour
2 teaspoons baking powder
1 cup brown sugar
1 cup chopped pecans or walnuts

Preheat the oven to 350°F. Mix together the sour cream and baking soda; set aside. Beat the butter and sugar. Add the eggs, flour, and baking powder, and beat just until moistened. Add the sour cream mixture, and gently combine. Pour half the batter into a greased 8 x 8 x 2" pan. Sprinkle with ½ cup of the brown sugar and ½ cup of the nuts. Pour the remaining batter over the nuts, and top with the remaining brown sugar and nuts. Bake 40 – 45 minutes. ***Yield: 10 servings.***

Rhubarb-Nut Streusel Coffee Cake

"Freezes well and is scrumptious — a Taste the Past favorite."
— Rosalie Nimmo

1½ cups sugar
3 tablespoons cornstarch
3 cups diced fresh rhubarb
¾ cup milk
1 tablespoon vinegar
2¼ cups all-purpose flour
¾ cup butter
½ teaspoon baking powder
½ teaspoon baking soda
½ cup finely chopped nuts
1 egg, beaten

Preheat the oven to 350°F. In a medium saucepan, combine ¾ cup of the sugar with the cornstarch. Stir in the rhubarb. Cook and stir over medium heat until the mixture comes to a boil and thickens; set aside to cool. Combine the milk and vinegar, and set aside. Combine the flour and the remaining sugar. Cut in the butter until the mixture is crumbly. Set aside ½ cup of the flour mixture. To the remainder, add the baking powder, baking soda, and nuts. Beat the egg into the milk mixture, and mix it into the flour mixture. Spread two-thirds of the batter over the bottom and halfway up the sides of a greased 9" springform pan. Spoon the rhubarb filling over the batter. Drop the remaining batter by small spoonfuls over the rhubarb. Sprinkle with the reserved flour mixture. Bake 50 minutes or until a toothpick inserted in the center comes out clean and the top springs back when lightly touched. ***Yield: 12 servings.***

Taste the Past Bed & Breakfast

Rosalie and Bryce Nimmo
PO Box 865, 281-2nd Street West
Drumheller, Alberta T0J 0Y0
Tel: (403) 823-5889
$$

ABOUT THE B&B

Return to a simpler era during a stay in one of Drumheller's original grand mansions, built at the turn of the century by Drumheller Valley's coal baron Jesse Gouge. The elegant dining room and sitting area are decorated with Rosalie's artwork and period antiques, which also adorn the four guest rooms. The entire home has been tastefully restored, and the atmosphere is one of old-world charm and elegance. A healthy gourmet breakfast, served in the sunny breakfast room, includes fruit, yogurt, muffins or scones, and a hot entrée. Taste the Past is located in downtown Drumheller, en route to the world-renowned Royal Tyrrell Museum of Palaeontology. Other activities available nearby include hiking through the badlands, visiting many dinosaur-related spots, golfing, camping, and fishing. Rosebud Dinner Theatre and the Canadian Badlands Passion Play are unique cultural attractions. Rosalie and Bryce are knowledgeable hosts and will help you plan your stay.

SEASON

all year

ACCOMMODATIONS

4 rooms with shared baths

Hawkins House Bed & Breakfast

Carla Pitzel and Garry Umbrich
303 Hawkins Street
Whitehorse, Yukon Y1A 1X5
Tel: (867) 668-7638
Fax: (867) 668-7632
$$$$

ABOUT THE B&B

To stay at the Hawkins House Bed & Breakfast is to share a once-in-a-lifetime Yukon experience with your hosts Carla, Garry, and their two sons. Each guest room in this custom-built, luxury Victorian B&B highlights a different Yukon theme and features private bath and balcony, oak floor, bar sink, refrigerator, cable TV, and VCR. Guests can take a Jacuzzi soak in the Fleur de Lys Room, watch videos about Native peoples in the First Nations Room, step back into gold rush days in the Victorian Tea Rose Room, or admire the splendid view of the SS Klondike *paddlewheeler and Canyon Mountain from the balcony of the Fireweed Room. Especially geared to the business traveler, Hawkins House provides the convenience of a private telephone line and answering machine, fax service, and a work table with a light and computer jack. Breakfast is a homemade feast of northern and international delights — from the home-smoked salmon pâté and moose sausage to jams, syrups, and sourdough pastries.*

SEASON

all year

ACCOMMODATIONS

4 rooms with private baths

Rosehip Torte

"This is our signature cake, which I traditionally make with rosehip jelly (but any jelly will do). Be careful slicing this cake — it's light as a feather." — Carla Pitzel

Dough (make 1 day in advance):
⅔ cup butter
⅔ cup sugar
1 egg
1½ cups all-purpose flour
1 cup ground hazelnuts or almonds

Whipped cream filling:
2 cups heavy cream
2 tablespoons sifted confectioners' sugar
1 teaspoon vanilla

Rosehip jelly (see recipe on page 325)
Rolled marzipan
Marzipan figurines
Fresh edible flowers

To make the dough, mix the butter, sugar, egg, flour, and nuts together in a bowl. Turn the dough onto a floured surface, and knead until it forms a nice soft ball. Wrap the dough in a plastic bag, and refrigerate for 1 day.

(continued on next page)

The next day, preheat the oven to 350°F. Cut 5 wax paper rounds to neatly fit the greased bottoms of 5 (10") springform pans. Lightly butter one side of the 5 wax paper rounds, and put them butter side up in each pan. Divide the dough into 5 equal pieces.

Put a mound of dough in each pan, and press it to the edges to make a thin layer of dough. Bake about 15 minutes (they're overdone if edges become too brown). Cool the cakes, and don't forget to peel off the wax paper!

For the filling, whip the cream until stiff. Add the confectioners' sugar and vanilla. Spread the rosehip jelly over the tops of all the layers. To assemble, put 1 layer on a cake plate. Spread a quarter of the whipped cream over the jelly. Repeat with the other 3 layers. On the top layer, cover the jelly with rolled marzipan. Decorate with marzipan figurines and fresh edible flowers. ***Yield: 12 servings.***

Spruceholme Inn

Marlene and Glenn Scullion
204 rue Principale
Fort-Coulonge, Québec J0X 1V0
Tel: (819) 683-5635
Fax: (819) 683-2139
$$$

ABOUT THE B&B

Built in 1875 by lumber baron George Bryson Jr., Spruceholme Inn is a historic Victorian stone mansion located in the Ottawa River Valley town of Fort-Coulonge. The inn is a leisurely drive from the nation's capital, Ottawa, only minutes from golfing, whitewater rafting, and skiing, and across the street from the Ottawa River where you can fish and, in winter, go skating. Operated by Marlene and Glenn Scullion, Spruceholme has been restored to its original glory and now operates as an elegant country inn with a licensed bar and a formal dining room. The six luxury guest suites are furnished with the mansion's original antiques. In years gone by, such distinguished guests as former Canadian prime minister Sir Wilfrid Laurier were entertained at Spruceholme. Marlene and Glenn, both recently retired from the broadcasting industry, work diligently to ensure their guests have a memorable stay. Glenn is an accomplished pianist and plays the inn's 1911 Steinway grand piano for guests each evening.

SEASON

all year

ACCOMMODATIONS

6 suites with private baths

Spanish Cheesecake with Strawberry-Rhubarb Topping

"Absolutely delicious and elegant." — Marlene Scullion

1 pound cream cheese
3 tablespoons butter
1½ cups granulated sugar
2 eggs
¼ cup all-purpose flour
1 teaspoon lemon zest
½ teaspoon ground cinnamon
½ teaspoon salt

Strawberry-rhubarb topping:
2 cups chopped rhubarb
2 cups fresh or thawed and drained frozen strawberries
Fresh lemon juice
Sugar

Confectioners' sugar

(continued on next page)

Preheat the oven to 400°F. Cream together the cream cheese, 1 tablespoon of the butter, and the granulated sugar (don't beat). Stir in the eggs, blending well after each addition. Add the flour, lemon zest, cinnamon, and salt. Mix well. Butter a round cake, flan, or springform pan with the remaining 2 tablespoons butter, and pour in the batter. Bake 12 minutes. Reduce the temperature to 350°F, and bake 25 – 30 minutes more. Cool. For the topping, simmer the rhubarb, strawberries, lemon juice, and sugar together until the rhubarb is tender. To serve, sprinkle the cake with confectioners' sugar, and cover with the topping. ***Tip:*** This sauce can be made ahead and served cold or warm. ***Yield: About 8 servings.***

Lake Crescent Inn

Evelyn and Bruce Warr
PO Box 69
Robert's Arm, Newfoundland
A0J 1R0
Tel: (709) 652-3067
Fax: (709) 652-3056
$

ABOUT THE B&B

When you think of Newfoundland, think peaceful lifestyle, clean air and rivers, and superb hospitality — all of which you'll find at Lake Crescent Inn. Walk along the quiet roads and beautiful beaches, visit fishers in the various communities along the route, or go iceberg or whale watching (in season). Boating trips can also be arranged, so why not give cod jigging or salmon fishing a try? Be sure to bring along your camera to capture the moment you reel in your first fish (you might even see "Cressie," the lake monster!). The inn offers four bedrooms and two bathrooms, one with whirlpool and shower. Breakfasts are a homemade feast of muffins, jams, jellies, and breads, and a special health-conscious menu is also available. A Jiggs dinner is served on Sundays from 5:00 pm, and a Fish Platter dinner is served on Fridays from 5:00 pm (other meals can be provided upon request).

SEASON

all year

ACCOMMODATIONS

4 rooms with shared baths

Sugarless, Butterless, Eggless Cake

2 cups raisins
2 cups water
1 cup dates
1 orange, chopped (including peel)
½ cup sunflower or olive oil
2 teaspoons ground cinnamon
2 teaspoons vanilla
1 teaspoon ground nutmeg
2¼ cups whole wheat flour
½ cup walnuts
2 teaspoons baking soda
1 teaspoon baking powder

Combine the raisins, water, dates, orange, oil, cinnamon, vanilla, and nutmeg, and boil for 10 minutes. Let cool. Preheat the oven to 300°F. In a separate bowl, combine the flour, walnuts, baking soda, and baking powder. Add the flour mixture to the fruit mixture, and stir just enough to moisten the dry ingredients. Place the batter in a greased 10" tube pan. Bake 60 minutes. ***Yield: About 16 servings.***

Swedish Rhubarb Meringue

"I grow rhubarb in my garden and I'm always on the lookout for delicious ways to serve it. This recipe hails from a Swedish B&B I visited, where I helped my hostess (who worked full time) with the cooking. It was a big hit with her guests and is now a big hit with mine." — Patricia Kroker

2 cups plus 4 tablespoons all-purpose flour
2 cups plus 7 tablespoons sugar
⅔ cup margarine
5 cups diced rhubarb
1 cup evaporated milk or heavy cream
4 eggs, separated
¼ teaspoon salt

Preheat the oven to 350°F. Mix together 2 cups of the flour, 2 tablespoons of the sugar, and the margarine, and press into a 13 x 9" pan. Prick the crust with a fork, and bake 10 minutes. Mix together the rhubarb, milk, egg yolks, and salt with 2 cups of the sugar and the remaining flour, and pour over the crust. Bake 45 minutes. To make the meringue, beat the egg whites until foamy with an electric mixer or by hand. While continuing to beat, add the remaining sugar 1 tablespoon at a time. The meringue is ready when stiff peaks form. Spoon the meringue over the rhubarb mixture and bake at 300°F – 350°F for 8 – 10 minutes, or until the meringue is browned. ***Yield: 12 servings.***

Gaeste-Haus Kroker

Patricia Kroker
PO Box 202
Bruderheim, Alberta T0B 0S0
Tel: (403) 796-3621
$$

ABOUT THE B&B

Only a short drive yet worlds away from the hustle and bustle of Edmonton, Gaeste-Haus Kroker is a charming and comfortable 1927 brick Victorian guest house. You can choose to enjoy the peaceful ambiance of the entire upper level or mingle with other guests in the parlor furnished in French Provincial style. Wind down your evening with a snack of homemade dessert. Awaken in the morning to freshly brewed coffee and a hearty breakfast served on fine china in the elegantly furnished dining room. Relax on the veranda or in front of the outdoor fireplace, and stroll about the spacious lawn and garden. A former registered nurse, town councilor, and town mayor, hostess Patricia Kroker enjoys gardening, baking, and traveling, and will make your visit an enjoyable and memorable experience. Area attractions include Elk Island National Park, West Edmonton Mall, Ukrainian Cultural Heritage Village, and Beaverhill Lake.

SEASON

April 1 – December 31

ACCOMMODATIONS

3 rooms with shared bath

White Pound Cake

Wooded Acres Bed & Breakfast

Elva and Skip Kennedy
4907 Rocky Point Road
Victoria, British Columbia V9C 4G2
Tel: (250) 478-8172 or
(250) 474-8959
$$$

ABOUT THE B&B

Elva and Skip's country house truly is a labor of love, made from scratch with logs from their property. The emptiness that settled in once their children had "grown and flown" inspired Elva and Skip to turn their dream home into an old-fashioned B&B. Secluded in three acres of forest, Wooded Acres invites you to relax in your own sheltered hot tub amid relics of bygone times. Enjoy a full breakfast of fresh-daily house specialties (including scones and biscuits) served at your convenience. Bedrooms are decorated with antiques, queen beds, and cozy down-filled duvets, while candlelight and lace add a special touch throughout the B&B. Nearby Victoria, British Columbia's capital, is known for its breathtaking scenery, beaches, and wilderness parks. The area offers a wealth of walking trails, golf courses, fishing and birdwatching areas, and numerous venues for the work of local artisans. Wooded Acres is located conveniently close to all amenities in Victoria (30 minutes away) and the rural splendor of Sooke (20 minutes away).

SEASON

all year

ACCOMMODATIONS

2 suites with private baths

1 cup butter
1½ cups granulated sugar
½ cup milk
½ cup warm water
1 teaspoon lemon juice
1 teaspoon vanilla
3 cups all-purpose flour
2 teaspoons baking powder
½ teaspoon salt
3 eggs

Confectioners' sugar
Orange slices
Lemon slices

Preheat the oven to 325°F. Cream the butter. Add the granulated sugar, and cream the mixture together. Add the milk slowly, and mix. Gradually add the warm water, lemon juice, and vanilla, and mix. Sift together the flour, baking powder, and salt, and add alternately with the eggs (one at a time) to the butter mixture. Beat well after each addition. Place the batter in a greased 9" tube pan, and bake 60 minutes. Let cool. Sprinkle the top with confectioners' sugar, and decorate with orange and lemon slices. ***Yield: 8 – 10 servings.***

Wild Strawberry Tarts with Coconut Topping

"I make the jam for this recipe with wild strawberries that are found growing throughout the countryside during July."
— Myra Roussy

1 cup warm water
1 egg
1 pound lard (2 cups)
4 cups all-purpose flour
3 tablespoons baking powder
½ teaspoon salt
Wild strawberry jam

Coconut topping (optional):
½ cup margarine
½ cup sugar
2 eggs
1 cup flaked unsweetened coconut
1 teaspoon vanilla

Preheat the oven to 375°F. Grease 3 regular-sized, 12-cup muffin pans. Combine the water, egg, and lard with an electric mixer. Combine the flour, baking powder, and salt, and gradually add to the lard mixture. Roll out the dough on a floured surface, and cut out circles large enough to line the muffin cups. Pat the circles of dough into the bottom and sides of the muffin cups. Place 1 teaspoon jam in each tart. For the optional topping, combine the margarine, sugar, and eggs. Add the coconut and vanilla, and mix well. Place 1 tablespoon of the coconut topping over the jam. Bake 10 – 15 minutes until the tart is golden. ***Variation:*** Try raspberry jam instead of strawberry. ***Yield: 36 tarts.***

Tranquil Acres B&B / Gîte à la ferme

Myra Roussy
PO Box 103, 252 route Lévesque
Port-Daniel, Québec G0C 2N0
Tel: (418) 396-3491
$

ABOUT THE B&B

Myra Roussy loves to show guests around her south-shore Gaspé working cattle farm and introduce them to all the animals, including cows, pigs, chickens, sheep, and a friendly band of cats (who love to have their pictures taken!). Located on a quiet secondary road just off the main highway (Route 132), the renovated farmhouse captures the true flavor of country style and offers a beautiful view of Baie des Chaleurs. Home-baked full breakfasts consist of dishes made with ingredients from the farm's fruit and vegetable garden. You can pitch in and help with the farm chores or simply relax in the spacious yard, soaking in the sights and smells of the countryside. The natural beauty of the Gaspé region is world renowned. Famous Percé Rock (one of the coast's main attractions) is a one-hour drive away, while the Paspébiac historic site and a spa specializing in seawater therapy is a 20-minute drive away. Other nearby attractions include the Bonaventure Island Bird Sanctuary, golf courses, and New Richmond historic village.

SEASON

all year

ACCOMMODATIONS

3 rooms with shared bath

Other Baked Goods & Desserts

Apple Pandowdy

"We like to spoil our guests with desserts at breakfast. These desserts are often old-time favorites, like this one from my mom."
— Glenda Carter

Shortcake dough:
2 cups all-purpose flour
4 teaspoons baking powder
½ teaspoon salt
⅓ cup margarine
1 tablespoon sugar
1 scant cup milk

Apple filling:
Sliced apples
1 cup sugar
Ground cinnamon
Ground nutmeg

Chocolate shavings
Yogurt

Preheat the oven to 450°F. Combine the flour, baking powder, and salt. Blend in the margarine with your fingers. Mix in the sugar and milk. Turn the dough out onto a floured surface, and roll the dough ½" thick to fit the baking dish.

(continued on next page)

Wyndswept Bed & Breakfast

Glenda and Bob Carter
Box 2683
Hinton, Alberta T7V 1Y2
Tel: (780) 866-3950
Fax: (780) 866-3951
E-mail: wyndswep@agt.net
$$ – $$$

ABOUT THE B&B

The Jasper area's first four-star B&B, Wyndswept Bed & Breakfast is built on the side of a hill in the Folding Mountain Range. From this vantage point, guests marvel at the 180-degree panoramic view of the Rocky Mountains, a nearby valley, and the spectacular sunrises and sunsets. Some 38 different wildflowers thrive on the hill. Wildlife such as bears, deer, elk, and bighorn sheep can be seen right outside the window while guests enjoy a five-course heart-healthy breakfast. The decor of each guest suite has a different theme, and all suites have private baths and luxurious bedding. At night, you can rest on hand-hewn benches by the cozy fire pit and watch the stars or listen to the howl of wolves and coyotes. Wyndswept is located in a quiet mountain village at the eastern edge of Jasper National Park. Your hosts are long-time residents who know the area well and can suggest points of interest. Glenda is retired after working for 30 years as a mental health therapist, while Bob is a quality control auditor and the resident star gazer.

SEASON

all year

ACCOMMODATIONS

2 suites with private baths

Place the sliced apples in the bottom of a greased 13 x 9" baking dish. Sprinkle the sugar and a little cinnamon and nutmeg on top of the fruit. Cover the fruit with the rolled shortcake dough. Moisten your fingers with water, and press the edges of the dough to the rim of the baking dish. Bake 10 minutes, reduce the temperature to 375°F, and bake another 15 – 20 minutes until the fruit is soft. Sprinkle some chocolate shavings over the top of the pandowdy, and serve immediately with yogurt. ***Tips:*** Any fruit can be used in the pandowdy, such as sliced peaches, cherries, or even canned fruit filling. You may need to add more sugar depending on how tart the fruit is. ***Yield: 8 servings.***

Apple Squares

"Because the Annapolis Valley is the apple growing region of Nova Scotia, desserts served at evening tea often feature one of the 10 local varieties. My own preference is for Idared and Gravenstein apples."
— Monica Cobb

1½ cups sugar
3 eggs
1 cup canola oil
1 teaspoon vanilla
2 cups all-purpose flour
1 teaspoon baking powder
1 tablespoon ground cinnamon
2 cups peeled, cored, and chopped apple

Preheat the oven to 350°F. Beat together the sugar and eggs. Add the oil and vanilla. In a separate bowl, mix the flour, baking powder, and cinnamon. Add the flour mixture to the egg mixture. Fold in the apple. Grease a 13 x 9" pan, and pour in the batter. Bake 40 minutes. Invert when cooled, and cut into squares. Store them in an airtight container. They will keep moist for about 5 days. ***Yield: About 18 (3 x 2") squares.***

Bread and Roses Country Inn

Monica and Richard Cobb
PO Box 177, 82 Victoria Street
Annapolis Royal, Nova Scotia
B0S 1A0
Tel: (902) 532-5727
$$

ABOUT THE B&B

Bread and Roses Country Inn is a rare Nova Scotia example of a brick Queen Anne revival house. Built circa 1882, this smoke-free inn has many fine design details, such as a large entrance hall with sweeping staircase, intricate woodwork, and etched glass windows. The nine guest rooms on three floors are all distinctively decorated with antiques. The owners' eclectic art collection, which includes whimsical Nova Scotia folk art, contemporary Canadian paintings, and Inuit sculpture, is displayed throughout the house. Breakfast includes Monica's brown bread and granola, local preserves, yogurt, juice, and tea or coffee. Guests enjoy gathering in the parlor each evening for tea and sweets and to share stories of their Nova Scotian adventures. Nearby are historic sites, museums, artists' studios, golf courses, walking trails, and excellent restaurants. Port-Royal, Canada's oldest permanent European settlement (1605) is a short drive away. Having traveled extensively throughout the Maritime provinces, Monica and Richard can provide touring tips tailored to your interests.

SEASON

March 1 – October 30

ACCOMMODATIONS

9 rooms with private baths

Humber Gallery Hospitality Home

Edna and Eldon Swyer
26 Roberts Drive
Little Rapids, Newfoundland
A2H 6C3
Mailing address: PO Box 15
Corner Brook, Newfoundland
A2H 6C3
Tel: (709) 634-2660
E-mail: eldonswyer@thezone.net
$$

ABOUT THE B&B

A popular stop for the British royal family, Little Rapids (near Corner Brook) is home to Humber Gallery, an impressive cedar abode with cathedral ceilings, fireplace, wraparound sun deck, two guest rooms with double beds, one guest room with twin beds, and one guest room with a queen bed. A nutritious breakfast is served, and other meals and use of the barbecue and picnic area can be arranged. An excellent spot for an overnight stay when going or coming from Gros Morne National Park, this B&B is in the heart of the Humber Valley Reserve near Marble Mountain Ski Resort, mini-golf facilities, "U-pick" strawberry farms, Bay of Islands tourist attractions, South Brook and Pasadena beaches on Deer Lake, and the Humber River. Edna and Eldon can provide maps, tourist literature, a licensed salmon fishing guide, and insider tips on area attractions.

SEASON

June – September;
February – March

ACCOMMODATIONS

1 room with private bath;
3 rooms with shared baths

Apricot-Fig Pudding

"A Christmas favorite in our home." — Edna Swyer

Granulated sugar
2 cups bread crumbs
2 cups raisins
2 eggs
1¼ cups all-purpose flour
1 cup brown sugar
1 cup chopped dried apricots
1 cup chopped walnuts
1 cup dried figs or dates
1 cup milk
1 cup suet (or vegetable oil or margarine)
¼ cup prune juice
1¼ teaspoons baking soda
1 teaspoon ground cinnamon
1 teaspoon ground cloves
1 teaspoon ground mace
1 teaspoon salt
1 teaspoon vanilla

Grease a large pudding mold. Sprinkle the sides with granulated sugar. Mix together the bread crumbs, raisins, eggs, flour, brown sugar, apricots, walnuts, figs, milk, suet, prune juice, baking soda, cinnamon, cloves, mace, salt, and vanilla, and place in the mold. Place the mold on a trivet in a heavy kettle over 1" boiling water on high heat. Partially cover the kettle so as to let some steam escape. As steam begins to escape, reduce the heat to low, and continue cooking for 1½ – 2 hours (replenish with boiling water as needed). Serve hot. ***Yield: 6 – 8 servings.***

Aussie Damper

"With its simple, basic ingredients, the damper is easily prepared over an open campfire and often used by drovers during cattle drives in the outback. It's served for breakfast with golden maple syrup or, as Australians call it, 'Cocky's Joy,' since 'Cocky' is slang for someone from the bush." — Carol Waters

2 cups self-rising flour*
1 cup whole wheat self-rising flour
2 teaspoons sugar
¼ teaspoon salt or to taste
½ cup milk
¾ cup (approximately) water
Milk or water and all-purpose flour for topping

**Note: Often used for quick breads and cakes, this is flour to which salt and baking powder have been added.*

Preheat the oven to 450°F – 475°F. Sift the self-rising flour, whole wheat flour, sugar, and salt into a bowl. Make a well in the center, and pour in the milk and most of the water, all at once. Mix with a knife to a moist, sticky dough. Add more water if necessary. Turn the dough onto a lightly floured surface, knead, divide into 8 round shapes, and place on greased baking sheets. Pat each shape out to a 6" circle. With a sharp knife, cut 2 slits about ½" across the dough like a cross (don't cut right to the edge). Brush the tops with milk or water, and sift a little extra flour over the tops. Bake 10 minutes, reduce the oven to 350°F – 375°F, and bake 20 – 30 minutes until golden brown. ***Yield: 8 servings.***

Australis Guest House

Carol and Brian Waters
35 Marlborough Avenue
Ottawa, Ontario K1N 8E6
Tel/Fax: (613) 235-8461
E-mail: waters@intranet.ca
www.bbcanada.com/1463.html
$$

ABOUT THE B&B

The first established and longest operating B&B in the Ottawa area, Australis is a multiple winner of the Ottawa Hospitality Award and has been recommended by Newsweek. *Located downtown on a quiet, tree-lined street, one block from the Rideau River (with its ducks and swans) and Strathcona Park, Australis is but a 20-minute walk from the Canadian Parliament Buildings. This stately, 60-year-old house has leaded windows, fireplaces, oak floors, and eight-foot high stained glass windows overlooking the hall. Three spacious guest rooms, including one room with private bath and one suite, display many of the hosts' collectibles gathered while living in different parts of the world. Hearty and delicious breakfasts, featuring award-winning home-baked breads and pastries, ensure you'll start the day just right. Off-street parking and free pick-up and delivery to and from the bus and train stations are available. Your hosts' Australian and English heritages combined with their time in Canada create a truly international and relaxed B&B experience.*

SEASON

all year

ACCOMMODATIONS

1 room with private bath;
2 rooms (including 1 suite) with shared bath

Le Gîte Park Avenue B&B

Anne-Marie and Irving Bansfield
54 Park Avenue
Ottawa, Ontario K2P 1B2
Tel: (613) 230-9131
$$

ABOUT THE B&B

A bright, airy ambiance and artistic decor await you at Park Avenue B&B, an elegant, brick 1906 home located in a charming residential area of downtown Ottawa, Canada's capital. In addition to high-quality beds done up in classic cotton and linen sheets and duvets, each guest room is furnished with a desk and swivel chair, a rocking chair, bookshelves, excellent lighting, and attractive works of art. Ideal for families, the third-floor suite has two bedrooms and a private bath. The mood throughout the house is one of relaxation and warmth. Park Avenue B&B is close to the Parliament Buildings, art galleries, and museums, and is only three minutes (by foot) from the Rideau Canal, which freezes into the world's longest skating rink. Ottawa has a number of exciting festivals and activities, including Winterlude, a winter carnival held each February. Anne-Marie and Irving make it a point to know what's going on when in Ottawa so they can advise their guests on what to see and do.

SEASON

all year

ACCOMMODATIONS

1 suite with private bath;
2 rooms with shared bath

"Bake" Biscuits

"Adding the coconut gives these delicious biscuits a wonderfully tropical taste." — Irving Bansfield

3 cups all-purpose flour
1½ tablespoons baking powder
1 teaspoon sugar
½ teaspoon salt
3 tablespoons shortening (or margarine or butter)
¾ cup lukewarm water
2 tablespoons pure creamed coconut (optional)

Salt cod (see recipe on page 281)

Preheat the oven to 375°F. Sift the flour, baking powder, sugar, and salt together. Cut in the shortening until the mixture resembles coarse meal. Add the water and optional creamed coconut, and toss the ingredients lightly with your fingertips. Turn the dough out onto a floured surface, and knead 1 – 2 minutes. Form the dough into a ball, then roll it into a round shape about 10" across and ¾" thick, either by hand or with a rolling pin (handle the dough briefly and lightly). Place the dough on a greased cookie sheet. Bake 35 – 40 minutes. Let it stand 10 minutes before cutting into wedges. Serve warm or at room temperature with salt cod (brule jol). ***Yield: 6 servings.***

Baked Lemon Pudding

1 cup sugar
¼ cup all-purpose flour
Salt
Zest of 1 lemon
2 egg yolks, beaten
1 cup milk
¼ cup lemon juice
2 egg whites, stiffly beaten

Preheat the oven to 350°F. Combine the sugar, flour, a pinch of salt, and the lemon zest. Stir in the egg yolks, milk, and lemon juice, and mix thoroughly. Fold in the beaten egg whites. Pour into an ungreased baking dish. Set the dish in a pan of hot water 1" deep. Bake 40 – 50 minutes until delicately browned. ***Yield: 6 servings.***

Le Gîte Park Avenue B&B

Anne-Marie and Irving Bansfield
54 Park Avenue
Ottawa, Ontario K2P 1B2
Tel: (613) 230-9131
$$

ABOUT THE B&B

A bright, airy ambiance and artistic decor await you at Park Avenue B&B, an elegant, brick 1906 home located in a charming residential area of downtown Ottawa, Canada's capital. In addition to high-quality beds done up in classic cotton and linen sheets and duvets, each guest room is furnished with a desk and swivel chair, a rocking chair, bookshelves, excellent lighting, and attractive works of art. Ideal for families, the third-floor suite has two bedrooms and a private bath. The mood throughout the house is one of relaxation and warmth. Park Avenue B&B is close to the Parliament Buildings, art galleries, and museums, and is only three minutes (by foot) from the Rideau Canal, which freezes into the world's longest skating rink. Ottawa has a number of exciting festivals and activities, including Winterlude, a winter carnival held each February. Anne-Marie and Irving make it a point to know what's going on when in Ottawa so they can advise their guests on what to see and do.

SEASON

all year

ACCOMMODATIONS

1 suite with private bath;
2 rooms with shared bath

Rowat's Waterside Bed and Breakfast

Marg and Jack Rowat
1397 Borland Road
Williams Lake, British Columbia
V2G 1M3
Tel: (604) 392-7395
$$

ABOUT THE B&B

Enjoy the tranquility of Rowat's Waterside B&B, located on Williams Lake right beside Scout Island Nature Center and Wildlife Reserve, in the heart of Cariboo Country. Walk the nature trails and return home to put your feet up and enjoy the view of the lake and marsh from the deck (this is a birdwatcher's paradise!). Rowat's Waterside is also within walking distance of places for mini-golf and parasailing, restaurants, and a stampede grounds, and a short drive away from downtown, golf and tennis facilities, and a sports arena. For something completely different, a one-and-a-half-hour drive will take you to the Ghost Town Museum of Barkerville, an old gold rush town. Rowat's accommodations include tastefully decorated rooms with private baths, a fireside guest lounge with TV, and air conditioning, purified water, and ample parking. Famous Cariboo Cowboy breakfasts are served in the dining room or deckside overlooking the marsh bird sanctuary. Hosts Marg and Jack are long-time residents of the Cariboo, and enjoy craft making, gardening, meeting people, and the great outdoors.

SEASON

all year

ACCOMMODATIONS

4 rooms with private baths

Cheesy Beaten Biscuits

4 cups all-purpose flour
4 teaspoons baking powder
1 teaspoon salt
½ cup butter
2 eggs, beaten
1½ – 2 cups milk
½ cup grated cheddar cheese

Preheat the oven to 450°F. Sift together the flour, baking powder, and salt. Add the butter, eggs, milk, and cheese, and mix briefly. Drop the batter by tablespoonfuls onto an ungreased cookie sheet. Bake until golden (about 12 minutes). ***Yield: 30 biscuits.***

Chocolate-Almond Squares

Whole graham crackers
1 cup flaked almonds
1 cup butter
1 cup brown sugar
1½ cups chocolate chips

Preheat the oven to 350°F. Line a greased 15 x 10" cookie sheet with the graham crackers. Sprinkle the almonds over the top. In a saucepan, bring the butter and brown sugar to a rolling boil, and continue to boil 3 minutes. Pour the butter mixture over the almonds, and bake 8 minutes. Remove from the oven, and sprinkle the chocolate chips over the top. Return to the oven just long enough to melt the chocolate, and then smooth it out with a spatula. Cool, and cut into squares. ***Yield: About 96 (1½ x 1") squares.***

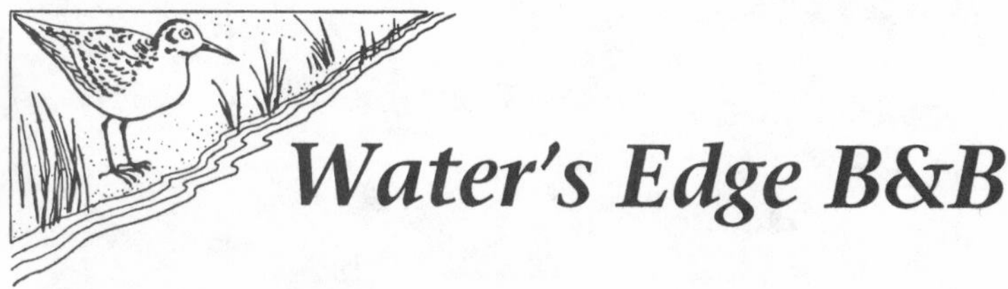

Water's Edge B&B

Mary Ellen and Ed Ironside
Box 635, 331 Park Street
Tofino, British Columbia
V0R 2Z0
Tel: (250) 725-1218
Fax (250) 725- 1219
$$ – $$$

ABOUT THE B&B

Water's Edge B&B, a contemporary cedar house, is set amid towering rainforest that frames views of small islands in Clayoquot Sound and the open Pacific Ocean. Stairs lead from the cliff-top location to rocky tidal pools directly below. Two beautiful beaches are reached by a short scramble along the rocks or by a five-minute stroll along a boardwalk to Tonquin Park. The home's builder was a boat carpenter, fisher, beachcomber, and sawmill operator, and his love of nature is evident in the design. The large windows and high wood ceilings frame the magnificent views. Tofino is a scenic fishing village, minutes from Pacific Rim National Park and Long Beach with its 13 miles of sandy beach. In the area you can walk the beach or hike in the rainforest, go fishing, diving, kayaking, or cycling, and play tennis or golf. Whale watching is a favorite pastime. Hosts Mary Ellen and Ed, who have lived in different parts of Canada and abroad, love traveling, reading, photography, gardening, and meeting people.

SEASON

all year

ACCOMMODATIONS

1 room with private bath;
2 rooms with shared bath

Chocolate Chip–Apple Cookies

Bread and Roses Country Inn

Monica and Richard Cobb
PO Box 177, 82 Victoria Street
Annapolis Royal, Nova Scotia
B0S 1A0
Tel: (902) 532-5727
$$

ABOUT THE B&B

Bread and Roses Country Inn is a rare Nova Scotia example of a brick Queen Anne revival house. Built circa 1882, this smoke-free inn has many fine design details, such as a large entrance hall with sweeping staircase, intricate woodwork, and etched glass windows. The nine guest rooms on three floors are all distinctively decorated with antiques. The owners' eclectic art collection, which includes whimsical Nova Scotia folk art, contemporary Canadian paintings, and Inuit sculpture, is displayed throughout the house. Breakfast includes Monica's brown bread and granola, local preserves, yogurt, juice, and tea or coffee. Guests enjoy gathering in the parlor each evening for tea and sweets and to share stories of their Nova Scotian adventures. Nearby are historic sites, museums, artists' studios, golf courses, walking trails, and excellent restaurants. Port-Royal, Canada's oldest permanent European settlement (1605) is a short drive away. Having traveled extensively throughout the Maritime provinces, Monica and Richard can provide touring tips tailored to your interests.

SEASON

March 1 – October 30

ACCOMMODATIONS

9 rooms with private baths

"Because the Annapolis Valley is the apple growing region of Nova Scotia, desserts served at evening tea often feature one of the 10 local varieties. My own preference is for Idared and Gravenstein apples."
— Monica Cobb

½ cup margarine
1 cup sugar
1 egg
1½ cups all-purpose flour
1 teaspoon ground ginger
½ teaspoon baking soda
1 cup peeled, cored, and grated apple
1 cup semisweet chocolate chips
½ cup quick-cooking rolled oats

Preheat the oven to 350°F. In a large bowl, cream together the margarine and sugar. Beat in the egg. In a separate bowl, mix together the flour, ginger, and baking soda. Stir the flour mixture into the butter mixture. Stir in the apple, chocolate chips, and oats. Drop the mixture by rounded teaspoonfuls onto a well-greased cookie sheet. Bake about 15 minutes. Store in an airtight container. ***Yield: 30 cookies.***

Chocolate Pudding

"Before retiring for the evening, I like to offer my guests this pudding as a nightcap along with tea or coffee." — Myra Roussy

2 cups mini marshmallows
½ cup whole milk
1¼ cups chocolate chips
1 cup whipped cream

Heat the marshmallows and milk over medium heat, and add the chocolate chips just before the marshmallows have melted. Cool, then add the whipped cream. Freeze in dessert cups. Allow the pudding to thaw 5 minutes before serving it. ***Tip:*** Do not use skim milk. ***Yield: 6 servings.***

Tranquil Acres B&B / Gîte à la ferme

Myra Roussy
PO Box 103, 252 route Lévesque
Port-Daniel, Québec G0C 2N0
Tel: (418) 396-3491
$

ABOUT THE B&B

Myra Roussy loves to show guests around her south-shore Gaspé working cattle farm and introduce them to all the animals, including cows, pigs, chickens, sheep, and a friendly band of cats (who love to have their pictures taken!). Located on a quiet secondary road just off the main highway (Route 132), the renovated farmhouse captures the true flavor of country style and offers a beautiful view of Baie des Chaleurs. Home-baked full breakfasts consist of dishes made with ingredients from the farm's fruit and vegetable garden. You can pitch in and help with the farm chores or simply relax in the spacious yard, soaking in the sights and smells of the countryside. The natural beauty of the Gaspé region is world renowned. Famous Percé Rock (one of the coast's main attractions) is a one-hour drive away, while the Paspébiac historic site and a spa specializing in seawater therapy is a 20-minute drive away. Other nearby attractions include the Bonaventure Island Bird Sanctuary, golf courses, and New Richmond historic village.

SEASON

all year

ACCOMMODATIONS

3 rooms with shared bath

Les Trois Érables

Madeleine and Jacques Mercier
PO Box 852, RR #2
Wakefield, Québec J0X 3G0
Tel: (819) 459-1118
$$

ABOUT THE B&B

Nestled among gentle rolling hills on the banks of the Gatineau River, the historic village of Wakefield is a gateway to beautiful Gatineau Park where you can find ample opportunities for hiking, skiing, or less arduous nature walks — especially beautiful in fall foliage season. Less than a half hour's drive takes you to the heart of Canada's national capital, Ottawa. Les Trois Érables was built at the turn of the century and was the home and office of three generations of village doctors until its transformation to a B&B in 1988. Rooms are tastefully decorated in soft colors and furnished for comfort and convenience. The sumptuous breakfasts attest to the fact that Madeleine loves to cook. Local restaurants, sports outfitters, and boutiques abound.

SEASON

all year

ACCOMMODATIONS

4 rooms with private baths

Cinnamon-Baked Pears

"Served as a first course on a cold and snowy morning, this fruit dish hits the spot every time with our guests." — Madeleine Mercier

6 medium pears
¾ cup fresh or thawed and drained frozen blueberries
¾ cup water
3 tablespoons packed brown sugar
1½ tablespoons lemon juice
½ teaspoon ground cinnamon

Preheat the oven to 350°F. Peel the pears, and cut them in half lengthwise; scoop out the core. Place the pears cut side down in a shallow baking dish, and sprinkle the blueberries around them. Combine the water, brown sugar, lemon juice, and cinnamon, and pour it over the pears. Bake, covered, about 45 minutes or until the pears are tender. Baste the pears occasionally with the pan juices. Serve 2 or 3 halves on a plate, and pour some juice and blueberries on top. ***Yield: 4 – 6 servings.***

Cinnamon Swirls

3 cups all-purpose flour
⅓ cup granulated sugar
5 teaspoons baking powder
½ teaspoon salt
¾ cup margarine
1 cup milk
1 egg, lightly beaten

Filling:
1 egg
4 tablespoons brown sugar
1½ teaspoons ground cinnamon
3 tablespoons Bran Buds cereal

Preheat the oven to 350°F. Combine the flour, granulated sugar, baking powder, and salt. Cut in the margarine until the mixture resembles crumbs. Mix the milk with the egg. Stir the milk mixture into the flour mixture, working it as little as possible. Place the dough on a floured surface, and knead about 12 times. Roll the dough out to an 18 x 9" rectangle. For the filling, beat the egg, and brush it over the dough. Sprinkle on the brown sugar, cinnamon, and Bran Buds. Roll the dough up like a jelly roll, and cut into 18 slices. Put each slice into a paper-lined muffin cup, or put the slices on a greased baking sheet. Bake 25 – 30 minutes. ***Yield: 18 servings.***

Rowat's Waterside Bed and Breakfast

Marg and Jack Rowat
1397 Borland Road
Williams Lake, British Columbia
V2G 1M3
Tel: (604) 392-7395
$$

ABOUT THE B&B

Enjoy the tranquility of Rowat's Waterside B&B, located on Williams Lake right beside Scout Island Nature Center and Wildlife Reserve, in the heart of Cariboo Country. Walk the nature trails and return home to put your feet up and enjoy the view of the lake and marsh from the deck (this is a birdwatcher's paradise!). Rowat's Waterside is also within walking distance of places for mini-golf and parasailing, restaurants, and a stampede grounds, and a short drive away from downtown, golf and tennis facilities, and a sports arena. For something completely different, a one-and-a-half-hour drive will take you to the Ghost Town Museum of Barkerville, an old gold rush town. Rowat's accommodations include tastefully decorated rooms with private baths, a fireside guest lounge with TV, and air conditioning, purified water, and ample parking. Famous Cariboo Cowboy breakfasts are served in the dining room or deckside overlooking the marsh bird sanctuary. Hosts Marg and Jack are long-time residents of the Cariboo, and enjoy craft making, gardening, meeting people, and the great outdoors.

SEASON

all year

ACCOMMODATIONS

4 rooms with private baths

Gwenmar Guest Home

Joy and Keith Smith
PO Box 59, RR #3
Brandon, Manitoba R7A 5Y3
Tel: (204) 728-7339
Fax: (204) 728-7336
E-mail: smithj@docker.com
$

ABOUT THE B&B

Space, privacy, and quiet is what you'll find at Gwenmar. This 1914 heritage home was the summer retreat of Manitoba's former Lieutenant Governor (from 1929 to 1934), J.D. McGregor, who named the estate after his daughter Gwen. Since 1980, Joy and Keith Smith have welcomed B&B guests to this relaxing countryside escape. Gwenmar breakfasts are memorable, particularly the home-baked bread and jams and jellies made from Gwenmar's wild berries. Joy, a home economist, is an avid gardener and a major contributor to Canada's heritage seed program, while Keith is a retired agrologist involved in overseas projects. In the summer, you can visit with them on the big, shaded veranda or go for walks on the beautiful grounds or in the valley. In the winter, sit by the fire or go cross-country skiing. Gwenmar is also a short drive from downtown Brandon, with shopping, restaurants, a water-slide, an air museum, golf courses, and the childhood home of Stone Angel *author Margaret Laurence.*

SEASON

all year

ACCOMMODATIONS

2 rooms with private baths;
2 rooms with shared bath

Cornmeal-Apple Wedges

"We like to accompany these wedges with our special yogurt, made with ½ cup toasted walnuts, 5 tablespoons maple syrup, and 2 cups plain yogurt." — Keith Smith

1½ cups all-purpose flour
⅔ cup cornmeal
⅓ cup brown sugar
1 tablespoon baking powder
1 teaspoon baking soda
¼ teaspoon salt
2 large apples, peeled, cored, and cut into chunks
½ cup currants or raisins
1¼ teaspoons ground cinnamon
Ground nutmeg
½ cup plain yogurt
¼ cup milk
2 whole eggs plus 1 egg white
2 tablespoons vegetable oil

Butter, jelly, or jam

Preheat the oven to 375°F. Mix together the flour, cornmeal, brown sugar, baking powder, baking soda, and salt. Toss together the apples, currants, cinnamon, and a pinch of nutmeg, and add to the flour mixture. In a separate bowl, mix the yogurt and milk together, and whisk in the eggs and oil. Pour the yogurt mixture into the flour mixture, and stir just until the dry ingredients are moistened. Pat the dough into a greased 9" round pan, leaving the top lumpy. Bake about 40 – 45 minutes. Cut into wedges, and serve warm with butter or jelly. These wedges can also be split, toasted, and served with jam. ***Yield: 6 – 8 servings.***

Danish Pastry Apple Bars

2½ cups all-purpose flour
1 teaspoon salt
1 cup shortening
1 egg, separated
Milk
1 cup cornflakes
8 – 10 tart apples such as Granny Smith, peeled, cored, and sliced (about 8 cups)
¾ – 1 cup granulated sugar
1 teaspoon ground cinnamon

Topping:
1 cup sifted confectioners' sugar
3 – 4 teaspoons milk

Preheat the oven to 375°F. Combine the flour and salt; cut in the shortening until the mixture resembles coarse meal. Beat the egg yolk in a measuring cup, adding enough milk to make ⅔ cup liquid. Mix well, and stir into the flour mixture. On a floured surface, roll half the dough out to a 17 x 12" rectangle. Fit the dough into the bottom and up the sides of a greased 15 x 10½ x 1" baking pan. Sprinkle with the cornflakes, and top with the apples. Combine the granulated sugar and cinnamon, and sprinkle over the top of the apples. Roll out the remaining dough, and place over the apples. Seal the edges, and cut slits in the top. Beat the egg white until frothy, and brush on the crust. Bake 50 minutes. Let cool 10 minutes. Cut into bars. Combine the confectioners' sugar and milk, and drizzle on the bars while they are still warm. ***Yield: 36 bars.***

Orchard Lane Bed & Breakfast

Yvonne Parker
13324 Middle Bench Road
Oyama, British Columbia V4V 2B4
Tel: (250) 548-3809
$$

ABOUT THE B&B

Smack dab between Kelowna and Vernon is Orchard Lane, a newly built Victorian B&B nestled in a private orchard. From the sprawling veranda is a panoramic view of the beautiful central Okanagan Valley, while nearby Kalamalka and Wood Lakes reflect the hills and distant mountains. Inside, a welcoming foyer and spiral staircase lead to romantic and comfortable bedrooms. Visitors lounge in the formal living room with fireplace, stroll through the flower gardens or nearby orchard, admire the terraced landscaping framed by giant trees, or take a refreshing dip in the outdoor hot tub. Your hostess, Yvonne, serves a full gourmet breakfast — made from produce grown in her garden — in the formal dining room or on the veranda. You'll quickly discover that one of her favorite hobbies is making crafts, which are displayed throughout the house. Alpine skiing, fishing, biking, hiking, and other recreational choices await you and there are golf courses and beaches aplenty to explore. This area is truly a corner of paradise.

SEASON

all year

ACCOMMODATIONS

2 rooms with shared bath;
1 room with private bath

Fairfield Farm Inn

Shae and Richard Griffith
10 Main Street West, Route 1
Middleton, Nova Scotia B0S 1P0
Tel/Fax: (800) 237-9896
or (902) 825-6989
$$

ABOUT THE B&B

Fairfield Farm Inn is situated on a 110-acre fruit and vegetable farm famous for its luscious melons. Built in 1886, this Annapolis Valley farmhouse has been completely restored and furnished in period antiques to enhance its original charm. The five guest rooms have cozy comforters, king- and queen-sized beds, and private baths. The Annapolis River and Slocum Brook are on the property, as are birdwatching and walking trails, pheasants, and other abundant wildlife. Shae and Richard take pride in offering Maritime hospitality and wholesome country breakfasts featuring fresh fruit picked from their farm and homemade jams and jellies. Shae is a member of the Acadia University Business School Advisory Board; Richard is a retired military officer. Their hobbies include gardening, antique hunting, reading, and traveling. A few minutes from picturesque fishing villages and the world's highest tides on the Bay of Fundy, Middleton boasts museums, restaurants, boutiques, and theater — all a short walking distance from the inn.

SEASON

all year
(winter by reservation only)

ACCOMMODATIONS

5 rooms with private baths

Fresh Fruit Cup

2 cups sugar
4 cups water
1 honeydew
1 cantaloupe
1 pineapple
2 oranges
1 grapefruit
Grapes
Kiwi

Heat the sugar and water in a pot until boiling and the sugar is dissolved. Cool. Prepare the fruit, and chop it into bite-sized pieces. Layer it in a gallon jar, and cover with the cooled sugar mixture. Refrigerate. ***Tip:*** You can vary the fruit combination depending on what's in season. Strawberries lose their color and ferment faster, and should be used only if you're going to serve all the fruit cup fairly quickly. ***Yield: 15 – 20 servings.***

Fruit Duff

"This recipe can be made with any fruit. I start the season with rhubarb and move through strawberries, raspberries, blueberries, and apples — all available at the local 'U-pick' or from our own garden."
— Carol Buckley

2 tablespoons butter
1 cup all-purpose flour
½ cup sugar
1 tablespoon baking powder
½ teaspoon salt
⅔ cup milk
2 cups sliced fruit or berries

Preheat the oven to 350°F. Melt the butter in a 7 or 8" ovenproof frying pan. Mix together the flour, sugar, baking powder, and salt. Mix in the milk. Spoon the batter over the melted butter. Top with the fruit. Bake 30 minutes. Cut into wedges, and serve warm. ***Tip:*** If using apple, sprinkle a little ground cinnamon and sugar on top before baking. ***Yield: 8 servings.***

The Old Rectory Bed & Breakfast

Carol and Ron Buckley
1519 Highway 358, RR #1
Port Williams, Nova Scotia B0P 1T0
Tel: (902) 542-1815
Fax: (902) 542-2346
E-mail: orectory@fox.nstn.ca
www.bbcanada.com/568.html
$$

ABOUT THE B&B

Share the warmth of this restored Victorian former rectory with its antiques, unique architecture, and three-acre operating apple orchard and gardens. Choose from one of three spacious bedrooms — one with private half-bath, and the others with shared full bath. Access to an additional bath is on the main floor. Your hosts are Ron, a retired geologist with knowledge of local "rock hounding" areas, and physiotherapist Carol, who enjoys preparing delicious hot breakfasts with homemade breads and preserves. Go on a three-hour mineral/fossil tour with Ron (for an additional fee), or visit with other guests over evening tea. The Old Rectory is close to historic Prescott House, Grand Pré Park, hiking trails, birdwatching areas, cultural activities (including the Atlantic Theatre Festival), and many fine restaurants.

SEASON

May 1 – October 31

ACCOMMODATIONS

1 room with private half-bath;
2 rooms with shared bath

Haus Treuburg

Elvi and Georg Kargoll
PO Box 92
Port Hood (Cape Breton Island),
Nova Scotia B0E 2W0
Tel: (902) 787-2116
Fax: (902) 787-3216
$$ – $$$

ABOUT THE B&B

Port Hood is a pretty little fishing port on Cape Breton Island, famous for lovely sandy beaches and the warmest waters in eastern Canada. It's no wonder, then, that Elvi and Georg Kargoll fell in love with this idyllic setting and decided to open a country inn. Decidedly European and with a distinctly German flair, Haus Treuburg offers two bright and attractively decorated rooms and one suite on the inn's second floor, each with private bath, telephone, and cable TV. There are also three cottages overlooking the ocean, each of which have a large sitting room, a kitchen (with microwave), a separate bedroom, a large full bath, telephone and cable TV, and a deck with a gas barbecue. Haus Treuburg's highly rated restaurant (with Georg as chef) serves a romantic candlelight four-course dinner to the soothing sound of classical music, while a German Sunday Morning Breakfast is served in the cozy bar. Bicycles are available for exploring the charming surroundings. Guided fishing tours are also offered.

SEASON

April 15 – December 31

ACCOMMODATIONS

3 rooms (including 1 suite) with private baths;
3 cottages with private baths

Georg's Famous Apple Strudel

"This is an old German recipe that has become a specialty of the inn's restaurant. People come from near and far for it." — Georg Kargoll

(Note: Elvi and Georg requested that this old family recipe not be converted from the original metric version. If necessary, please consult the metric conversion chart on page 339.)

Dough:
250 grams all-purpose flour
3 tablespoons vegetable oil
Salt
Water as needed (about 3 tablespoons)

Filling:
2 kilograms apples (McIntosh or Red Delicious recommended)
125 grams granulated sugar
80 grams bread crumbs
65 grams chopped almonds
65 grams raisins
1 teaspoon ground cinnamon
½ teaspoon vanilla
Heavy cream
2 tablespoons melted butter

(continued on next page)

Confectioners' sugar
Vanilla ice cream
Whipped cream

Combine the flour, oil, and a little salt, and knead with enough water to form a nonsticking dough. Set aside. Peel, core, and slice the apples, and mix them with the sugar, bread crumbs, almonds, raisins, cinnamon, and vanilla. Preheat the oven to 350°F. Roll out the dough into a very thin rectangle — so thin that you could read a love letter through it!

Brush some heavy cream over the dough. Put the filling lengthwise on half of the dough, and start rolling it, filling side first. Put the strudel on a greased baking sheet, and brush the top with the melted butter. Bake 40 minutes. Top with some confectioners' sugar. Serve warm with vanilla ice cream and whipped cream. ***Yield: 10 – 15 servings.***

Ginger Scones

"There are never any leftovers when I make these delicious scones."
— Sharon Spraggett

2 cups all-purpose flour
4 teaspoons baking powder
¼ cup sugar
½ teaspoon salt
½ cup cold butter or margarine
⅓ cup chopped preserved ginger
⅔ cup milk
1 egg white
Sugar

Preheat the oven to 450°F. In a large bowl, mix the flour, baking powder, sugar, and salt. Cut in the butter until the mixture is crumbly. Add the ginger and milk just until the dough sticks together. Turn out onto an ungreased cookie sheet, and pat into a round. Flatten with your hand to an 8" circle. Cut just through into 8 or 10 wedges. Brush with egg white, and sprinkle with sugar. Bake 10 – 15 minutes. ***Yield: 8 or 10 scones.***

Hipwood House B&B

Sharon and Malcolm Spraggett
PO Box 211, 1763 Hipwood Road
Shawnigan Lake, British Columbia
V0R 2W0
Tel/Fax: (250) 743-7855
E-mail: hipwoodh@cvnet.net
www.cvnet.net/cowb&b/hipwood/
$$

ABOUT THE B&B

Thinking of traveling to beautiful Vancouver Island? If so, take the breathtaking 45-minute drive north of Victoria to the quaint village of Shawnigan Lake, and you'll come upon a peaceful country B&B called Hipwood House. Unwind in one of three spacious guest rooms, enjoy a refreshing cup of tea in the garden, or stroll the trails, including a 50-foot suspension bridge, on Hipwood's two acres. There's also a putting green and horseshoes and badminton — if you need to work off that full country breakfast! You're also a five-minute walk away from the public beach, local artists' gallery, and museum, and close to boat and water sport rentals on the lake, a seaplane for magnificent air tours, fishing, golf, tennis, and restaurants. Many interesting and picturesque areas are within a half-hour drive. Lifelong residents of Vancouver Island, Sharon and Malcolm are knowledgeable about the area and will help make your stay extra special.

SEASON

all year

ACCOMMODATIONS

1 room with private bath;
2 rooms with shared bath

Ginger Snaps

"These cookies are terrific with tea." — Yvonne Parker

¾ cup shortening
1 cup sugar
1 egg
¼ cup molasses
2 cups all-purpose flour
2 teaspoons baking soda
1 teaspoon ground cinnamon
½ teaspoon ground cloves
½ teaspoon ground ginger
½ teaspoon salt
Sugar

Melt the shortening, and let cool. Add the sugar, egg, and molasses, and beat well. In a bowl, sift together the flour, baking soda, cinnamon, cloves, ginger, and salt. Add the egg mixture to the flour mixture, and mix until combined. Chill the dough.

Preheat the oven to 350°F. Remove the dough from the refrigerator. Form into 1" balls, and roll them in sugar (do not flatten). Place on a greased cookie sheet, and bake 8 – 10 minutes. ***Yield: 36 cookies.***

Orchard Lane Bed & Breakfast

Yvonne Parker
13324 Middle Bench Road
Oyama, British Columbia V4V 2B4
Tel: (250) 548-3809
$$

ABOUT THE B&B

Smack dab between Kelowna and Vernon is Orchard Lane, a newly built Victorian B&B nestled in a private orchard. From the sprawling veranda is a panoramic view of the beautiful central Okanagan Valley, while nearby Kalamalka and Wood Lakes reflect the hills and distant mountains. Inside, a welcoming foyer and spiral staircase lead to romantic and comfortable bedrooms. Visitors lounge in the formal living room with fireplace, stroll through the flower gardens or nearby orchard, admire the terraced landscaping framed by giant trees, or take a refreshing dip in the outdoor hot tub. Your hostess, Yvonne, serves a full gourmet breakfast — made from produce grown in her garden — in the formal dining room or on the veranda. You'll quickly discover that one of her favorite hobbies is making crafts, which are displayed throughout the house. Alpine skiing, fishing, biking, hiking, and other recreational choices await you and there are golf courses and beaches aplenty to explore. This area is truly a corner of paradise.

SEASON

all year

ACCOMMODATIONS

2 rooms with shared bath;
1 room with private bath

Glacé Lace Cookies

"These thin, crisp wafers last a long time." — Anne-Marie Bansfield

½ cup softened butter
2 cups brown sugar
2 eggs
¾ cup all-purpose flour
2 teaspoons baking powder
½ teaspoon salt

Preheat the oven to 375°F. Cream the butter with the sugar using your fingers. Beat in the eggs, one at a time. Stir in the flour, baking powder, and salt. Spread foil on baking sheets, and butter lightly. Drop the dough by scant teaspoonfuls, about 2" apart (don't flatten — the cookies will spread while baking). Bake 5 – 6 minutes until the cookies are caramel colored. Test for doneness by lifting one off the foil with a spatula. If the cookie sticks to the foil, bake a little longer. When done, place the baking sheets in the refrigerator to chill for 5 minutes, then peel the cookies off the foil (don't try to remove them while they're still hot). ***Tip:*** Store the cookies in tin containers. ***Yield: 12 dozen cookies.***

Le Gîte Park Avenue B&B

Anne-Marie and Irving Bansfield
54 Park Avenue
Ottawa, Ontario K2P 1B2
Tel: (613) 230-9131
$$

ABOUT THE B&B

A bright, airy ambiance and artistic decor await you at Park Avenue B&B, an elegant, brick 1906 home located in a charming residential area of downtown Ottawa, Canada's capital. In addition to high-quality beds done up in classic cotton and linen sheets and duvets, each guest room is furnished with a desk and swivel chair, a rocking chair, bookshelves, excellent lighting, and attractive works of art. Ideal for families, the third-floor suite has two bedrooms and a private bath. The mood throughout the house is one of relaxation and warmth. Park Avenue B&B is close to the Parliament Buildings, art galleries, and museums, and is only three minutes (by foot) from the Rideau Canal, which freezes into the world's longest skating rink. Ottawa has a number of exciting festivals and activities, including Winterlude, a winter carnival held each February. Anne-Marie and Irving make it a point to know what's going on when in Ottawa so they can advise their guests on what to see and do.

SEASON

all year

ACCOMMODATIONS

1 suite with private bath;
2 rooms with shared bath

Heritage Scones

3 cups all-purpose flour
1 cup brown sugar
3 teaspoons baking powder
½ teaspoon salt
1 cup margarine
1 cup milk
1 egg, separated
1 cup raisins or currants
Granulated sugar

Preheat the oven to 400°F. Mix together the flour, brown sugar, baking powder, and salt. Work in the margarine with a fork until well blended. Beat the milk and egg yolk together, and add to the margarine mixture. Add the raisins, and mix well. On a floured surface, roll the dough into a 1" thick circle. Spread with the egg white, and sprinkle with sugar. Cut the dough into triangles, and place them on an ungreased baking sheet. Bake 15 minutes. ***Yield: 24 scones.***

Park View Bed & Breakfast

Gladys and Carson Langille
254 Cameron Street
Moncton, New Brunswick E1C 5Z3
Tel: (506) 382-4504
$$

ABOUT THE B&B

This art deco home was built in 1940 as a residence for Mrs. Inez Robinson, owner of Moncton's first business college. The architectural plans came from the 1939 New York World's Fair, and this was the first art deco home in Moncton. The curved living room windows look out on beautiful Victoria Park in the city's center. Opened as a B&B in 1989, this charming home has three guest rooms with cable TV, telephones, and exquisite shared bath, spacious living room with fireplace, elegant dining room, and cozy kitchen. Your hosts provide a warm welcome, a hearty, home-cooked breakfast of your choice, and a wealth of information about the area. Gladys is a part-time school teacher, while Carson enjoys playing bridge and painting landscapes. A collection of works by local artists graces their walls. Nearby is superb dining, shopping, beaches, parks, museums, galleries, theater, a must-see tidal bore (where the tide goes up and down very quickly), and the famous Magnetic Hill (you'll never believe this phenomenon unless you experience it yourself!).

SEASON

all year

ACCOMMODATIONS

3 rooms with shared bath

Brio Haus

Diana and Les Habkirk
3005 Brio Entrance
Whistler, British Columbia V0N 1B3
Tel: (800) 331-BRIO (2746)
or (604) 932-3313
E-mail: briohaus@whistler.net
$$ – $$$

ABOUT THE B&B

Brio Haus is an intimate B&B located in Canada's premier ski resort area. Enjoy charming rooms, fitted with cozy goose down duvets, in a European-style alpine home, and awake to a full home-baked breakfast, often featuring one of the pear specialties of the house. After skiing, hiking, canoeing, or horseback riding, you can prepare your own snacks and dinners in the guest kitchen loaded with amenities. After that, warm yourself by the evening fire in the guest lounge and watch a variety of complimentary movies. Or, ease sore muscles after an active day with a soak in the Jacuzzi moon tub and sauna. Brio Haus is centrally located, an easy walk to Whistler Village and ski lifts via the Valley Trail, and right across the street from the golf course. Diana and Les spent many years as a bus tour guide team in the Canadian Rockies before opening their lodge in 1989. Les now runs the local transit system and Diana works full time seeing to the needs of her B&B guests.

SEASON

all year

ACCOMMODATIONS

3 rooms with shared bath

Honey-Glazed Pear Turnovers

"Pears were always a special treat when I was growing up in Kansas, and this recipe originates with my mother. My sister loved the fruit so much that her childhood nickname was (you guessed it) 'Pear.' "
— Diana Habkirk

3 pears, peeled, cored, and diced
½ cup chopped pecans
¼ cup plus 2 tablespoons honey
1½ tablespoons lemon juice
1 tablespoon all-purpose flour
1 teaspoon ground cinnamon
Ground ginger
1 egg white
3 tablespoons water
17-ounce package frozen puff pastry
1 tablespoon butter

Preheat the oven to 350°F. Combine the pears, pecans, 2 tablespoons honey, lemon juice, flour, cinnamon, and a pinch of ginger in a bowl. In a separate bowl, combine the egg white and 1 tablespoon of the water, and blend. Thaw the pastry sheets. Unfold and cut each sheet into 4 squares. Place 2 tablespoons of the pear mixture in the lower right-hand corner of the pastry square. Moisten the edges with the egg mixture, and fold in half. Press the edges together firmly with a fork. Brush the top with the egg mixture. Place the turnovers on a greased baking sheet. Bake 20 minutes. Meanwhile, combine the remaining water, remaining honey, and butter in a saucepan. Bring to a boil without stirring for 2 minutes. Baste the turnovers with this glaze. Continue cooking another 10 minutes or until golden. Baste again, and serve. ***Yield: 8 turnovers.***

Jelly Roll

"If you raise chickens and get lots of extra 'cackleberries,' you can use the egg yolks for this recipe and leftover egg whites for my angel food cake (see recipe on page 99), both great for afternoon or after-dinner treats." — Jim Saville

10 egg yolks
2 whole eggs
3 tablespoons water
1 teaspoon lemon juice
1 cup sugar
1 cup all-purpose flour
1 teaspoon baking powder
1 teaspoon cream of tartar
Jam or pie filling

Preheat the oven to 350°F. To the egg yolks and whole eggs, add the water and lemon juice, and beat well. Add the sugar, and beat some more. In a separate bowl, combine the flour, baking powder, and cream of tartar. Add the flour mixture to the egg mixture, and beat until smooth. Line a rectangular, well-greased cookie sheet with well-greased waxed paper, and pour in the batter. Bake 10 minutes. Flip out onto a clean, wet tea towel, and immediately peel off the waxed paper. Spread the jam lengthwise across the jelly roll, then roll up (short end to short end). ***Yield: 12 servings.***

Spring Valley Guest Ranch

Jim Saville
PO Box 10
Ravenscrag, Saskatchewan
S0N 0T0
Tel: (306) 295-4124
$$

ABOUT THE B&B

Come enjoy an afternoon visit or an overnight stay at Spring Valley Guest Ranch. This three-story, 1913 home is nestled in a tall grove of cottonwood poplars near a spring-fed stream in a pleasant wooded valley with many varieties of flora and fauna. There are more than a thousand acres of hills and valleys to explore, either on foot or on horseback. You are invited to dine, choosing from a unique menu, in the licensed Country Tea Room, which houses over 200 duck replicas. Poultry, sheep, horses, and a donkey can be visited in the barnyard. The craft shop in the log cabin is filled with treasures of leather, wood, and pottery and with knitted and beaded crafts — all made by local artists. An excellent area for naturalists, photographers, and hikers, Ravenscrag is only 20 minutes from Cypress Hills Provincial Park, on the Alberta border.

SEASON

all year

ACCOMMODATIONS

4 rooms with shared baths;
1 log cabin with shared bath

Gîte à la ferme MACDALE Bed and Breakfast

Anne and Gordon MacWhirter
365 Route 132, Hope, PO Box 803
Paspébiac, Québec G0C 2K0
Tel: (418) 752-5270
$

ABOUT THE B&B

For a relaxing holiday, visit the Gaspé Peninsula and MACDALE Bed and Breakfast. Situated overlooking Baie des Chaleurs on a beef farm that has been active for five generations, this spacious three-story home offers two family rooms and a variety of guest accommodations. The aroma of fresh coffee and assorted muffins and pastries will awaken you and whet your appetite for an old-fashioned home-baked breakfast that includes farm-fresh eggs. Thanks to MACDALE's central location, tourist attractions such as world-famous Percé Rock and Forillon Park are well within day-trip driving distance. A seawater therapy resort is just minutes away, as are many museums, points of historical interest, and sports facilities. Anne is a first grade teacher while Gordon has recently retired from teaching junior high school mathematics.

SEASON

all year

ACCOMMODATIONS

1 loft with private bath;
4 rooms with shared baths

Jiffy Pudding

"As the name suggests, this pudding can be made in a jiffy. It's so easy and so good!" — Anne MacWhirter

1 cup all-purpose flour
¾ cup brown sugar
½ cup milk
⅓ cup raisins
2 teaspoons baking powder

Topping:
2 cups boiling water
¾ cup brown sugar
2 tablespoons butter
½ teaspoon vanilla

Preheat the oven to 350°F. Mix together the flour, brown sugar, milk, raisins, and baking powder, and pour into a buttered 8" square baking dish. For the topping, mix together the water, brown sugar, butter, and vanilla, and pour over the batter. Bake 30 minutes. Serve warm. ***Yield: 6 – 8 servings.***

Lemon-Buttermilk Sorbet

2 cups buttermilk
¾ cup white corn syrup
¼ cup honey
Juice and zest of 2 lemons

Fresh mint leaves

Beat together the buttermilk, corn syrup, honey, and lemon juice and zest. Chill at least 30 minutes. Pour the mixture into an ice cream maker, and follow the manufacturer's directions. When the sorbet is ready, scoop it out, and freeze it in a plastic container. Allow the sorbet to soften for 15 minutes (or microwave it 40 seconds on the defrost setting) before serving. Serve in a martini glass, and garnish with a fresh mint leaf. ***Yield: 8 (single-scoop) servings.***

Weston Lake Inn Bed & Breakfast

Susan Evans and Ted Harrison
813 Beaver Point Road
Salt Spring Island, British Columbia
V8K lX9
Tel: (250) 653-4311
$$$

ABOUT THE B&B

Perched on a knoll of well-tended flowering trees and shrubs overlooking Weston Lake, the inn is a serene and comfortable adult getaway on the rural south end of Salt Spring Island. The three tastefully decorated guest bedrooms have private baths, down duvets, and fresh flower bouquets. Original Canadian art and beautiful petit point (done by host Ted) grace the rooms. Guests have the exclusive use of a cozy fireside lounge with library, TV, and VCR, and an outdoor hot tub overlooking the lake. Creative breakfasts feature fresh eggs from the inn's chickens and produce from the large organic garden, such as berries, herbs, and asparagus in season. Near Victoria, Salt Spring Island offers a mild climate, exceptional beauty, a thriving community of artists and craftspeople, and an abundance of outdoor activities. Since opening Weston Lake Inn in 1986, hosts Susan and Ted have been fine-tuning their B&B craft, restoring the house, landscaping, and enjoying their 10-acre paradise with guests. Susan loves gardening, while Ted loves sailing and offers charters aboard their 36-foot sloop.

SEASON

all year

ACCOMMODATIONS

3 rooms with private baths

Fraser House

Sheila and Dennis Derksen
PO Box 211, 33 1st Street East
Letellier, Manitoba R0G 1C0
Tel: (204) 737-2284
$

ABOUT THE B&B

Memories are made at this elegant and romantic 1916 home. Hardwood floors, area rugs, and antique furniture enhance the home's Victorian decor. Spacious rooms combined with great hospitality make your stay most enjoyable. Relax with a beverage and home-baked goodies in the parlor or on the veranda or patio. Breakfast may consist of a puffy egg pancake or freshly baked croissants and muffins, along with the season's fresh fruit, served in the formal dining room. Fraser House is located just a few minutes north of the US border in the heart of Manitoba's bustling agricultural area, and is near places to golf, fish, shop, and ski. Sheila enjoys craft projects and holds painting classes during the winter months, while Dennis enjoys carpentry and is employed as a fertilizer dealer.

SEASON

all year

ACCOMMODATIONS

2 rooms with shared bath

Maple Twist Rolls

¾ cup milk
¼ cup margarine
2¾ – 3 cups all-purpose flour
3 tablespoons granulated sugar
1 package active dry yeast (1 tablespoon) dissolved in ¼ cup lukewarm water
1 egg
1 teaspoon maple extract
½ teaspoon salt

Filling:
½ cup granulated sugar
⅓ cup chopped pecans
1 teaspoon ground cinnamon
¼ cup melted margarine

Icing:
1 cup confectioners' sugar
2 tablespoons melted margarine
1 tablespoon milk or water
½ teaspoon maple extract

In a small saucepan, heat the milk and margarine until lukewarm. In a large mixer bowl, blend the milk mixture, 1 cup of the flour, and the granulated sugar, yeast mixture, egg, maple extract, and salt at low speed until the dry ingredients are moistened. Beat 2 minutes.

(continued on next page)

By hand, stir in the remaining flour to form a soft dough. Knead it on a floured surface until smooth and elastic (about 2 minutes). Place the dough in a lightly buttered bowl, turning it to coat it with butter. Cover the dough, and let it rise in a warm place until it has doubled in size.

For the filling, combine the granulated sugar, pecans, and cinnamon in a small bowl, and set aside. Lightly grease a 12" round pizza pan. Punch the dough down, divide it into 3 pieces, and shape them into balls. Roll or press 1 ball of dough into the bottom of the prepared pizza pan. Brush the dough with about one-third of the melted margarine, then sprinkle with one-third of the pecan mixture. Roll out the other 2 balls of dough, and add layers of dough, melted margarine, and the pecan mixture to the first layer.

To shape the rolls, place a glass about 2" in diameter in the center of the dough. With scissors, cut from the outside edge to the glass, forming 16 pie-shaped wedges. Twist each wedge 4 times. Remove the glass. Let the dough rise until it has doubled in size. Bake the rolls in a preheated 350°F oven for 20 minutes. Cool 5 minutes. In a small bowl, blend together the confectioners' sugar, margarine, milk, and maple extract until smooth. Break off the rolls, and drizzle them with the icing.
Yield: 16 rolls.

Caron House (1837)

Mary and Mike Caron
PO Box 143
Williamstown, Ontario K0C 2J0
Tel: (613) 347-7338
$$

ABOUT THE B&B

Caron House (1837) is a romantic historic brick home located in the quaint village of Williamstown (established in 1784). Beautifully decorated and furnished with antiques, the house has many of its original features — working fireplaces, inside shutters, tin ceilings, and wide pine floorboards. The upstairs is reserved for guests only. Two rooms with shared bath are individually decorated with Laura Ashley wallpaper, antique linens, hooked rugs, quilts, and collectibles. Guests can relax in the Keeping Room (a colonial term for "gathering place") or in the living room. A candlelit full gourmet breakfast — accompanied by classical music — is served in the dining room graced by fine china, silverware, and crystal. Outside, you'll marvel at the herb and Victorian gardens, relax on the antique wicker furniture on the back veranda, and enjoy the lovely yards, complete with trellis, brick patio, and gazebo. Caron House is one hour's drive from either Montréal or Ottawa; nearby attractions include Upper Canada Village, artisans' studios, a bird sanctuary, tennis courts, places to go cycling, and good restaurants. Mary and Mike enjoy traveling, antique hunting, cooking, gardening, and history.

SEASON

all year

ACCOMMODATIONS

2 rooms with shared bath

Mary's Baked Apple

"The Seaway Valley is home of the McIntosh Red Apple, at its peak in the fall when the local 'Apples and Art Studio and Heritage Tour' is held (the last weekend in September). At that time, studios and heritage sites open their doors and invite the public to enjoy arts of the past and arts in the making. It's also when I like to serve my baked apple recipe — art, if I may say so myself, that can be eaten with more than the eye." — Mary Caron

4 McIntosh apples
4 tablespoons raisins
4 teaspoons brown sugar
4 teaspoons butter
2 teaspoons orange zest
Ground cinnamon
Ground nutmeg
Reconstituted orange juice

Sour cream or yogurt

The night before serving, core the apples and set them upright in an electric crock pot. In the center of each apple, layer the raisins, brown sugar, butter, orange zest, and a pinch of cinnamon and nutmeg. Pour in enough orange juice to fill the pot up to the middle of the apples. Cook them in the crock pot on low overnight. In the morning, top each apple with a dollop of sour cream or yogurt. ***Yield: 4 servings.***

Nana's Tea Biscuits

"In the 1940s, we lived in a Cape Breton coal mining town where money was scarce. Our grandmother made these biscuits and served them with molasses as a snack or dessert. Molasses was the peanut butter of our childhood and it's still a comfort food for expatriate Cape Bretoners." — Innis and Sheila MacDonald

3 cups all-purpose flour
¼ cup sugar
3 teaspoons baking powder
2 teaspoons cream of tartar
1 teaspoon baking soda
1 teaspoon salt
¾ cup shortening
1¼ cups milk

Sharp cheddar cheese

Preheat the oven to 400°F. Sift together the flour, sugar, baking powder, cream of tartar, baking soda, and salt. Cut in the shortening with a pastry blender or 2 knives until the mixture resembles coarse meal. Add the milk and stir briefly, just until mixed. Roll out the dough ½" thick on a floured surface. Cut into rounds with a 2" biscuit cutter. Bake the biscuits on a lightly greased cookie sheet until they spring back when pressed lightly (about 12 minutes). Sharp cheddar cheese is a great accompaniment. ***Yield: 16 biscuits.***

Fresh Start Bed & Breakfast

Innis and Sheila MacDonald
2720 Gottingen Street
Halifax, Nova Scotia B3K 3C7
Tel: (902) 453-6616
$ – $$

ABOUT THE B&B

Fresh Start Bed & Breakfast is an 1895 Victorian mansion, one of the few North End houses to escape destruction by the Halifax Explosion of 1917. It's located in an interesting area populated by families, artists, craftspeople, and students. Citadel Hill, historic properties, and the uniquely designed Hydrostone District are within walking distance. Halifax is a friendly city with many restaurants, live theater, wonderful crafts, and a lively nightlife. In July, visitors come for the International Tattoo Festival and, in August, for the International Buskers Festival. Conveniently located on a bus route, informal Fresh Start lets guests decide when to check in and check out. Laundry service and off-street parking are available, and breakfast tastes great! Guests enjoy relaxing in solitary quiet, visiting with the hosts and other guests, reading in the library, or watching TV. The two owners are sisters and nurses. They are also enthusiastic grandmothers and travelers! Innis likes gardening, crafts, and social activism, while Sheila likes cooking and reading.

SEASON

all year

ACCOMMODATIONS

2 rooms with private baths;
6 rooms with shared baths

DeWitt's Bed and Breakfast

Irene DeWitt and Wendy Kelly
RR #1
Airdrie, Alberta T4B 2A3
Tel: (403) 948-5356
Fax: (403) 912-0788
E-mail: dewitbnb@cadvision.com
$$

ABOUT THE B&B

A relaxing stay in the country awaits you at DeWitt's Bed and Breakfast. Enjoy a hearty, home-cooked breakfast either on the flower filled patio or in the dining room, from which the Rocky Mountains can be seen. The three bedrooms are simple yet elegant: The Evergreen Room has a huge picture window, twin beds, and a private bathroom; The Knotty Pine Room has a double bed and a shared bathroom; and The Whispering Spruce Room has a queen bed and a shared bathroom. DeWitt's B&B is located a short distance west of Airdrie and within 20 minutes of Calgary and the international airport. It's an hour's drive to the scenic Kananaskis country, on the way to Canmore and Banff National Park. Nearby attractions include the Calgary Stampede, Calgary Zoo, and Glenbow Museum.

SEASON

all year

ACCOMMODATIONS

1 room with private bath;
2 rooms with shared baths

No-Fry Doughnuts

2 packages active dry yeast (2 tablespoons)
¼ cup warm water
2 eggs
1½ cups lukewarm milk, scalded and cooled
½ cup sugar
⅓ cup shortening
1 teaspoon ground nutmeg
1 teaspoon salt
¼ teaspoon ground cinnamon
4½ cups all-purpose flour
¼ cup melted margarine
Cinnamon sugar

Preheat the oven to 425°F. In a large mixer bowl, dissolve the yeast in the warm water. Add the eggs, milk, sugar, shortening, nutmeg, salt, cinnamon, and 2 cups of the flour. Blend for 30 seconds on top speed, stopping occasionally to scrape the sides of the bowl. Stir in the remaining flour until the dough is smooth, again stopping occasionally to scrape the sides of the bowl. Cover and let rise in a warm place until the dough has doubled in size. Turn the dough out onto a well-floured, cloth-covered surface. Roll the dough around lightly to coat it with flour (the dough will be soft to handle). Roll the dough ½" thick. Cut out doughnuts with a 2½" doughnut cutter, and place them 2" apart on a greased baking sheet. Brush them with margarine. Cover the doughnuts, and let them rise until they have doubled in size. Bake the doughnuts 8 – 10 minutes until they are golden brown. Immediately brush them with margarine, then coat them in cinnamon sugar. ***Yield: About 20 doughnuts.***

Oatmeal Cookies

"We love to serve these cookies to arriving guests on the porch with tea, coffee, or a cool drink." — Monique Sanders

2 cups all-purpose flour
1 teaspoon baking powder
1 teaspoon baking soda
½ teaspoon salt
¼ teaspoon ground cinnamon
⅛ teaspoon ground mace
1⅓ cups butter (preferably unsalted)
2 cups dark brown sugar
⅔ cup plus 2 tablespoons granulated sugar
2 eggs
1 tablespoon vanilla
4½ cups quick-cooking rolled oats

Preheat the oven to 350°F. Generously grease several baking sheets. Combine the flour, baking powder, baking soda, salt, cinnamon, and mace, and set aside. In a separate large bowl, beat the butter with an electric mixer on medium speed until softened. Add the brown sugar and ⅔ cup of the granulated sugar, and beat until fluffy and smooth. Beat in the eggs and vanilla. Beat in the flour mixture. Mix in the oats until thoroughly incorporated. Roll the dough into 1½" balls, and place them about 3" apart on the prepared baking sheets. Using the bottom of a glass that has been lightly greased and dipped in the remaining granulated sugar, flatten the balls into 2½" rounds (dip the glass in sugar after flattening each cookie). Place the baking sheets in the upper third of the oven, and bake 10 – 12 minutes or until the cookies are slightly browned. Let the cookies cool on the baking sheets for 3 – 4 minutes. Transfer the cookies to wire racks, and let them cool completely. ***Tip:*** Store the cookies in an airtight container up to 10 days. They also freeze well. ***Yield: About 48 cookies.***

Limestone & Lilacs

Monique and John Sanders
1775 Highway #38
Kingston, Ontario K7P 2Y7
Tel: (613) 545-0222
E-mail: john.sanders@sympatico.ca
$$

ABOUT THE B&B

Limestone & Lilacs rests on 27 picturesque acres on the northwest outskirts of Kingston. The romantic 1820s limestone farmhouse has been elegantly restored and stands out among the many limestone homes for which Kingston is known. The house has high ceilings, and the interior limestone walls are the perfect backdrop for graceful furnishings and Canadiana. A full gourmet breakfast is served in the elegant dining room. Kingston's waterfront area is only 12 minutes away, and from there you can cruise the famous Thousand Islands. Visit Kingston's 17 museums and Fort Henry — built during the War of 1812 — or shop in various boutiques. Monique and John, who speak English and French, opened their B&B in 1995 after working for corporations in Montréal, Toronto, and Pennsylvania.

SEASON

all year

ACCOMMODATIONS

3 rooms with shared baths

Bruce Gables B&B

Elsie and Jorn Christensen
PO Box 448, 410 Berford Street
Wiarton, Ontario N0H 2T0
Tel: (519) 534-0429
Fax: (519) 534-0779
$$

ABOUT THE B&B

Whether in French, German, Spanish, Danish, or English, Elsie and Jorn bid you "welcome" to Bruce Gables, their spacious turn-of-the-century home. Relax in the large living room, which has been restored to its Victorian splendor and furnished with period furniture and antiques. Two of the three large bedrooms have bay windows that overlook the town of Wiarton and the clear blue waters of Colpoy's Bay. A hearty breakfast, served in the elegant dining room, is your choice of crêpes, pancakes, waffles, French toast, eggs Benedict or Florentine, omelets, or any other style of eggs. In the garden, picnic tables and a gas barbecue are available for the guests to use. Known as the "gateway to the Bruce," the town of Wiarton makes a perfect headquarters for exploring the Bruce Peninsula. With Georgian Bay to the east and Lake Huron to the west, the Bruce offers abundant water recreation, not to mention some of the most breathtaking scenery in Ontario from its high limestone bluffs. In addition, the area's provincial parks are natural habitats for many varieties of birds and animals.

SEASON

May – October

ACCOMMODATIONS

3 rooms with shared baths

Papaya Scones

⅔ cup buttermilk or plain yogurt (have an additional ¼ cup on hand)
1 egg
3 cups all-purpose flour
½ cup sugar
4 teaspoons baking powder
½ teaspoon baking soda
½ teaspoon salt
½ cup butter
½ cup chopped dried papaya
¼ cup currants
1 teaspoon orange zest
1 tablespoon softened butter

Butter
Preserves
Devonshire cream

Preheat the oven to 375°F. Pour the buttermilk into a measuring cup, and beat in the egg. In a large bowl, blend together the flour, sugar, baking powder, baking soda, and salt. With a pastry blender or 2 knives, cut the butter into the flour mixture until it forms fine granules. Add the papaya, currants, and orange zest, and stir to mix. Add the buttermilk mixture all at once, and stir until a soft dough forms (you may have to add up to ¼ cup buttermilk). Turn the dough out onto a lightly floured surface, and knead 5 – 6 times, or just until well mixed. Roll or pat out the dough to about 1" thick. Dip the rim of a 2" small glass in flour, and cut out the scones. Place the scones on an ungreased cookie sheet. Bake 15 – 20 minutes. Brush the tops with softened butter. Serve warm with butter, preserves, and Devonshire cream. ***Yield: 12 – 15 scones.***

Pat's Leftover Bread Pudding

"After wondering what to do with a variety of leftover muffins and breads — should I feed them to Chloe (my hungry pup) or to the birds? — I thought of concocting this delicious recipe. It reminds me of the Christmas puddings I used to enjoy when I was a youngster."
— Pat Le Baron

2 eggs
2 cups milk
½ cup sugar
½ teaspoon ground cinnamon
¼ teaspoon ground nutmeg
4 cups stale bread and/or muffin cubes
¼ cup raisins

Whipped cream or vanilla ice cream

Beat the eggs. Add the milk, sugar, cinnamon, and nutmeg, and mix. Oil a 2-quart baking casserole. Arrange bread and / or muffin cubes in the dish with the raisins, and cover with the egg mixture. Let stand until well soaked (about 15 minutes). Bake in a preheated 350°F oven for 25 – 35 minutes until a knife inserted in the pudding's center comes out clean. Serve warm with whipped cream or vanilla ice cream. ***Tips:*** If the bread or muffins aren't stale, put them in the oven for 5 – 10 minutes to dry them out. You can bake this pudding in 2 (1-quart) casseroles. ***Yield: 8 servings.***

Willow House B&B / La Maison des Saules

Pat Le Baron and Allan Watson
30 Western Avenue, PO Box 906
Sutton, Québec J0E 2K0
Tel: (514) 538-0035
$$

ABOUT THE B&B

A lovely 96-year-old Loyalist-style home with views of a running brook and a pond, Willow House is situated in the hub of an artisans community with many local arts and crafts shops nearby. Pat's claim to fame is home baking, and her specialties include ginger-lemon, blueberry, poppy seed, and carrot-bran muffins, and squash, oatmeal, and granola breads. (Suppers or lunches can be arranged on request.) Other Willow House niceties include a private garden where you can watch many species of birds come and go, and a cozy lounge where you can while away the hours listening to classical music (with Pat's miniature collie, Chloe, to keep you quiet company). Situated in the Eastern Townships, Sutton is a popular getaway for cycling, hiking, walking, golf, boating, skiing, antique and outlet shopping, and admiring spectacular fall foliage. About one-and-three-quarter hours from Montréal and a half hour from the Vermont border, Willow House welcomes both children and pets and permits smoking in some areas of the B&B.

SEASON

all year

ACCOMMODATIONS

4 rooms with shared baths

Morrison Manor

Nancy and Jerry Morrison
RR #1
Morpeth, Ontario N0P 1X0
Tel: (519) 674-3431
$$

ABOUT THE B&B

Built in 1989 especially as a B&B, Morrison Manor is a warm and charming three-story hand-crafted log home just a few minutes from the natural environment of Rondeau Provincial Park. On the first floor of the manor is a cozy living room with a fireplace. A full country breakfast is served in the large dining room where fresh herbs hang overhead. Six guest bedrooms are on the second floor, and two large private suites that overlook fields, a pond, and the full length of Rondeau Bay are on the third floor. Each room has a different country style, and a door that opens onto a large porch. Besides the park, which is a bird-watcher's paradise, the area features a winery, buffalo farm, art gallery, cultural center, antique shops, car races, seasonal festivals, and much more. Nancy, a secondary school teacher, and Jerry, a quality-control technician, enjoy cooking, gardening, traveling, theatergoing, birdwatching, walking, decorating, and playing shuffleboard.

SEASON

all year

ACCOMMODATIONS

2 suites with private baths;
6 rooms with shared baths

Peach Cobbler

"This peach cobbler always reminds me of the time I served it to five aviators (as they called themselves) from Paris, who didn't have to tell me it was delicious — their loud 'erotic' moaning and groaning made it obvious! I was thrilled that they liked it so much and, at the same time, a bit embarrassed by their reaction." — Nancy Morrison

1 cup melted butter or margarine
2 (28-ounce) cans peaches
1 yellow cake mix (no substitution)
Ground cinnamon

Preheat the oven to 350°F. Place ½ cup of the melted butter in the bottom of a 12 x 9" glass dish. Add the peaches and most of the juice. Add the cake mix over the top without mixing, then add the rest of the butter. Sprinkle with cinnamon. Bake until the delicious smell drives you crazy, and the top is browned. ***Yield: 10 – 12 servings.***

Raisin Buns

"The perfect buns for tea." — Pearl Hiscock

3 cups all-purpose flour
¼ cup sugar
5 teaspoons baking powder
1 cup butter
½ cup raisins
2 eggs
1½ cups water

Preheat the oven to 425°F. Combine the flour, sugar, and baking powder, and cut in the butter. Add the raisins. Beat the eggs well, add with the water to the flour mixture, and mix to form a soft dough. Place the dough on a floured surface, and roll out to a ½" thickness. Cut out the buns with a 2"-diameter cookie cutter or a glass with its rim dipped in flour. Place them on greased baking pans. Bake about 15 minutes.
Yield: 36 buns.

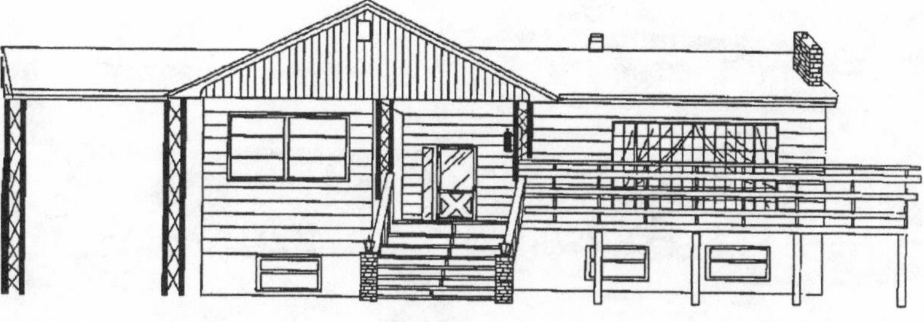

Brookside Hospitality Home

Pearl and Lloyd Hiscock
PO Box 104
Sunnyside, Newfoundland A0B 3J0
Tel: (709) 472-4515
$

ABOUT THE B&B

You'll be welcomed like family at Brookside Hospitality Home, a well-maintained ranch-style dwelling in the rural community of Sunnyside. Pearl and Lloyd have lived in Sunnyside practically all their lives and know what Newfoundland hospitality is all about. Get to know them over a cup of tea or coffee, which is provided along with a bedtime snack. In the morning, make your way to the breakfast nook, which overlooks the water, where homemade bread and jam, cereals, and juices await you. Radio, cable TV, laundry facilities, and ample parking are also available. Let your well-informed hosts direct you to the best sights in the province. Lloyd is a boat enthusiast and you may want to look in on his latest boat building project in the shed. Pearl keeps busy with her household responsibilities. Brookside is about one-and-a-half hours' drive from the Argentia Ferry to North Sydney, Nova Scotia, and one hour's drive from St. John's, capital of Newfoundland.

SEASON

all year

ACCOMMODATIONS

2 rooms with shared bath

Rhubarb and Apple Compote

"Guests from Japan were curious about what rhubarb looked like after they had been served this compote. Because of communication difficulties, we resorted to bringing a stick of rhubarb from the garden to the dining room table for demonstration purposes. It turns out that the type of rhubarb grown in Japan is used as a vegetable dish."
— Judy Hill

1 pound fresh or thawed and drained frozen rhubarb
1 large apple, peeled, cored, and thinly sliced
¼ cup granulated sugar (plus additional for adjusting taste)
Juice and zest of 1 orange

Plain yogurt or sour cream
Brown sugar

Cut the rhubarb into 1" lengths. In a saucepan, combine the rhubarb, apple, granulated sugar, and orange juice and zest. Cover and bring to a boil. Reduce the heat and simmer for 10 minutes or until the fruit is soft. Add granulated sugar to taste. Top each serving with yogurt or sour cream, and sprinkle with brown sugar. ***Tip:*** Raisins or other dried or fresh fruit can be added to the compote before it is cooked. ***Yield: 8 – 10 servings.***

The Shipwright Inn

Judy and Jordan Hill
51 Fitzroy Street
Charlottetown,
Prince Edward Island C1A 1R4
Tel: (902) 368-1905
Fax: (902) 628-1905
E-mail: shipwright@isn.net
www.isn.net/ShipwrightInn
$$$ – $$$$

ABOUT THE B&B

The Shipwright Inn is an elegant Victorian home built in the 1860s by the accomplished Charlottetown shipbuilder James Douse. This award-winning heritage inn is located in Olde Charlottetown, one block east of Queen Street and within a three-minute walk of the historic waterfront area, dining, and shopping. In keeping with its shipbuilding heritage, The Shipwright Inn's decor has a nautical theme. While savoring breakfast beneath the dining room chandelier, you might imagine the rope-insignia china (circa 1810) in use at the captain's table of a clipper ship. Your hosts Judy and Jordan Hill have carefully collected period antiques, art work, Victorian memorabilia, family quilts, and old books and artifacts related to the sea for your enjoyment. The seven guest rooms have polished pine floors, some of which were previously ship's planking that was reused by the home's builder. Each bedroom features a private bath, goose down duvets, a TV and telephone, a ceiling fan, and air conditioning. All rooms are smoke free.

SEASON

all year

ACCOMMODATIONS

7 rooms with private baths

Rhubarb Sauce Drop Cookies

½ cup margarine
1 cup sugar
1 egg
1¾ cups all-purpose flour
1 teaspoon ground cinnamon
½ teaspoon baking powder
½ teaspoon baking soda
½ teaspoon salt
¼ teaspoon ground cloves
¼ teaspoon ground nutmeg
1 cup quick-cooking rolled oats
½ cup raisins
1 cup rhubarb sauce (recipe follows)

Preheat the oven to 350°F – 375°F. Cream the margarine and sugar together. Stir in the egg. Sift together the flour, cinnamon, baking powder, baking soda, salt, cloves, and nutmeg. Mix in the rolled oats and raisins. Add the flour mixture to the margarine mixture in 3 portions alternately with the rhubarb sauce in 2 portions, mixing well after each addition. Drop dough by teaspoonfuls onto greased baking sheets. Bake about 12 minutes. ***Yield: 36 cookies.***

Rhubarb sauce:
3 cups cubed fresh rhubarb
1 cup water
¾ cup sugar

Boil the rhubarb in the water for 10 minutes. Add the sugar. Stir and let cool.

Bay View Farm / La Ferme Bay View

Helen and Garnett Sawyer
PO Box 21,
337 New Carlisle West, Route 132
New Carlisle, Québec G0C 1Z0
Tel: (418) 752-2725/6718
$

ABOUT THE B&B

Situated between New Carlisle and Bonaventure, Bay View Farm offers country hospitality in a beautiful seaside environment on the rugged Baie des Chaleurs coastline of Québec's Gaspé Peninsula. Seaside accommodations include five comfortable guest rooms and a fully equipped cottage. At breakfast, enjoy Bay View's farm-fresh eggs, meat, homemade muffins, scones, jams, jellies, and beverages, as well as fresh fruits and vegetables in season from the farm's garden and orchards. Additional meals are available on request at reasonable rates. Handicrafts are on display throughout the house. Enjoy the breathtaking panoramic seascapes, participate in the Bay View Folk Festival (second weekend of August) with folk music and dancing, or visit Percé Rock and the archaeological caves of Saint-Elzéar.

SEASON

May – November

ACCOMMODATIONS

5 rooms with shared baths;
1 private cottage with private bath

Bluenose Country Vacation Farm

Jo and Kenneth Mader
PO Box 173
Qu'Appelle, Saskatchewan S0G 4A0
Tel: (306) 699-7192
$$

ABOUT THE B&B

For an old-fashioned welcome where Mother Nature wraps you in her arms, there's no place like Bluenose Country Vacation Farm. Step back in history as you admire the English-style split fieldstone home — a striking landmark on the prairie landscape since 1904. Stroll through the farmyard, pet the farm animals, see the large farm machinery new and old, and spend some time in the Agriculture Education Center, with hands-on displays and model farm machinery for children to play with. After a refreshing swim in the indoor heated pool, try your hand at mini-golf while the children frolic in the playground. In early morning, the call of a meadowlark breaks the stillness and you're eventually coaxed to the breakfast table by the smells of homemade bread and sizzling bacon. Country high tea is served from May to September, and lunch and dinner meals can also be arranged. Bluenose is a short drive from picturesque Qu'Appelle Valley with its sparkling lakes and sandy beaches, and a few minutes from the town's stores and attractions.

SEASON

all year

ACCOMMODATIONS

6 rooms with private baths

Saskatoon Dumplings

"This recipe was an old standby of my mother-in-law, Lena Mader, who was an excellent cook and mother of eight boys! It's now become a specialty in our Country Tea Room." — Jo Mader

Dough:
1 cup all-purpose flour
2 teaspoons sugar
1 heaping teaspoon baking powder
Salt
2 tablespoons canola oil or melted butter
Milk as needed

Fruit sauce:
2 cups Saskatoon berries or blueberries
1 cup water
½ cup sugar

Vanilla ice cream

Mix together the flour, sugar, baking powder, a pinch of salt, and the oil with enough milk to produce a very thick batter; set aside. In a heavy saucepan, mix the berries, water, and sugar, and bring to a boil. At once, drop the dumpling dough by heaping spoonfuls into the fruit. Cover and simmer about 15 minutes. Serve hot with a scoop of vanilla ice cream. ***Yield: 5 – 6 servings.***

Scandinavian Kringler

"This is an excellent morning treat for my B&B guests."
— Kathy Chaplin

Crust:
½ cup chilled butter
1 cup all-purpose flour
2 tablespoons ice water

Puff filling:
1 cup water
½ cup butter
1 cup all-purpose flour
3 eggs
½ teaspoon almond extract

Frosting:
1 cup confectioners' sugar
1 tablespoon softened butter
2 – 3 tablespoons milk or cream (any type)
½ teaspoon almond extract or 1½ teaspoons vanilla

Sliced almonds

(continued on next page)

Chaplin's Country B&B

Kathy and Ron Chaplin
RR #5, Box 43
Saskatoon, Saskatchewan S7K 3J8
Tel/Fax: (306) 931-3353
E-mail: chaplinr@duke.usask.ca
www.dbs2.com/chaplins
$

ABOUT THE B&B

Experience the wide open spaces and blue sky of Canada's prairies at Chaplin's Country B&B, a working farm with Jersey cows, pigs, sheep, goats, and chickens. Enjoy a rest on the veranda and view awesome sunsets, or stroll through the barnyard and watch the evening milking. This gracious country home has a handmade spiral staircase, knotty pine paneling, and prairie antiques. For privacy, the guest bedrooms, TV lounge, and bathroom are all on the second floor. Chaplin's country breakfast, including French toast with homemade syrups, sausage, fresh fruit in season, and beverages, is a real eye-opener, while an evening snack of apple cake and hot cider always hits the spot. Saskatoon, only 15 minutes away, offers many fine restaurants, shops, and attractions. Other area diversions include the Western Development Museum, Wanuskewin Heritage Park, University of Saskatchewan, and numerous provincial parks and golf courses. Kathy and Ron pride themselves on their prairie hospitality and comfortable facilities.

SEASON

all year

ACCOMMODATIONS

3 rooms with shared bath

Preheat the oven to 350°F. In a small bowl, cut the butter into the flour, using a pastry blender (or 2 knives), until the particles are the size of small peas. Sprinkle with the water, 1 tablespoon at a time. Stir with a fork just until a soft dough forms. Divide the dough in half. On a greased cookie sheet, roll out each half into a 12 x 3" strip. For the filling, heat the water and butter to boiling in a medium saucepan. Remove from the heat, and immediately stir in the flour until the mixture is smooth. Add the eggs, one at a time, and beat until smooth. Stir in the almond extract. Divide the batter in half, and spoon over each crust, spreading to within ¾" of the edges. Bake 50 – 60 minutes or until golden brown. Immediately remove from the pan, and cool (the puffed top will shrink and fall). In a small bowl, blend together the confectioners' sugar, butter, milk, and almond extract until smooth. Spread frosting on each kringler. Sprinkle with the almonds, then slice. ***Yield: 16 – 20 servings.***

Sourdough Cinnamon Rolls

"A guest gave me this recipe and a cup of starter that was 25 years old at the time. I have since kept it going and have, in turn, given it away to other guests." — Nancy Perkins

1 cup sourdough sponge batter*
¼ cup vegetable oil
4 tablespoons brown sugar
2 cups all-purpose flour
2 teaspoons baking powder
1 teaspoon baking soda
¼ teaspoon salt

Filling:
1 cup brown sugar
3 tablespoons margarine or butter
1 teaspoon ground cinnamon

White frosting (see recipe on page 308)

**Note: In the evening (or at least 12 hours before using), make the sponge (see pages 88 – 89).*

Preheat the oven to 350°F. Put the sponge, oil, and brown sugar in a bowl, and mix together. Add the flour, baking powder, baking soda, and salt, and mix into a soft dough. Place the dough on a floured surface, and roll into a rectangle ½" thick. For the filling, combine the brown sugar, margarine, and cinnamon, and spread over the dough. Roll the dough up like a jelly roll, and cut into 1" slices. Place the rolls on greased cookie sheets, spaced about 1" apart, and press them down lightly with your hand. Bake 20 – 25 minutes. Serve warm with dribbled white frosting. ***Yield: 24 rolls.***

Bayberry Cliff Inn

Nancy and Don Perkins
RR #4, Little Sands
Murray River,
Prince Edward Island C0A 1W0
Tel: (800) 668-3395 or
(902) 962-3395
$$ – $$$

ABOUT THE B&B

Bayberry Cliff Inn is named for the fragrant bayberry bushes that cover the rugged 40-foot cliff on which the inn sits. Incorporating two reconstructed post and beam barns, the inn features intriguing architectural details such as individually shaped rooms and multiple-level living spaces. Bedrooms, lofts, and sitting areas are filled with handmade quilts, antique furniture, and paintings, the result of a lifetime of collecting beautiful things. A large library and breakfast area are on the ground level. Don's hash browns and bacon and Nancy's sourdough pancakes and blueberry muffins all consistently get rave reviews. Don is a retired teacher and Nancy is a marine painter (who has made sure the changeable ocean can be seen from every level of the B&B). Bayberry Cliff Inn activities include enjoying up to 35 different wildflowers, sitting in the whimsical tree perch to watch for marine life, inner-tubing, swimming, and beachcombing. You may cook your own meals on the gas grill or choose from many excellent restaurants a scant 15-minute drive away.

SEASON

May 10 – September 30

ACCOMMODATIONS

3 rooms with private baths;
1 room with shared bath

Taste the Past Bed & Breakfast

Rosalie and Bryce Nimmo
PO Box 865, 281-2nd Street West
Drumheller, Alberta T0J 0Y0
Tel: (403) 823-5889
$$

ABOUT THE B&B

Return to a simpler era during a stay in one of Drumheller's original grand mansions, built at the turn of the century by Drumheller Valley's coal baron Jesse Gouge. The elegant dining room and sitting area are decorated with Rosalie's artwork and period antiques, which also adorn the four guest rooms. The entire home has been tastefully restored, and the atmosphere is one of old-world charm and elegance. A healthy gourmet breakfast, served in the sunny breakfast room, includes fruit, yogurt, muffins or scones, and a hot entrée. Taste the Past is located in downtown Drumheller, en route to the world-renowned Royal Tyrrell Museum of Palaeontology. Other activities available nearby include hiking through the badlands, visiting many dinosaur-related spots, golfing, camping, and fishing. Rosebud Dinner Theatre and the Canadian Badlands Passion Play are unique cultural attractions. Rosalie and Bryce are knowledgeable hosts and will help you plan your stay.

SEASON

all year

ACCOMMODATIONS

4 rooms with shared baths

Spiced Pear and Cranberry Compote

"Breakfast at Taste the Past always begins with a fruit dish. This compote is a delightful, refreshing start to the day, is simple to prepare ahead of time, and keeps well in the refrigerator for several days (if there is ever any left to keep!)." — Rosalie Nimmo

2 cups dry white wine or apple juice
½ cup sugar (or to taste, if using apple juice)
Peel of ½ lemon, cut into strips
Peel of ½ orange, cut into strips
8 whole cloves
2 cinnamon sticks
8 ripe firm pears, peeled, cored, and quartered
1½ cups fresh or frozen thawed cranberries

In a medium saucepan, combine the wine, sugar, lemon peel, orange peel, cloves, and cinnamon sticks. Bring to a boil, and stir until the sugar is dissolved. Add the pears, and simmer 10 – 12 minutes or just until the pears yield when pierced with a knife. Add the cranberrries, and simmer 1 – 2 minutes more or until their skins start to pop (do not overcook). Remove the saucepan from the heat, and let cool. Transfer to a serving bowl, cover, and refrigerate. Remove the cinnamon sticks, cloves, and peel before serving. ***Yield: 6 – 8 servings.***

Strawberry Squares

Bottom crust:
½ cup margarine
¼ cup brown sugar
1 cup all-purpose flour
½ cup chopped walnuts or pecans

Filling:
1 cup thawed frozen strawberries in syrup
½ cup granulated sugar
Small package strawberry Jell-O
2 packages Dream Whip dessert topping mix

Preheat the oven to 375°F. Combine the margarine, brown sugar, flour, and walnuts, and press into a 9 x 9" greased pan. Bake 12 minutes. Cool. For the filling, combine the strawberries, granulated sugar, and Jell-O in a saucepan, and bring just to a boil. Remove from the heat, and cool. Prepare 1 package of Dream Whip, and add it to the cooled strawberry mixture. Spread the strawberry mixture over the bottom crust, and chill. Cut into squares. Before serving, prepare the other package of Dream Whip, and spread it on the squares. ***Tip:*** You can double the recipe for a 13 x 9" pan (about 24 squares) or even do a triple batch for a nice thick square. ***Yield: About 16 squares.***

Fairfield Farm Inn

Shae and Richard Griffith
10 Main Street West, Route 1
Middleton, Nova Scotia B0S 1P0
Tel/Fax: (800) 237-9896
or (902) 825-6989
$$

ABOUT THE B&B

Fairfield Farm Inn is situated on a 110-acre fruit and vegetable farm famous for its luscious melons. Built in 1886, this Annapolis Valley farmhouse has been completely restored and furnished in period antiques to enhance its original charm. The five guest rooms have cozy comforters, king- and queen-sized beds, and private baths. The Annapolis River and Slocum Brook are on the property, as are birdwatching and walking trails, pheasants, and other abundant wildlife. Shae and Richard take pride in offering Maritime hospitality and wholesome country breakfasts featuring fresh fruit picked from their farm and homemade jams and jellies. Shae is a member of the Acadia University Business School Advisory Board; Richard is a retired military officer. Their hobbies include gardening, antique hunting, reading, and traveling. A few minutes from picturesque fishing villages and the world's highest tides on the Bay of Fundy, Middleton boasts museums, restaurants, boutiques, and theater — all a short walking distance from the inn.

SEASON

all year
(winter by reservation only)

ACCOMMODATIONS

5 rooms with private baths

Domaine-sur-Mer

Eveline Haché
Box 1, Site 13, RR3
Bouctouche, New Brunswick
E0A 1G0
Tel: (506) 743-6582
Fax: (506) 743-8392
E-mail: domaine@auracom.com
$$

ABOUT THE B&B

This B&B has so many windows that guests sometimes feel they are having breakfast in the garden with the gold finches and hummingbirds that feed nearby. From the ocean, which can be seen from any of the B&B's three guest rooms, come refreshing sea breezes and the constant murmur of waves. For a great day at the beach or for a leisurely stroll, host Eveline Haché recommends the Irving Nature Park with its boardwalk and white sand dunes. The Eco-Centre is another popular spot and is staffed by professional biologists and interpreters from May to November. Domaine-sur-Mer is only 10 minutes from le Pays de la Sagouine in Bouctouche, home of the famous Acadian character made popular by the internationally renowned author Antonine Maillet. To complete your Acadian adventure, you can arrange for Eveline (who is knowledgeable about Acadian culture and history) to give you a hands-on lesson in cooking lobster — part of a multiday package that includes a lobster dinner and a seafood picnic for two.

SEASON

all year

ACCOMMODATIONS

3 rooms with private baths

Tender Mayo Biscuits

4 cups all-purpose flour
7 teaspoons baking powder
½ cup mayonnaise
2 cups milk
1 egg
Salt

Preheat the oven to 425°F. Combine the flour, baking powder, and mayonnaise. Add the milk, egg, and a pinch of salt, and mix just until the dry ingredients are moistened. Turn the dough out onto a lightly floured surface, and pat the dough to a thickness of ½". Cut out biscuits with a floured 2" cookie cutter. Place the biscuits on an ungreased baking sheet, and bake 12 – 14 minutes until golden. ***Yield: About 24 biscuits.***

Ten-Fruit Salad

"Initially, this eye-catching fruit salad was served to our vegetarian guests, but it quickly became a standard appetizer for all of our guests." — Ken Fisher

15 seedless green grapes, halved
15 seedless red grapes, halved
1 apple (not too sweet), peeled, cored, and sliced
1 banana, peeled and sliced
1 kiwi, peeled, quartered, and sliced
1 pear, pealed, cored, quartered, and sliced
1 seedless navel orange, peeled, sectioned, and halved
¼ canteloupe, balled
¼ honeydew, balled
¼ cup wild blueberries
6 – 8 strawberries, hulled and sliced

Mint leaves

In a large glass bowl (for visibility), gently combine the green grapes, red grapes, apple, banana, kiwi, pear, orange, canteloupe, and honeydew. Place the blueberries in the center of the fruit salad. Arrange the strawberry slices around the blueberries. Garnish with mint leaves, and serve. *Tip:* Don't make this salad more than 30 minutes before serving it, or the fruit will be soggy and the apple may turn brown. ***Yield: 4 servings.***

Wanaki-on-the-Ottawa

Ken Fisher
133 avenue des Plages
Pontiac (Luskville), Québec J0X 2G0
Tel: (819) 455-9295
Fax: (819) 455-9213
E-mail: kfisher@magi.com
$$

ABOUT THE B&B

The Algonquin word wanaki *means "a serene state of being," which is an apt description of a stay at Wanaki-on-the-Ottawa. Located at the end of a rural wooded cul-de-sac, Wanaki offers quiet seclusion in a new, large home. Wanaki's decks, porches, and three guest rooms overlook a private sandy beach and offer a panoramic view of the Ottawa River and dramatic sunsets. In winter, guests can skate, snowshoe, snowmobile, cross-country ski, or relax in front of the fireplace. In summer, guests can swim, sail, canoe, fish, or enjoy an evening around the campfire. Year round, guests can keep in shape right on the premises — at Wanaki's indoor swim spa and exercise room. Nearby attractions include Luskville Falls and Gatineau Park. Breakfasts are sumptuous, include fresh fruit, and are catered to all tastes. The house is wood-heated in winter and air conditioned in summer. Wanaki — only 30 minutes from downtown Ottawa in scenic Pontiac County, Québec — is an ideal setting for retreats, parties, and family reunions.*

SEASON

all year

ACCOMMODATIONS

3 rooms with shared baths

Weston Lake Inn Bed & Breakfast

Susan Evans and Ted Harrison
813 Beaver Point Road
Salt Spring Island, British Columbia
V8K IX9
Tel: (250) 653-4311
$$$

ABOUT THE B&B

Perched on a knoll of well-tended flowering trees and shrubs overlooking Weston Lake, the inn is a serene and comfortable adult getaway on the rural south end of Salt Spring Island. The three tastefully decorated guest bedrooms have private baths, down duvets, and fresh flower bouquets. Original Canadian art and beautiful petit point (done by host Ted) grace the rooms. Guests have the exclusive use of a cozy fireside lounge with library, TV, and VCR, and an outdoor hot tub overlooking the lake. Creative breakfasts feature fresh eggs from the inn's chickens and produce from the large organic garden, such as berries, herbs, and asparagus in season. Near Victoria, Salt Spring Island offers a mild climate, exceptional beauty, a thriving community of artists and craftspeople, and an abundance of outdoor activities. Since opening Weston Lake Inn in 1986, hosts Susan and Ted have been fine-tuning their B&B craft, restoring the house, landscaping, and enjoying their 10-acre paradise with guests. Susan loves gardening, while Ted loves sailing and offers charters aboard their 36-foot sloop.

SEASON

all year

ACCOMMODATIONS

3 rooms with private baths

Three-Cheese Scones

"While we have made adaptations to the originals over time, we gratefully acknowledge that many of our best ideas have come from our guests!" — Susan Evans

½ cup grated Emmental cheese
½ cup grated sharp cheddar cheese
½ cup freshly grated Parmesan cheese
1 whole egg
1 egg, separated
½ cup light cream
2 cups all-purpose flour
4 teaspoons baking powder
½ teaspoon salt
¼ cup very cold unsalted butter

Preheat the oven to 425°F. Mix the Emmental, cheddar, and ¼ cup of the Parmesan cheese in a large bowl. In a small bowl, beat a whole egg, egg yolk, and the cream until blended. In the bowl of a food processor, mix the flour, baking powder, and salt, then cut in the butter (if you don't have a food processor, use 2 knives). Add the flour mixture to the cheeses, and mix briefly. Add the egg mixture all at once, and stir with a fork. Press the dough into a ball, and knead gently on a floured surface up to 10 times. Roll into a circle ½" thick. Transfer the dough to a lightly greased baking sheet, brush with the egg white, score into 12 wedges, and sprinkle with the remaining Parmesan cheese. Bake 12 – 15 minutes. ***Yield: 12 scones.***

Yogurt Scones

"Using the lemon zest makes great biscuits for strawberry shortcakes." — Elaine Landray

2 cups all-purpose flour
2 tablespoons sugar
1 tablespoon baking powder
½ teaspoon baking soda
½ teaspoon salt
½ cup butter or margarine
1 cup plain yogurt

Options:
½ cup grated cheddar cheese or a combination of 2 – 3 kinds of cheese (Asiago, Parmesan, and mozzarella recommended)
½ cup raisins or dried cranberries
1 teaspoon lemon zest

Preheat the oven to 400°F. Mix together the flour, sugar, baking powder, baking soda, and salt. Cut in the butter with a pastry blender or 2 knives until blended. Add whichever option you are using (cheese, raisins, cranberries, or lemon zest). Mix in the yogurt, and form the dough into a loose ball. Roll the dough out on a floured surface to about ½" thick. Cut out the biscuits with a 2" cookie cutter. Place them on an ungreased cookie sheet, and bake 12 minutes. ***Yield: 18 scones.***

Linden House B&B

Elaine and Phil Landray
PO Box 1586, 389 Simcoe Street
Niagara-on-the-Lake, Ontario
L0S 1J0
Tel: (905) 468-3923
Fax: (905) 468-8946
E-mail: linden@niagara.com
$$$

ABOUT THE B&B

A warm welcome awaits you at Linden House, a new Cape Cod-style, air conditioned home with private guest wing featuring two rooms with queen beds and one room with twin/king bed. All rooms have private ensuite bathrooms. In the queen rooms are brass beds and cream wicker furniture, while the twin/king room highlights the nautical atmosphere with Cape Cod wicker. On the same level as the bedrooms is a guest lounge with television, VCR, games, and books, or you can choose to enjoy the garden or relax in the gazebo. Smoke-free Linden House offers convenient on-site parking and is located in the old town, just four short blocks from Queen Street with its shopping and theaters. In summer, enjoy water recreation on Lake Ontario or top-notch theater at the Shaw Festival. Your hosts, Elaine and Phil, serve such sumptuous breakfasts — featuring seasonal Niagara fruit — that their guests claim they don't need lunch!

SEASON

all year

ACCOMMODATIONS

3 rooms with private baths

French Toast, Pancakes, & Waffles

Apple-Cinnamon French Toast

5 tablespoons butter
2 – 3 large baking apples, peeled, cored, and sliced
1 cup brown sugar
2 tablespoons maple syrup
1 teaspoon ground cinnamon
½ teaspoon ground allspice
8 (1"-thick) slices French bread
3 – 4 eggs
1 cup milk
1 teaspoon vanilla

Confectioners' sugar

Prepare this French toast in the evening, and bake it the next morning. In a large frying pan, melt the butter over medium heat and add the apple slices. Cook and stir occasionally until tender. Add the brown sugar, maple syrup, cinnamon, and allspice. Cook, stirring, until the sugar dissolves. Pour the apple mixture into a 13 x 9" glass baking dish. Place the bread on top. In a separate bowl, combine the eggs, milk, and vanilla, and pour over the bread. Cover the dish with plastic wrap, and refrigerate overnight. In the morning, remove from the refrigerator 45 minutes before baking. Preheat the oven to 375°F. Remove the plastic wrap, and bake the French toast 30 – 35 minutes or until firm and the top is golden. Cool in the pan 5 minutes. Cut out the French toast slices, and invert them onto warmed plates. Cover with the apple and sauce from the dish. Dust with confectioners' sugar, and serve immediately. ***Tip:*** If you prefer the dish to be less sweet, use ½ cup brown sugar instead of 1 cup. ***Yield: 8 servings.***

Tall Cedars Bed & Breakfast

Dwyla and Ed Beglaw
720 Robinson Street
Coquitlam, British Columbia
V3J 4G1
Tel/Fax: (604) 936-6016
E-mail: tallcedars_bnb@bc.sympatico.ca
www/bbcanada.com/2490.html
$$

ABOUT THE B&B

For Dwyla and Ed Beglaw, operating a B&B is not just a business, it's an adventure! Seasoned B&B innkeepers, for over 11 years they have welcomed guests from all over the world to their gracious family home located 20 minutes from Vancouver. Tall fir and cedar trees surround the house, and, in summer, the walkway is bordered with beautiful flower beds. Guest rooms have queen or twin beds, ceiling fans, and comfy eiderdowns. Guests can choose from a full or continental breakfast. Tall Cedars is close to Simon Fraser University and Burrard Inlet and is minutes from serene Como Lake — ideal for strolling, jogging, and fishing — Rocky Point Park — a great spot for rollerblading, cycling, and boating — shops, movie theaters, and a restaurant that serves the best fish and chips this side of England. At the end of the day, guests can wind down on the lit, covered flower garden balcony (where smoking is permitted) and enjoy refreshments.

SEASON

all year

ACCOMMODATIONS

1 room with private bath;
2 rooms with shared bath

The Old Rectory Bed & Breakfast

Carol and Ron Buckley
1519 Highway 358, RR #1
Port Williams, Nova Scotia B0P 1T0
Tel: (902) 542-1815
Fax: (902) 542-2346
E-mail: orectory@fox.nstn.ca
www.bbcanada.com/568.html
$$

ABOUT THE B&B

Share the warmth of this restored Victorian former rectory with its antiques, unique architecture, and three-acre operating apple orchard and gardens. Choose from one of three spacious bedrooms — one with private half-bath, and the others with shared full bath. Access to an additional bath is on the main floor. Your hosts are Ron, a retired geologist with knowledge of local "rock hounding" areas, and physiotherapist Carol, who enjoys preparing delicious hot breakfasts with homemade breads and preserves. Go on a three-hour mineral/fossil tour with Ron (for an additional fee), or visit with other guests over evening tea. The Old Rectory is close to historic Prescott House, Grand Pré Park, hiking trails, birdwatching areas, cultural activities (including the Atlantic Theatre Festival), and many fine restaurants.

SEASON

May 1 – October 31

ACCOMMODATIONS

1 room with private half-bath;
2 rooms with shared bath

Apple-Cinnamon Molasses Pancakes

"Molasses has been used locally as a sweetener since the days of trade with the West Indies. It adds a unique flavor to these pancakes."
— Carol Buckley

¾ cup all-purpose flour
¾ cup whole wheat flour
3 teaspoons baking powder
½ teaspoon baking soda
½ teaspoon ground cinnamon
½ teaspoon salt
2 large apples, cored and peeled
1¼ cups sweet or sour milk
1 egg
¼ cup molasses

Hot applesauce
Maple syrup

Mix together the all-purpose flour, whole wheat flour, baking powder, baking soda, cinnamon, and salt. Grate the apples into the flour mixture. In a separate bowl, beat together the milk, egg, and molasses. Add the milk mixture to the flour mixture, and stir just until smooth (don't over-mix). Cook about ¼ cup batter per pancake on a hot griddle. Serve with hot applesauce and maple syrup. ***Yield: 10 medium-sized pancakes.***

Avocado and Chicken Crêpes

8 crêpes (see recipe on page 231)
5 tablespoons butter or margarine
5 tablespoons all-purpose flour
1 cup milk
¾ cup chicken broth
¼ cup dry white wine
½ cup grated mozzarella cheese
3 tablespoons chopped parsley
1 teaspoon salt
½ teaspoon Worcestershire sauce
¼ teaspoon pepper
1½ cups cooked diced chicken
¼ cup sliced black olives

8 – 12 avocado slices
Grated mozzarella cheese
Paprika

Preheat the oven to 350°F. Prepare the crêpes. Melt the butter in a saucepan, and stir in the flour. Add the milk, broth, and wine. Cook, stirring constantly, until the sauce is thick and smooth. Add the cheese, and stir until melted. Add the parsley, salt, Worcestershire sauce, and pepper. Combine the chicken and olives in a bowl. Mix in 1 cup of the cheese sauce. Divide the chicken mixture evenly among the crêpes, and roll them up. Place the crêpes seam-side down in a single layer in a greased shallow baking dish. Bake, uncovered, for 15 – 20 minutes or until very hot and lightly browned on top. Before serving, top each crêpe with avocado slices, and pour the remaining cheese sauce over the crêpes. Sprinkle them with mozzarella cheese, and dust with paprika. If you wish, garnish the plates with extra slices of avocado. ***Yield: 4 servings.***

Caron House (1837)

Mary and Mike Caron
PO Box 143
Williamstown, Ontario K0C 2J0
Tel: (613) 347-7338
$$

ABOUT THE B&B

Caron House (1837) is a romantic historic brick home located in the quaint village of Williamstown (established in 1784). Beautifully decorated and furnished with antiques, the house has many of its original features — working fireplaces, inside shutters, tin ceilings, and wide pine floorboards. The upstairs is reserved for guests only. Two rooms with shared bath are individually decorated with Laura Ashley wallpaper, antique linens, hooked rugs, quilts, and collectibles. Guests can relax in the Keeping Room (a colonial term for "gathering place") or in the living room. A candlelit full gourmet breakfast — accompanied by classical music — is served in the dining room graced by fine china, silverware, and crystal. Outside, you'll marvel at the herb and Victorian gardens, relax on the antique wicker furniture on the back veranda, and enjoy the lovely yards, complete with trellis, brick patio, and gazebo. Caron House is one hour's drive from either Montréal or Ottawa; nearby attractions include Upper Canada Village, artisans' studios, a bird sanctuary, tennis courts, places to go cycling, and good restaurants. Mary and Mike enjoy traveling, antique hunting, cooking, gardening, and history.

SEASON

all year

ACCOMMODATIONS

2 rooms with shared bath

Sanford House Bed & Breakfast

Elizabeth and Charlie Le Ber
PO Box 1825, 20 Platt Street
Brighton, Ontario K0K 1H0
Tel/Fax: (613) 475-3930
$$

ABOUT THE B&B

Sitting majestically on the crest of a hill, Sanford House Bed & Breakfast is a red-brick Victorian home close to Main Street in the friendly town of Brighton. This century-old home with turret and covered veranda has offstreet parking, a separate guest entrance, and three large, bright, and comfortable air conditioned bedrooms. Guests can choose to relax in the round turret room; in the lounge with television, VCR, videos, board games, and books; in the spacious, bright Victorian parlor; or on the veranda. Delicious home-baked breakfasts, often spotlighting apples grown in nearby orchards, are served in the guest dining room. It's a short drive to beautiful Presqu'ile Provincial Park's sandy beaches, nature trails, fine birdwatching areas, and marsh boardwalk. If antique hunting is a passion, there are numerous antique shops right in Brighton and in the surrounding area. Applefest, a celebration of the harvest in September, is a particularly lovely time to visit the area. When not entertaining their B&B guests, Elizabeth and Charlie enjoy cycling and nature walks.

SEASON

all year

ACCOMMODATIONS

3 rooms with shared bath

Baked French Toast à l'Orange

6 slices bread, 1" thick and crusts removed
8 eggs
2 cups milk
2 tablespoons orange juice concentrate

Orange marmalade sauce:
½ cup orange marmalade
¼ cup butter

Cooked sliced bacon

Cut each bread slice in half diagonally. Allow the bread to dry out for a few hours by standing the slices on their edges. Place the bread flat in a shallow glass 13 x 9" dish. Stir together the egg, milk, and orange juice concentrate until smooth. Pour the egg mixture over the bread. Turn the bread over once. Cover and refrigerate until the liquid is absorbed (or overnight). Preheat the oven to 350°F. Butter another 13 x 9" baking dish, and place the bread flat inside. Bake 35 minutes. For the sauce, combine the marmalade and butter, and heat in a saucepan or in the microwave until hot. Stir well to blend. Pour the sauce over the baked French toast, and serve immediately with cooked sliced bacon. ***Yield: 4 – 6 servings.***

Banana-Oatmeal Waffles

1 cup all-purpose flour
1 cup large-flake rolled oats
3 tablespoons brown sugar
1 tablespoon baking powder
½ teaspoon baking soda
½ teaspoon ground cinnamon
Freshly grated nutmeg
1½ cups buttermilk
2 eggs
2 bananas, sliced
¼ cup melted unsalted butter

Sliced bananas
Warm maple syrup
Sour cream (optional)
Confectioners' sugar

Preheat a waffle iron. Combine the flour, oats, brown sugar, baking powder, baking soda, cinnamon, and a pinch of freshly grated nutmeg in a large bowl. Whisk the buttermilk and eggs together in a separate bowl. Stir the buttermilk mixture into the flour mixture (don't overmix). Stir in the bananas and melted butter. Bake the waffles according to the manufacturer's directions. Transfer them to serving plates, and top with sliced bananas, warm maple syrup, and a dollop of optional sour cream. Dust with confectioners' sugar. ***Yield: 8 waffles.***

Mecklenburgh Inn

Suzi Fraser
78 Queen Street
Chester, Nova Scotia B0J 1J0
Tel/Fax: (902) 275-4638
www.destination-ns.com/
lighthouse/mecklenburgh
$$

ABOUT THE B&B

Constructed by shipwrights in 1890, Mecklenburgh Inn is located in the heart of seaside Chester, which has catered to summer visitors and sailing enthusiasts for over 150 years. Sleep in the spacious and comfortably appointed bedrooms filled with period furniture and other interesting objects Suzi has collected over the years, then enjoy a delicious breakfast while you plan the day ahead. You might wander the historic village streets, stopping to watch the yacht races on Mahone Bay, or browse through craft shops and boutiques. Or, maybe a sailboat ride, bicycle ride, or game of golf or tennis would be more your style. Later, relax on the balcony while the sun sets over the western shore of the bay and village activity lulls. You might consider an evening meal at one of the excellent restaurants in the area or catch a play at the Chester Playhouse. At the end of the day, the living room is the perfect place to wind down chatting by the fire or perusing travel books and magazines.

SEASON

May 24 – November 7

ACCOMMODATIONS

4 rooms with shared baths

Les Trois Érables

Madeleine and Jacques Mercier
PO Box 852, RR #2
Wakefield, Québec J0X 3G0
Tel: (819) 459-1118
$$

ABOUT THE B&B

Nestled among gentle rolling hills on the banks of the Gatineau River, the historic village of Wakefield is a gateway to beautiful Gatineau Park where you can find ample opportunities for hiking, skiing, or less arduous nature walks — especially beautiful in fall foliage season. Less than a half hour's drive takes you to the heart of Canada's national capital, Ottawa. Les Trois Érables was built at the turn of the century and was the home and office of three generations of village doctors until its transformation to a B&B in 1988. Rooms are tastefully decorated in soft colors and furnished for comfort and convenience. The sumptuous breakfasts attest to the fact that Madeleine loves to cook. Local restaurants, sports outfitters, and boutiques abound.

SEASON

all year

ACCOMMODATIONS

4 rooms with private baths

Blueberry-Stuffed French Toast

12 slices home-style white bread, crusts removed and slices cut into 1" cubes
2 (8-ounce) packages cold cream cheese, cut into 1" cubes
1 cup fresh blueberries
12 eggs
2 cups milk
⅓ cup maple syrup

Sauce:
1 cup sugar
2 tablespoons cornstarch
1 cup water
1 cup fresh blueberries
1 tablespoon butter

Arrange half the bread cubes in a buttered 13 x 9" glass baking dish. Scatter the cream cheese cubes over the bread, and sprinkle the blueberries over the cream cheese. Arrange the remaining bread cubes over the blueberries. In a large bowl, whisk together the eggs, milk, and syrup. Pour the egg mixture evenly over the bread mixture. Cover the dish with tin foil, and refrigerate overnight. In the morning, remove the bread mixture from the refrigerator, and let stand 45 minutes.

(continued on next page)

Preheat the oven to 350°F. Bake the bread mixture, covered, for 30 minutes. Remove the foil, and bake 30 minutes more or until the French toast is puffed and golden.

To prepare the sauce, stir together the sugar, cornstarch, and water in a small saucepan. Cook over moderately high heat, stirring occasionally, for 5 minutes or until the sugar mixture has thickened. Stir in the blueberries and simmer, stirring occasionally, for 10 minutes or until the berries have burst. Add the butter, and stir the sauce until the butter has melted. Serve the sauce hot over the blueberry-stuffed French toast.
Yield: 6 – 8 servings.

The Green Door Bed & Breakfast

Doloris Paquin
PO Box 335, 376 Berford Street
Wiarton, Ontario N0H 2T0
Tel: (519) 534-4710
$ – $$

ABOUT THE B&B

"Completely comfortable, wonderfully welcoming," is how one recent guest described The Green Door. Built at the turn of the century, this red-brick, stately, restored Victorian house is situated on Wiarton's main street and is within a few minutes' walk of shops and restaurants. The main floor has a dining room and a charming and spacious living room with bay windows. Up the wooden staircase are three guest bedrooms, two with double beds and one with two single beds, as well as a large guest bathroom. The high ceilings and spacious rooms lend an airy feeling to this B&B with all the comforts and coziness of home. Outside, enjoy the large garden, maple-shaded deck, and barbecue facilities.

SEASON

all year

ACCOMMODATIONS

1 room with private bath;
2 rooms with shared bath

Bruce Trail Breakfast Pancakes

"These pancakes are named for the celebrated hiking trail on the Bruce Peninsula, just a short distance away." — Doloris Paquin

1¾ cups milk
½ cup quick-cooking rolled oats
1 cup all-purpose flour
¾ cup whole wheat flour
2 tablespoons sugar
1 tablespoon baking powder
½ teaspoon ground cinnamon
½ teaspoon salt
2 eggs
2 tablespoons vegetable oil
2 teaspoons vanilla

Combine the milk and oats, and let stand 5 minutes. Mix together the all-purpose flour, whole wheat flour, sugar, baking powder, cinnamon, and salt in a large bowl. Beat the eggs, oil, and vanilla into the oats mixture with a whisk just until blended. Stir the egg mixture into the flour mixture just until the dry ingredients are moistened (don't worry about lumps). Lightly grease a skillet, and place it on medium heat. Using about ⅓ cup batter for each one, cook the pancakes until bubbles form on the surface. Turn them, and brown on the other side. ***Yield: 8 medium-sized pancakes.***

Cheddar and Bacon Crêpes

2 eggs
⅔ cup milk
½ cup all-purpose flour
¼ teaspoon salt
1 teaspoon vegetable oil
¾ cup grated sharp cheddar cheese
18 slices bacon, cooked

Combine the eggs, milk, flour, and salt in an electric mixer. Heat a 6" crêpe pan, and pour in the oil. Pour in enough batter to thinly coat the bottom of the pan. When the underside of the crêpe is brown and the edges begin to curl, flip the crêpe and brown the other side. If the crêpes begin to stick, add more oil to the pan. Place 2 tablespoons of the cheddar across the middle of the crêpe. Fold the crêpe over, and top with 3 slices of bacon. Repeat with the remaining ingredients. Serve immediately. ***Yield: 6 servings.***

Marshlands Inn

Diane and Peter Weedon
55 Bridge Street
Sackville, New Brunswick E4L 3N8
Tel: (506) 536-0170
Fax: (506) 536-0721
E-mail: marshlds@nbnet.nb.ca
$$

ABOUT THE B&B

In operation for over 60 years, Marshlands Inn was built in 1854 by William Crane as a wedding gift for his daughter. Crane, a man of some wealth, was a merchant and ship builder and is believed to be the financier of Samuel Cunard's first steamship. Over the years, the inn has been the stopping place of many visiting celebrities, including the Queen of England. The front lawns are shaded by the oldest white birch trees in Atlantic Canada, while the rhododendron in the front flower bed dates back almost 100 years. Surrounding the inn are eight acres of land, home to pheasants, ducks, muskrats, and songbirds. Fireplaces, easy chairs, and art grace the parlors. Guest rooms are furnished with antiques, and the bathrooms in the main house have claw-footed bathtubs. Marshlands Inn's excellent dining room has been cited in Anne Hardy's Where to Eat in Canada *for more than 25 consecutive years. While in Sackville, you can stroll along the boardwalk in the Waterfowl Park, walk the campus of Mount Allison University, or visit the Sackville Harness Shop for handmade horse leathers.*

SEASON

all year

ACCOMMODATIONS

18 rooms with private baths

Caron House (1837)

Mary and Mike Caron
PO Box 143
Williamstown, Ontario K0C 2J0
Tel: (613) 347-7338
$$

ABOUT THE B&B

Caron House (1837) is a romantic historic brick home located in the quaint village of Williamstown (established in 1784). Beautifully decorated and furnished with antiques, the house has many of its original features — working fireplaces, inside shutters, tin ceilings, and wide pine floorboards. The upstairs is reserved for guests only. Two rooms with shared bath are individually decorated with Laura Ashley wallpaper, antique linens, hooked rugs, quilts, and collectibles. Guests can relax in the Keeping Room (a colonial term for "gathering place") or in the living room. A candlelit full gourmet breakfast — accompanied by classical music — is served in the dining room graced by fine china, silverware, and crystal. Outside, you'll marvel at the herb and Victorian gardens, relax on the antique wicker furniture on the back veranda, and enjoy the lovely yards, complete with trellis, brick patio, and gazebo. Caron House is one hour's drive from either Montréal or Ottawa; nearby attractions include Upper Canada Village, artisans' studios, a bird sanctuary, tennis courts, places to go cycling, and good restaurants. Mary and Mike enjoy traveling, antique hunting, cooking, gardening, and history.

SEASON

all year

ACCOMMODATIONS

2 rooms with shared bath

Cherry Breakfast Puff Pancakes

Butter
1 egg
⅓ cup all-purpose flour
⅓ cup milk
Ground nutmeg

Cherry pie filling, heated
Confectioners' sugar
Warmed maple syrup

Preheat the oven to 400°F. Place a pat of butter in each of 2 (5½ x 3½") casserole dishes, and put the dishes in the oven until the butter has melted. Combine the egg, flour, milk, and a pinch of nutmeg, and mix slightly. Pour equal amounts of the batter into each dish, and return them to the oven for about 15 – 20 minutes, until the pancakes are puffed and golden. Pour heated cherry pie filling (or filling of your choice) into the center of each puff, and top with confectioners' sugar. Serve with warmed maple syrup. ***Yield: 2 puff pancakes.***

Dutch Cinnamon-Apple Pancake

"This spectacular-looking dish puffs up high around the edges to the delight of hungry guests." — Marj Wilkie

⅓ cup brown sugar
¼ cup butter
2 teaspoons ground cinnamon
1 Granny Smith or Golden Delicious apple, peeled, cored, and thinly sliced
4 eggs
¾ cup milk
¾ cup all-purpose flour
Salt

Confectioners' sugar
Maple syrup, orange-ginger sauce (see recipe on page 320), jam, or topping of your choice

Preheat the oven to 425°F. Put the brown sugar, butter, and cinnamon into a 10" ovenproof skillet, and heat in the oven about 6 minutes until very hot and bubbly (don't burn). Add the apple slices. Return the skillet to the oven for 3 minutes. Meanwhile, beat together the eggs, milk, flour, and a pinch of salt. Slowly pour the egg mixture over the apples, distributing the batter evenly. Return the skillet to the oven for 25 minutes or until the pancake has browned and puffed high at the sides. Cut it into 6, and sprinkle with confectioners' sugar. Serve with maple syrup, orange-ginger sauce, jam, or a topping of your choice.
Tip: This dish is even more impressive when the batter is baked in 6 oval ramekins. ***Yield: 6 servings.***

The Lookout at Schooner Cove

Marj and Herb Wilkie
3381 Dolphin Drive
Nanoose Bay, British Columbia
V9P 9H7
Tel/Fax: (250) 468-9796
www.pixsell.bc.ca/bb/1169.htm
$$

ABOUT THE B&B

Situated halfway between Victoria and Tofino on unspoiled Vancouver Island, this West Coast contemporary cedar home stands in a woodsy setting of rocks and tall evergreens. The wrap-around deck affords a 180-degree view of the Strait of Georgia and the majestic mountains beyond. Relax and savor this "little bit of heaven" or hike, golf, kayak, sail, fish, or sightsee. Take a day trip to the wild western shore of the island and Pacific Rim National Park or head south to charming Victoria. The vacation suite will accommodate four people and, with its private entrance and deck and fully equipped kitchen, makes a popular headquarters for an island stay. Hearty breakfasts are served in the dining room overlooking the ocean. After running a store in New York's Catskill Mountains for 17 years, Marj (from Australia) and Herb (from the US) established The Lookout in 1988 and enjoy helping their guests have a memorable stay.

SEASON

May – October
(or by arrangement)

ACCOMMODATIONS

1 vacation suite with private bath;
1 room with private bath;
1 room with shared bath

Fairmount Bed and Breakfast

Susan Proven
Box 633
Minnedosa, Manitoba R0J 1E0
Tel/Fax: (204) 874-2165
$$

ABOUT THE B&B

Fairmount Bed and Breakfast is located between Minnedosa and Riding Mountain National Park. The hills, valleys, and sloughs (prairie water holes) make the area one of the most beautiful in the province. From the dining room and all three guest rooms, you can see geese and ducks on the nearby slough and at night hear the sounds of frogs and other creatures. Relax watching the sheep graze in the pastures, or take a short hike to where the deep ruts made by Red River carts that followed the Carlton Trail can still be seen. The 1914 two-and-a-half-story house, which is crowned by lightning rods, features stained glass windows and maple flooring and is furnished in early Canadiana. A visit to Fairmount is like a trip back in time, especially when it comes to meals. Host Susan Proven specializes in food made from scratch with locally produced farm products. When she's not in the kitchen, in the garden, or out with the sheep, Susan produces radio documentaries drawing inspiration from the people of the countryside.

SEASON

all year

ACCOMMODATIONS

3 rooms with shared bath

Flax Seed Waffles

"Waffles usually have more fat than pancakes so they won't stick. This recipe substitutes flax seed for some of the oil, which produces a unique nutty flavor and light texture. Rich in Omega-3 fatty acids, flax seed grows well in the fertile land surrounding the B&B."
— Susan Proven

2 eggs, separated
⅔ cup flax seed*
1¾ cups milk
1 tablespoon vegetable oil
1 cup all-purpose flour
2 tablespoons sugar
1 tablespoon baking powder
1 teaspoon salt

**Note: Flax seed can be purchased in health food stores.*

Beat the egg whites until they stand in soft peaks; set aside. Place the flax seed in a blender or food processor, grind the seed until it is reduced to a fine powder, and place in a bowl. Add the egg yolks, milk, and oil, and mix. In another bowl, combine the flour, sugar, baking powder, and salt. Add the flax mixture, and blend until smooth. Fold in the egg whites. Cook the batter according to the waffle iron manufacturer's directions. ***Yield: 4 waffles.***

French Toast Raphael

6 cups white bread cubes (1 x 1") with crusts removed
6 ounces cream cheese, cut into small cubes
6 eggs, well beaten
1 cup milk
⅓ cup dark maple syrup
½ teaspoon ground cinnamon

Cooked bacon or pork breakfast sausage

Place half of the bread cubes in a greased 8 x 8" pan. Dot with the cream cheese, and cover with the remaining bread. Combine the eggs, milk, maple syrup, and cinnamon, and pour over the bread. Cover with plastic wrap, and refrigerate overnight. In the morning, remove the dish from the refrigerator, and let stand 45 minutes. Preheat the oven to 375°F, and bake 45 minutes until the French toast is puffy and golden. Serve immediately with cooked bacon or sausage. ***Yield: 4 servings.***

Dorrington Bed & Breakfast

Pat Gray
13851 19A Avenue
White Rock, British Columbia
V4A 9M2
Tel: (604) 535-4408
Fax: (604) 535-4409
www.bbcanada.com/508.html
$$ – $$$

ABOUT THE B&B

A luxurious escape a short drive from Vancouver, Dorrington is a wonderful base for exploring the city and its surrounding area. Each guest room has a different theme: The Victorian is graced by a double four-poster bed and period decor; The St. Andrews has a unique queen bed hewn from maple branches, and contains many original souvenirs of this famous Scottish golf links; The Windsor is 700 square feet of luxury with a brass, canopied queen bed, fireplace, sitting area, and marble bathroom with a double Jacuzzi tub. A full breakfast is served in the Hunt Salon or on the patio overlooking the gardens, tennis court, pond, and outside hot tub. White Rock beach with its promenade and fine eateries is three minutes away, while ferries to Victoria and the Gulf Islands are 30 minutes away. If you wish, you can use Dorrington's side-by-side tandem bike for a picnic in one of the many nearby heritage forests. Pat is the director of marketing for a calendar manufacturer/distributor.

SEASON

all year

ACCOMMODATIONS

3 rooms (including 1 suite) with private baths

Barbara Ann's Bed 'n Breakfast Vacation Farm

Barbara Ann and Ted Witzaney
PO Box 156
Denzil, Saskatchewan S0L 0S0
Tel: (306) 358-4814
$

ABOUT THE B&B

Specially geared for families, Barbara Ann's B&B is located on the Witzaney farm, where they've been raising crops and hogs since 1911. The petting zoo includes traditional farm animals and more exotic ones, including a llama and Muscovy ducks. Barbara Ann's breakfast (and other meals served on request) feature farm-fresh milk, eggs, cheese, and vegetables; home-baked goods, such as buns, pies, and cookies; homemade jams, jellies, relishes, and pickles; and pork raised on the farm. Homemade sausages are the specialty of the house. Picnic and barbecue facilities, a sandbox and swing set, a horseshoe pit, lawn bowling and badminton equipment, and an 18-hole miniature golf course are all on the property. When not tending to guests, Barbara Ann enjoys sewing and craft making, while Ted enjoys woodworking. Both like to spend time with their 10 grandchildren. Denzil is about a half-hour drive west of Unity, Saskatchewan, and a 45-minute drive east of Provost, Alberta.

SEASON

all year

ACCOMMODATIONS

2 rooms with shared bath

French Toast with Apricot Sauce

"If we have fresh cream on hand, I like to serve it along with this dish." — Barbara Ann Witzaney

2 eggs
½ cup milk
4 tablespoons sugar
¼ teaspoon vanilla
8-ounce can apricots in syrup
Juice of ½ lemon
8 slices white bread, each cut in half
2 – 4 tablespoons butter or margarine

Whisk the eggs with the milk, then stir in the sugar and vanilla; set aside. Purée the apricots and their syrup in a blender or food processor. Stir in the lemon juice, and heat the purée over moderate heat; keep warm. Dip the bread in the egg mixture, and fry on both sides in butter until golden brown. Arrange the French toast slices on warmed plates, and pour apricot sauce over them. Serve immediately. ***Yield: 4 servings.***

French Toast with Honey-Yogurt Sauce

Honey-yogurt sauce:
¼ cup low-fat plain yogurt
1 teaspoon honey

French toast:
1 egg
⅓ cup skim milk
½ teaspoon orange zest
¼ teaspoon vanilla
Salt
4 slices white or whole wheat bread
½ teaspoon margarine

Ground nutmeg

In a small bowl, combine the yogurt and honey; set aside. In a shallow bowl, beat together the egg, milk, orange zest, vanilla, and a pinch of salt. Dip each bread slice into the egg mixture, coating each side well. In a large nonstick skillet, melt the margarine over medium heat. Cook the bread for 2 minutes per side or until golden brown. Sprinkle with nutmeg, and serve with honey-yogurt sauce. ***Yield: 2 servings.***

Gwenmar Guest Home

Joy and Keith Smith
PO Box 59, RR #3
Brandon, Manitoba R7A 5Y3
Tel: (204) 728-7339
Fax: (204) 728-7336
E-mail: smithj@docker.com
$

ABOUT THE B&B

Space, privacy, and quiet is what you'll find at Gwenmar. This 1914 heritage home was the summer retreat of Manitoba's former Lieutenant Governor (from 1929 to 1934), J.D. McGregor, who named the estate after his daughter Gwen. Since 1980, Joy and Keith Smith have welcomed B&B guests to this relaxing countryside escape. Gwenmar breakfasts are memorable, particularly the home-baked bread and jams and jellies made from Gwenmar's wild berries. Joy, a home economist, is an avid gardener and a major contributor to Canada's heritage seed program, while Keith is a retired agrologist involved in overseas projects. In the summer, you can visit with them on the big, shaded veranda or go for walks on the beautiful grounds or in the valley. In the winter, sit by the fire or go cross-country skiing. Gwenmar is also a short drive from downtown Brandon, with shopping, restaurants, a water-slide, an air museum, golf courses, and the childhood home of Stone Angel *author Margaret Laurence.*

SEASON

all year

ACCOMMODATIONS

2 rooms with private baths;
2 rooms with shared bath

Fried Porridge Pancakes

"We always hope for leftovers when these are served. They go very well as a snack with mid-morning coffee." — Sheila Jackson

2¼ cups quick-cooking rolled oats
3 cups milk
3 eggs
⅓ cup butter, melted
1½ tablespoons brown sugar
1 teaspoon salt
1½ cups whole wheat flour
1½ tablespoons baking powder
1½ teaspoons ground cinnamon
¼ cup wheat germ

Yogurt and fruit, maple syrup, or jam

Preheat the oven to 250°F. Soak the oats in the milk for 10 – 15 minutes; set aside. Beat the eggs, and add the butter, brown sugar, and salt. In a separate bowl, sift the flour, baking powder, and cinnamon together, then add the wheat germ. Stir the oat mixture and the flour mixture into the egg mixture. Let stand 5 – 10 minutes. Ladle the batter onto a hot, lightly greased griddle, and cook the pancakes, turning them once when bubbles appear and the underside is golden. Keep the pancakes warm in the oven, covered with a clean cloth, until all the batter has been cooked. Serve them hot with yogurt and fruit or maple syrup, or cold with jam. ***Yield: 4 large- or 8 small-sized pancakes.***

Seaboard Bed & Breakfast

Sheila and Barrie Jackson
2629 Crowell Road
East Lawrencetown, Nova Scotia
B2Z 1P4
Tel: (800) SEA-6566 or
(902) 827-3747
$ – $$

ABOUT THE B&B

Seaboard Bed & Breakfast at Lawrencetown Beach is a renovated farmhouse built around 1917. Now the home of Sheila and Barrie Jackson, this large white house across the road from Porter's Lake and the Atlantic Ocean has been an area landmark for many years. Local attractions include international-caliber surfing from a sand beach; birdwatching from the shore or nearby hills, at a local marsh, or along walking trails; and fishing, canoeing, windsurfing, and — in season — skating and cross-country skiing. Seaboard is only 35 minutes from Halifax airport and 30 minutes from the cities of Halifax and Dartmouth, where you can enjoy the casino, restaurants, theaters, and special events. Sheila and Barrie are both keen Scottish country dancers and have aptly named their guest rooms after favorite dances. There are two semi-private bathrooms for the exclusive use of guests. A varied and full home-cooked breakfast is served in the sunny dining room overlooking the lake and sea, while tea and coffee are offered in the lounge or on the porch.

SEASON

all year

ACCOMMODATIONS

3 rooms with shared baths

Fruit Pancakes

"A generous helping of Canadian bacon and any garnish you like will make this one of your favorites." — Isabel Christie

1 tablespoon butter
1 cup sugar
2 eggs, well beaten
2 cups all-purpose flour
2 teaspoons baking powder
Salt
½ – ¾ cup milk
1 teaspoon vanilla
Fresh fruit

Hot applesauce or apple juice thickened with cornstarch
Ground cinnamon

Cream the butter and sugar. Add the eggs, and combine. In a separate bowl, combine the flour, baking powder, and salt, and add to the egg mixture alternately with the milk. Add the vanilla, and mix briefly. Using about ¼ cup batter, fry on a hot griddle or in a crêpe pan. Top the pancakes or fill the crêpes with any fruit in season (strawberries or blueberries in summer, apples in winter). Serve with hot applesauce or apple juice thickened with cornstarch, and sprinkle cinnamon on top. *Yield: 12 pancakes.*

Riverdell Estate

Clare and Isabel Christie
68 Ross Road
Dartmouth, Nova Scotia B2Z 1B4
Tel/Fax: (902) 434-7880
$$ – $$$

ABOUT THE B&B

Nestled among the trees beside a babbling brook, Riverdell offers modern luxury with good, old-fashioned hospitality. Antiques, collectibles, and handmade quilts adorn this charming Cape Cod home. The large rooms with private or shared baths include two "special occasion" suites — both with a double whirlpool and one with a fireplace. There's lots of space to read, relax, or birdwatch from the sunny Florida Room where your homemade breakfast is served. All this is within minutes of the ocean beach, golf course, and Dartmouth and Halifax — two cities full of adventure. Whatever your leisure interests may be, your knowledgeable hosts Clare and Isabel will ensure you get the most out of your stay.

SEASON

all year

ACCOMMODATIONS

4 rooms with private baths;
2 rooms with shared baths

Cobble House Bed & Breakfast

Ingrid and Simon Vermegen
3105 Cameron-Taggart Road, RR #1
Cobble Hill, British Columbia
V0R 1L0
Tel/Fax: (250) 743-2672
E-mail: stay@cobble-house.com
www.cobble-house.com
$$

ABOUT THE B&B

Cobble House Bed & Breakfast is located on southeastern Vancouver Island, in a rural area with wineries and many recreational opportunities. Victoria and the world-famous Butchart Gardens are about an hour away, as is ferry access from Washington State and mainland British Columbia. The new home, which was designed and built by the hosts, is in a private 40-acre forest with a creek. The atmosphere is warm, welcoming, and relaxing. The very spacious and colorful Hummingbird, Jay, and Heron rooms are decorated with wicker and antiques. Your host Simon is a former executive chef and can prepare dinners for guests by prior arrangement. The family, which includes two beloved dogs, has lots of hobbies and interests — antique car restoration, miniature train collecting, reading, crafts, decorative painting, antique collecting — but never enough time to enjoy them all!

SEASON

all year

ACCOMMODATIONS

3 rooms with private baths

Grilled Sabayon Fruit Crêpes

"Our main goal is to serve a well-prepared, delicious breakfast geared to our guests' preferences." — Simon Vermegen

Crêpes:
1 cup milk
1 egg
1 cup all-purpose flour
Salt
Vegetable oil

Fruit filling:
2 medium apples, peeled, cored, and cubed
2 oranges, peeled and chopped
½ cup orange juice
Zest of 1 lemon
2 teaspoons cornstarch
1 cup fresh or thawed and drained frozen blueberries

Maple syrup sabayon:
3 eggs
2 teaspoons brandy
¼ cup maple syrup

20 raspberries for decoration

(continued on next page)

Mix the milk, egg, flour, and a pinch of salt together well, making sure no lumps remain. Heat a small, preferably Teflon-coated, frying pan. Put a little vegetable oil in the pan, and add one-quarter of the batter. Cook until the crêpe is golden brown. Repeat with the rest of the batter to make 4 crêpes.

For the filling, place the apple, orange, orange juice, and lemon zest in a saucepan, and bring to a quick boil. Add the cornstarch, turn the heat down to low, and add the blueberries. Keep the filling warm. Place a rack at the highest level in the oven, and turn on the broiler.

For the sabayon, combine the eggs, brandy, and maple syrup in a stainless steel bowl. Bring a saucepan of water to a boil, then turn the heat down to low. Place the bowl over the water, and beat the egg mixture with a whip until it is foamy and firm.

To serve, place each crêpe on an ovenproof plate, put some of the fruit filling in the crêpe, and fold it over the filling. Spoon some of the sabayon on top. Place the plates in the oven to brown the sabayon (this happens quite quickly — watch it!). When the sabayon has browned, remove the plates, and decorate the crêpes with the raspberries. ***Yield: 4 servings.***

Anna's Bed and Breakfast

Anna and Robert Doorenbos
204 Wolf Street
Thompson, Manitoba R8N 1J7
Tel: (204) 677-5075
$ – $$

ABOUT THE B&B

Visit Anna's Bed and Breakfast to experience what Canadian Dutch hospitality is all about. This adult-oriented and smoke-free B&B offers a private guest suite with its own entrance and parking space, two single beds, private bath, kitchenette, and den with TV and telephone. Anna enjoys cooking and will get your day off to a delicious start with a full breakfast served in the main dining room. Oriental meals are another specialty and, along with traditional meals, are available for an additional charge. The greenhouse, which is connected to the cozy and informal living room, opens onto the deck and lends a summer atmosphere to the home — even in the dead of winter! Thompson is the home base of travelers to fly-in fishing lodges and Churchill (Manitoba) and other northern communities. It also boasts the longest alpine ski season in Manitoba. Guest pick-up can be arranged as well as scenic touring by car. Your hosts Anna and Robert moved to Canada from Holland and have lived in Thompson since 1971. Robert, an award-winning visual artist, comes from Egypt and Anna from Indonesia.

SEASON

all year

ACCOMMODATIONS

1 suite with private bath

Heart-Healthy Buttermilk Pancakes

"Both my husband Robert and I are health conscious, so I've become well versed in heart-healthy cooking . . . without compromising taste. I developed this recipe from one I learned in Winnipeg from a cook in a coffee shop." — Anna Doorenbos

2 cups all-purpose flour
2 cups buttermilk
2 egg whites
2 tablespoons polyunsaturated vegetable oil, such as corn, sunflower, or canola oil
1 teaspoon baking powder
1 teaspoon baking soda
¼ – ½ teaspoon salt
Polyunsaturated vegetable oil or low-fat cooking spray for frying

Maple syrup, fruit syrup, or honey

Mix together the flour, buttermilk, egg whites, oil, baking powder, baking soda, and salt just enough to make a lumpy batter. Heat a skillet lightly greased with oil or cooking spray to medium, and ladle the batter onto the skillet. Turn the pancakes once when bubbles appear and the underside is golden. Serve the pancakes with maple syrup, fruit syrup, or honey. ***Tip:*** Try adding blueberries or slivers of apple to the batter. ***Yield: 16 pancakes.***

Henderson Hotcakes with Chokecherry Syrup

"While making chokecherry jelly one year, I made a mistake and the jelly didn't set. However, we tried the concoction on pancakes and it was a hit! I make the syrup from the chokecherries we pick in the surrounding bush." — Jeanette Henderson

2 cups all-purpose flour
½ cup bran, oat bran, or whole wheat flour
¼ cup sugar
2 tablespoons baking powder
1½ teaspoons salt
2 eggs, beaten
1¾ cups milk
¼ cup vegetable oil

Chokecherry syrup (recipe follows)

Combine the flour, bran, sugar, baking powder, and salt. In a separate bowl, combine the eggs, milk, and oil. Add the egg mixture to the flour mixture, and stir just until the dry ingredients are moistened (don't overmix). Using ¼ – ⅓ cup batter for each one, cook the pancakes on a greased griddle, turning them once when bubbles appear and the underside is golden. Top with chokecherry syrup. ***Yield: 12 – 16 pancakes.***

(continued on next page)

Henderson Hollow

Jeanette and Garry Henderson
RR #1
Austin, Manitoba R0H 0C0
Tel: (204) 466-2857
$

ABOUT THE B&B

A piece of heaven and a heavenly getaway, Henderson Hollow is a cozy country home set in beautiful, rolling, wooded hills. Simply relax on the large deck or in the screened sun porch surrounded by nature's beauty and abundant wildlife, or enjoy many indoor and outdoor activities (depending on the season). Full home-cooked meals include home-baked bread and cinnamon rolls, and dishes featuring garden-fresh fruits and vegetables. The house is filled with antiques and decorated with many homemade crafts for you to enjoy (or purchase, if you desire). Nearby points of interest include the Austin Agricultural Museum (largest in western Canada), Spruce Woods Provincial Park, Margaret Laurence Museum, and the Thomas Seton Centre. Your hosts' interests include golfing in summer at the many beautiful — and challenging! — golf courses nearby, and cross-country skiing in winter right from the back door.

SEASON

all year

ACCOMMODATIONS

1 room with private bath;
2 rooms with shared bath;
campground facilities

Chokecherry syrup:
8 cups sugar
6½ cups chokecherry juice (recipe follows)
1 cup cornstarch
1 cup water

Boil the sugar and chokecherry juice for 5 minutes. Dissolve the cornstarch in the water, and add to the chokecherry mixture. Boil 5 minutes, and seal in sterilized jars. ***Variation:*** You can substitute blueberries or pincherries for the chokecherries. ***Yield: About 9 cups.***

Chokecherry juice:
4 quarts chokecherries
2½ – 3 cups water

Simmer the chokecherries in the water for 15 minutes. Mash the chokecherries, place them in a cheesecloth bag, and allow the juice to drain from the pulp.

Lemon French Toast with Strawberry Sauce

12 slices Italian or French bread (don't use ends)
16-ounce jar lemon spread
6 eggs, beaten
½ cup milk
2 tablespoons butter or margarine

Strawberry sauce:
1-pound package frozen sliced strawberries in syrup, thawed
2 tablespoons cold water
2 teaspoons cornstarch

Spread 6 of the bread slices with lemon spread; cover with the remaining bread. In a shallow bowl, mix the eggs and milk. Dip each sandwich in the egg mixture (let it soak in a bit), and fry them in butter until golden. Meanwhile, heat the strawberries and syrup in a small saucepan. Mix the cold water with the cornstarch in a cup, and add to the strawberry mixture, stirring constantly until the sauce has thickened. To serve, slice each French toast sandwich in half diagonally, and spoon some sauce over the slices. ***Yield: 6 servings.***

Harbour House Bed & Breakfast Inn

Paula Franklin
615 Lakeshore Drive
Cold Lake, Alberta T9M 1A2
Tel: (403) 639-2337
$$ – $$$

ABOUT THE B&B

Built in 1989 to complement the Cold Lake Marina, Harbour House is patterned after the Old Coast Guard Station in Virginia Beach, Virginia. The house has the charm of old New England. Climb the stairs to the viewing tower for a panoramic view of Cold Lake, Alberta's seventh largest lake. Settle into one of 11 individually decorated rooms (most facing the lake), and rest assured of a comfortable night's sleep under feather duvets or hand-stitched quilts. Awake to a breathtaking sunrise over the lake and the aroma of the inn's famous sticky buns or other home-baked goods, served with fresh fruit specialties and juice. Nearby Cold Lake Provincial Park is home to many bird species. Harbour House is within walking distance of the lake, with its opportunities for fishing and boating. Nearby you can go mini-golfing and regular golfing, bowling, skiing, and browsing in antique and craft shops.

SEASON

all year

ACCOMMODATIONS

5 rooms with private baths;
6 rooms with shared baths

Courtney Leanne Bed and Breakfast

Louise Studer
3428 Dieppe Street
Saskatoon, Saskatchewan S7M 3S9
Tel: (306) 382-0444
$ – $$

ABOUT THE B&B

Courtney Leanne Bed and Breakfast is located on the west side of Saskatoon in a quiet neighborhood with large lots. Large, comfortable bedrooms are decorated with quilts and afghans, and homemade soaps are provided in the shared baths. Homemade jams, jellies, and muffins complement a full breakfast that, weather permitting, is served out on the deck overlooking the flower beds, pond, and creek. Situated close to golf courses, the city's downtown, a commuter rail station, and the John G. Diefenbaker Airport, Courtney Leanne offers a piano, billiard table, and display of local crafts on site and cross-country skiing nearby. In addition to running her B&B and meeting new people, hostess Louise Studer takes pleasure in gardening, interior design, and craft making.

SEASON

all year

ACCOMMODATIONS

3 rooms with shared baths

Mom's Dandelion Pancakes

4 eggs
2 cups milk
1½ cups all-purpose flour
4 teaspoons baking powder
1 heaping tablespoon sugar
½ teaspoon salt

Dandelion syrup (recipe follows)

Beat the eggs until light and fluffy. Add the milk, flour, baking powder, sugar, and salt, and mix well. Using ¼ – ½ cup batter for each one, cook the pancakes on a greased griddle, turning them once when bubbles appear and the underside is golden. Top with dandelion syrup. ***Yield: About 12 large pancakes.***

Dandelion syrup:
250 dandelion flowers*
Juice of 1 lemon
8 cups water
5 cups sugar

**Note: If picking dandelions in the wild, ensure that the area hasn't been sprayed with pesticides or fertilizer.*

(continued on next page)

Wash the dandelion flowers well, and place them in a large pot. Add the lemon juice and water and bring to a boil. Cover and simmer 60 minutes. Remove from the heat and let stand, covered, overnight. Strain and add the sugar to the dandelion liquid. Bring to a boil, reduce the heat, and simmer vigorously for 90 minutes or until the dandelion liquid has the consistency of maple syrup. Store any extra syrup in a sealed glass jar in the refrigerator. ***Tip:*** Make big batches of the syrup, and seal it in sterilized jars as you would preserves. Refrigerate open jars of syrup. ***Yield: 4 cups.***

Rowat's Waterside Bed and Breakfast

Marg and Jack Rowat
1397 Borland Road
Williams Lake, British Columbia
V2G 1M3
Tel: (604) 392-7395
$$

ABOUT THE B&B

Enjoy the tranquility of Rowat's Waterside B&B, located on Williams Lake right beside Scout Island Nature Center and Wildlife Reserve, in the heart of Cariboo Country. Walk the nature trails and return home to put your feet up and enjoy the view of the lake and marsh from the deck (this is a birdwatcher's paradise!). Rowat's Waterside is also within walking distance of places for mini-golf and parasailing, restaurants, and a stampede grounds, and a short drive away from downtown, golf and tennis facilities, and a sports arena. For something completely different, a one-and-a-half-hour drive will take you to the Ghost Town Museum of Barkerville, an old gold rush town. Rowat's accommodations include tastefully decorated rooms with private baths, a fireside guest lounge with TV, and air conditioning, purified water, and ample parking. Famous Cariboo Cowboy breakfasts are served in the dining room or deckside overlooking the marsh bird sanctuary. Hosts Marg and Jack are long-time residents of the Cariboo, and enjoy craft making, gardening, meeting people, and the great outdoors.

SEASON

all year

ACCOMMODATIONS

4 rooms with private baths

Mushroom Puff Pancake

1 cup sliced mushrooms
½ cup plus 1 tablespoon butter
4 green onions, chopped
6 medium eggs
¼ teaspoon salt
2 cups milk
1 cup all-purpose flour
¾ cup small-curd cottage cheese
¼ cup grated Parmesan cheese
1 teaspoon baking powder

½ cup grated sharp cheddar or mozzarella cheese
Salsa (see recipes on page 285 and page 295)

Preheat the oven to 450°F. Sauté the mushrooms on medium-low heat in 1 tablespoon butter, stirring often until just brown. Add the green onion, and cook 1 minute; set aside. Cut ½ cup butter into small pieces, put into a 10" cast-iron skillet or 13 x 9" baking dish, and place in the oven to melt the butter. Combine the eggs and salt in a bowl, and beat at high speed for 1 minute. Continue mixing while adding the milk, flour, cottage cheese, Parmesan cheese, and baking powder. Fold in the mushroom mixture. Pour the batter into the hot skillet, and bake 35 minutes until it has puffed and lightly browned. Let stand 5 minutes before cutting into 6. Sprinkle with grated cheese. Serve with salsa. ***Yield: 6 servings.***

Oatmeal Pancakes with Chunky Apple-Maple Sauce

"For this recipe, I use organically grown apples picked right from my garden." — Margaret Whetter

2 cups milk
1½ cups quick-cooking rolled oats
1 cup all-purpose flour
2 tablespoons sugar
2½ teaspoons baking powder
1 teaspoon salt
2 eggs, beaten
½ cup vegetable oil

Chunky apple-maple sauce:
6 apples, peeled, cored, and cut into chunks
½ cup maple syrup
1 tablespoon butter
1 teaspoon ground cinnamon
1 teaspoon lemon juice
Ground nutmeg

(continued on next page)

River Park Farm

Margaret Whetter
PO Box 310
Hartney, Manitoba R0M 0X0
Tel/Fax: (204) 858-2407
$$

ABOUT THE B&B

River Park Farm is a Victorian guest home built in 1910 on 10 acres of lawn and garden on the banks of the Souris River. Recently restored and redecorated, the heritage farmstead has a cozy and casual charm that often sparks memories of childhood visits to a grandma's home in the country. Guests can glimpse deer, raccoons, woodchucks, and many birds while breakfasting on the veranda or in the sun room. Grain elevators in the distance are silhouetted against beautiful prairie sunrises and sunsets. There are walking trails along the river, a nearby golf course and swimming pool, and canoes available either for professionally led or self-guided trips. Margaret Whetter, the owner and hostess, is a home economist who considers cooking an art form and an act of love. She finds the opportunity to share the stories of her guests' lives a great privilege.

SEASON

all year

ACCOMMODATIONS

4 rooms with shared baths;
7-bed attic room with private bath

Pour the milk over the oats, and let stand 5 minutes. Sift together the flour, sugar, baking powder, and salt. Add the flour mixture with the eggs and oil to the oat mixture, and stir just until the dry ingredients are moistened. Ladle small amounts of the batter onto a hot, greased skillet. Turn the pancakes when bubbles appear, and the undersides are golden brown. ***Tip:*** Don't hesitate to add goodies (apples, bananas, almond-flavored Saskatoon berries, or blueberries) to the batter.

For the sauce, combine the apple, maple syrup, butter, cinnamon, lemon juice, and a pinch of nutmeg in a saucepan. Bring the apple mixture to a boil, and cook until the apple is tender (6 – 8 minutes). Serve the hot sauce over the pancakes. For extra pizzazz, flame the sauce with 2 tablespoons rum. ***Tip:*** This topping is also great over vanilla ice cream. ***Yield: About 12 pancakes.***

Old-fashioned Waffles with Sauce

2 eggs, separated
1½ cups milk
2 tablespoons vegetable oil
2 cups all-purpose flour
4 teaspoons baking powder
1 tablespoon sugar
1 teaspoon salt

Sauce:
½ cup sugar
½ cup reserved waffle batter
2 cups scalded milk
1 teaspoon vanilla

Fresh fruit

Preheat a Belgian waffle maker. In a small bowl, beat the egg whites until stiff. Set aside. In a separate bowl, beat the egg yolks until creamy. Add the milk and oil to the egg yolks, and beat. In a separate bowl, combine the flour, baking powder, sugar, and salt, and gradually add to the milk mixture, beating until smooth. Gently fold in the egg whites. Reserve ½ cup batter for the sauce. Cook the batter according to the waffle iron manufacturer's directions.

For the sauce, combine the sugar and waffle batter. Add the sugar mixture to the milk (in a 4-cup bowl or measuring cup), and microwave for 2 minutes. Stir, microwave for 2 more minutes, and stir again. Continue to cook the sauce in the microwave, checking at 1-minute intervals, until it has a pudding-like consistency. Stir in the vanilla. Serve the sauce over the waffles, and garnish with fresh fruit. ***Yield: 5 – 6 waffles.***

Longview Bed & Breakfast

Charlene and Bob Siemens
PO Box 53
Fiske, Saskatchewan S0L 1C0
Tel: (306) 377-4786
$

ABOUT THE B&B

Peaceful surroundings, nature walks, farm-fresh meals, and barnyard animals are what you can expect at Longview, a working prairie farm southwest of Saskatoon. While listening to the howl of the coyote, fall asleep in your private guest cottage with its own bath and deck, then wake up to the crow of the rooster. Join hosts Charlene and Bob in their home for a hearty breakfast (and other meals if requested) — all of which take advantage of the produce, eggs, and meat from the farm. For those who want to really get away from it all, Longview offers a rustic cottage surrounded by a grove of trees and a choir of birds. A short drive away, you can find ancient petroglyphs and teepee rings. Your hosts especially welcome families, and enjoy visiting with their guests and sharing their love of the land.

SEASON

May – September

ACCOMMODATIONS

1 private cottage (3 rooms with shared bath);
1 rustic cabin

Orchard Lane Bed & Breakfast

Yvonne Parker
13324 Middle Bench Road
Oyama, British Columbia V4V 2B4
Tel: (250) 548-3809
$$

ABOUT THE B&B

Smack dab between Kelowna and Vernon is Orchard Lane, a newly built Victorian B&B nestled in a private orchard. From the sprawling veranda is a panoramic view of the beautiful central Okanagan Valley, while nearby Kalamalka and Wood Lakes reflect the hills and distant mountains. Inside, a welcoming foyer and spiral staircase lead to romantic and comfortable bedrooms. Visitors lounge in the formal living room with fireplace, stroll through the flower gardens or nearby orchard, admire the terraced landscaping framed by giant trees, or take a refreshing dip in the outdoor hot tub. Your hostess, Yvonne, serves a full gourmet breakfast — made from produce grown in her garden — in the formal dining room or on the veranda. You'll quickly discover that one of her favorite hobbies is making crafts, which are displayed throughout the house. Alpine skiing, fishing, biking, hiking, and other recreational choices await you and there are golf courses and beaches aplenty to explore. This area is truly a corner of paradise.

SEASON

all year

ACCOMMODATIONS

2 rooms with shared bath;
1 room with private bath

Orchard Lane Waffles

"This recipe can either be halved or made ahead and frozen."
— Yvonne Parker

1 pound butter (2 cups)
4½ cups brown sugar
12 eggs
½ cup evaporated skim milk
2 tablespoons vanilla
5 cups all-purpose flour
5 teaspoons baking powder
1 teaspoon salt

Whipped cream
Fresh fruit, strawberry jam, or maple syrup

In a large bowl, cream the butter and sugar. Add the eggs, milk, and vanilla, and mix. In a separate bowl, sift together the flour, baking powder, and salt. Add the flour mixture to the egg mixture, and combine. Cook the batter according to the waffle iron manufacturer's directions. Serve with some whipped cream and fresh fruit, strawberry jam, or maple syrup. ***Yield: About 36 waffles.***

Partridgeberry and Blueberry Pancakes

1 whole egg or 2 egg whites, well beaten
1 cup milk
3 tablespoons melted butter or margarine
1¼ cups all-purpose flour
2 teaspoons baking powder
2 tablespoons sugar
½ cup blueberries
½ cup partridgeberries*
Vegetable oil or butter

Maple syrup, heated partridgeberry jam, or berry sauce

**Note: Partridgeberries are also known as mountain cranberries or creeping cranberries. If necessary, substitute coarsely chopped plain cranberries for partridgeberries.*

Beat the egg with the milk and butter. Gradually stir in the flour, baking powder, and sugar (don't overmix). Fold in the berries. Fry ½ cup batter per pancake in oil, turning once when bubbles appear and the undersides are golden. Serve with maple syrup, heated partridgeberry jam, or berry sauce. ***Yield: 10 – 12 pancakes.***

Lake Crescent Inn

Evelyn and Bruce Warr
PO Box 69
Robert's Arm, Newfoundland
A0J 1R0
Tel: (709) 652-3067
Fax: (709) 652-3056
$

ABOUT THE B&B

When you think of Newfoundland, think peaceful lifestyle, clean air and rivers, and superb hospitality — all of which you'll find at Lake Crescent Inn. Walk along the quiet roads and beautiful beaches, visit fishers in the various communities along the route, or go iceberg or whale watching (in season). Boating trips can also be arranged, so why not give cod jigging or salmon fishing a try? Be sure to bring along your camera to capture the moment you reel in your first fish (you might even see "Cressie," the lake monster!). The inn offers four bedrooms and two bathrooms, one with whirlpool and shower. Breakfasts are a homemade feast of muffins, jams, jellies, and breads, and a special health-conscious menu is also available. A Jiggs dinner is served on Sundays from 5:00 pm, and a Fish Platter dinner is served on Fridays from 5:00 pm (other meals can be provided upon request).

SEASON

all year

ACCOMMODATIONS

4 rooms with shared baths

Linden House B&B

Elaine and Phil Landray
PO Box 1586, 389 Simcoe Street
Niagara-on-the-Lake, Ontario
L0S IJ0
Tel: (905) 468-3923
Fax: (905) 468-8946
E-mail: linden@niagara.com
$$$

ABOUT THE B&B

A warm welcome awaits you at Linden House, a new Cape Cod-style, air conditioned home with private guest wing featuring two rooms with queen beds and one room with twin/king bed. All rooms have private ensuite bathrooms. In the queen rooms are brass beds and cream wicker furniture, while the twin/king room highlights the nautical atmosphere with Cape Cod wicker. On the same level as the bedrooms is a guest lounge with television, VCR, games, and books, or you can choose to enjoy the garden or relax in the gazebo. Smoke-free Linden House offers convenient on-site parking and is located in the old town, just four short blocks from Queen Street with its shopping and theaters. In summer, enjoy water recreation on Lake Ontario or top-notch theater at the Shaw Festival. Your hosts, Elaine and Phil, serve such sumptuous breakfasts — featuring seasonal Niagara fruit — that their guests claim they don't need lunch!

SEASON

all year

ACCOMMODATIONS

3 rooms with private baths

Peaches and Cream French Toast

"A wonderful use for the world's best peaches, grown right here on the Niagara Peninsula." — Elaine Landray

Peach butter:
⅓ cup peach preserves
¼ cup softened butter

French toast:
3 eggs
3 tablespoons peach preserves
¾ cup half-and-half
6 slices French bread, each ½" thick
4 tablespoons butter

Confectioners' sugar
2 peaches, peeled, pitted, and sliced
Toasted almonds
Maple syrup

For the peach butter, beat the peach preserves and softened butter together with an electric mixer until fluffy. Chill the peach butter until ready to serve.

(continued on next page)

For the French toast, whisk together the eggs and the peach preserves in a small bowl. Beat in the half-and-half. Place the bread slices in a single layer in a 13 x 9" baking dish. Pour the egg mixture over the bread. Cover and refrigerate a few hours or overnight until most of the liquid is absorbed.

Melt 2 tablespoons of the butter in a large skillet. Add 3 of the bread slices, and cook over medium-high heat until browned, turning once. Remove them from the skillet, and keep warm. Repeat with the remaining bread slices and butter. Serve the French toast sprinkled with confectioners' sugar, and topped with peach slices, toasted almonds, maple syrup, and the peach butter (use a melon baller to serve it). ***Yield: 4 – 6 servings.***

River Park Farm

Margaret Whetter
PO Box 310
Hartney, Manitoba R0M 0X0
Tel/Fax: (204) 858-2407
$$

ABOUT THE B&B

River Park Farm is a Victorian guest home built in 1910 on 10 acres of lawn and garden on the banks of the Souris River. Recently restored and redecorated, the heritage farmstead has a cozy and casual charm that often sparks memories of childhood visits to a grandma's home in the country. Guests can glimpse deer, raccoons, woodchucks, and many birds while breakfasting on the veranda or in the sun room. Grain elevators in the distance are silhouetted against beautiful prairie sunrises and sunsets. There are walking trails along the river, a nearby golf course and swimming pool, and canoes available either for professionally led or self-guided trips. Margaret Whetter, the owner and hostess, is a home economist who considers cooking an art form and an act of love. She finds the opportunity to share the stories of her guests' lives a great privilege.

SEASON

all year

ACCOMMODATIONS

4 rooms with shared baths;
7-bed attic room with private bath

Saskatoon Breakfast Puff Pancakes

"I use Saskatoon berries because they are a wonderful almond-flavored wild berry found in the Prairies. However, any berry may be substituted." — Margaret Whetter

6 teaspoons butter
4 eggs
1 cup all-purpose flour
1 cup milk
Ground nutmeg
Saskatoon berry filling (recipe follows) or other berry filling

Confectioners' sugar

Preheat the oven to 425°F. Place 1 teaspoon of the butter in each cup of a 6-cup muffin pan (or in 6 individual ramekins), and put the pan in the oven until the butter is melted and the pan is hot. Mix together the eggs, flour, milk, and a pinch of nutmeg until slightly lumpy. Pour the batter into the hot muffin cups. Put 1 tablespoon of the berry filling into each muffin cup. Bake 20 minutes until the pancakes are puffed and golden. To serve, spoon some warm berry filling on each of 6 plates, place a puff pancake on the filling, and dust with confectioners' sugar. ***Yield: 6 puff pancakes.***

Saskatoon berry filling:
2 cups Saskatoon berries
¾ cup sugar
½ cup water
2 tablespoons cornstarch

Combine the berries, sugar, water, and cornstarch in a saucepan, and cook until the sauce thickens and becomes clear.

Sourdough Pancakes

"Sourdough pancakes are traditional Yukon breakfast fare during our February winter carnival (appropriately called Sourdough Rendezvous), New Year's Day, and on special occasions throughout the year." — Carla Pitzel

4 cups sourdough sponge batter*
1 egg
1 tablespoon sugar
1 tablespoon vegetable oil
1 teaspoon salt
1 teaspoon baking soda
1 tablespoon water

Maple syrup, or strawberries and whipped cream

**Note: In the evening (or at least 12 hours before using), make the sponge batter (see pages 88 – 89).*

Reserve 1 cup of the sponge batter, and return it to your starter container. Add the egg, sugar, oil, and salt to the remaining sponge, and beat with a fork to blend (if the batter seems a little stiff, add another egg). Just before cooking the pancakes, dissolve the baking soda in the water, then add the baking soda mixture to the batter. Using 3 tablespoons batter for each one, cook the pancakes on a hot, greased griddle. Turn them once when bubbles appear and the undersides are golden. Serve with maple syrup, or strawberries and whipped cream. ***Yield: 15 medium-sized pancakes.***

Hawkins House Bed & Breakfast

Carla Pitzel and Garry Umbrich
303 Hawkins Street
Whitehorse, Yukon Y1A 1X5
Tel: (867) 668-7638
Fax: (867) 668-7632
$$$$

ABOUT THE B&B

To stay at the Hawkins House Bed & Breakfast is to share a once-in-a-lifetime Yukon experience with your hosts Carla, Garry, and their two sons. Each guest room in this custom-built, luxury Victorian B&B highlights a different Yukon theme and features private bath and balcony, oak floor, bar sink, refrigerator, cable TV, and VCR. Guests can take a Jacuzzi soak in the Fleur de Lys Room, watch videos about Native peoples in the First Nations Room, step back into gold rush days in the Victorian Tea Rose Room, or admire the splendid view of the SS Klondike *paddlewheeler and Canyon Mountain from the balcony of the Fireweed Room. Especially geared to the business traveler, Hawkins House provides the convenience of a private telephone line and answering machine, fax service, and a work table with a light and computer jack. Breakfast is a homemade feast of northern and international delights — from the home-smoked salmon pâté and moose sausage to jams, syrups, and sourdough pastries.*

SEASON

all year

ACCOMMODATIONS

4 rooms with private baths

Sanford House Bed & Breakfast

Elizabeth and Charlie Le Ber
PO Box 1825, 20 Platt Street
Brighton, Ontario K0K lH0
Tel/Fax: (613) 475-3930
$$

ABOUT THE B&B

Sitting majestically on the crest of a hill, Sanford House Bed & Breakfast is a red-brick Victorian home close to Main Street in the friendly town of Brighton. This century-old home with turret and covered veranda has offstreet parking, a separate guest entrance, and three large, bright, and comfortable air conditioned bedrooms. Guests can choose to relax in the round turret room; in the lounge with television, VCR, videos, board games, and books; in the spacious, bright Victorian parlor; or on the veranda. Delicious home-baked breakfasts, often spotlighting apples grown in nearby orchards, are served in the guest dining room. It's a short drive to beautiful Presqu'ile Provincial Park's sandy beaches, nature trails, fine birdwatching areas, and marsh boardwalk. If antique hunting is a passion, there are numerous antique shops right in Brighton and in the surrounding area. Applefest, a celebration of the harvest in September, is a particularly lovely time to visit the area. When not entertaining their B&B guests, Elizabeth and Charlie enjoy cycling and nature walks.

SEASON

all year

ACCOMMODATIONS

3 rooms with shared bath

Spartan Apple–Cinnamon Crêpes

"In the Brighton area, the beauty of spring apple blossoms in surrounding orchards gives way to colorful autumn baskets filled with the harvested apple crop at fruit stands. Sanford House offers a bowl of this magnificent fruit in season and features them in some of the hot breakfast entrées." — Elizabeth and Charlie Le Ber

3 eggs
1½ cups milk
1 cup all-purpose flour
4 tablespoons melted butter
2 tablespoons Calvados*
2 tablespoons granulated sugar

Spartan apple–cinnamon filling:
12 Spartan apples, peeled, cored, and sliced
2 cups brown sugar
⅓ cup water
6 tablespoons butter
1½ teaspoons ground cinnamon

Confectioners' sugar

**Note: Calvados is an apple brandy from Normandy in France.*

(continued on next page)

Whisk the eggs. Add the milk, and blend well. Stir in the flour, butter, Calvados, and granulated sugar, and beat until the batter is smooth and free of lumps. Refrigerate the batter overnight. Remove the batter from the refrigerator, and whisk again. Pour a thin layer of batter over the bottom of a hot, buttered 5½" skillet, and cook at medium heat for 1½ minutes. Turn and cook about 30 seconds. Transfer to a towel. Repeat with the remaining batter.

For the filling, combine the apple, brown sugar, water, butter, and cinnamon in a microwave-safe casserole. Cook uncovered in the microwave on high power for 12 minutes, stirring twice. Place some filling in the center of each crêpe, and fold the 2 sides over. As the crêpes are filled, keep them warm, folded side down. To serve, place 2 filled crêpes on a heated plate with a little of the juices from the filling, and dust with confectioners' sugar. ***Yield: About 7 servings.***

Domaine-sur-Mer

Eveline Haché
Box 1, Site 13, RR3
Bouctouche, New Brunswick
E0A 1G0
Tel: (506) 743-6582
Fax: (506) 743-8392
E-mail: domaine@auracom.com
$$

ABOUT THE B&B

This B&B has so many windows that guests sometimes feel they are having breakfast in the garden with the gold finches and hummingbirds that feed nearby. From the ocean, which can be seen from any of the B&B's three guest rooms, come refreshing sea breezes and the constant murmur of waves. For a great day at the beach or for a leisurely stroll, host Eveline Haché recommends the Irving Nature Park with its boardwalk and white sand dunes. The Eco-Centre is another popular spot and is staffed by professional biologists and interpreters from May to November. Domaine-sur-Mer is only 10 minutes from le Pays de la Sagouine in Bouctouche, home of the famous Acadian character made popular by the internationally renowned author Antonine Maillet. To complete your Acadian adventure, you can arrange for Eveline (who is knowledgeable about Acadian culture and history) to give you a hands-on lesson in cooking lobster — part of a multiday package that includes a lobster dinner and a seafood picnic for two.

SEASON

all year

ACCOMMODATIONS

3 rooms with private baths

Spelt Pancakes

"This is a healthful, stick-to-your-ribs recipe. Spelt is the most ancient cereal grain used for cooking and baking, and is cited several times in the Bible. Spelt flour is energizing as well as nutritional."
— Eveline Haché

1 cup buckwheat flour
1 cup spelt flour*
2 cups buttermilk
1 egg
Salt
⅓ cup boiling water
¾ teaspoon baking soda
Blueberries or raspberries (optional)

**Note: Spelt flour can be found in health or bulk food stores. Use all-purpose flour as a substitute.*

Combine the buckwheat flour and spelt flour. Add the buttermilk, egg, and a pinch of salt, and mix with a fork. Just before you're ready to cook the pancakes, mix the boiling water and baking soda, and combine with the flour mixture. Gently mix in the optional berries. Cook the pancakes on a hot, greased griddle until they are puffed up and dry around the edges. Turn the pancakes, and cook the other side until golden brown.
Yield: About 8 medium-sized pancakes.

Strawberry-Almond French Toast

Strawberry-almond sauce:
10-ounce package frozen strawberries, thawed
Water
½ cup sugar
2 tablespoons cornstarch
½ cup toasted sliced almonds

French toast:
6 eggs
2 cups milk
½ cup all-purpose flour
1½ tablespoons sugar
¼ teaspoon ground nutmeg
¼ teaspoon salt
18 slices French bread, 1" thick
1 tablespoon butter or margarine

Drain the strawberries, and reserve the berries and the liquid. Add enough water to the strawberry liquid to measure 1 cup. Combine the sugar and cornstarch in a saucepan; gradually add the strawberry liquid. Cook, stirring constantly, until the mixture is clear and thickened. Stir in the reserved strawberries and the almonds. In a large bowl, mix the eggs, milk, flour, sugar, nutmeg, and salt with a rotary beater until the batter is smooth. Soak the bread in the batter until the bread is saturated. Heat the butter in a large skillet, and carefully place the bread slices in it (if overcrowded, use a second skillet). Cook over medium-low heat until each side is golden brown. Serve with the strawberry-almond sauce.
Yield: 6 servings.

Park View Bed & Breakfast

Gladys and Carson Langille
254 Cameron Street
Moncton, New Brunswick E1C 5Z3
Tel: (506) 382-4504
$$

ABOUT THE B&B

This art deco home was built in 1940 as a residence for Mrs. Inez Robinson, owner of Moncton's first business college. The architectural plans came from the 1939 New York World's Fair, and this was the first art deco home in Moncton. The curved living room windows look out on beautiful Victoria Park in the city's center. Opened as a B&B in 1989, this charming home has three guest rooms with cable TV, telephones, and exquisite shared bath, spacious living room with fireplace, elegant dining room, and cozy kitchen. Your hosts provide a warm welcome, a hearty, home-cooked breakfast of your choice, and a wealth of information about the area. Gladys is a part-time school teacher, while Carson enjoys playing bridge and painting landscapes. A collection of works by local artists graces their walls. Nearby is superb dining, shopping, beaches, parks, museums, galleries, theater, a must-see tidal bore (where the tide goes up and down very quickly), and the famous Magnetic Hill (you'll never believe this phenomenon unless you experience it yourself!).

SEASON

all year

ACCOMMODATIONS

3 rooms with shared bath

Lakewinds

Jane and Stephen Locke
PO Box 1483, 328 Queen Street
Niagara-on-the-Lake, Ontario
L0S 1J0
Tel: (905) 468-1888
Fax: (905) 468-1061
E-mail: lakewind@niagara.com
www.lakewinds.niagara.com
$$$$

ABOUT THE B&B

A special experience awaits you at Lakewinds, a circa-1881, restored Victorian manor operated by Jane and Stephen Locke. Situated on an acre of quiet trees and gardens, Lakewinds offers unparalleled views of the Niagara-on-the-Lake Golf Club and Lake Ontario. The guest rooms, elegantly appointed with antiques, have been designed for comfort and privacy and feature private baths. Guests are invited to the games room for billiards or cards and, in summer, can enjoy refreshing dips in the heated pool or simply relax in rocking chairs on the veranda. Sumptuous breakfasts feature fruits, vegetables, and herbs from Jane's garden. Only one-and-a-half hours south of Toronto, Niagara-on-the-Lake is a charming town offering world-class theater, shops, fine restaurants, and beautiful parks — all with a turn-of-the-century ambiance. The many estate wineries in the area offer tours and tastings, while golf courses, tennis courts, and countless hiking and biking trails await the active visitor.

SEASON

all year

ACCOMMODATIONS

6 rooms with private baths

Sweet Potato Pancakes

3 eggs
2 large sweet potatoes, peeled and grated
1 cup chopped green onion
⅓ cup all-purpose flour
1½ tablespoons minced hot pepper (such as jalapeño)
1 teaspoon orange zest
Pepper
Salt
Vegetable oil

Sour cream or crème fraîche
Chopped green onion

In a large bowl, combine the eggs, sweet potato, onion, flour, hot pepper, orange zest, and a pinch of pepper and salt. Heat a little oil in a large skillet over medium heat. Use about ¼ cup of sweet potato mixture to make small round pancakes about 3" in diameter. Turn the pancakes after 3 – 5 minutes or when the edges are lightly browned, and cook another 3 – 5 minutes. Keep warm while cooking the rest of the pancakes. Serve with a dollop of sour cream or crème fraîche and a sprinkle of chopped green onion. ***Tip:*** These pancakes are very nice served with cooked sweet cured ham. ***Yield: 25 – 30 small-sized pancakes.***

Veggie and Cheese Puff Pancake

3 tablespoons butter
2 eggs, beaten
½ cup all-purpose flour
½ cup milk
¼ teaspoon salt
2 cups chopped broccoli
1 cup finely chopped red onion
1 cup chopped tomato
1½ cups grated cheddar cheese

Fresh fruit salad
Croissants

Heat the oven to 425°F. In a 9" glass pie pan, melt 1 tablespoon of the butter. In a small bowl, stir together the eggs, flour, milk, and salt. Pour the egg mixture into the pie pan. Bake 12 – 15 minutes. Meanwhile, melt the remaining butter in a skillet. Add the broccoli, onion, and tomato, and cook at medium heat until the vegetables are tender. Sprinkle ½ cup of the cheese on the cooked pancake, followed by the vegetables, then the remaining cheese. Return the pancake to the oven for 2 minutes to melt the cheese. Cut the pancake into 4. Serve with fresh fruit salad and croissants. ***Yield: 4 servings.***

Fraser House

Sheila and Dennis Derksen
PO Box 211, 33 1st Street East
Letellier, Manitoba R0G 1C0
Tel: (204) 737-2284
$

ABOUT THE B&B

Memories are made at this elegant and romantic 1916 home. Hardwood floors, area rugs, and antique furniture enhance the home's Victorian decor. Spacious rooms combined with great hospitality make your stay most enjoyable. Relax with a beverage and home-baked goodies in the parlor or on the veranda or patio. Breakfast may consist of a puffy egg pancake or freshly baked croissants and muffins, along with the season's fresh fruit, served in the formal dining room. Fraser House is located just a few minutes north of the US border in the heart of Manitoba's bustling agricultural area, and is near places to golf, fish, shop, and ski. Sheila enjoys craft projects and holds painting classes during the winter months, while Dennis enjoys carpentry and is employed as a fertilizer dealer.

SEASON

all year

ACCOMMODATIONS

2 rooms with shared bath

Caron House (1837)

Mary and Mike Caron
PO Box 143
Williamstown, Ontario K0C 2J0
Tel: (613) 347-7338
$$

ABOUT THE B&B

Caron House (1837) is a romantic historic brick home located in the quaint village of Williamstown (established in 1784). Beautifully decorated and furnished with antiques, the house has many of its original features — working fireplaces, inside shutters, tin ceilings, and wide pine floorboards. The upstairs is reserved for guests only. Two rooms with shared bath are individually decorated with Laura Ashley wallpaper, antique linens, hooked rugs, quilts, and collectibles. Guests can relax in the Keeping Room (a colonial term for "gathering place") or in the living room. A candlelit full gourmet breakfast — accompanied by classical music — is served in the dining room graced by fine china, silverware, and crystal. Outside, you'll marvel at the herb and Victorian gardens, relax on the antique wicker furniture on the back veranda, and enjoy the lovely yards, complete with trellis, brick patio, and gazebo. Caron House is one hour's drive from either Montréal or Ottawa; nearby attractions include Upper Canada Village, artisans' studios, a bird sanctuary, tennis courts, places to go cycling, and good restaurants. Mary and Mike enjoy traveling, antique hunting, cooking, gardening, and history.

SEASON

all year

ACCOMMODATIONS

2 rooms with shared bath

Whole Wheat Crêpes

"Delicious crêpes with a wholesome texture that I like to use for my avocado and chicken crêpe recipe (on page 192)." — Mary Caron

1¼ cups milk
1 cup whole wheat flour
3 eggs
2 tablespoons melted butter or margarine, cooled
¼ teaspoon salt
Butter

Place the milk, flour, eggs, melted butter, and salt in a blender, and blend for about 1 minute at high speed. Scrape down the sides of the jar with a spatula, and blend at high speed for another 15 seconds. Pour the batter into a bowl, cover, and refrigerate 60 minutes or more. Place 1 tablespoon butter in a crêpe pan over medium heat. When the butter bubbles, swirl it around to coat the pan. Pour in enough batter to thinly coat the bottom of the pan. Turn the crêpe when the underside is brown and the edges begin to curl. After about 1 minute, the crêpe should be done. Repeat with the remaining batter. Stack the crêpes between wax paper or paper towels, and set aside or freeze until needed. ***Yield: 18 crêpes.***

Wild Wiarton Berry Waffles

"These wonderfully light waffles are a breakfast favorite. We serve them heart shaped." — *Elsie Christensen*

3 eggs, separated
¾ cup milk
¾ cup sour cream
½ cup melted butter or margarine
1 teaspoon vanilla
1½ cups all-purpose flour
2 teaspoons baking powder
½ teaspoon baking soda
½ teaspoon salt

Berries
Confectioners' sugar

Beat the egg whites until stiff. In a large bowl, beat the egg yolks. Add the milk, sour cream, butter, and vanilla to the egg yolks, and beat well. In a separate bowl, combine the flour, baking powder, baking soda, and salt. Sift the flour mixture into the egg yolk mixture, and beat well. Fold the egg whites into the batter carefully. Bake the waffles on a hot, greased waffle iron according to the manufacturer's directions. Top with berries, and sprinkle with confectioners' sugar. ***Yield: 8 waffles.***

Bruce Gables B&B

Elsie and Jorn Christensen
PO Box 448, 410 Berford Street
Wiarton, Ontario N0H 2T0
Tel: (519) 534-0429
Fax: (519) 534-0779
$$

ABOUT THE B&B

Whether in French, German, Spanish, Danish, or English, Elsie and Jorn bid you "welcome" to Bruce Gables, their spacious turn-of-the-century home. Relax in the large living room, which has been restored to its Victorian splendor and furnished with period furniture and antiques. Two of the three large bedrooms have bay windows that overlook the town of Wiarton and the clear blue waters of Colpoy's Bay. A hearty breakfast, served in the elegant dining room, is your choice of crêpes, pancakes, waffles, French toast, eggs Benedict or Florentine, omelets, or any other style of eggs. In the garden, picnic tables and a gas barbecue are available for the guests to use. Known as the "gateway to the Bruce," the town of Wiarton makes a perfect headquarters for exploring the Bruce Peninsula. With Georgian Bay to the east and Lake Huron to the west, the Bruce offers abundant water recreation, not to mention some of the most breathtaking scenery in Ontario from its high limestone bluffs. In addition, the area's provincial parks are natural habitats for many varieties of birds and animals.

SEASON

May – October

ACCOMMODATIONS

3 rooms with shared baths

Zucchini Pancakes with Béchamel Sauce

(Recipe from Joan Peggs Eggs, *written and published by Joan Peggs)*

1 cup all-purpose flour
1 cup whole wheat flour
4 teaspoons baking powder
2 tablespoons sugar
1½ cups grated zucchini
½ medium onion, chopped
½ – 1 teaspoon Italian seasoning or a mixture of dried oregano, marjoram, and basil
2 eggs
1 cup milk
¼ cup vegetable oil

Béchamel sauce (recipe follows)

Sift together the all-purpose flour, whole wheat flour, baking powder, and sugar. In a large mixing bowl, mix together the zucchini, onion, and Italian seasoning. Add the flour mixture to the zucchini mixture, and combine. Place the eggs, milk, and oil in a blender jar, and blend for 15 seconds. Add the egg mixture to the zucchini mixture, and stir gently with a fork until just mixed (extra milk may be required). Using ¼ cup batter for each one, cook the pancakes in a lightly greased frying pan on medium heat (or in an electric frying pan set at 350°F). Turn them when the surface is covered with bubbles, and the underside is golden brown.

(continued on next page)

The Inn on St. Andrews

Joan Peggs
231 St. Andrews Street
Victoria, British Columbia V8V 2N1
Tel: (800) 668-5993 or (604) 384-8613
Fax: (604) 384-6063
E-mail: joan_peggs@bc.sympatico.ca.
www.bctravel.com/andrews.html
$$

ABOUT THE B&B

The Inn on St. Andrews is as lovely today as when it was built in 1913 by Edith Carr, eldest sister of the famous Canadian artist and author Emily Carr. This Tudor-style heritage property features elegant woodwork, stained and beveled glass, and large bright bedrooms. After a wholesome breakfast in the formal dining room, you can congregate in the sunroom overlooking the east garden or on the sun deck overlooking the west garden, in the cozy TV room, or in the larger drawing room. The inn is ideally located in James Bay, close to Victoria's inner harbor with ferry and seaplane terminals, the Parliament buildings, the Royal British Columbia Museum, famed Empress Hotel, and downtown shops. A short walk brings you to Beacon Hill Park and the oceanfront. Your host Joan Peggs believes in modern comfort and old-fashioned hospitality, and provides guests with her own map highlighting walking and driving destinations and recommended restaurants.

SEASON

all year

ACCOMMODATIONS

1 room with private bath;
2 rooms with shared bath

Cook them until the undersides are golden brown. Serve with béchamel sauce flavored with Parmesan cheese. ***Tip:*** Leftover pancakes may be frozen. ***Yield: 16 – 20 pancakes.***

Béchamel sauce:
2 tablespoons margarine
2 tablespoons all-purpose flour
Pepper
Salt
1 cup milk

Bring some water to a boil in the bottom section of a double boiler. Place the margarine in the top section of the double boiler, and place it over the bottom section. When the margarine has melted, remove the top section of the double boiler, add the flour and a pinch of pepper and salt, and stir well. Add the milk, and stir well. Place the top section of the double boiler over the bottom section, and cook the sauce, stirring constantly, until it thickens to the desired consistency.

If cheese is to be added (see variation below), add it as the sauce begins to thicken. To prevent further thickening, remove the top section of the double boiler from the bottom section. Cover the sauce with plastic wrap or brush it with melted margarine to prevent a skin from forming on the surface. ***Variation:*** For a cheese sauce, add ½ cup grated cheese (sharp cheddar, Parmesan, or Swiss). Cayenne pepper and paprika can be added with cheddar cheese; nutmeg can be added with Parmesan and Swiss cheese. ***Tips:*** Extra béchamel sauce can be frozen (6-ounce yogurt containers work best). Place the frozen sauce in the refrigerator to thaw overnight. Use a double boiler or a microwave to reheat the sauce. If the sauce is too thick, add a small amount of milk. ***Yield: 1 cup.***

Quiches, Omelets, Frittatas, & Casseroles

Asparagus and Crab Strata

¼ cup softened butter
6 slices white bread
1 cup grated cheddar cheese
1 cup chopped and cooked fresh asparagus
1 cup cooked crab meat, fresh or canned
4 eggs
1¼ cups milk
1½ tablespoons chopped parsley
½ teaspoon paprika
½ teaspoon salt
Pepper

Preheat the oven to 350°F. Grease an 8 x 8" baking dish. Spread butter on one side of the bread slices. Arrange 3 slices of bread in the dish, buttered side down (if necessary, trim the bread to fit). Layer the cheese, asparagus, and crab meat over the bread. Place the remaining bread slices, buttered side up, over the crab meat. Combine the eggs, milk, parsley, paprika, salt, and a pinch of pepper. Pour the egg mixture evenly over the bread. Let stand for 10 minutes. Bake 35 – 45 minutes or until a knife inserted in the center comes out clean. ***Yield: 6 servings.***

Fraser House

Sheila and Dennis Derksen
PO Box 211, 33 1st Street East
Letellier, Manitoba R0G 1C0
Tel: (204) 737-2284
$

ABOUT THE B&B

Memories are made at this elegant and romantic 1916 home. Hardwood floors, area rugs, and antique furniture enhance the home's Victorian decor. Spacious rooms combined with great hospitality make your stay most enjoyable. Relax with a beverage and home-baked goodies in the parlor or on the veranda or patio. Breakfast may consist of a puffy egg pancake or freshly baked croissants and muffins, along with the season's fresh fruit, served in the formal dining room. Fraser House is located just a few minutes north of the US border in the heart of Manitoba's bustling agricultural area, and is near places to golf, fish, shop, and ski. Sheila enjoys craft projects and holds painting classes during the winter months, while Dennis enjoys carpentry and is employed as a fertilizer dealer.

SEASON

all year

ACCOMMODATIONS

2 rooms with shared bath

Les Trois Érables

Madeleine and Jacques Mercier
PO Box 852, RR #2
Wakefield, Québec J0X 3G0
Tel: (819) 459-1118
$$

ABOUT THE B&B

Nestled among gentle rolling hills on the banks of the Gatineau River, the historic village of Wakefield is a gateway to beautiful Gatineau Park where you can find ample opportunities for hiking, skiing, or less arduous nature walks — especially beautiful in fall foliage season. Less than a half hour's drive takes you to the heart of Canada's national capital, Ottawa. Les Trois Érables was built at the turn of the century and was the home and office of three generations of village doctors until its transformation to a B&B in 1988. Rooms are tastefully decorated in soft colors and furnished for comfort and convenience. The sumptuous breakfasts attest to the fact that Madeleine loves to cook. Local restaurants, sports outfitters, and boutiques abound.

SEASON

all year

ACCOMMODATIONS

4 rooms with private baths

Asparagus, Gruyère, and Tarragon Souffléd Omelet

½ pound trimmed asparagus
1 medium red onion, thinly sliced
1½ tablespoons unsalted butter
Sugar
⅔ cup grated Gruyère cheese
1 tablespoon minced tarragon leaves
Pepper
Salt
4 eggs, separated
2 tablespoons all-purpose flour

Preheat the oven to 375°F. In a 10" nonstick and ovenproof skillet, simmer the asparagus in enough water to cover for 3 – 5 minutes or until just tender. Drain the asparagus, rinse it under cold water, and pat it dry with paper towels. Cut the asparagus into ¼" pieces, and transfer them to a bowl. In the skillet, cook the onion with 1 tablespoon of the butter over medium heat, stirring frequently, for 5 minutes. Add a pinch of sugar and cook, stirring, for 3 – 5 minutes or until the onion is golden. Add the onion to the asparagus. Add the cheese and tarragon, season with a little pepper and salt, and mix thoroughly. Set aside.

(continued on next page)

Clean the skillet, and melt the remaining butter in it over medium heat. Tilt the skillet to coat the entire surface with butter, then remove the skillet from the heat. In a bowl, whisk the egg yolks with the flour and a little pepper and salt until the mixture is thick and lemon colored.

In another bowl, beat the egg whites with a pinch of salt until they just hold stiff peaks. Fold the egg whites into the yolk mixture gently but thoroughly, and spread the egg mixture evenly in the skillet. Bake the omelet in the middle of the oven for 7 minutes or until it has puffed up. Spoon the asparagus mixture across the middle of the omelet and, with a spatula, fold the omelet in half to enclose the filling. Bake the omelet 1 minute more or until the cheese has melted. Cut the omelet in half. *Yield: 2 servings.*

The Lookout at Schooner Cove

Marj and Herb Wilkie
3381 Dolphin Drive
Nanoose Bay, British Columbia
V9P 9H7
Tel/Fax: (250) 468-9796
www.pixsell.bc.ca/bb/1169.htm
$$

ABOUT THE B&B

Situated halfway between Victoria and Tofino on unspoiled Vancouver Island, this West Coast contemporary cedar home stands in a woodsy setting of rocks and tall evergreens. The wrap-around deck affords a 180-degree view of the Strait of Georgia and the majestic mountains beyond. Relax and savor this "little bit of heaven" or hike, golf, kayak, sail, fish, or sightsee. Take a day trip to the wild western shore of the island and Pacific Rim National Park or head south to charming Victoria. The vacation suite will accommodate four people and, with its private entrance and deck and fully equipped kitchen, makes a popular headquarters for an island stay. Hearty breakfasts are served in the dining room overlooking the ocean. After running a store in New York's Catskill Mountains for 17 years, Marj (from Australia) and Herb (from the US) established The Lookout in 1988 and enjoy helping their guests have a memorable stay.

SEASON

May – October
(or by arrangement)

ACCOMMODATIONS

1 vacation suite with private bath;
1 room with private bath;
1 room with shared bath

Bacon and Egg Casserole

"Creates a flavorful beginning to the day, not to mention that my cholesterol-conscious guests appreciate the fact that they each get less than an egg per serving." — Marj Wilkie

2 cups grated medium or sharp cheddar cheese
1 cup crumbled cooked bacon or ham chunks
2 tablespoons dried onion
6 eggs
3 cups milk
1½ cups powdered biscuit mix
½ cup melted butter
½ teaspoon pepper
½ teaspoon powdered mustard

Preheat the oven to 400°F. Butter a 13 x 9" casserole. Sprinkle the bottom of the casserole with the cheese, bacon, and onion. In a bowl, combine the eggs, milk, biscuit mix, butter, pepper, and mustard, and slowly pour into the casserole. Bake 25 – 30 minutes. ***Yield: 8 servings.***

Barbara Ann's Omelet

3 slices bacon, cut into small pieces
2 small potatoes, peeled and sliced into ¼" slices
8 large spinach leaves, stems removed and sliced into ¼" strips
6 eggs, lightly beaten
½ cup plain yogurt
Pepper
Salt

Heat the bacon briefly in a 10" skillet. Add the potatoes, and fry until the bacon is crisp and the potatoes are tender and lightly browned. Add the spinach, then place the spinach mixture in a small bowl. In a separate bowl, combine the eggs, the yogurt, and a pinch of pepper and salt, and pour one-third of the mixture into the skillet. Cook over low heat without stirring. As the eggs set on the bottom, lift the edges of the omelet to let the uncooked liquid run underneath. When the omelet has set, place one-third of the spinach mixture on one side of the omelet, and fold the other side over it. Repeat the procedure twice more with the remaining egg mixture and spinach mixture, using a little vegetable oil to grease the skillet if necessary. Serve immediately. ***Yield: 3 omelets.***

Barbara Ann's Bed 'n Breakfast Vacation Farm

Barbara Ann and Ted Witzaney
PO Box 156
Denzil, Saskatchewan S0L 0S0
Tel: (306) 358-4814
$

ABOUT THE B&B

Specially geared for families, Barbara Ann's B&B is located on the Witzaney farm, where they've been raising crops and hogs since 1911. The petting zoo includes traditional farm animals and more exotic ones, including a llama and Muscovy ducks. Barbara Ann's breakfast (and other meals served on request) feature farm-fresh milk, eggs, cheese, and vegetables; home-baked goods, such as buns, pies, and cookies; homemade jams, jellies, relishes, and pickles; and pork raised on the farm. Homemade sausages are the specialty of the house. Picnic and barbecue facilities, a sandbox and swing set, a horseshoe pit, lawn bowling and badminton equipment, and an 18-hole miniature golf course are all on the property. When not tending to guests, Barbara Ann enjoys sewing and craft making, while Ted enjoys woodworking. Both like to spend time with their 10 grandchildren. Denzil is about a half-hour drive west of Unity, Saskatchewan, and a 45-minute drive east of Provost, Alberta.

SEASON

all year

ACCOMMODATIONS

2 rooms with shared bath

Mecklenburgh Inn

Suzi Fraser
78 Queen Street
Chester, Nova Scotia B0J 1J0
Tel/Fax: (902) 275-4638
www.destination-ns.com/
lighthouse/mecklenburgh
$$

ABOUT THE B&B

Constructed by shipwrights in 1890, Mecklenburgh Inn is located in the heart of seaside Chester, which has catered to summer visitors and sailing enthusiasts for over 150 years. Sleep in the spacious and comfortably appointed bedrooms filled with period furniture and other interesting objects Suzi has collected over the years, then enjoy a delicious breakfast while you plan the day ahead. You might wander the historic village streets, stopping to watch the yacht races on Mahone Bay, or browse through craft shops and boutiques. Or, maybe a sailboat ride, bicycle ride, or game of golf or tennis would be more your style. Later, relax on the balcony while the sun sets over the western shore of the bay and village activity lulls. You might consider an evening meal at one of the excellent restaurants in the area or catch a play at the Chester Playhouse. At the end of the day, the living room is the perfect place to wind down chatting by the fire or perusing travel books and magazines.

SEASON

May 24 – November 7

ACCOMMODATIONS

4 rooms with shared baths

Breakfast Casserole

10 eggs
3 cups creamed cottage cheese
3 scallions, chopped
2 cups grated cheddar cheese
2 cups sour cream
1 cup cooked corn kernels
½ cup chopped mild green chilies
½ cup melted butter
½ cup all-purpose flour
1 teaspoon baking powder

Preheat the oven to 350°F. In a large bowl, mix together the eggs, cottage cheese, scallions, cheddar cheese, sour cream, corn, chilies, and butter. In a separate bowl, combine the flour and baking powder. Combine the flour mixture with the egg mixture. Pour the egg mixture into a greased 13 x 9" pan, and bake 45 minutes. *Yield: 12 servings.*

Breakfast Pie

"The following recipe comes from the New Sweden Church 100th Anniversary Cookbook (1894 – 1994), *my husband Winston's first country parish. It's simple, easy, and guests find it really tasty."* — *Vera Sproule*

2½ cups thawed and grated frozen hash browns (or use grated leftover hash browns)
5 eggs
1½ cups grated cheddar cheese
1 green onion, sliced
1 teaspoon salt
⅓ cup milk
½ cup chopped mushrooms
½ cup creamed cottage cheese
⅛ teaspoon pepper
Tabasco
½ cup cornflakes
½ cup crumbled cooked bacon or finely diced cooked ham

Preheat the oven to 325°F. Press the hash browns into a 9" greased pie plate to form a crust. In a large bowl, beat the eggs until they are foamy. Stir in the cheddar cheese, onion, salt, milk, mushrooms, cottage cheese, pepper, and a dash of Tabasco. Pour the batter into the pie plate. Top with the cornflakes and bacon, and bake 40 – 50 minutes. Let stand 3 – 4 minutes before cutting. ***Yield: 4 – 5 servings.***

Sproule Heritage Place B&B

Vera and Winston Sproule
PO Box 43, Site 14, RR #1
Strathmore, Alberta T1P 1J6
Tel: (403) 934-3219
$$

ABOUT THE B&B

While Sproule Heritage Place B&B has been featured by both Hallmark USA and Alberta Government Telephone in their television commercials, this farm actually had less high-profile beginnings. In 1909, the site was little more than a well-trodden buffalo trail when the Scheer family settled on the open prairie east of Calgary. Years later, the stately house and barn became a landmark to travelers on a road that today is the Trans-Canada Highway. Vera and Winston Sproule purchased the farm in 1985 and began extensive renovations to restore its 1920s elegance. As a result, the site has been declared an Alberta Registered Historic Resource. Artisans and designers of furniture and quilts, Vera and Winston (a country pastor for four years in Yukon and 24 years in Alberta) assure you a comfortable bed in one of three charming bedrooms and an interesting breakfast.

SEASON

all year

ACCOMMODATIONS

1 room with private bath;
2 rooms with shared bath

Barbara Ann's Bed 'n Breakfast Vacation Farm

Barbara Ann and Ted Witzaney
PO Box 156
Denzil, Saskatchewan S0L 0S0
Tel: (306) 358-4814
$

ABOUT THE B&B

Specially geared for families, Barbara Ann's B&B is located on the Witzaney farm, where they've been raising crops and hogs since 1911. The petting zoo includes traditional farm animals and more exotic ones, including a llama and Muscovy ducks. Barbara Ann's breakfast (and other meals served on request) feature farm-fresh milk, eggs, cheese, and vegetables; home-baked goods, such as buns, pies, and cookies; homemade jams, jellies, relishes, and pickles; and pork raised on the farm. Homemade sausages are the specialty of the house. Picnic and barbecue facilities, a sandbox and swing set, a horseshoe pit, lawn bowling and badminton equipment, and an 18-hole miniature golf course are all on the property. When not tending to guests, Barbara Ann enjoys sewing and craft making, while Ted enjoys woodworking. Both like to spend time with their 10 grandchildren. Denzil is about a half-hour drive west of Unity, Saskatchewan, and a 45-minute drive east of Provost, Alberta.

SEASON

all year

ACCOMMODATIONS

2 rooms with shared bath

Broccoli and Cheese Quiche

9" unbaked pie shell
¼ cup grated Parmesan cheese
2 cups finely chopped broccoli
1 cup grated Swiss cheese
¼ cup sliced scallions
3 eggs
⅔ cup chicken broth
½ cup heavy cream
½ teaspoon salt
¼ teaspoon Tabasco

Preheat the oven to 450°F. Prick the bottom and corners of the pie shell with a fork, and bake 5 minutes. Remove it from the oven, and sprinkle with 2 tablespoons of the Parmesan cheese. Layer half the broccoli over the Parmesan cheese. Over that, layer half the Swiss cheese and scallions. Add layers of the remaining broccoli, Swiss cheese, and scallions. In a bowl, beat the eggs, then add the chicken broth, cream, salt, and Tabasco, and mix well. Pour the egg mixture over the layers in the pastry shell. Sprinkle with the remaining Parmesan cheese. Bake 10 minutes, then reduce the temperature to 325°F, and bake 20 – 25 minutes or until a knife inserted in the center of the quiche comes out clean. Let stand 5 – 10 minutes before cutting. ***Yield: 8 servings.***

Crispin Apple and Sausage Quiche

"In the Brighton area, the beauty of spring apple blossoms in surrounding orchards gives way to colorful autumn baskets filled with the harvested apple crop at fruit stands. Sanford House offers a bowl of this magnificent fruit in season and features them in some of the hot breakfast entrées." — Elizabeth and Charlie Le Ber

Crust:
6 tablespoons cold butter
2 tablespoons lard
1¼ cups all-purpose flour
3 tablespoons ice water

Filling:
8 pork breakfast sausages
1 Crispin or Granny Smith apple, peeled, cored, and chopped
1 tablespoon butter
½ cup grated medium cheddar cheese
2 egg yolks
1 whole egg
1 cup milk

(continued on next page)

Sanford House Bed & Breakfast

Elizabeth and Charlie Le Ber
PO Box 1825, 20 Platt Street
Brighton, Ontario K0K 1H0
Tel/Fax: (613) 475-3930
$$

ABOUT THE B&B

Sitting majestically on the crest of a hill, Sanford House Bed & Breakfast is a red-brick Victorian home close to Main Street in the friendly town of Brighton. This century-old home with turret and covered veranda has offstreet parking, a separate guest entrance, and three large, bright, and comfortable air conditioned bedrooms. Guests can choose to relax in the round turret room; in the lounge with television, VCR, videos, board games, and books; in the spacious, bright Victorian parlor; or on the veranda. Delicious home-baked breakfasts, often spotlighting apples grown in nearby orchards, are served in the guest dining room. It's a short drive to beautiful Presqu'ile Provincial Park's sandy beaches, nature trails, fine birdwatching areas, and marsh boardwalk. If antique hunting is a passion, there are numerous antique shops right in Brighton and in the surrounding area. Applefest, a celebration of the harvest in September, is a particularly lovely time to visit the area. When not entertaining their B&B guests, Elizabeth and Charlie enjoy cycling and nature walks.

SEASON

all year

ACCOMMODATIONS

3 rooms with shared bath

Blend the butter and lard together well with a pastry blender or 2 knives, then work in the flour. Using your fingers, blend the mixture well. Make a well in the center of the flour mixture, and gradually add the ice water while stirring quickly. Gather the dough into a ball, wrap it in plastic wrap, and refrigerate it 2 hours. Roll out the dough on a lightly floured surface, and place it in a 9" or 10" round, fluted quiche dish.

Preheat the oven to 350°F. For the filling, remove the sausage meat from the casings, and sauté it until it is cooked through and crumbles. Drain the meat first in a colander, then on paper towels. Place the meat in the pie crust. Sauté the apple in the butter until the apple is soft, then distribute it over the sausage. Sprinkle the cheese over the apple. In a bowl, beat together the egg yolks, whole egg, and milk, and pour the egg mixture over the cheese, apple, and sausage. Bake 50 – 60 minutes or until the pie is somewhat firm in the center, and the top is golden. Serve warm. ***Yield: 4 servings.***

Dilled Smoked Salmon Quiche

1 medium onion, chopped
2 tablespoons butter
2 tablespoons all-purpose flour
4 eggs
2 cups milk or light cream
1 teaspoon dried dill weed
¼ teaspoon powdered mustard
¼ teaspoon Spike seasoning*
Ground nutmeg
Tabasco
6 ounces grated cheddar, Swiss, or Monterey Jack cheese, chilled
¾ cup flaked smoked salmon

**Note: Spike is a seasoning mixture available at health food stores.*

Preheat the oven to 350°F. Microwave the onion and butter in a glass, microwave-safe quiche dish on high for 2 minutes. Add the flour, and stir. In a bowl, beat the eggs, milk, dill, mustard, Spike, a pinch of nutmeg, and a dash of Tabasco until combined. Pour the egg mixture into a quiche dish. Sprinkle the cheese and salmon on top. Bake 35 – 45 minutes. Let stand 5 minutes before cutting. ***Yield: 6 servings.***

An Ocean View Bed & Breakfast

Yvette and Ralf Craig
715 Suffolk Street
Victoria, British Columbia V9A 3J5
Tel: (800) 342-9986 or (250) 386-7330
Fax: (250) 389-0280
E-mail: 74561.3556@compuserve.com
www.islandnet.com/~relic/oceanvw.html
$$ – $$$$

ABOUT THE B&B

Feel the ocean breeze and admire the sweeping views of the Strait of Juan de Fuca and the snow-capped Olympic Mountains from the deck of this modern, Mediterranean-style B&B. Only minutes from Victoria's many attractions, Ocean View offers four whimsical guest rooms, each with private entrance and bath, king or queen bed, TV, bar refrigerator, and French door entrance to a garden patio. Some rooms have an electric fireplace and a canopy bed. Breakfast includes a variety of egg dishes or pancakes, fruit salad, granola muesli, yogurt, beverages, and homemade breads and jams. Chat with guests from around the world at the large dining room table, seat yourself in the more intimate sunroom, or relax in the hot tub or on the gazebo sundeck. Stroll the scenic ocean boardwalk to Chinatown, Market Square, the Inner Harbour, the famed Empress Hotel, and a wide assortment of museums, restaurants, theaters, and pubs.

SEASON

all year

ACCOMMODATIONS

4 rooms with private baths

The Green Door Bed & Breakfast

Doloris Paquin
PO Box 335, 376 Berford Street
Wiarton, Ontario N0H 2T0
Tel: (519) 534-4710

$ – $$

ABOUT THE B&B

"Completely comfortable, wonderfully welcoming," is how one recent guest described The Green Door. Built at the turn of the century, this red-brick, stately, restored Victorian house is situated on Wiarton's main street and is within a few minutes' walk of shops and restaurants. The main floor has a charming dining room and a spacious living room with bay windows. Up the wooden staircase are three guest bedrooms, two with double beds and one with two single beds, as well as a large guest bathroom. The high ceilings and spacious rooms lend an airy feeling to this B&B with all the comforts and coziness of home. Outside, enjoy the large garden, maple-shaded deck, and barbecue facilities.

SEASON

all year

ACCOMMODATIONS

1 room with private bath;
2 rooms with shared bath

Doloris's Individual Baked Omelet

¼ cup grated sharp cheddar cheese
¼ cup grated Swiss cheese
2 eggs, beaten
2 tablespoons milk
½ teaspoon dried minced onion
Pepper
Salt
Paprika

Preheat the oven to 350°F. Sprinkle the cheddar and Swiss cheese evenly on the bottom of a greased 4" baking dish. Mix together the eggs, milk, onion, and a pinch of pepper and salt, and pour over the cheese. Sprinkle with paprika. Bake 20 – 30 minutes. *Yield: 1 serving.*

Eggs Florentine

"No need to call my guests for breakfast when this dish is baking in the oven — its wonderful aromas do the job for me!"
— Sharon Spraggett

1 tablespoon vegetable oil
2 bunches spinach, washed and dried
1 large clove garlic, finely chopped
¾ teaspoon salt
2 tablespoons half-and-half
3 tablespoons butter
⅓ cup plus 2 tablespoons grated Swiss cheese
1½ tablespoons all-purpose flour
¼ teaspoon pepper
1 cup milk
6 eggs

Preheat the oven to 350°F. In a large frying pan, heat the oil. Add the spinach and garlic, and cover. Cook just until the spinach has wilted. Drain the spinach well, and chop it. Return it to the pan, and add ½ teaspoon of the salt, the half-and-half, and 1 tablespoon of the butter. Mix well. Turn the spinach mixture into an 8 x 8" baking dish, and sprinkle with 2 tablespoons of the cheese. Melt the remaining butter in a saucepan, remove it from the heat, and add the flour, remaining salt, and pepper. Stir the butter mixture until smooth. Stir in the milk. Bring the sauce to a boil, stirring constantly. Carefully break the eggs over the cheese and spinach in the dish. Cover with the sauce, and sprinkle on the remaining cheese. Bake uncovered for 15 – 20 minutes or until the eggs are set and the top is golden. ***Yield: 6 servings.***

Hipwood House B&B

Sharon and Malcolm Spraggett
PO Box 211, 1763 Hipwood Road
Shawnigan Lake, British Columbia
V0R 2W0
Tel/Fax: (250) 743-7855
E-mail: hipwoodh@cvnet.net
www.cvnet.net/cowb&b/hipwood/
$$

ABOUT THE B&B

Thinking of traveling to beautiful Vancouver Island? If so, take the breathtaking 45-minute drive north of Victoria to the quaint village of Shawnigan Lake, and you'll come upon a peaceful country B&B called Hipwood House. Unwind in one of three spacious guest rooms, enjoy a refreshing cup of tea in the garden, or stroll the trails, including a 50-foot suspension bridge, on Hipwood's two acres. There's also a putting green and horseshoes and badminton — if you need to work off that full country breakfast! You're also a five-minute walk away from the public beach, local artists' gallery, and museum, and close to boat and water sport rentals on the lake, a seaplane for magnificent air tours, fishing, golf, tennis, and restaurants. Many interesting and picturesque areas are within a half-hour drive. Lifelong residents of Vancouver Island, Sharon and Malcolm are knowledgeable about the area and will help make your stay extra special.

SEASON

all year

ACCOMMODATIONS

1 room with private bath;
2 rooms with shared bath

Fairmount Bed and Breakfast

Susan Proven
Box 633
Minnedosa, Manitoba R0J 1E0
Tel/Fax: (204) 874-2165
$$

ABOUT THE B&B

Fairmount Bed and Breakfast is located between Minnedosa and Riding Mountain National Park. The hills, valleys, and sloughs (prairie water holes) make the area one of the most beautiful in the province. From the dining room and all three guest rooms, you can see geese and ducks on the nearby slough and at night hear the sounds of frogs and other creatures. Relax watching the sheep graze in the pastures, or take a short hike to where the deep ruts made by Red River carts that followed the Carlton Trail can still be seen. The 1914 two-and-a-half-story house, which is crowned by lightning rods, features stained glass windows and maple flooring and is furnished in early Canadiana. A visit to Fairmount is like a trip back in time, especially when it comes to meals. Host Susan Proven specializes in food made from scratch with locally produced farm products. When she's not in the kitchen, in the garden, or out with the sheep, Susan produces radio documentaries drawing inspiration from the people of the countryside.

SEASON

all year

ACCOMMODATIONS

3 rooms with shared bath

Fairmount Frittata

"Each season brings ever-changing ingredient combinations for this frittata. During the summer, the garden is full of zucchini, peppers, tomatoes, and broccoli. In the winter, the freezer, cold room, and pantry shelves yield dried tomatoes, basil, potatoes, and onions, and canned local trout." — Susan Proven

1 medium potato, peeled and diced
8 eggs
½ cup milk
½ teaspoon dried basil
½ teaspoon salt
Pepper
2 tablespoons vegetable oil
1 clove garlic, minced
1 green pepper or small zucchini, diced
1 medium onion, chopped
¼ cup dried tomatoes or 1 fresh tomato, sliced
½ cup grated cheddar or Swiss cheese

Microwave the potato in ¼ cup water on high power for 4 minutes. Drain. Beat together the eggs, milk, basil, salt, and a little pepper. Heat the oil in a cast-iron frying pan, and sauté the garlic, green pepper, and onion for 3 minutes. Add the potato, and sauté 2 minutes more. Pour the egg mixture into the pan, cover with the tomato, and cook over low heat for 10 minutes. Sprinkle the top with the cheese, and place under the broiler for about 2 minutes until the cheese begins to bubble and turn brown. Cut the frittata into wedges, and serve immediately. ***Yield: 4 servings.***

Fiddlehead Quiche

9" unbaked pie shell
8-ounce package cream cheese, cubed
1 cup milk
4 eggs, beaten
¼ cup chopped onion
1 cup chopped mushrooms
2 tablespoons margarine
10-ounce package frozen fiddleheads*
2 cups grated Swiss cheese
Paprika
Pepper
Salt
6 slices crisply cooked bacon, crumbled

**Note: Fiddleheads are the young, tightly coiled shoots of the Ostrich fern, and are available fresh in the spring and frozen year round.*

Preheat the oven to 400°F. Prick the bottom and sides of the pie shell with a fork. Bake 12 – 15 minutes or until lightly browned. Combine the cream cheese and milk in a saucepan; stir over low heat until smooth. Gradually add the cream cheese mixture to the eggs, mixing until well blended. In a skillet, sauté the onion, then the mushrooms, in the margarine; remove the onion mixture from the skillet. Steam or boil the fiddleheads until cooked al dente, and drain. Add the onion mixture, fiddleheads, cheese, and a pinch of paprika, pepper, and salt to the cream cheese mixture. Mix well, and pour into the pastry shell. Top with the crumbled bacon. Reduce the temperature to 350°F and bake 35 – 40 minutes or until set. ***Yield: 8 servings.***

Park View Bed & Breakfast

Gladys and Carson Langille
254 Cameron Street
Moncton, New Brunswick E1C 5Z3
Tel: (506) 382-4504
$$

ABOUT THE B&B

This art deco home was built in 1940 as a residence for Mrs. Inez Robinson, owner of Moncton's first business college. The architectural plans came from the 1939 New York World's Fair, and this was the first art deco home in Moncton. The curved living room windows look out on beautiful Victoria Park in the city's center. Opened as a B&B in 1989, this charming home has three guest rooms with cable TV, telephones, and exquisite shared bath, spacious living room with fireplace, elegant dining room, and cozy kitchen. Your hosts provide a warm welcome, a hearty, home-cooked breakfast of your choice, and a wealth of information about the area. Gladys is a part-time school teacher, while Carson enjoys playing bridge and painting landscapes. A collection of works by local artists graces their walls. Nearby is superb dining, shopping, beaches, parks, museums, galleries, theater, a must-see tidal bore (where the tide goes up and down very quickly), and the famous Magnetic Hill (you'll never believe this phenomenon unless you experience it yourself!).

SEASON

all year

ACCOMMODATIONS

3 rooms with shared bath

River Run Cottage & Breakfast

Janice and Bill Harkley
4551 River Road West
Ladner, British Columbia V4K 1R9
Tel: (604) 946-7778
Fax: (604) 940-1970
$$$$

ABOUT THE B&B

Described in Vancouver Best Places *as "a jewel on the Fraser" and rated "four kisses" in* Best Places to Kiss in the Northwest, *River Run is a romantic, tranquil getaway 30 minutes south of downtown Vancouver. Individual waterfront cottages with private decks overlooking the Fraser river and the mountains have wood-burning fireplaces, CD players, telephones, bathrobes, and cozy furnishings. All have private baths. One cottage is equipped with a Jacuzzi tub for two, and another with a soaker tub on the deck. Breakfast is delivered to the cottages at the time specified by guests and includes freshly squeezed juice, home-baked goods, and a variety of entrées. Bicycles, rowboats, and a double kayak are available for guests to explore the delta and the nearby Reifel Migratory Bird Sanctuary. By car, River Run is a 10-minute drive from ferries to Victoria and the Gulf Islands and a 20-minute drive from Vancouver International Airport.*

SEASON

all year

ACCOMMODATIONS

3 cottages with private baths

Fresh Salmon and Leek Quiche

"We're fortunate to have salmon easily available, since the river we live on is one of the most important salmon rivers in British Columbia. Often, after barbecuing, we use some of the leftover fish for this quiche." — Jan Harkley

Crust:

1¼ cups all-purpose flour
¼ teaspoon salt
¼ cup unsalted butter
2 tablespoons lard
1 egg, beaten

Filling:

1 – 2 leeks, well rinsed, with white and tender greens cut into matchstick-sized pieces
2 tablespoons butter
1 cup cooked fresh salmon, deboned
1 tablespoon snipped dill or 1 teaspoon dried dill weed
1 cup grated Swiss cheese
4 eggs
1⅓ cups half-and-half
½ teaspoon powdered mustard
½ teaspoon salt

(continued on next page)

Preheat the oven to 450°F. To make the crust, mix together the flour and salt. Cut in the butter and lard. Mix in the egg. Roll the dough out on a floured surface, and place in a 9" pie pan. In a frying pan, sauté the leeks in the butter until they are translucent. Remove them from the heat, and mix in the salmon and dill. Spread the salmon mixture evenly over the pie crust, and sprinkle the cheese over the salmon mixture. In a separate bowl, beat together the eggs, half-and-half, mustard, and salt. Pour the egg mixture over the cheese. Bake 10 minutes, reduce the temperature to 350°F, and bake another 25 minutes or until the center of the quiche is firm. ***Yield: 6 servings.***

Le Gîte Park Avenue B&B

Anne-Marie and Irving Bansfield
54 Park Avenue
Ottawa, Ontario K2P 1B2
Tel: (613) 230-9131
$$

ABOUT THE B&B

A bright, airy ambiance and artistic decor await you at Park Avenue B&B, an elegant, brick 1906 home located in a charming residential area of downtown Ottawa, Canada's capital. In addition to high-quality beds done up in classic cotton and linen sheets and duvets, each guest room is furnished with a desk and swivel chair, a rocking chair, bookshelves, excellent lighting, and attractive works of art. Ideal for families, the third-floor suite has two bedrooms and a private bath. The mood throughout the house is one of relaxation and warmth. Park Avenue B&B is close to the Parliament Buildings, art galleries, and museums, and is only three minutes (by foot) from the Rideau Canal, which freezes into the world's longest skating rink. Ottawa has a number of exciting festivals and activities, including Winterlude, a winter carnival held each February. Anne-Marie and Irving make it a point to know what's going on when in Ottawa so they can advise their guests on what to see and do.

SEASON

all year

ACCOMMODATIONS

1 suite with private bath;
2 rooms with shared bath

Frittata with Four Cheeses

2 tablespoons butter or margarine
1 onion, finely diced
½ cup diced cooked ham
¼ cup diced cooked potatoes
½ cup vegetables, such as diced red and green pepper, mushrooms, and corn kernels
Chopped basil
Chopped parsley
4 eggs
2 tablespoons milk
¾ cup grated cheese (Swiss, Gruyère, Monterey Jack, and mozzarella combined)
Pepper
Salt
Snipped chives or green onion

Preheat the oven to 400°F. In a large, ovenproof skillet, heat the butter and sauté the onion. Add the ham, potatoes, vegetables, and some chopped basil and parsley, and cook a few minutes. Lightly whisk the eggs with the milk, then add the cheese and a pinch of pepper and salt. Remove the skillet from the heat, and pour in the egg mixture. Top with some snipped chives, and bake 15 – 20 minutes until the frittata has browned and the center is set. ***Yield: 6 servings.***

Gouda-Baked Eggs with Roasted Red Pepper Coulis

"When serving groups, this baked omelet is easier and faster than making fried omelets one at a time. I like to serve it over a pool of roasted red pepper coulis or a mild salsa." — Jane Locke

Roasted red pepper coulis:
2 cloves garlic, chopped
1 onion, chopped
2 tablespoons olive oil
2 cups peeled, seeded, and chopped tomato
1 – 2 fresh hot chilies, seeded and chopped
1 tablespoon lime juice
½ teaspoon dried oregano
Salt
Sugar
Freshly ground pepper
1 sweet red pepper, roasted, peeled, and seeded

(continued on next page)

Lakewinds

Jane and Stephen Locke
PO Box 1483, 328 Queen Street
Niagara-on-the-Lake, Ontario
L0S 1J0
Tel: (905) 468-1888
Fax: (905) 468-1061
E-mail: lakewind@niagara.com
www.lakewinds.niagara.com
$$$$

ABOUT THE B&B

A special experience awaits you at Lakewinds, a circa-1881, restored Victorian manor operated by Jane and Stephen Locke. Situated on an acre of quiet trees and gardens, Lakewinds offers unparalleled views of the Niagara-on-the-Lake Golf Club and Lake Ontario. The guest rooms, elegantly appointed with antiques, have been designed for comfort and privacy and feature private baths. Guests are invited to the games room for billiards or cards and, in summer, can enjoy refreshing dips in the heated pool or simply relax in rocking chairs on the veranda. Sumptuous breakfasts feature fruits, vegetables, and herbs from Jane's garden. Only one-and-a-half hours south of Toronto, Niagara-on-the-Lake is a charming town offering world-class theater, shops, fine restaurants, and beautiful parks — all with a turn-of-the-century ambiance. The many estate wineries in the area offer tours and tastings, while golf courses, tennis courts, and countless hiking and biking trails await the active visitor.

SEASON

all year

ACCOMMODATIONS

6 rooms with private baths

Gouda-baked eggs:
4 shallots, finely chopped
3 cloves garlic, chopped
1 teaspoon dried thyme
1 teaspoon – 1 tablespoon butter
9 eggs, beaten
½ cup grated Gouda cheese

To make the coulis, sauté the garlic and onion in the oil until they are soft. Add the tomato, chilies, lime juice, oregano, a pinch of salt and sugar, and a little freshly ground pepper, and simmer about 2 minutes. Add the red pepper, and purée the mixture in a blender until smooth.

To make the baked eggs, preheat the oven to 350°F. Sauté the shallots, garlic, and thyme in the butter. Add the shallot mixture to the beaten eggs. Pour the egg mixture into a greased 9" pie or quiche dish. Bake 15 minutes. Remove, sprinkle with the cheese, and bake another 15 minutes. Serve immediately with roasted red pepper coulis.
Yield: 4 – 6 servings.

Hot Sausage Squares

"A wonderful dish for brunch or served as an appetizer."
— Rosalie Nimmo

1 pound Italian hot sausage
½ cup chopped onion
2 cups Bisquick biscuit mix
1 heaping cup grated Swiss cheese
¾ cup grated Parmesan cheese
1 egg, beaten
⅔ cup milk
¼ cup mayonnaise
¼ cup Pace brand picante sauce
2 tablespoons chopped parsley
1½ teaspoons salt

Jalapeño jelly
Fresh fruit

Preheat the oven to 400°F. Cook the sausage and onion together until the meat has browned. In a large bowl, combine the Bisquick, Swiss cheese, ½ cup of the Parmesan cheese, egg, milk, mayonnaise, picante sauce, parsley, and salt. Add the sausage mixture, and combine. Grease an 8 x 12" glass baking dish, place the sausage mixture in the dish, and sprinkle with the remaining Parmesan cheese. Bake 25 – 30 minutes. Serve with jalapeño jelly and fresh fruit. ***Tip:*** Owen's brand hot sausage works best in this recipe. ***Yield: 6 – 8 servings.***

Taste the Past Bed & Breakfast

Rosalie and Bryce Nimmo
PO Box 865, 281-2nd Street West
Drumheller, Alberta T0J 0Y0
Tel: (403) 823-5889
$$

ABOUT THE B&B

Return to a simpler era during a stay in one of Drumheller's original grand mansions, built at the turn of the century by Drumheller Valley's coal baron Jesse Gouge. The elegant dining room and sitting area are decorated with Rosalie's artwork and period antiques, which also adorn the four guest rooms. The entire home has been tastefully restored, and the atmosphere is one of old-world charm and elegance. A healthy gourmet breakfast, served in the sunny breakfast room, includes fruit, yogurt, muffins or scones, and a hot entrée. Taste the Past is located in downtown Drumheller, en route to the world-renowned Royal Tyrrell Museum of Palaeontology. Other activities available nearby include hiking through the badlands, visiting many dinosaur-related spots, golfing, camping, and fishing. Rosebud Dinner Theatre and the Canadian Badlands Passion Play are unique cultural attractions. Rosalie and Bryce are knowledgeable hosts and will help you plan your stay.

SEASON

all year

ACCOMMODATIONS

4 rooms with shared baths

Lakewinds

Jane and Stephen Locke
PO Box 1483, 328 Queen Street
Niagara-on-the-Lake, Ontario
L0S 1J0
Tel: (905) 468-1888
Fax: (905) 468-1061
E-mail: lakewind@niagara.com
www.lakewinds.niagara.com
$$$$

ABOUT THE B&B

A special experience awaits you at Lakewinds, a circa-1881, restored Victorian manor operated by Jane and Stephen Locke. Situated on an acre of quiet trees and gardens, Lakewinds offers unparalleled views of the Niagara-on-the-Lake Golf Club and Lake Ontario. The guest rooms, elegantly appointed with antiques, have been designed for comfort and privacy and feature private baths. Guests are invited to the games room for billiards or cards and, in summer, can enjoy refreshing dips in the heated pool or simply relax in rocking chairs on the veranda. Sumptuous breakfasts feature fruits, vegetables, and herbs from Jane's garden. Only one-and-a-half hours south of Toronto, Niagara-on-the-Lake is a charming town offering world-class theater, shops, fine restaurants, and beautiful parks — all with a turn-of-the-century ambiance. The many estate wineries in the area offer tours and tastings, while golf courses, tennis courts, and countless hiking and biking trails await the active visitor.

SEASON

all year

ACCOMMODATIONS

6 rooms with private baths

Leek and Sage Quiche

1 package cream of leek soup (Knorr brand recommended)
2 cups milk
5 eggs, beaten
2 cups half-and-half
¼ cup chopped sage
4 leaves phyllo dough
Melted butter
3 tablespoons bread crumbs
1½ cups grated cheese (a mixture of Gruyère, cheddar, and Emmental is best)

Sage sprigs

Combine the soup mix with the milk, and heat until the soup is boiling and thick. Cool it to room temperature (this may be done the night before). Preheat the oven to 375°F. Add the eggs, half-and-half, and chopped sage to the soup. Brush each leaf of phyllo with melted butter, and place them in a deep, 9" pie dish, folding and fluting the overhanging edges for a frilly effect. Sprinkle the bread crumbs, then the cheese, over the phyllo. Pour the egg mixture over the cheese, and bake 60 minutes. Let stand 10 minutes before cutting. Garnish with sage sprigs. ***Variation:*** Try basil or parsley instead of sage. ***Yield: 8 servings.***

Moose Jaw Minuet

16 slices brown bread, crusts removed
6 – 8 slices Black Forest ham, edges trimmed
¼ – ½ pound grated sharp cheddar cheese
6 eggs
3 cups homogenized milk
¼ cup finely chopped onion
2 teaspoons Worcestershire sauce
1 teaspoon powdered mustard
Pepper
Salt
Tabasco
¼ cup margarine
1 cup crushed cornflakes or Special K cereal

Cover the bottom of a greased 13 x 9" pan with half of the bread slices. Layer the ham, then the grated cheese, over the bread slices. Cover the cheese with the remaining bread slices. Beat together the eggs, milk, onion, Worcestershire sauce, mustard, a pinch of pepper and salt, and a dash of Tabasco, and pour the egg mixture over the bread slices. Seal the pan with plastic wrap, and let stand in the refrigerator overnight. In the morning, remove the pan from the refrigerator 45 minutes before baking. Preheat the oven to 350°F. Melt the margarine, and pour it over the crushed cornflakes. Sprinkle the cornflake mixture over the bread mixture, and bake, uncovered, for 60 minutes. Let stand 10 minutes before serving. ***Yield: 8 servings.***

Latimer on Oxford

Pat and Bill Latimer
37 Oxford Street West
Moose Jaw, Saskatchewan S6H 2N2
Tel: (306) 692-5481
$ – $$

ABOUT THE B&B

Built in 1911, this faithfully restored foursquare neo-Greek revival home greets you with Corinthian columns decorated with cherubs, which support the front balcony. The solid oak front door with acanthus leaf appliqué and beveled oval glass encourages you to come inside. Interior oak picture frame floors, leaded glass windows, pocket doors, and plate rails recall an era when quality craft, natural materials, and functional design ruled the day. Choose either the Oriental, Western, or Victorian guest rooms with shared bath, or the elegant Violet guest room with private bath. Also on the site is a little red coach house with exposed beams and a hay loft. Plan your visit to coincide with the Moose Jaw Minuet breakfast and your morning is begun with a cheer. A specialty produced by the heartland oven are golden brown rusks. Temple Gardens Thermo Mineral Spa, the museum and public library, City Hall, shops, and restaurants are a 10-minute walk downtown. Your hosts' interests include art, literature, and music.

SEASON

all year

ACCOMMODATIONS

1 room with private bath;
3 rooms with shared bath

Otella's Guest House

Ella van Dinther and Otto Schwab
42 Altura Road
Kelowna, British Columbia V1V 1B6
Tel: (250) 763-4922
Fax: (250) 763-4982
Reservations: (888) 858-8596
$$ – $$$$

ABOUT THE B&B

Enjoy luxury, nature, and gourmet cuisine at this romantic estate near world-class wineries, golf courses, sandy beaches, and downtown Kelowna. Otella's Guest House is located in a serene, parklike setting with a panoramic view of orchards, mountains, and the Okanagan Valley, and is adjacent to Knox Mountain Park's hiking trails. The landscaped garden is dotted with patios, benches, and chairs, which invite you to stop and enjoy the sun, flowers, birds, and butterflies. The three-story, air conditioned home was completely renovated as a B&B. The spacious guest rooms are comfortably furnished with queen or twin beds, down duvets, a sitting area, window seats, and a telephone and TV. Host-chef Otto Schwab prepares gourmet breakfasts that are served on the vine-covered patio or in the elegant dining room. Your hosts are wine enthusiasts and speak Dutch and German. Otella's Guest House is adult oriented and smoke- and pet-free.

SEASON

all year

ACCOMMODATIONS

2 rooms with private baths;
2-bedroom suite with private bath

Otella's Quiche in Potato Basket

"This no-dough quiche is great for breakfast or served with a salad for lunch." — Chef Otto Schwab

4 tablespoons butter
8 medium potatoes, peeled and grated
1 tablespoon vegetable oil or butter
½ pound bacon, cut into small strips
⅓ cup finely chopped green onion or snipped chives
3 – 4 ounces cheddar cheese, grated or diced
9 eggs
Ground coriander
Ground nutmeg
Pepper
Salt

Parsley sprigs
Sliced tomato

Heat 2 tablespoons of the butter in a large frying pan. Add the grated potato, and fry for about 10 minutes until golden brown, stirring with a wooden spoon. Add the remaining butter, and fry another 10 minutes until the potato is three-quarters cooked; remove from the heat.

(continued on next page)

Grease 12 large muffin cups with the vegetable oil. Press a thin layer of potato on the bottom and up the sides of each cup. Set aside until 60 minutes before serving (this process can be done 1 or 2 days in advance; simply cover the muffin pan with plastic wrap and store in the refrigerator until ready to use).

Preheat the oven to 375°F. Bake the potato cups for 10 – 15 minutes or until they are crisp. In the meantime, fry the bacon. Before the bacon becomes crisp, add the green onion and continue frying. After about 2 minutes, when the bacon is slightly crisp, remove the bacon mixture from the heat and drain the fat. Add some grated cheese to each baked potato cup. Bake for 3 minutes or until the cheese has melted. In a bowl, whisk the eggs and a pinch of coriander, nutmeg, pepper, and salt for 1 minute. Add some of the bacon mixture to each potato cup, followed by the egg mixture. Bake 10 – 15 minutes or until the egg is firm. Remove the quiches from the pan with a butter knife. Garnish with parsley sprigs and tomato, and serve immediately. ***Yield: 6 servings.***

Gîte à la ferme MACDALE Bed and Breakfast

Anne and Gordon MacWhirter
365 Route 132, Hope, PO Box 803
Paspébiac, Québec G0C 2K0
Tel: (418) 752-5270
$

ABOUT THE B&B

For a relaxing holiday, visit the Gaspé Peninsula and MACDALE Bed and Breakfast. Situated overlooking Baie des Chaleurs on a beef farm that has been active for five generations, this spacious three-story home offers two family rooms and a variety of guest accommodations. The aroma of fresh coffee and assorted muffins and pastries will awaken you and whet your appetite for an old-fashioned home-baked breakfast that includes farm-fresh eggs. Thanks to MACDALE's central location, tourist attractions such as world-famous Percé Rock and Forillon Park are well within day-trip driving distance. A seawater therapy resort is just minutes away, as are many museums, points of historical interest, and sports facilities. Anne is a first grade teacher while Gordon has recently retired from teaching junior high school mathematics.

SEASON

all year

ACCOMMODATIONS

1 loft with private bath;
4 rooms with shared baths

Overnight Sausage Omelet

1 pound pork breakfast sausage
6 slices white bread, crusts removed, cubed
1 cup grated cheddar or Emmental cheese
4 eggs
2 cups milk
½ teaspoon powdered mustard
½ teaspoon salt

Boil the sausage for 20 minutes, then cut it into bite-sized pieces. Grease a 12 x 8" casserole. Layer ⅓ of each of the bread, then the sausage, then the cheese, in the casserole. Repeat with the remaining bread, sausage, and cheese. Beat the eggs until foamy. Add the milk, mustard, and salt to the eggs, and mix well. Pour the egg mixture over the layered ingredients in the casserole. Cover and place in the refrigerator overnight. Remove the casserole from the refrigerator about 45 minutes before baking. Preheat the oven to 350°F. Bake the casserole, uncovered, for 90 minutes. Serve immediately. ***Yield: 8 – 10 servings.***

Reuben Bread Pudding with Maple-Onion Jam

(Recipe from Open Kitchen: A Chef's Day at The Inn at Bay Fortune *by Michael Smith, Callawind Publications)*

4 slices rye bread, cut into ½" cubes (about 4 cups)
1 cup milk
2 tablespoons coarse grained mustard
1 tablespoon Dijon mustard
¼ teaspoon ground caraway seeds
¼ teaspoon pepper
½ teaspoon salt
2 whole eggs
1 egg yolk
6 ounces cooked corned beef, cut into ½" cubes (about 1 cup)
½ cup sauerkraut
¼ cup snipped chives

Maple-onion jam:
1 large onion, sliced
2 tablespoons olive oil
½ cup maple syrup
¼ teaspoon salt

Preheat the oven to 350°F. Grease 4 (8-ounce) ramekins with cooking spray. Place the bread cubes on a baking sheet, and bake 15 – 20 minutes until they are completely toasted and golden brown. In a saucepan, heat the milk, mustards, caraway, pepper, and salt until the mixture simmers. Remove from heat.

(continued on next page)

The Inn at Bay Fortune

David Wilmer and Michael Smith
Bay Fortune
Prince Edward Island C0A 2B0
Tel: (902) 687-3745
Fax: (902) 687-3540
$$$ – $$$$

ABOUT THE B&B

Built in 1910 as the summer home of Broadway playwright Elmer Harris, this inn has enjoyed a place in the Bay Fortune artists' community ever since. In 1989, innkeeper David Wilmer restored the home to its former splendor, taking full advantage of its location overlooking Bay Fortune and the Northumberland Strait beyond. Uniquely decorated with a combination of island antiques and pieces created by local craftspeople, the 17 guest suites all have private baths and a view of the sea, and most have a fireplace in the sitting area. The dining room is the highest rated in Atlantic Canada by Where to Eat in Canada. *Chef Michael Smith has earned an international reputation for his focus on fresh island ingredients, and his contemporary cuisine is recognized for its lively combinations and detailed methods. The Inn at Bay Fortune is close to top-flight golf courses and deep-sea fishing, and less than an hour from Charlottetown, with its active nightlife and some of Canada's best theater.*

SEASON

May – October

ACCOMMODATIONS

17 suites with private baths

Whisk the whole eggs and egg yolk together in a large bowl. Slowly add the milk mixture, and whisk to combine. Add the bread cubes, corned beef, sauerkraut, and chives, and combine. Let stand 20 minutes. Bring a kettle of water to the boil. Divide the batter among the ramekins. Place them in a pan, and fill it with the hot water to two-thirds the depth of the pudding. Bake about 45 minutes until the edges of the puddings pull away from the ramekins and the pudding centers are set.

For the maple-onion jam, in a skillet, cook the onion slowly in the oil, stirring frequently, until the onion is caramelized to a deep, golden brown. As it cooks, gradually lower the heat to avoid burning the onion. (This step takes patience!). When the onion is brown, add the maple syrup and simmer 5 minutes. Remove from heat, and season with the salt.

To serve, unmold the puddings onto 4 warm plates, and serve with warm maple-onion jam. ***Tips:*** The pudding can also be placed in a 1-quart baking dish and baked about 5 – 10 minutes longer. The jam can be made ahead and refrigerated. It's also great served cold as a condiment. ***Yield: 4 servings.***

Sausage and Hash Brown Casserole

"For the hash brown lovers of the world, this is different and delicious." — Marj Wilkie

16-ounce package frozen shredded hash browns, thawed
5 eggs
¼ cup milk
2 tablespoons chopped onion
1 tablespoon chopped parsley
1 teaspoon powdered mustard
½ teaspoon salt
¼ teaspoon pepper
1 cup grated sharp cheddar cheese
8 pork breakfast sausages
4 tomato slices, cut in halves

Preheat the oven to 350°F. Partially cook the hash browns. Combine the eggs, milk, onion, parsley, mustard, salt, and pepper. Pour the egg mixture over the potatoes in a 13 x 9" baking dish. Sprinkle with ½ cup of the cheese. Bake 15 – 20 minutes. Meanwhile, cook the sausages. Arrange the sausages down the center of the potatoes. Sprinkle with the remaining cheese. Place 4 half slices of tomato along each side of the sausages. Return the casserole to the oven until the cheese melts. ***Yield: 4 servings.***

The Lookout at Schooner Cove

Marj and Herb Wilkie
3381 Dolphin Drive
Nanoose Bay, British Columbia
V9P 9H7
Tel/Fax: (250) 468-9796
www.pixsell.bc.ca/bb/1169.htm
$$

ABOUT THE B&B

Situated halfway between Victoria and Tofino on unspoiled Vancouver Island, this West Coast contemporary cedar home stands in a woodsy setting of rocks and tall evergreens. The wrap-around deck affords a 180-degree view of the Strait of Georgia and the majestic mountains beyond. Relax and savor this "little bit of heaven" or hike, golf, kayak, sail, fish, or sightsee. Take a day trip to the wild western shore of the island and Pacific Rim National Park or head south to charming Victoria. The vacation suite will accommodate four people and, with its private entrance and deck and fully equipped kitchen, makes a popular headquarters for an island stay. Hearty breakfasts are served in the dining room overlooking the ocean. After running a store in New York's Catskill Mountains for 17 years, Marj (from Australia) and Herb (from the US) established The Lookout in 1988 and enjoy helping their guests have a memorable stay.

SEASON

May – October
(or by arrangement)

ACCOMMODATIONS

1 vacation suite with private bath;
1 room with private bath;
1 room with shared bath

Captain's Quarters B&B

Linda and Arnie Aylward
RR #1
South Gillies, Ontario P0T 2V0
Tel: (807) 475-5630
$$

ABOUT THE B&B

Named in honor of the Aylward sea captains from Nova Scotia, Captain's Quarters is an intimate country bed and breakfast located southwest of the city of Thunder Bay, and a short drive from ski hills, amethyst mines, and fine dining. The modern log home features rustic yet gracious bedrooms with queen beds and private baths. Hiking, cross-country skiing, and golf can be done on the property. Expansion plans include a solarium with a hot tub. Pancakes with strawberries and whipped cream highlight an extensive and varied breakfast menu created from fresh, high-quality products. Another menu favorite, Nova Scotia crab toasties, reflects the B&B's maritime theme and the East Coast heritage of the host. Golf, gardening, sewing, and crafts are among Linda and Arnie's hobbies.

SEASON

all year

ACCOMMODATIONS

2 rooms with private baths

Shrimp and Dill Quiche

¾ cup grated mozzarella cheese
½ cup coarsely chopped cooked shrimp (canned is fine)
2 tablespoons finely chopped red pepper
1 tablespoon finely chopped green onion
24 small- or 18 medium-sized pastry shells (Crisco brand recommended)
2 eggs
⅔ cup light cream
½ teaspoon dried dill weed
Pepper
Salt

Preheat the oven to 375°F. Sprinkle the cheese, shrimp, red pepper, and green onion evenly into the pastry shells. Beat the eggs with the cream, dill, and a pinch of pepper and salt. Pour the egg mixture into the pastry shells, and bake 20 – 25 minutes. Serve warm. ***Variation:*** Use crab meat instead of shrimp. ***Yield: 24 small- or 18 medium-sized tarts.***

Spinach Omelet

2 (10-ounce) packages frozen spinach, partially thawed
¼ cup butter
¼ cup all-purpose flour
1 teaspoon salt
⅛ teaspoon pepper
2 cups half-and-half
6 – 8 thick slices bacon, cut into ¼" pieces and sautéed until partially crisp
3 green onions, chopped
1¼ cups grated Swiss cheese

6 omelets (recipe follows)

Coarsely chopped parsley

In a saucepan, cook the partially thawed spinach and drain. In another saucepan or large cast-iron skillet, melt the butter over low heat, and stir in the flour, salt, and pepper until blended. Increase the heat to medium, and gradually stir in the half-and-half. Cook, stirring constantly, until the cream mixture has thickened. Add the cooked spinach, bacon, onion, and 1 cup of the cheese. Cook, stirring, just until the cheese melts. Remove from the heat. Spoon about ¼ cup of the spinach filling onto each omelet, and fold. Sprinkle the omelet immediately with some of the remaining cheese (so it melts) and some chopped parsley. Repeat with the other omelets. *Tip:* This filling can be used with crêpes too. ***Yield: 6 servings.***

(continued on next page)

Fraser House

Sheila and Dennis Derksen
PO Box 211, 33 1st Street East
Letellier, Manitoba R0G 1C0
Tel: (204) 737-2284
$

ABOUT THE B&B

Memories are made at this elegant and romantic 1916 home. Hardwood floors, area rugs, and antique furniture enhance the home's Victorian decor. Spacious rooms combined with great hospitality make your stay most enjoyable. Relax with a beverage and home-baked goodies in the parlor or on the veranda or patio. Breakfast may consist of a puffy egg pancake or freshly baked croissants and muffins, along with the season's fresh fruit, served in the formal dining room. Fraser House is located just a few minutes north of the US border in the heart of Manitoba's bustling agricultural area, and is near places to golf, fish, shop, and ski. Sheila enjoys craft projects and holds painting classes during the winter months, while Dennis enjoys carpentry and is employed as a fertilizer dealer.

SEASON

all year

ACCOMMODATIONS

2 rooms with shared bath

Omelet:
2 eggs
2 tablespoons water
Pepper
Salt
1 tablespoon butter

Beat together the eggs and water. Season with a little pepper and salt. Melt the butter in a pan over medium-high heat (don't let it get brown). When the foaming butter starts to subside, pour in the egg mixture. It should set at the edges at once. With a spatula, gently push the cooked portions toward the center, and tilt and rotate the pan to allow any uncooked egg to flow into the spaces. Continue cooking until the top of the omelet just sets, and is moist and creamy. ***Yield: 1 omelet.***

Spinach Pie with Pine Nuts

4 cups roughly chopped spinach
1⅓ cups grated Swiss cheese
½ cup finely chopped onion
2 tablespoons pine nuts
4 eggs
1⅓ cups milk
1 cup biscuit mix
Ground nutmeg

Preheat the oven to 400°F. Lightly grease 4 individual casseroles. Layer the spinach, cheese, onion, and pine nuts in each casserole. Blend the eggs, milk, biscuit mix, and a sprinkle of nutmeg in a blender for 20 seconds. Pour the egg mixture over the spinach mixture. Bake 20 – 25 minutes or until firm. Serve immediately, before the pies deflate.
Yield: 4 servings.

The Catalpa Tree

Connie Ellis
2217 London Line
Sarnia, Ontario N7T 7H2
Tel: (800) 276-5135 or
(519) 542-5008
Fax: (519) 541-0297
$

ABOUT THE B&B

Built in 1894 by the host's great-grandfather, William Beatty, this family home displays true Victorian fashion, complete with gingerbread trim. The house, which is situated on a 100-acre crop farm, has been lovingly maintained in its original form. The B&B's decor complements the design of the house but also incorporates modern conveniences such as gas fireplaces and central air conditioning. Furnishings are a warm mix of contemporary and traditional pieces. A full gourmet breakfast is served in the parlor. The original dining room is now a lounge where guests can visit, relax with a good book, watch a favorite television program, enjoy a video, or play a game. A golf course is located at the end of the lane. In the area are many historical points of interest, a community theater, a water amusement park, a harness racing track, and places to go fishing, swimming, and boating. Picnic lunches or dinner are available by advance request.

SEASON

all year

ACCOMMODATIONS

3 rooms with shared bath

Sir William Mackenzie Inn

Joan and Paul Scott
PO Box 255, Highway 48
Kirkfield, Ontario K0M 2B0
Tel/Fax: (705) 438-1278
$$ – $$$

ABOUT THE B&B

Born in a Kirkfield log cabin in 1849, Canadian Northern Railway founder Sir William Mackenzie built his first mansion in Kirkfield in 1888, which became an exciting hub of hospitality for Mackenzie family guests. Today, this carefully restored 40-room home is now a B&B, offering large bedrooms — many with fireplaces. A full hot breakfast awaits your rising, after which you can visit in the popular Games Room. Take the time to explore the Sculpture Garden and the estate's 13 acres of tree-shaded lawns and beautiful woods, which create a relaxed atmosphere and form a magnificent backdrop for photographs. A restaurant is also located on the grounds. Innkeeper Paul Scott delights in relating the history of the estate and its original owner, "The Railway King of Canada," to his guests while leading the mansion tour. Sir William Mackenzie Inn is situated a few minutes from the Kirkfield Lift Locks (world's second largest), and is near places for boating, swimming, golfing, birdwatching, horseback riding, cycling, and go-carting, as well as a gambling casino.

SEASON

May 1 – October 20

ACCOMMODATIONS

7 rooms with private baths;
5 rooms with shared baths

Vegetable Casserole Surprise

"This vegetable casserole evolved from necessity. One day, we had unexpected company and an almost empty refrigerator. Our solution was to combine all the bits and pieces we had into a casserole that would serve 10. Everyone loved it and we have since been serving it regularly. You can add and subtract amounts according to your tastes and group size. We have prepared this dish for dinners of up to 100 people." — Joan Scott

2 cups medium-finely chopped cabbage
4 carrots, cut into bite-sized pieces
2 broccoli stalks, cut into bite-sized pieces
1 green pepper, cut into bite-sized pieces
1 onion, cut into bite-sized pieces
1 red pepper, cut into bite-sized pieces
½ head cauliflower, cut into bite-sized pieces
1 zucchini, 6" long, cut into bite-sized pieces
¼ pound sliced mushrooms
3 cloves garlic, finely chopped
3 tablespoons finely chopped ginger
Dried basil
Pepper
Salt

(continued on next page)

10-ounce can of cream soup (mushroom, chicken, or broccoli)
½ cup milk
3 slices mozzarella cheese
Sliced mushrooms or tomato wedges

Preheat the oven to 350°F. Steam the cabbage until just barely cooked (leave crisp). Place the cabbage in a gratin pan or rectangular glass casserole. Steam the carrot, broccoli, green pepper, onion, red pepper, and cauliflower until crisp (again, don't overcook). Add the zucchini, mushrooms, garlic, and ginger near the end of the cooking period to avoid overcooking. Stir in a little dried basil, pepper, and salt. Spread the vegetable mixture over the cabbage. Combine the soup with the milk, and pour over the vegetable mixture. Garnish with the cheese slices and some sliced mushrooms. Bake about 15 minutes. ***Tip:*** This casserole is great for a hot brunch on its own or when served with rice and breast of chicken. ***Yield: 8 – 10 generous servings.***

Vegetable Cheese Omelet

4 green onions, finely chopped
3 tomatoes, finely chopped
1 green pepper, finely chopped
¼ pound mushrooms, finely chopped
Butter
8 eggs, lightly beaten
8 ounces sharp cheddar cheese, grated

Snipped chives
Whole wheat toast
Jam

Preheat the oven broiler. Sauté the onion, tomato, green pepper, and mushrooms in butter in a large ovenproof frying pan. Gently pour in the eggs. Cook over low heat until the bottom of the omelet is set. Place the omelet under the broiler for 3 – 4 minutes. As the omelet puffs up (it should remain pale yellow), remove it and sprinkle it with the cheese. Return the omelet to the broiler until the cheese has melted. The omelet will puff up beautifully. Cut the omelet in half, and garnish with the chives. Serve with whole wheat toast and jam. ***Yield: 2 servings.***

Bay View Farm / La Ferme Bay View

Helen and Garnett Sawyer
PO Box 21,
337 New Carlisle West, Route 132
New Carlisle, Québec G0C 1Z0
Tel: (418) 752-2725/6718
$

ABOUT THE B&B

Situated between New Carlisle and Bonaventure, Bay View Farm offers country hospitality in a beautiful seaside environment on the rugged Baie des Chaleurs coastline of Québec's Gaspé Peninsula. Seaside accommodations include five comfortable guest rooms and a fully equipped cottage. At breakfast, enjoy Bay View's farm-fresh eggs, meat, homemade muffins, scones, jams, jellies, and beverages, as well as fresh fruits and vegetables in season from the farm's garden and orchards. Additional meals are available on request at reasonable rates. Handicrafts are on display throughout the house. Enjoy the breathtaking panoramic seascapes, participate in the Bay View Folk Festival (second weekend of August) with folk music and dancing, or visit Percé Rock and the archaeological caves of Saint-Elzéar.

SEASON

May – November

ACCOMMODATIONS

5 rooms with shared baths;
1 private cottage with private bath

Vegetable Garden Bake

"Since I love to use recipes that call for ingredients I can pick fresh from my garden, this has become one of my favorites. It seems to be a favorite of my guests too since I get lots of compliments every time it's served. I like to dish it up with freshly baked cheese biscuits and pork breakfast sausage." — Patricia Kroker

5 eggs
⅔ cup vegetable oil
1 tablespoon dried parsley
¾ teaspoon salt
¼ teaspoon pepper
⅔ cup grated Parmesan cheese
3½ cups grated zucchini
1¼ cups chopped onion
¼ cup grated carrot
1¼ cups biscuit mix

Preheat the oven to 350°F. Beat the eggs until frothy in a large mixing bowl. Mix in the oil, parsley, salt, and pepper. Stir in the cheese, then the zucchini, onion, and carrot. Add the biscuit mix, and combine. Pour the batter into a greased 9" shallow casserole, and bake about 35 minutes. ***Yield: 8 servings.***

Gaeste-Haus Kroker

Patricia Kroker
PO Box 202
Bruderheim, Alberta T0B 0S0
Tel: (403) 796-3621
$$

ABOUT THE B&B

Only a short drive yet worlds away from the hustle and bustle of Edmonton, Gaeste-Haus Kroker is a charming and comfortable 1927 brick Victorian guest house. You can choose to enjoy the peaceful ambiance of the entire upper level or mingle with other guests in the parlor furnished in French Provincial style. Wind down your evening with a snack of homemade dessert. Awaken in the morning to freshly brewed coffee and a hearty breakfast served on fine china in the elegantly furnished dining room. Relax on the veranda or in front of the outdoor fireplace, and stroll about the spacious lawn and garden. A former registered nurse, town councilor, and town mayor, hostess Patricia Kroker enjoys gardening, baking, and traveling, and will make your visit an enjoyable and memorable experience. Area attractions include Elk Island National Park, West Edmonton Mall, Ukrainian Cultural Heritage Village, and Beaverhill Lake.

SEASON

April 1 – December 31

ACCOMMODATIONS

3 rooms with shared bath

Spruceholme Inn

Marlene and Glenn Scullion
204 rue Principale
Fort-Coulonge, Québec J0X 1V0
Tel: (819) 683-5635
Fax: (819) 683-2139
$$$

ABOUT THE B&B

Built in 1875 by lumber baron George Bryson Jr., Spruceholme Inn is a historic Victorian stone mansion located in the Ottawa River Valley town of Fort-Coulonge. The inn is a leisurely drive from the nation's capital, Ottawa, only minutes from golfing, whitewater rafting, and skiing, and across the street from the Ottawa River where you can fish and, in winter, go skating. Operated by Marlene and Glenn Scullion, Spruceholme has been restored to its original glory and now operates as an elegant country inn with a licensed bar and a formal dining room. The six luxury guest suites are furnished with the mansion's original antiques. In years gone by, such distinguished guests as former Canadian prime minister Sir Wilfrid Laurier were entertained at Spruceholme. Marlene and Glenn, both recently retired from the broadcasting industry, work diligently to ensure their guests have a memorable stay. Glenn is an accomplished pianist and plays the inn's 1911 Steinway grand piano for guests each evening.

SEASON

all year

ACCOMMODATIONS

6 suites with private baths

Zucchini Crescent Pie

4 cups thinly sliced unpeeled zucchini
1 cup chopped onion
½ cup margarine
⅓ cup chopped parsley
½ teaspoon pepper
½ teaspoon salt
¼ teaspoon dried basil
¼ teaspoon dried oregano
¼ teaspoon garlic powder
2 eggs, well beaten
8 ounces mozzarella cheese, grated
8-ounce package crescent dinner rolls
2 teaspoons prepared mustard

Preheat the oven to 375°F. Sauté the zucchini and onion until tender in the margarine. Stir in the parsley, pepper, salt, basil, oregano, and garlic powder. In a large bowl, blend the eggs with the cheese. Stir in the vegetable mixture. Separate the pieces of crescent dough, and press them over the bottom and up the sides of an ungreased 9" pie pan to form a crust. Spread the crust with the mustard. Pour the vegetable mixture evenly over the crust. Bake 18 – 20 minutes. Let stand 10 minutes before cutting. ***Yield: 6 – 8 servings.***

Egg, Cheese, Meat, & Fish Main Dishes

Baked Stuffed Salmon in Egg Sauce

3 tablespoons lemon juice
3 teaspoons salt
1 Atlantic salmon, 5 – 8 pounds, cleaned and scaled
⅓ cup butter
1 – 2 medium onions, chopped
½ cup chopped celery
½ cup grated carrot
2 cups white or whole wheat bread crumbs
1 teaspoon dried savory or sage
¼ teaspoon pepper
1 egg, beaten
Vegetable oil

Egg sauce:
¼ cup butter
¼ cup all-purpose flour
1½ cups milk
½ – 1 teaspoon salt
Pepper
2 eggs, hard-boiled and chopped
Chopped parsley

(continued on next page)

Humber Gallery Hospitality Home

Edna and Eldon Swyer
26 Roberts Drive
Little Rapids, Newfoundland
A2H 6C3
Mailing address: PO Box 15
Corner Brook, Newfoundland
A2H 6C3
Tel: (709) 634-2660
E-mail: eldonswyer@thezone.net
$$

ABOUT THE B&B

A popular stop for the British royal family, Little Rapids (near Corner Brook) is home to Humber Gallery, an impressive cedar abode with cathedral ceilings, fireplace, wraparound sun deck, two guest rooms with double beds, one guest room with twin beds, and one guest room with a queen bed. A nutritious breakfast is served, and other meals and use of the barbecue and picnic area can be arranged. An excellent spot for an overnight stay when going or coming from Gros Morne National Park, this B&B is in the heart of the Humber Valley Reserve near Marble Mountain Ski Resort, mini-golf facilities, "U-pick" strawberry farms, Bay of Islands tourist attractions, South Brook and Pasadena beaches on Deer Lake, and the Humber River. Edna and Eldon can provide maps, tourist literature, a licensed salmon fishing guide, and insider tips on area attractions.

SEASON

June – September;
February – March

ACCOMMODATIONS

1 room with private bath;
3 rooms with shared baths

Preheat the oven to 425°F. Combine the lemon juice with 2 teaspoons of the salt. Rub the salmon inside and out with the lemon juice mixture. Melt the butter in a saucepan. Add the onion and celery, and cook over medium-low heat until soft (about 10 minutes). In a bowl, combine the onion mixture with the carrot, bread crumbs, savory, remaining salt, and pepper. Add the beaten egg, and mix well. Stuff the salmon with the bread crumb mixture, and skewer or sew closed. Brush the surface of the salmon with oil. Place the salmon on a lightly greased baking sheet. Bake allowing 10 minutes per inch of thickness of stuffed fish. Baste with oil during the baking. The salmon is ready when the flesh is no longer translucent and can be pulled away from the backbone with a knife. Let stand 5 – 10 minutes while you cook the egg sauce.

In a heavy saucepan, melt the butter over medium-low heat. Stir in the flour until the mixture is smooth, and remove from the heat. Gradually stir in half of the milk. Return the sauce to the heat, and beat until smooth and shiny. Gradually add the remaining milk, salt, and pepper to taste. Cook 2 – 3 minutes until the sauce is smooth and shiny. Add the chopped egg and a little chopped parsley. Place the hot egg sauce in a dish, and serve with the salmon. ***Yield: 8 servings.***

Basil Tomato and Egg

1 tomato
Chopped basil or fresh pesto
Olive oil
Freshly grated white pepper
Salt
Butter
2 eggs, beaten

2 basil leaves

Cut off the top of the tomato. Gently squeeze the tomato to remove the juice with the seeds, then chop the tomato into small pieces. Sauté the tomato and some chopped basil for a couple of minutes in some olive oil. Add some freshly grated white pepper and some salt, and mix. Add some butter and the eggs, and scramble the eggs. Divide the egg mixture between 2 plates, garnish with a basil leaf, and serve immediately.
Yield:* *2 servings.

Montréal Oasis

Lena Blondel
3000 Breslay Road
Montréal, Québec H3Y 2G7
Tel: (514) 935-2312
$$

ABOUT THE B&B

In pilgrim days, the evergreen tree was a sign of shelter, good food, and warm hospitality. It's fitting, then, that two towering evergreens frame the door to Montréal Oasis. This charming B&B with original leaded windows and slanted ceilings is located in downtown Montréal's west end, close to the Fine Arts Museum, chic Crescent Street and Greene Avenue shopping and restaurants, and the "main drag," St. Catherine Street. The beautiful and safe neighborhood with its spacious Elizabethan-style houses and pretty gardens is locally referred to as the Priest Farm district — once a holiday resort for priests. Originally from Sweden, your world-traveled hostess Lena has lived in many countries around the globe, which is evident from the African, Asian, and Swedish art that graces the B&B. The three guest rooms feature Scandinavian and Québecois furniture. Lena loves good food, and serves three-course gourmet breakfasts featuring delicious, fresh ingredients. A friendly Siamese cat resides on the main floor.

SEASON

all year

ACCOMMODATIONS

3 rooms with shared baths

Harbour House Bed & Breakfast Inn

Paula Franklin
615 Lakeshore Drive
Cold Lake, Alberta T9M 1A2
Tel: (403) 639-2337
$$ – $$$

ABOUT THE B&B

Built in 1989 to complement the Cold Lake Marina, Harbour House is patterned after the Old Coast Guard Station in Virginia Beach, Virginia. The house has the charm of old New England. Climb the stairs to the viewing tower for a panoramic view of Cold Lake, Alberta's seventh largest lake. Settle into one of 11 individually decorated rooms (most facing the lake), and rest assured of a comfortable night's sleep under feather duvets or hand-stitched quilts. Awake to a breathtaking sunrise over the lake and the aroma of the inn's famous sticky buns or other home-baked goods, served with fresh fruit specialties and juice. Nearby Cold Lake Provincial Park is home to many bird species. Harbour House is within walking distance of the lake, with its opportunities for fishing and boating. Nearby you can go mini-golfing and regular golfing, bowling, skiing, and browsing in antique and craft shops.

SEASON

all year

ACCOMMODATIONS

5 rooms with private baths;
6 rooms with shared baths

Breakfast Burritos

"I used to make this in pita bread, but one day the store was out of pita, so I decided to try tortillas. Lo and behold, they became breakfast burritos!" — Paula Franklin

4 eggs, beaten
¼ cup milk
2 slices cooked ham, chopped
1 green onion, chopped
Pepper
Salt
2 teaspoons butter or margarine
2 large flour tortillas
½ cup grated cheddar cheese

Salsa (see recipes on page 285 and page 295)

Mix together the eggs, milk, ham, onion, and a pinch of pepper and salt in a bowl. Melt the butter in a skillet, and scramble the egg mixture. Pile half of the egg mixture down the center of each tortilla, leaving 1" of space at each end. Fold one end of the tortilla over the egg mixture, then fold the sides over. Place the burrito seam-side down on a plate, and sprinkle the cheese over it. Microwave 60 – 90 seconds or until the cheese has melted. Serve with salsa. ***Yield: 2 servings.***

Breakfast in One

"For vegetarians, simply omit the bacon or ham." — Elaine Landray

6 slices bread, crusts removed
Butter
1 cup grated Gruyère or Emmental cheese
1 cup cooked chopped ham or crumbled bacon
6 eggs
Pepper
Salt
6 teaspoons heavy cream

Preheat the oven to 375°F. Roll the bread slices with a rolling pin. Butter both sides, and press the slices into a 6-cup muffin pan (a Texas muffin pan works best). Bake 15 minutes.

Reduce the oven temperature to 350°F. Reserve a little of the cheese, and put the rest in the bottoms of the toast cups. Sprinkle the ham over the cheese. Break an egg carefully into each cup. Add a little pepper and salt, a dot of butter, and 1 teaspoon of the cream to each cup. Top with the remaining cheese, and bake 18 – 20 minutes. ***Yield: 6 servings.***

Linden House B&B

Elaine and Phil Landray
PO Box 1586, 389 Simcoe Street
Niagara-on-the-Lake, Ontario
L0S IJ0
Tel: (905) 468-3923
Fax: (905) 468-8946
E-mail: linden@niagara.com
$$$

ABOUT THE B&B

A warm welcome awaits you at Linden House, a new Cape Cod-style, air conditioned home with private guest wing featuring two rooms with queen beds and one room with twin/king bed. All rooms have private ensuite bathrooms. In the queen rooms are brass beds and cream wicker furniture, while the twin/king room highlights the nautical atmosphere with Cape Cod wicker. On the same level as the bedrooms is a guest lounge with television, VCR, games, and books, or you can choose to enjoy the garden or relax in the gazebo. Smoke-free Linden House offers convenient on-site parking and is located in the old town, just four short blocks from Queen Street with its shopping and theaters. In summer, enjoy water recreation on Lake Ontario or top-notch theater at the Shaw Festival. Your hosts, Elaine and Phil, serve such sumptuous breakfasts — featuring seasonal Niagara fruit — that their guests claim they don't need lunch!

SEASON

all year

ACCOMMODATIONS

3 rooms with private baths

Le Gîte Park Avenue B&B

Anne-Marie and Irving Bansfield
54 Park Avenue
Ottawa, Ontario K2P 1B2
Tel: (613) 230-9131
$$

ABOUT THE B&B

A bright, airy ambiance and artistic decor await you at Park Avenue B&B, an elegant, brick 1906 home located in a charming residential area of downtown Ottawa, Canada's capital. In addition to high-quality beds done up in classic cotton and linen sheets and duvets, each guest room is furnished with a desk and swivel chair, a rocking chair, bookshelves, excellent lighting, and attractive works of art. Ideal for families, the third-floor suite has two bedrooms and a private bath. The mood throughout the house is one of relaxation and warmth. Park Avenue B&B is close to the Parliament Buildings, art galleries, and museums, and is only three minutes (by foot) from the Rideau Canal, which freezes into the world's longest skating rink. Ottawa has a number of exciting festivals and activities, including Winterlude, a winter carnival held each February. Anne-Marie and Irving make it a point to know what's going on when in Ottawa so they can advise their guests on what to see and do.

SEASON

all year

ACCOMMODATIONS

1 suite with private bath;
2 rooms with shared bath

Brule Jol (Salt Cod)

"This nutritious salt cod dish originates from my West Indian roots. It's usually accompanied by 'bake' biscuits." — Irving Bansfield

1 pound (approximately) boneless salt cod
3 – 4 tablespoons finely chopped green onion and/or snipped chives
3 – 4 tablespoons finely chopped red and/or yellow pepper
3 tablespoons olive oil
Juice of 1 lemon or lime
Lettuce leaves
2 tomatoes, sliced or cut into wedges
1 avocado, cut into slender wedges (optional)

Lemon slices
"Bake" biscuits (see recipe on page 145)

Soak the fish overnight in just enough water to cover it. Drain. Place the fish in a deep skillet, and cover it again with cold water. Bring the fish mixture almost to a boil — as it starts to simmer, remove it from the heat, rinse the fish under cold water, and drain. Shred the fish into a bowl. Add the onion and pepper. Combine the oil and lemon juice, and drizzle over the fish, reserving a little. Arrange the fish on some lettuce leaves on a platter. Surround the fish with the tomatoes and optional avocado, and drizzle the reserved oil mixture over the dish. Garnish with lemon slices. Serve with "bake" biscuits. ***Tip:*** If your taste buds delight in piquant flavor, add a few drops of hot pepper sauce to the dressing. ***Yield: 6 servings.***

Dutch Toastie

"A Dutch toastie is great at any time of the day. We serve them to our Tea Room patrons for lunch and to our B&B guests for a hearty breakfast." — Bonnie Evans

1 slice Black Forest ham
1 pineapple ring
1 slice bread
4 – 6 spears cooked asparagus
2 thin slices cheese (Swiss or Gruyère)

Place the ham, then the pineapple, on the bread. Top with the asparagus and cheese. Heat under the broiler until the cheese has melted. ***Yield: 1 serving.***

Cornelius White House Bed & Breakfast

Bonnie and Frank Evans
8 Wellington Street
Bloomfield, Ontario K0K 1G0
Tel/Fax: (613) 393-2282
$ – $$

ABOUT THE B&B

Located on the historic Loyalist Parkway at the west end of a farming community in picturesque Prince Edward County, the Cornelius White House is named for its original owner, a Dutch settler who built this charming red-brick house in 1862. Today, a sense of history and design combine with European furnishings and accents to create a unique B&B. Three guest rooms on the second floor open onto the sitting room below, which has a cathedral ceiling. There is also a suite on the main floor. The house is air conditioned and is a smoke-free environment. A full breakfast of fruit, a hot main course, and fresh baked goods is served in the Dutch Treat Tea Room. Outstanding restaurants are nearby, as well as antique and craft shops, galleries, studios, and museums. Cornelius White House is just 10 minutes from Sandbanks and Outlet Beach Provincial Parks, famous for the largest freshwater sand dunes in the world. Prince Edward County, with its panoramic views and gentle rolling hills, is a cyclist's dream come true.

SEASON

all year

ACCOMMODATIONS

2 rooms with private baths;
2 rooms with shared bath

Wyndswept Bed & Breakfast

Glenda and Bob Carter
Box 2683
Hinton, Alberta T7V 1Y2
Tel: (780) 866-3950
Fax: (780) 866-3951
E-mail: wyndswep@agt.net
$$ – $$$

ABOUT THE B&B

The Jasper area's first four-star B&B, Wyndswept Bed & Breakfast is built on the side of a hill in the Folding Mountain Range. From this vantage point, guests marvel at the 180-degree panoramic view of the Rocky Mountains, a nearby valley, and the spectacular sunrises and sunsets. Some 38 different wildflowers thrive on the hill. Wildlife such as bears, deer, elk, and bighorn sheep can be seen right outside the window while guests enjoy a five-course heart-healthy breakfast. The decor of each guest suite has a different theme, and all suites have private baths and luxurious bedding. At night, you can rest on hand-hewn benches by the cozy fire pit and watch the stars or listen to the howl of wolves and coyotes. Wyndswept is located in a quiet mountain village at the eastern edge of Jasper National Park. Your hosts are long-time residents who know the area well and can suggest points of interest. Glenda is retired after working for 30 years as a mental health therapist, while Bob is a quality control auditor and the resident star gazer.

SEASON

all year

ACCOMMODATIONS

2 suites with private baths

Eggs in Tomato Cups

4 firm tomatoes (of uniform shape)
Dried basil
Pepper
Salt
Diced ham
4 eggs
Grated Parmesan cheese

Hash browns
Biscuits

Preheat the oven to 400°F. Pour boiling water over the tomatoes. Remove the skins and stem ends, and scoop out the centers to make cups. Drain them, and sprinkle the inside of each with some basil, pepper, salt, and ham. Break an egg into each cup, and top with Parmesan cheese. Place the tomato cups in a baking dish, and bake about 10 minutes or until the eggs are set. Serve with hash browns and biscuits. ***Tip:*** Add some chopped sun-dried tomatoes. ***Yield: 4 servings.***

Eggs Mexicana with Salsa

"We enjoyed this dish so much when visiting Mexico that we decided to adapt it for our Henderson Hollow guests." — Jeanette Henderson

8 eggs, beaten
2 tablespoons water
1 hot pepper, diced (such as jalapeño)
1 medium tomato, diced (juice and seeds removed)
1 small onion, diced
½ green pepper, diced
1 tablespoon butter or vegetable oil

Salsa (recipe follows)

Beat the eggs and water together. Sauté the hot pepper, tomato, onion, and green pepper in the butter just until the vegetables are tender (don't brown). Stir in the egg mixture and continue stirring until cooked. Serve with salsa. ***Tip:*** If you don't want your eggs too hot, leave the hot pepper whole and remove it before serving this dish. ***Yield: 4 servings.***

(continued on next page)

Henderson Hollow

Jeanette and Garry Henderson
RR #1
Austin, Manitoba R0H 0C0
Tel: (204) 466-2857
$

ABOUT THE B&B

A piece of heaven and a heavenly getaway, Henderson Hollow is a cozy country home set in beautiful, rolling, wooded hills. Simply relax on the large deck or in the screened sun porch surrounded by nature's beauty and abundant wildlife, or enjoy many indoor and outdoor activities (depending on the season). Full home-cooked meals include home-baked bread and cinnamon rolls, and dishes featuring garden-fresh fruits and vegetables. The house is filled with antiques and decorated with many homemade crafts for you to enjoy (or purchase, if you desire). Nearby points of interest include the Austin Agricultural Museum (largest in western Canada), Spruce Woods Provincial Park, Margaret Laurence Museum, and the Thomas Seton Centre. Your hosts' interests include golfing in summer at the many beautiful — and challenging! — golf courses nearby, and cross-country skiing in winter right from the back door.

SEASON

all year

ACCOMMODATIONS

1 room with private bath;
2 rooms with shared bath;
campground facilities

Salsa:

6 cups peeled, coarsely diced tomatoes
3 large onions, chopped
1 – 2 cloves garlic, minced
1 large green pepper, diced
¼ cup diced hot pepper (such as jalapeño)
½ cup cider vinegar or white vinegar
2 tablespoons sugar
2 teaspoons dried parsley
1½ teaspoons salt
1 teaspoon dried basil
1 teaspoon dried oregano
1 cup cooked black beans (optional)
1 cup cooked corn kernels (optional)
2 tablespoons cornstarch
¼ cup water

In a saucepan, combine the tomato, onion, garlic, green pepper, hot pepper, vinegar, sugar, parsley, salt, basil, and oregano. Bring the tomato mixture to a boil and simmer 30 minutes or until the vegetables are tender. Add the optional black beans and corn. Dissolve the cornstarch in the water and stir into the vegetable mixture. Cook another 10 minutes. Seal the salsa in sterilized jars. Refrigerate once a jar has been opened. ***Yield: About 8 cups.***

Finnish Miners' Pasties

"Given to me by my Finnish father, this recipe was a favorite 'all-in-one' lunch for Finnish miners. The meat is at one end and the dessert at the other! These are great to pack for hikes or picnics."
— *Nancy Perkins*

Dough:
1 cup shortening
1¼ cups boiling water
1 teaspoon salt
4½ – 5 cups all-purpose flour

Meat filling:
3 slices bacon, diced
3 small potatoes, diced
1 carrot, grated
1 small onion, diced
Pepper
Salt

Apple filling:
4 medium apples, peeled, cored, and diced
2 tablespoons sugar
2 teaspoons all-purpose flour
½ teaspoon ground cinnamon
⅛ teaspoon salt

Bacon grease

(continued on next page)

Bayberry Cliff Inn

Nancy and Don Perkins
RR #4, Little Sands
Murray River,
Prince Edward Island C0A 1W0
Tel: (800) 668-3395 or
(902) 962-3395
$$ – $$$

ABOUT THE B&B

Bayberry Cliff Inn is named for the fragrant bayberry bushes that cover the rugged 40-foot cliff on which the inn sits. Incorporating two reconstructed post and beam barns, the inn features intriguing architectural details such as individually shaped rooms and multiple-level living spaces. Bedrooms, lofts, and sitting areas are filled with handmade quilts, antique furniture, and paintings, the result of a lifetime of collecting beautiful things. A large library and breakfast area are on the ground level. Don's hash browns and bacon and Nancy's sourdough pancakes and blueberry muffins all consistently get rave reviews. Don is a retired teacher and Nancy is a marine painter (who has made sure the changeable ocean can be seen from every level of the B&B). Bayberry Cliff Inn activities include enjoying up to 35 different wildflowers, sitting in the whimsical tree perch to watch for marine life, inner-tubing, swimming, and beachcombing. You may cook your own meals on the gas grill or choose from many excellent restaurants a scant 15-minute drive away.

SEASON

May 10 – September 30

ACCOMMODATIONS

3 rooms with private baths;
1 room with shared bath

Mix the shortening with the boiling water and salt. Add just enough flour to make a stiff dough. Chill 60 minutes. Preheat the oven to 350°F. On a floured surface, roll pieces of dough into 4½" circles; set aside. For the meat filling, combine the bacon, potato, carrot, onion, and a little pepper and salt in a bowl. For the apple filling, combine the apple, sugar, flour, cinnamon, and salt in a separate bowl. To assemble the pasties, put 1 tablespoon meat filling on one side of the circles of dough, and 1 tablespoon apple filling on the other side. Raise the edges of the dough, and pinch them together. Put the pasties pinched-side down on a greased baking sheet, and pat into the shape of a finger roll. Brush the tops with bacon grease, and bake 60 minutes. ***Yield: 20 – 24 pasties.***

Maritime Morning Eggs

2 English muffins
Mayonnaise
4 slices cooked ham
4 eggs, poached
4 slices cheese, cut into strips

Preheat the oven to 350°F. Split the muffins with a fork, and spread each half generously with mayonnaise. Top each half with a slice of ham. Place the muffins in a covered baking dish, and warm them in the oven about 15 minutes. Top each muffin with a well-drained poached egg, and arrange cheese strips in a lattice design on top of the egg. Return the muffins to the oven and bake, uncovered, just until the cheese melts. *Tip:* A quick method is to warm the muffins topped with mayonnaise and ham in a microwave, place the egg and cheese on top, and broil briefly. ***Yield: 4 servings.***

Fairfield Farm Inn

Shae and Richard Griffith
10 Main Street West, Route 1
Middleton, Nova Scotia B0S 1P0
Tel/Fax: (800) 237-9896
or (902) 825-6989
$$

ABOUT THE B&B

Fairfield Farm Inn is situated on a 110-acre fruit and vegetable farm famous for its luscious melons. Built in 1886, this Annapolis Valley farmhouse has been completely restored and furnished in period antiques to enhance its original charm. The five guest rooms have cozy comforters, king- and queen-sized beds, and private baths. The Annapolis River and Slocum Brook are on the property, as are birdwatching and walking trails, pheasants, and other abundant wildlife. Shae and Richard take pride in offering Maritime hospitality and wholesome country breakfasts featuring fresh fruit picked from their farm and homemade jams and jellies. Shae is a member of the Acadia University Business School Advisory Board; Richard is a retired military officer. Their hobbies include gardening, antique hunting, reading, and traveling. A few minutes from picturesque fishing villages and the world's highest tides on the Bay of Fundy, Middleton boasts museums, restaurants, boutiques, and theater — all a short walking distance from the inn.

SEASON

all year
(winter by reservation only)

ACCOMMODATIONS

5 rooms with private baths

Dorrington Bed & Breakfast

Pat Gray
13851 19A Avenue
White Rock, British Columbia
V4A 9M2
Tel: (604) 535-4408
Fax: (604) 535-4409
www.bbcanada.com/508.html
$$ – $$$

ABOUT THE B&B

A luxurious escape a short drive from Vancouver, Dorrington is a wonderful base for exploring the city and its surrounding area. Each guest room has a different theme: The Victorian is graced by a double four-poster bed and period decor; The St. Andrews has a unique queen bed hewn from maple branches, and contains many original souvenirs of this famous Scottish golf links; The Windsor is 700 square feet of luxury with a brass, canopied queen bed, fireplace, sitting area, and marble bathroom with a double Jacuzzi tub. A full breakfast is served in the Hunt Salon or on the patio overlooking the gardens, tennis court, pond, and outside hot tub. White Rock beach with its promenade and fine eateries is three minutes away, while ferries to Victoria and the Gulf Islands are 30 minutes away. If you wish, you can use Dorrington's side-by-side tandem bike for a picnic in one of the many nearby heritage forests. Pat is the director of marketing for a calendar manufacturer/distributor.

SEASON

all year

ACCOMMODATIONS

3 rooms (including 1 suite) with private baths

Nest Eggs

2 – 3 thin slices Black Forest ham
1 egg
1 tablespoon half-and-half
1 heaping tablespoon grated Swiss cheese
Dried basil
English muffin half

Preheat the oven to 350°F. Grease a 4" ramekin or custard dish. Line it with the ham, and break the egg over it. Add the half-and-half, and sprinkle it with the cheese and a little basil. Bake 20 minutes. Toward the end of the baking time, toast the muffin half, and serve the egg on top. ***Yield: 1 serving.***

Nova Scotia Crab Toasties

"This recipe reflects the East Coast influence of our B&B."
— Arnie Aylward

12 ounces cooked king crab meat, chopped (canned is fine)
¾ cup finely diced celery
¼ – ½ cup mayonnaise
½ teaspoon dried dill weed
3 English muffins, halved
6 slices cheddar cheese

Preheat the oven to 350°F. Mix the crab, celery, mayonnaise, and dill. Set aside. Lightly toast the English muffin halves. Spread the crab mixture evenly on the muffin halves, and top each with a slice of cheese. Place the toasties on a baking sheet, and bake 10 – 12 minutes. ***Yield: 6 servings.***

Captain's Quarters B&B

Linda and Arnie Aylward
RR #1
South Gillies, Ontario P0T 2V0
Tel: (807) 475-5630
$$

ABOUT THE B&B

Named in honor of the Aylward sea captains from Nova Scotia, Captain's Quarters is an intimate country bed and breakfast located southwest of the city of Thunder Bay, and a short drive from ski hills, amethyst mines, and fine dining. The modern log home features rustic yet gracious bedrooms with queen beds and private baths. Hiking, cross-country skiing, and golf can be done on the property. Expansion plans include a solarium with a hot tub. Pancakes with strawberries and whipped cream highlight an extensive and varied breakfast menu created from fresh, high-quality products. Another menu favorite, Nova Scotia crab toasties, reflects the B&B's maritime theme and the East Coast heritage of the host. Golf, gardening, sewing, and crafts are among Linda and Arnie's hobbies.

SEASON

all year

ACCOMMODATIONS

2 rooms with private baths

Montréal Oasis

Lena Blondel
3000 Breslay Road
Montréal, Québec H3Y 2G7
Tel: (514) 935-2312
$$

ABOUT THE B&B

In pilgrim days, the evergreen tree was a sign of shelter, good food, and warm hospitality. It's fitting, then, that two towering evergreens frame the door to Montréal Oasis. This charming B&B with original leaded windows and slanted ceilings is located in downtown Montréal's west end, close to the Fine Arts Museum, chic Crescent Street and Greene Avenue shopping and restaurants, and the "main drag," St. Catherine Street. The beautiful and safe neighborhood with its spacious Elizabethan-style houses and pretty gardens is locally referred to as the Priest Farm district — once a holiday resort for priests. Originally from Sweden, your world-traveled hostess Lena has lived in many countries around the globe, which is evident from the African, Asian, and Swedish art that graces the B&B. The three guest rooms feature Scandinavian and Québecois furniture. Lena loves good food, and serves three-course gourmet breakfasts featuring delicious, fresh ingredients. A friendly Siamese cat resides on the main floor.

SEASON

all year

ACCOMMODATIONS

3 rooms with shared baths

Oasis Poached Eggs

1 teaspoon mixed chopped parsley, chopped cilantro*, and snipped chives
1 teaspoon butter
Lemon juice
1 egg, poached
White, black, red, and green crushed peppercorns

Toasted English muffins
Dark bread

**Note: Cilantro is also known as coriander.*

Place the herb mixture and the butter in a small dish, and melt the butter in a microwave. Mix in a few drops of lemon juice. Place the herb mixture over the poached egg, and top with the peppercorn mixture. ***Tip:*** If using unsalted butter, add some sea salt to the butter mixture. Serve with a basket of toasted English muffins and dark bread. ***Yield: 1 serving.***

Pesto and Cheese Bagel Melt

"This is a good hot breakfast on a warm summer morning. Guests take the leftovers and have them cold for lunch while they are hiking one of our many spectacular trails." — Glenda Carter

Low-fat cream cheese
4 onion or pesto bagels, halved
Pesto
Tomatoes, thinly sliced
Freshly ground pepper
Dried basil
Grated Swiss and cheddar cheese, mixed
Grated jalapeño cheese

Spread a thin layer of cream cheese over each bagel half, followed by a layer of pesto. Top with some tomato slices. Sprinkle with pepper, basil, cheddar and Swiss cheese, and jalapeño cheese. Broil in the oven until the cheese has melted. ***Yield: 4 servings.***

Wyndswept Bed & Breakfast

Glenda and Bob Carter
Box 2683
Hinton, Alberta T7V 1Y2
Tel: (780) 866-3950
Fax: (780) 866-3951
E-mail: wyndswep@agt.net
$$ – $$$

ABOUT THE B&B

The Jasper area's first four-star B&B, Wyndswept Bed & Breakfast is built on the side of a hill in the Folding Mountain Range. From this vantage point, guests marvel at the 180-degree panoramic view of the Rocky Mountains, a nearby valley, and the spectacular sunrises and sunsets. Some 38 different wildflowers thrive on the hill. Wildlife such as bears, deer, elk, and bighorn sheep can be seen right outside the window while guests enjoy a five-course heart-healthy breakfast. The decor of each guest suite has a different theme, and all suites have private baths and luxurious bedding. At night, you can rest on hand-hewn benches by the cozy fire pit and watch the stars or listen to the howl of wolves and coyotes. Wyndswept is located in a quiet mountain village at the eastern edge of Jasper National Park. Your hosts are long-time residents who know the area well and can suggest points of interest. Glenda is retired after working for 30 years as a mental health therapist, while Bob is a quality control auditor and the resident star gazer.

SEASON

all year

ACCOMMODATIONS

2 suites with private baths

Caron House (1837)

Mary and Mike Caron
PO Box 143
Williamstown, Ontario K0C 2J0
Tel: (613) 347-7338
$$

ABOUT THE B&B

Caron House (1837) is a romantic historic brick home located in the quaint village of Williamstown (established in 1784). Beautifully decorated and furnished with antiques, the house has many of its original features — working fireplaces, inside shutters, tin ceilings, and wide pine floorboards. The upstairs is reserved for guests only. Two rooms with shared bath are individually decorated with Laura Ashley wallpaper, antique linens, hooked rugs, quilts, and collectibles. Guests can relax in the Keeping Room (a colonial term for "gathering place") or in the living room. A candlelit full gourmet breakfast — accompanied by classical music — is served in the dining room graced by fine china, silverware, and crystal. Outside, you'll marvel at the herb and Victorian gardens, relax on the antique wicker furniture on the back veranda, and enjoy the lovely yards, complete with trellis, brick patio, and gazebo. Caron House is one hour's drive from either Montréal or Ottawa; nearby attractions include Upper Canada Village, artisans' studios, a bird sanctuary, tennis courts, places to go cycling, and good restaurants. Mary and Mike enjoy traveling, antique hunting, cooking, gardening, and history.

SEASON

all year

ACCOMMODATIONS

2 rooms with shared bath

Poached Eggs on Black Bean Cakes with Sour Cream

Black bean cakes:
3 cups cooked drained black beans (or canned)
2 tablespoons plus 2 teaspoons olive oil
½ cup chopped onion
1 clove garlic, minced
2 eggs, well beaten
½ teaspoon salt
¼ teaspoon pepper
⅛ teaspoon cayenne
⅛ teaspoon chili powder
1 cup cornmeal
1 tablespoon butter

Poached eggs:
8 eggs

Sour cream

(continued on next page)

To make the bean cakes, chop the black beans finely in a blender. Place them in a bowl, and set aside. In a skillet, heat the 2 teaspoons of oil. Sauté the onion and garlic a few minutes until tender. Add the onion mixture to the beans. Blend in the egg, salt, pepper, cayenne, and chili powder. Stir in ½ cup of the cornmeal. Form the bean mixture into 8 balls, and roll them in the remaining cornmeal. Flatten the balls into patties about ¾" thick and 3" wide. In a skillet, heat the butter and the 2 tablespoons of oil. Cook the patties over medium-low heat 4 – 5 minutes on each side.

To poach the eggs, half fill a saucepan with water. Bring the water to a boil, then reduce to a simmer. Break 1 egg into a small dish, then slide the egg into the water. Repeat with 3 more eggs. Simmer the eggs, uncovered, for 3 – 5 minutes. Remove them with a slotted spoon. Repeat with the remaining eggs.

To serve, spread a dollop of sour cream over each of 4 plates, place 2 bean cakes in the center of each plate, and top with a poached egg. Place a dollop of sour cream on each egg. ***Yield: 4 servings.***

River Run Cottage & Breakfast

Janice and Bill Harkley
4551 River Road West
Ladner, British Columbia V4K 1R9
Tel: (604) 946-7778
Fax: (604) 940-1970
$$$$

ABOUT THE B&B

Described in Vancouver Best Places *as "a jewel on the Fraser" and rated "four kisses" in* Best Places to Kiss in the Northwest, *River Run is a romantic, tranquil getaway 30 minutes south of downtown Vancouver. Individual waterfront cottages with private decks overlooking the Fraser river and the mountains have wood-burning fireplaces, CD players, telephones, bathrobes, and cozy furnishings. All have private baths. One cottage is equipped with a Jacuzzi tub for two, and another with a soaker tub on the deck. Breakfast is delivered to the cottages at the time specified by guests and includes freshly squeezed juice, home-baked goods, and a variety of entrées. Bicycles, rowboats, and a double kayak are available for guests to explore the delta and the nearby Reifel Migratory Bird Sanctuary. By car, River Run is a 10-minute drive from ferries to Victoria and the Gulf Islands and a 20-minute drive from Vancouver International Airport.*

SEASON

all year

ACCOMMODATIONS

3 cottages with private baths

River Run Eggs

"One of our all-time favorite breakfasts is this gem created by owner Bill Harkley. It takes about half an hour of preparation but the results are well worth it."
— Karen Bond, Innkeeper of River Run Cottage & Breakfast

2 English muffins, halved
4 eggs, poached
Miracle Whip salad dressing or mayonnaise
River Run salsa (recipe follows)
Grated medium cheddar cheese

Warm the muffin halves in the toaster. Meanwhile, poach the eggs. Spread each muffin half with Miracle Whip, and place the muffins on a pre-warmed, ovenproof plate. Spread some salsa over each muffin half, top with a poached egg, and sprinkle with grated cheddar cheese. Place the muffin halves under the broiler until the cheese melts, and serve immediately. ***Yield: 2 servings.***

River Run salsa:
4 Roma (Italian) tomatoes, finely chopped
1 serrano pepper, minced
1 tablespoon olive oil with chili peppers (or plain)
⅓ cup finely chopped white onion
¼ cup chopped cilantro*
Juice of ½ lime
Salt

**Note: Cilantro is also known as coriander.*

Combine the tomato, serrano pepper, oil, onion, cilantro, lime juice, and a pinch of salt. Stir gently, and place in the refrigerator.

Scrambled Egg Packets

"I like to use tomato-basil tortillas for this recipe." — Connie Ellis

2 teaspoons unsalted margarine
16 small mushrooms, thinly sliced
2 teaspoons finely chopped onion
8 eggs, lightly beaten
4 (10") flour tortillas
Pepper
Salt
Dried marjoram
1 cup grated medium cheddar or Swiss cheese

Sliced tomato
Lettuce
Parsley sprigs
Salsa (optional)
Sour cream (optional)

Preheat the oven to 325°F. Melt the margarine in a large cast-iron frying pan. Add the mushrooms and onion, and sauté until slightly softened. Add the eggs, and cook until the desired consistency, stirring constantly. Keeping the tortillas flat, wrap them in foil and heat them in the oven for 5 minutes. Place some of the scrambled egg mixture in the center of the warmed tortilla, and season with pepper, salt, and marjoram. Sprinkle with the cheese. Fold over the edges of the tortilla to form a packet, wrap with foil, and heat in the oven for 10 minutes. Place each tortilla on a warmed plate with a garnish of tomato, lettuce, and parsley. Serve with optional salsa and sour cream. ***Yield: 4 servings.***

The Catalpa Tree

Connie Ellis
2217 London Line
Sarnia, Ontario N7T 7H2
Tel: (800) 276-5135 or
(519) 542-5008
Fax: (519) 541-0297
$

ABOUT THE B&B

Built in 1894 by the host's great-grandfather, William Beatty, this family home displays true Victorian fashion, complete with gingerbread trim. The house, which is situated on a 100-acre crop farm, has been lovingly maintained in its original form. The B&B's decor complements the design of the house but also incorporates modern conveniences such as gas fireplaces and central air conditioning. Furnishings are a warm mix of contemporary and traditional pieces. A full gourmet breakfast is served in the parlor. The original dining room is now a lounge where guests can visit, relax with a good book, watch a favorite television program, enjoy a video, or play a game. A golf course is located at the end of the lane. In the area are many historical points of interest, a community theater, a water amusement park, a harness racing track, and places to go fishing, swimming, and boating. Picnic lunches or dinner are available by advance request.

SEASON

all year

ACCOMMODATIONS

3 rooms with shared bath

The Lookout at Schooner Cove

Marj and Herb Wilkie
3381 Dolphin Drive
Nanoose Bay, British Columbia
V9P 9H7
Tel/Fax: (250) 468-9796
www.pixsell.bc.ca/bb/1169.htm
$$

ABOUT THE B&B

Situated halfway between Victoria and Tofino on unspoiled Vancouver Island, this West Coast contemporary cedar home stands in a woodsy setting of rocks and tall evergreens. The wrap-around deck affords a 180-degree view of the Strait of Georgia and the majestic mountains beyond. Relax and savor this "little bit of heaven" or hike, golf, kayak, sail, fish, or sightsee. Take a day trip to the wild western shore of the island and Pacific Rim National Park or head south to charming Victoria. The vacation suite will accommodate four people and, with its private entrance and deck and fully equipped kitchen, makes a popular headquarters for an island stay. Hearty breakfasts are served in the dining room overlooking the ocean. After running a store in New York's Catskill Mountains for 17 years, Marj (from Australia) and Herb (from the US) established The Lookout in 1988 and enjoy helping their guests have a memorable stay.

SEASON

May – October
(or by arrangement)

ACCOMMODATIONS

1 vacation suite with private bath;
1 room with private bath;
1 room with shared bath

Smoked Salmon Hollandaise

"You can't beat this when the fish are biting!" — Marj Wilkie

1 biscuit, freshly baked
4 ounces smoked salmon, warmed
2 eggs, poached
2 tomato slices
Quick hollandaise sauce (recipe follows)

Halve the biscuit and pile each half high with warmed smoked salmon. Place a poached egg on top of each half, and add a slice of tomato. Pour hollandaise sauce over all. ***Yield: 1 serving.***

Quick hollandaise sauce:
¾ cup butter or margarine
¼ teaspoon salt
Cayenne
1½ tablespoons lemon juice
3 egg yolks

Place the butter in the top of a double boiler. Beat until creamy. Add salt and a pinch of cayenne. Add the lemon juice, a few drops at a time, beating constantly. Add the egg yolks one at a time, and beat until the mixture is light and fluffy. Place over hot — but not boiling — water for a few minutes, stirring constantly, until the sauce is glossy (water shouldn't touch the top section of the double boiler). ***Tip:*** If you leave the sauce too long, it will separate. ***Yield: About 1 cup.***

Sweet and Sour Maritime Catch

Sweet and sour sauce:
½ cup water
2 carrots, cut into small pieces
⅓ cup white vinegar
½ cup brown sugar
2 tablespoons cornstarch
2 tablespoons soy sauce
8-ounce can pineapple chunks
1 green pepper, finely chopped

Battered fish:
1½ pounds cod fillets
¾ cup water
⅔ cup all-purpose flour
1½ teaspoons salt
½ teaspoon baking powder
Butter

In a small saucepan, heat the water to boiling and cook the carrots for 8 – 10 minutes. In another pan, mix together the vinegar, brown sugar, cornstarch, and soy sauce. Stir in the carrots with the liquid, the pineapple chunks and juice, and the green pepper. Heat the carrot mixture to boiling, stirring constantly. Boil and stir 1 minute more. Keep warm. Rinse the cod fillets, and pat them dry. Mix together the water, flour, salt, and baking powder. Dip the fish in the batter, and pan fry in butter. Top with the sweet and sour sauce, and serve immediately. ***Yield: 4 servings.***

Lake Crescent Inn

Evelyn and Bruce Warr
PO Box 69
Robert's Arm, Newfoundland
A0J 1R0
Tel: (709) 652-3067
Fax: (709) 652-3056
$

ABOUT THE B&B

When you think of Newfoundland, think peaceful lifestyle, clean air and rivers, and superb hospitality — all of which you'll find at Lake Crescent Inn. Walk along the quiet roads and beautiful beaches, visit fishers in the various communities along the route, or go iceberg or whale watching (in season). Boating trips can also be arranged, so why not give cod jigging or salmon fishing a try? Be sure to bring along your camera to capture the moment you reel in your first fish (you might even see "Cressie," the lake monster!). The inn offers four bedrooms and two bathrooms, one with whirlpool and shower. Breakfasts are a homemade feast of muffins, jams, jellies, and breads, and a special health-conscious menu is also available. A Jiggs dinner is served on Sundays from 5:00 pm, and a Fish Platter dinner is served on Fridays from 5:00 pm (other meals can be provided upon request).

SEASON

all year

ACCOMMODATIONS

4 rooms with shared baths

Spruceholme Inn

Marlene and Glenn Scullion
204 rue Principale
Fort-Coulonge, Québec J0X 1V0
Tel: (819) 683-5635
Fax: (819) 683-2139
$$$

ABOUT THE B&B

Built in 1875 by lumber baron George Bryson Jr., Spruceholme Inn is a historic Victorian stone mansion located in the Ottawa River Valley town of Fort-Coulonge. The inn is a leisurely drive from the nation's capital, Ottawa, only minutes from golfing, whitewater rafting, and skiing, and across the street from the Ottawa River where you can fish and, in winter, go skating. Operated by Marlene and Glenn Scullion, Spruceholme has been restored to its original glory and now operates as an elegant country inn with a licensed bar and a formal dining room. The six luxury guest suites are furnished with the mansion's original antiques. In years gone by, such distinguished guests as former Canadian prime minister Sir Wilfrid Laurier were entertained at Spruceholme. Marlene and Glenn, both recently retired from the broadcasting industry, work diligently to ensure their guests have a memorable stay. Glenn is an accomplished pianist and plays the inn's 1911 Steinway grand piano for guests each evening.

SEASON

all year

ACCOMMODATIONS

6 suites with private baths

Turkey and Mushroom Croustades

"These are wonderful for happy hour or afternoon tea!"
— Marlene Scullion

20 slices white bread, crusts removed
Melted butter

Filling:
¼ cup butter
1 cup finely chopped mushrooms
1 small onion, finely chopped
6½-ounce can turkey flakes, drained and flaked with a fork
3 tablespoons all-purpose flour
1 cup milk
1 teaspoon lemon juice
½ teaspoon salt
Cayenne
Freshly ground black pepper

Chopped parsley

Preheat the oven to 350°F. Brush both sides of each bread slice with melted butter. Press the slices gently into muffin cups. Bake the croustades for 15 – 20 minutes or until golden.

(continued on next page)

In a medium saucepan, melt the butter over medium heat. Sauté the mushrooms and onion until the onion is transparent. Stir in the turkey. Sprinkle the turkey mixture with the flour, and blend well. Add the milk gradually. Continue stirring until the turkey mixture thickens and comes to a boil. Remove from the heat, and stir in the lemon juice, salt, and a pinch of cayenne and black pepper. Place some of the turkey mixture in each croustade, place them on a cookie sheet, and heat them in the oven for 10 minutes or until the filling is bubbly. Sprinkle the croustades with chopped parsley, and serve hot. ***Tip:*** The croustades can be made ahead and frozen unfilled. ***Yield: 20 croustades.***

The Inn on St. Andrews

Joan Peggs
231 St. Andrews Street
Victoria, British Columbia V8V 2N1
Tel: (800) 668-5993 or (604) 384-8613
Fax: (604) 384-6063
E-mail: joan_peggs@
bc.sympatico.ca.
www.bctravel.com/andrews.html

$$

ABOUT THE B&B

The Inn on St. Andrews is as lovely today as when it was built in 1913 by Edith Carr, eldest sister of the famous Canadian artist and author Emily Carr. This Tudor-style heritage property features elegant woodwork, stained and beveled glass, and large bright bedrooms. After a wholesome breakfast in the formal dining room, you can congregate in the sunroom overlooking the east garden or on the sun deck overlooking the west garden, in the cozy TV room, or in the larger drawing room. The inn is ideally located in James Bay, close to Victoria's inner harbor with ferry and seaplane terminals, the Parliament buildings, the Royal British Columbia Museum, famed Empress Hotel, and downtown shops. A short walk brings you to Beacon Hill Park and the oceanfront. Your host Joan Peggs believes in modern comfort and old-fashioned hospitality, and provides guests with her own map highlighting walking and driving destinations and recommended restaurants.

SEASON

all year

ACCOMMODATIONS

1 room with private bath;
2 rooms with shared bath

Vegetable Custard

(Recipe from Joan Peggs Eggs, *written and published by Joan Peggs)*

4 slices onion, chopped
¼ cup chopped vegetables, such as cauliflower (combine with a colorful vegetable for appearance), spinach, Swiss chard, zucchini, green or red pepper, or broccoli
¾ cup milk
3 eggs
½ teaspoon paprika
Grated cheese or seasoned bread crumbs

Chopped parsley
Buttered toast wedges

Preheat the oven to 350°F. Lightly grease 4 custard dishes. Place the onion and vegetable in a microwave-safe dish. Heat 1 minute in the microwave on medium-high. Divide the vegetable mixture among the prepared custard dishes. Scald the milk in the microwave. Mix together the egg and paprika. Add the scalded milk to the egg mixture, stirring constantly. Pour the egg mixture over the vegetables. Sprinkle with grated cheese. Place the custard dishes in a pan of water (1" deep), and bake 15 – 20 minutes until a knife inserted into the custard's center comes out clean. Garnish with the parsley, and serve on buttered toast wedges. ***Yield: 4 servings.***

Wake-up Pizza

"I serve this pizza with scrambled eggs and find that guests usually ask for just a small piece more!" — Mary Ellen Ironside

8-ounce package refrigerated crescent rolls
1 cup chopped smoked salmon
1 cup sliced mushrooms
1 cup grated mozzarella cheese
1 cup grated cheddar cheese

Preheat the oven to 350°F. Separate the crescent roll dough into 8 triangles. Place the triangles on an ungreased 12" pizza pan so that the narrowest point of each triangle faces the center of the pan. Press the dough over the bottom and sides of the pan to form a crust. Make sure the edges of the triangles are pressed together well. Bake 10 minutes. Distribute the salmon over the crust, and sprinkle on the mushrooms and mozzarella and cheddar cheese. Bake 10 – 15 minutes until the cheese has melted. ***Variation:*** Cooked shrimp or cooked and crumbled pork sausage can be substituted for the smoked salmon. ***Yield: 8 servings.***

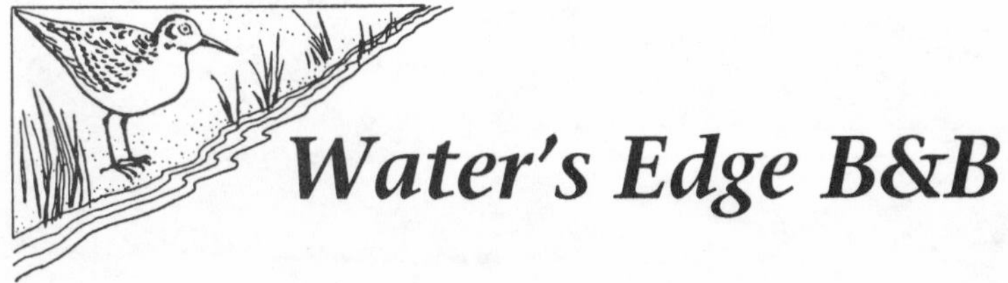

Water's Edge B&B

Mary Ellen and Ed Ironside
Box 635, 331 Park Street
Tofino, British Columbia V0R 2Z0
Tel: (250) 725-1218
Fax (250) 725- 1219
$$ – $$$

ABOUT THE B&B

Water's Edge B&B, a contemporary cedar house, is set amid towering rainforest that frames views of small islands in Clayoquot Sound and the open Pacific Ocean. Stairs lead from the cliff-top location to rocky tidal pools directly below. Two beautiful beaches are reached by a short scramble along the rocks or by a five-minute stroll along a boardwalk to Tonquin Park. The home's builder was a boat carpenter, fisher, beachcomber, and sawmill operator, and his love of nature is evident in the design. The large windows and high wood ceilings frame the magnificent views. Tofino is a scenic fishing village, minutes from Pacific Rim National Park and Long Beach with its 13 miles of sandy beach. In the area you can walk the beach or hike in the rainforest, go fishing, diving, kayaking, or cycling, and play tennis or golf. Whale watching is a favorite pastime. Hosts Mary Ellen and Ed, who have lived in different parts of Canada and abroad, love traveling, reading, photography, gardening, and meeting people.

SEASON

all year

ACCOMMODATIONS

1 room with private bath;
2 rooms with shared bath

Spreads & Toppings

Angels' Hair Preserves (Carrot Marmalade)

"This 19th-century recipe is as heavenly as its name! Guests enjoy it on muffins or fruit bread." — Mary Caron

1 orange
2 – 3 lemons
1¼ cups water
5 cups coarsely grated carrot
7 cups sugar
1 pouch liquid fruit pectin

Cut up the orange and 1 of the lemons; discard the seeds. Chop the fruit finely, and place it in a medium saucepan. Squeeze the remaining lemons to obtain ¼ cup juice. Add the lemon juice and water to the fruit mixture, and bring to a boil. Reduce the heat, cover the fruit mixture, and simmer 20 minutes, stirring occasionally. Add the carrot to the fruit mixture, and combine. Place the fruit mixture in a 6 – 8 quart pot. Stir in the sugar, and bring to a full, rolling boil, stirring constantly. Quickly stir in the pectin. Boil hard for 1 minute, stirring. Remove the pot from the heat, and skim off any foam from the surface of the fruit mixture. Ladle the fruit mixture into hot, sterilized jars, leaving ¼" head space, and seal them tightly. Store in a cool, dark, dry place. ***Yield: 8 half pints.***

Caron House (1837)

Mary and Mike Caron
PO Box 143
Williamstown, Ontario K0C 2J0
Tel: (613) 347-7338
$$

ABOUT THE B&B

Caron House (1837) is a romantic historic brick home located in the quaint village of Williamstown (established in 1784). Beautifully decorated and furnished with antiques, the house has many of its original features — working fireplaces, inside shutters, tin ceilings, and wide pine floorboards. The upstairs is reserved for guests only. Two rooms with shared bath are individually decorated with Laura Ashley wallpaper, antique linens, hooked rugs, quilts, and collectibles. Guests can relax in the Keeping Room (a colonial term for "gathering place") or in the living room. A candlelit full gourmet breakfast — accompanied by classical music — is served in the dining room graced by fine china, silverware, and crystal. Outside, you'll marvel at the herb and Victorian gardens, relax on the antique wicker furniture on the back veranda, and enjoy the lovely yards, complete with trellis, brick patio, and gazebo. Caron House is one hour's drive from either Montréal or Ottawa; nearby attractions include Upper Canada Village, artisans' studios, a bird sanctuary, tennis courts, places to go cycling, and good restaurants. Mary and Mike enjoy traveling, antique hunting, cooking, gardening, and history.

SEASON

all year

ACCOMMODATIONS

2 rooms with shared bath

Lakewinds

Jane and Stephen Locke
PO Box 1483, 328 Queen Street
Niagara-on-the-Lake, Ontario
L0S 1J0
Tel: (905) 468-1888
Fax: (905) 468-1061
E-mail: lakewind@niagara.com
www.lakewinds.niagara.com
$$$$

ABOUT THE B&B

A special experience awaits you at Lakewinds, a circa-1881, restored Victorian manor operated by Jane and Stephen Locke. Situated on an acre of quiet trees and gardens, Lakewinds offers unparalleled views of the Niagara-on-the-Lake Golf Club and Lake Ontario. The guest rooms, elegantly appointed with antiques, have been designed for comfort and privacy and feature private baths. Guests are invited to the games room for billiards or cards and, in summer, can enjoy refreshing dips in the heated pool or simply relax in rocking chairs on the veranda. Sumptuous breakfasts feature fruits, vegetables, and herbs from Jane's garden. Only one-and-a-half hours south of Toronto, Niagara-on-the-Lake is a charming town offering world-class theater, shops, fine restaurants, and beautiful parks — all with a turn-of-the-century ambiance. The many estate wineries in the area offer tours and tastings, while golf courses, tennis courts, and countless hiking and biking trails await the active visitor.

SEASON

all year

ACCOMMODATIONS

6 rooms with private baths

Apple Butter

8 cups apple cider
2 quarts apples (20 – 24 medium), peeled, cored, and sliced
2 cups sugar
1 cup corn syrup
1 teaspoon ground cinnamon

Boil the cider until it has been reduced to 4 cups. Add the apple to the cider, and cook slowly, stirring most of the time, until the mixture begins to thicken. Add the sugar, corn syrup, and cinnamon. Continue cooking on low heat, stirring occasionally, for 2 – 3 hours until a small sample, when cooled on a plate, has a consistency suitable for spreading. ***Variation:*** Try 1 cup cooked pumpkin instead of corn syrup. ***Yield: 10 – 12 cups.***

Applesauce Cream

⅔ cup heavy cream
½ cup applesauce
¼ cup sifted confectioners' sugar
1 tablespoon lemon juice

Whip the cream at medium speed with an electric mixer until soft peaks form. Fold in the applesauce, confectioners' sugar, and lemon juice. Cover and chill. Serve with waffles or pancakes. ***Yield: 1½ cups.***

Bay View Farm / La Ferme Bay View

Helen and Garnett Sawyer
PO Box 21,
337 New Carlisle West, Route 132
New Carlisle, Québec G0C 1Z0
Tel: (418) 752-2725/6718
$

ABOUT THE B&B

Situated between New Carlisle and Bonaventure, Bay View Farm offers country hospitality in a beautiful seaside environment on the rugged Baie des Chaleurs coastline of Québec's Gaspé Peninsula. Seaside accommodations include five comfortable guest rooms and a fully equipped cottage. At breakfast, enjoy Bay View's farm-fresh eggs, meat, homemade muffins, scones, jams, jellies, and beverages, as well as fresh fruits and vegetables in season from the farm's garden and orchards. Additional meals are available on request at reasonable rates. Handicrafts are on display throughout the house. Enjoy the breathtaking panoramic seascapes, participate in the Bay View Folk Festival (second weekend of August) with folk music and dancing, or visit Percé Rock and the archaeological caves of Saint-Elzéar.

SEASON

May – November

ACCOMMODATIONS

5 rooms with shared baths;
1 private cottage with private bath

Montréal Oasis

Lena Blondel
3000 Breslay Road
Montréal, Québec H3Y 2G7
Tel: (514) 935-2312
$$

ABOUT THE B&B

In pilgrim days, the evergreen tree was a sign of shelter, good food, and warm hospitality. It's fitting, then, that two towering evergreens frame the door to Montréal Oasis. This charming B&B with original leaded windows and slanted ceilings is located in downtown Montréal's west end, close to the Fine Arts Museum, chic Crescent Street and Greene Avenue shopping and restaurants, and the "main drag," St. Catherine Street. The beautiful and safe neighborhood with its spacious Elizabethan-style houses and pretty gardens is locally referred to as the Priest Farm district — once a holiday resort for priests. Originally from Sweden, your world-traveled hostess Lena has lived in many countries around the globe, which is evident from the African, Asian, and Swedish art that graces the B&B. The three guest rooms feature Scandinavian and Québecois furniture. Lena loves good food, and serves three-course gourmet breakfasts featuring delicious, fresh ingredients. A friendly Siamese cat resides on the main floor.

SEASON

all year

ACCOMMODATIONS

3 rooms with shared baths

Beet Sauce

"A guest, chef, and teacher of gourmet cooking in Stratford, Ontario, gave me this unique recipe, which looks stunning on a poached egg. Even if you don't like beets, I guarantee you'll like this sauce!"
— Lena Blondel

2¼ pounds beets, cooked
Olive oil
Dijon mustard
Pepper
Salt
Snipped dill (optional)

Liquefy the beets in a juicer. In a saucepan, reduce the juice over low heat until it begins to get thick (at least 15 – 20 minutes). Stir in enough olive oil to achieve a consistency the same as that of mayonnaise. Add some Dijon mustard, pepper, and salt to taste. The sauce should now be thick, creamy, and dark red. Add the optional dill. Serve the beet sauce over poached eggs. ***Yield: About ½ cup.***

Best Ever White Frosting

"This never-fail recipe is great on carrot cake, muffins, and quick breads. Even if you leave it out on the counter, it will not run."
— Linda Aylward

⅔ cup milk
3 tablespoons all-purpose flour
½ cup butter
½ cup shortening
¾ cup sugar
1½ teaspoons vanilla
¼ teaspoon salt

In a 1-quart saucepan, mix together the milk and flour over medium heat. Cook until the milk mixture boils, stirring constantly, and continue to boil 1 minute. Cool the milk mixture slightly. Using a mixer at low speed, beat the butter, shortening, and sugar until blended. At high speed, continue beating the butter mixture until it is light and fluffy. Reduce the speed to low, add the milk mixture, vanilla, and salt. At high speed, beat until the frosting is very fluffy. ***Yield: About 2½ cups.***

Captain's Quarters B&B

Linda and Arnie Aylward
RR #1
South Gillies, Ontario P0T 2V0
Tel: (807) 475-5630
$$

ABOUT THE B&B

Named in honor of the Aylward sea captains from Nova Scotia, Captain's Quarters is an intimate country bed and breakfast located southwest of the city of Thunder Bay, and a short drive from ski hills, amethyst mines, and fine dining. The modern log home features rustic yet gracious bedrooms with queen beds and private baths. Hiking, cross-country skiing, and golf can be done on the property. Expansion plans include a solarium with a hot tub. Pancakes with strawberries and whipped cream highlight an extensive and varied breakfast menu created from fresh, high-quality products. Another menu favorite, Nova Scotia crab toasties, reflects the B&B's maritime theme and the East Coast heritage of the host. Golf, gardening, sewing, and crafts are among Linda and Arnie's hobbies.

SEASON

all year

ACCOMMODATIONS

2 rooms with private baths

Weston Lake Inn Bed & Breakfast

Susan Evans and Ted Harrison
813 Beaver Point Road
Salt Spring Island, British Columbia
V8K lX9
Tel: (250) 653-4311
$$$

ABOUT THE B&B

Perched on a knoll of well-tended flowering trees and shrubs overlooking Weston Lake, the inn is a serene and comfortable adult getaway on the rural south end of Salt Spring Island. The three tastefully decorated guest bedrooms have private baths, down duvets, and fresh flower bouquets. Original Canadian art and beautiful petit point (done by host Ted) grace the rooms. Guests have the exclusive use of a cozy fireside lounge with library, TV, and VCR, and an outdoor hot tub overlooking the lake. Creative breakfasts feature fresh eggs from the inn's chickens and produce from the large organic garden, such as berries, herbs, and asparagus in season. Near Victoria, Salt Spring Island offers a mild climate, exceptional beauty, a thriving community of artists and craftspeople, and an abundance of outdoor activities. Since opening Weston Lake Inn in 1986, hosts Susan and Ted have been fine-tuning their B&B craft, restoring the house, landscaping, and enjoying their 10-acre paradise with guests. Susan loves gardening, while Ted loves sailing and offers charters aboard their 36-foot sloop.

SEASON

all year

ACCOMMODATIONS

3 rooms with private baths

Blueberry-Cointreau Jam

4 cups blueberries
3 cups sugar
3 tablespoons lime juice
2 tablespoons Cointreau

Place the blueberries and sugar in a heavy saucepan over low heat, and stir constantly until the sugar dissolves. Boil 20 – 25 minutes. Add the lime juice and Cointreau, and boil 3 minutes longer. Place a spoonful of the blueberry mixture on a plate, allow it to cool slightly, and check the consistency. If the blueberry mixture has reached the consistency of jam, remove the pot from the heat, skim any foam from the surface of the jam, pour it into sterilized jars, and seal with paraffin wax. Store the jam in a cool, dark, dry place. ***Yield: 2 pints.***

Blueberry Hill Sauce

2 cups blueberries
¼ cup maple syrup
1 heaping tablespoon cornstarch mixed with a little cold water
2 tablespoons Cointreau

Combine the blueberries and maple syrup in a small saucepan. Bring just to a boil on medium heat. Add the cornstarch, and stir until thick, at least 1 minute. Remove the pan from the heat, and stir the Cointreau into the blueberry mixture. Serve warm on pancakes, French toast, or waffles. Store the sauce in the refrigerator for up to 1 week, or freeze. ***Yield: 2 cups.***

Weston Lake Inn Bed & Breakfast

Susan Evans and Ted Harrison
813 Beaver Point Road
Salt Spring Island, British Columbia
V8K 1X9
Tel: (250) 653-4311
$$$

ABOUT THE B&B

Perched on a knoll of well-tended flowering trees and shrubs overlooking Weston Lake, the inn is a serene and comfortable adult getaway on the rural south end of Salt Spring Island. The three tastefully decorated guest bedrooms have private baths, down duvets, and fresh flower bouquets. Original Canadian art and beautiful petit point (done by host Ted) grace the rooms. Guests have the exclusive use of a cozy fireside lounge with library, TV, and VCR, and an outdoor hot tub overlooking the lake. Creative breakfasts feature fresh eggs from the inn's chickens and produce from the large organic garden, such as berries, herbs, and asparagus in season. Near Victoria, Salt Spring Island offers a mild climate, exceptional beauty, a thriving community of artists and craftspeople, and an abundance of outdoor activities. Since opening Weston Lake Inn in 1986, hosts Susan and Ted have been fine-tuning their B&B craft, restoring the house, landscaping, and enjoying their 10-acre paradise with guests. Susan loves gardening, while Ted loves sailing and offers charters aboard their 36-foot sloop.

SEASON

all year

ACCOMMODATIONS

3 rooms with private baths

Spring Valley Guest Ranch

Jim Saville
PO Box 10
Ravenscrag, Saskatchewan S0N 0T0
Tel: (306) 295-4124
$$

ABOUT THE B&B

Come enjoy an afternoon visit or an overnight stay at Spring Valley Guest Ranch. This three-story, 1913 home is nestled in a tall grove of cottonwood poplars near a spring-fed stream in a pleasant wooded valley with many varieties of flora and fauna. There are more than a thousand acres of hills and valleys to explore, either on foot or on horseback. You are invited to dine, choosing from a unique menu, in the licensed Country Tea Room, which houses over 200 duck replicas. Poultry, sheep, horses, and a donkey can be visited in the barnyard. The craft shop in the log cabin is filled with treasures of leather, wood, and pottery and with knitted and beaded crafts — all made by local artists. An excellent area for naturalists, photographers, and hikers, Ravenscrag is only 20 minutes from Cypress Hills Provincial Park, on the Alberta border.

SEASON

all year

ACCOMMODATIONS

4 rooms with shared baths;
1 log cabin with shared bath

Dad's Jam

"This favorite of my father was passed down through our family from my paternal grandmother. When I first opened my B&B in 1988, I offered a variety of jams. This one was always the winner, so now it's the only one I make." — Jim Saville

3¼ cups dried apricots
4 pounds rhubarb, chopped in ½" pieces
8 cups sugar
1 unpeeled lemon, chopped
2 unpeeled oranges, chopped

Soak the apricots overnight in enough water to cover them. Set aside the soaking water, and cut the apricots into quarters. Combine the rhubarb, sugar, and apricots and 1 cup of the reserved soaking water, and boil gently for 30 minutes, stirring to prevent scorching. Add the lemon and oranges, and boil until the mixture is thick and jellylike. Pour the jam into hot, sterilized jars, and seal tightly. Store in a cool, dark, dry place. ***Tips:*** Use the heaviest pot you have; it will help prevent the jam from sticking and scorching. You can substitute zucchini for the rhubarb.
Yield: 8 pints.

Flavored Butters

(Recipes from Joan Peggs Eggs, *written and published by Joan Peggs)*

Whipped orange butter:
½ cup softened butter
2 tablespoons concentrated orange juice
2 teaspoons confectioners' sugar
1 teaspoon grated fresh ginger

In a small bowl, beat the butter until fluffy. Add the concentrated orange juice, confectioners' sugar, and ginger, and beat until combined. ***Tip:*** Keeps well in the refrigerator. ***Yield: ½ cup.***

Cinnamon-honey butter:
¼ cup honey
¼ cup softened butter
1 teaspoon ground cinnamon

Beat the honey, butter, and cinnamon in a small bowl until combined. ***Variation:*** Use 1 teaspoon ground nutmeg or 1 teaspoon ground ginger in place of the cinnamon. ***Tip:*** Keeps well in the refrigerator. ***Yield: ½ cup.***

Nut butter:
½ cup softened butter
¼ cup ground nuts (almonds, hazelnuts, or walnuts)
1 tablespoon confectioners' sugar
1 teaspoon vanilla (optional)

In a small bowl, combine the butter and nuts. Blend in the confectioners' sugar and optional vanilla. ***Tip:*** Keeps well in the refrigerator. ***Yield: ¾ cup.***

The Inn on St. Andrews

Joan Peggs
231 St. Andrews Street
Victoria, British Columbia V8V 2N1
Tel: (800) 668-5993 or (604) 384-8613
Fax: (604) 384-6063
E-mail: joan_peggs@
bc.sympatico.ca.
www.bctravel.com/andrews.html
$$

ABOUT THE B&B

The Inn on St. Andrews is as lovely today as when it was built in 1913 by Edith Carr, eldest sister of the famous Canadian artist and author Emily Carr. This Tudor-style heritage property features elegant woodwork, stained and beveled glass, and large bright bedrooms. After a wholesome breakfast in the formal dining room, you can congregate in the sunroom overlooking the east garden or on the sun deck overlooking the west garden, in the cozy TV room, or in the larger drawing room. The inn is ideally located in James Bay, close to Victoria's inner harbor with ferry and seaplane terminals, the Parliament buildings, the Royal British Columbia Museum, famed Empress Hotel, and downtown shops. A short walk brings you to Beacon Hill Park and the oceanfront. Your host Joan Peggs believes in modern comfort and old-fashioned hospitality, and provides guests with her own map highlighting walking and driving destinations and recommended restaurants.

SEASON

all year

ACCOMMODATIONS

1 room with private bath;
2 rooms with shared bath

Gwenmar Guest Home

Joy and Keith Smith
PO Box 59, RR #3
Brandon, Manitoba R7A 5Y3
Tel: (204) 728-7339
Fax: (204) 728-7336
E-mail: smithj@docker.com
$

ABOUT THE B&B

Space, privacy, and quiet is what you'll find at Gwenmar. This 1914 heritage home was the summer retreat of Manitoba's former Lieutenant Governor (from 1929 to 1934), J.D. McGregor, who named the estate after his daughter Gwen. Since 1980, Joy and Keith Smith have welcomed B&B guests to this relaxing countryside escape. Gwenmar breakfasts are memorable, particularly the home-baked bread and jams and jellies made from Gwenmar's wild berries. Joy, a home economist, is an avid gardener and a major contributor to Canada's heritage seed program, while Keith is a retired agrologist involved in overseas projects. In the summer, you can visit with them on the big, shaded veranda or go for walks on the beautiful grounds or in the valley. In the winter, sit by the fire or go cross-country skiing. Gwenmar is also a short drive from downtown Brandon, with shopping, restaurants, a water-slide, an air museum, golf courses, and the childhood home of Stone Angel *author Margaret Laurence.*

SEASON

all year

ACCOMMODATIONS

2 rooms with private baths;
2 rooms with shared bath

Gooseberry-Orange Marmalade

1 orange, quartered and thinly sliced
¾ cup water
6 cups gooseberries
4 cups sugar
3 tablespoons lemon juice

Simmer the orange in the water for 30 – 45 minutes until tender. Add the gooseberries. Boil another 10 minutes. Add the sugar and lemon juice. Bring the mixture to a full, rolling boil over high heat, and boil 10 – 12 minutes, stirring frequently. Stir another 2 – 5 minutes to suspend the fruit (so it doesn't all end up at the bottom). Place the marmalade in sterilized jars, and seal tightly. Store in a cool, dark, dry place. ***Yield: 3 pints.***

Herbed Cookie Cutter Butter

"I cut loon- and heart-shaped butter to serve with my old-fashioned tea biscuits."— Penny Grimshaw

Unsalted butter, cut into ½" slabs
Freshly chopped or dried herbs

Cut the slabs of butter into interesting shapes with cookie cutters. Arrange the shapes on a plate, and sprinkle herbs over them. ***Tip:*** Cut the butter into shapes immediately after it's removed from the refrigerator.

Elgin Manor B&B

Penny and Dave Grimshaw
RR #2
Port Sandfield, Ontario P0B 1J0
Tel: (705) 765-5325
$$ – $$$$

ABOUT THE B&B

Nestled on a quiet bay of picturesque Lake Joseph is the unique and heartwarming Elgin Manor B&B, a 1920s Tudor home surrounded by English gardens and a water's edge fireplace. As you relax in a wooden Muskoka chair, you're sure to see some antique wooden launches, for which the Muskoka Lakes are famous, or perhaps the old steamship Segwun *pass by. The manor is decorated with antiques throughout and handmade quilts grace each guest room. Launch excursions and old-fashioned picnic lunches packed in wicker baskets can be arranged. Elgin Manor B&B is situated in the heart of Muskoka cottage country (two hours north of Toronto), an area that offers year-round activities — from summer nature walks, fishing, swimming, canoeing, and midnight strolls under a million glistening stars to tours of local artisans' studios, ice skating, and snowshoeing and cross-country skiing in the panoramic countryside.*

SEASON

all year

ACCOMMODATIONS

3 rooms with private baths;
1 honeymoon cabin
with private bath

Cornelius White House Bed & Breakfast

Bonnie and Frank Evans
8 Wellington Street
Bloomfield, Ontario K0K 1G0
Tel/Fax: (613) 393-2282
$ – $$

ABOUT THE B&B

Located on the historic Loyalist Parkway at the west end of a farming community in picturesque Prince Edward County, the Cornelius White House is named for its original owner, a Dutch settler who built this charming red-brick house in 1862. Today, a sense of history and design combine with European furnishings and accents to create a unique B&B. Three guest rooms on the second floor open onto the sitting room below, which has a cathedral ceiling. There is also a suite on the main floor. The house is air conditioned and is a smoke-free environment. A full breakfast of fruit, a hot main course, and fresh baked goods is served in the Dutch Treat Tea Room. Outstanding restaurants are nearby, as well as antique and craft shops, galleries, studios, and museums. Cornelius White House is just 10 minutes from Sandbanks and Outlet Beach Provincial Parks, famous for the largest freshwater sand dunes in the world. Prince Edward County, with its panoramic views and gentle rolling hills, is a cyclist's dream come true.

SEASON

all year

ACCOMMODATIONS

2 rooms with private baths;
2 rooms with shared bath

Homestyle Boursin

"For a while, Boursin cheese was unavailable in Canada due to its high bacterial content, which didn't meet Canadian standards. I started making my own version, which uses fresh herbs grown in my kitchen window and tastes very much like the original — delicious!" — Bonnie Evans

1 pound softened cream cheese
¼ cup mayonnaise
2 tablespoons finely snipped dill
1 tablespoon finely chopped parsley
1 tablespoon finely snipped chives
2 teaspoons Dijon mustard
1 garlic clove, minced

Crackers or bagels

Combine the cream cheese, mayonnaise, dill, parsley, chives, mustard, and garlic, and beat with an electric mixer until thoroughly blended. Spoon into a 2-cup mold lined with aluminum foil (or place in a small crockery serving bowl). Turn out onto a small serving plate, and peel off the foil. Serve with crackers or bagels. ***Tip:*** This cheese is best when made 1 or 2 days ahead. ***Yield: 2 cups.***

Island Clotted Cream Topping

"This is basically a substitute for Devonshire cream enjoyed by the British with tea and scones. Needless to say, our guests from the British Isles consider this a great treat and find our approach of serving it with coffee cake a novel variation on an old theme."
— Judy Hill

4-ounce package cream cheese
3 tablespoons brown sugar
Salt
1 cup heavy cream

Combine the cream cheese, brown sugar, a pinch of salt, and 3 tablespoons of the heavy cream. Beat until fluffy. Whip the remaining cream until soft peaks form. Fold the whipped cream into the cream cheese mixture. Chill, and serve with The Shipwright Inn's apple streusel coffee cake (see recipe on page 100) or as a dip with fresh strawberries. ***Yield:* *2 cups.***

The Shipwright Inn

Judy and Jordan Hill
51 Fitzroy Street
Charlottetown,
Prince Edward Island C1A 1R4
Tel: (902) 368-1905
Fax: (902) 628-1905
E-mail: shipwright@isn.net
www.isn.net/ShipwrightInn
$$$ – $$$$

ABOUT THE B&B

The Shipwright Inn is an elegant Victorian home built in the 1860s by the accomplished Charlottetown shipbuilder James Douse. This award-winning heritage inn is located in Olde Charlottetown, one block east of Queen Street and within a three-minute walk of the historic waterfront area, dining, and shopping. In keeping with its shipbuilding heritage, The Shipwright Inn's decor has a nautical theme. While savoring breakfast beneath the dining room chandelier, you might imagine the rope-insignia china (circa 1810) in use at the captain's table of a clipper ship. Your hosts Judy and Jordan Hill have carefully collected period antiques, art work, Victorian memorabilia, family quilts, and old books and artifacts related to the sea for your enjoyment. The seven guest rooms have polished pine floors, some of which were previously ship's planking that was reused by the home's builder. Each bedroom features a private bath, goose down duvets, a TV and telephone, a ceiling fan, and air conditioning. All rooms are smoke free.

SEASON

all year

ACCOMMODATIONS

7 rooms with private baths

Lake Crescent Inn

Evelyn and Bruce Warr
PO Box 69
Robert's Arm, Newfoundland
A0J 1R0
Tel: (709) 652-3067
Fax: (709) 652-3056
$

ABOUT THE B&B

When you think of Newfoundland, think peaceful lifestyle, clean air and rivers, and superb hospitality — all of which you'll find at Lake Crescent Inn. Walk along the quiet roads and beautiful beaches, visit fishers in the various communities along the route, or go iceberg or whale watching (in season). Boating trips can also be arranged, so why not give cod jigging or salmon fishing a try? Be sure to bring along your camera to capture the moment you reel in your first fish (you might even see "Cressie," the lake monster!). The inn offers four bedrooms and two bathrooms, one with whirlpool and shower. Breakfasts are a homemade feast of muffins, jams, jellies, and breads, and a special health-conscious menu is also available. A Jiggs dinner is served on Sundays from 5:00 pm, and a Fish Platter dinner is served on Fridays from 5:00 pm (other meals can be provided upon request).

SEASON

all year

ACCOMMODATIONS

4 rooms with shared baths

Low-Calorie Vegetable Dip

3 cups plain yogurt
2 cups light Miracle Whip salad dressing or light mayonnaise
Dried dill weed
Dried minced onion

Fresh raw vegetables

Mix the yogurt and Miracle Whip together in a bowl. Add some dill weed and minced onion to taste. Serve with fresh raw vegetables. ***Tip:*** This dip will keep in the refrigerator for several days. ***Yield: 5 cups.***

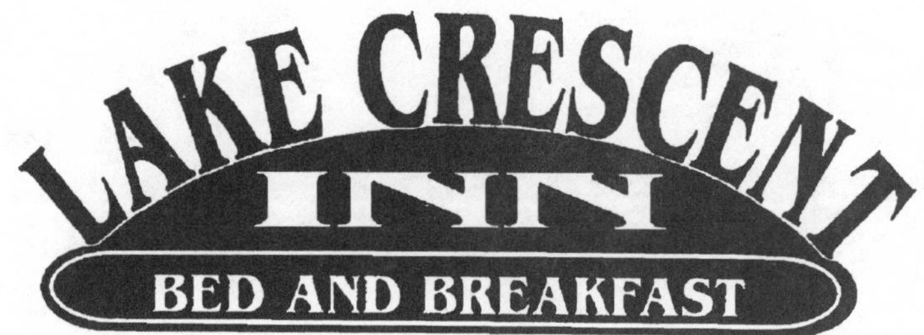

Ma's Rhubarb Marmalade

"My grandmother served me this rhubarb marmalade when I was a little girl."— Janice Trowsdale

12 cups chopped rhubarb
8 cups sugar
Juice and grated peel of 3 oranges and 2 lemons
19-ounce can crushed pineapple

Combine the rhubarb and sugar, and let stand overnight. In the morning, add the orange and lemon juice and peel and the pineapple with its juice. Boil the rhubarb mixture gently for 30 minutes or until thick. Pour the marmalade into sterilized jars, and seal tightly. Store in a cool, dark, dry place. ***Yield: About 7 pints.***

Hilltop Acres Bed & Breakfast

Janice and Wayne Trowsdale
Route 166
Bideford, Prince Edward Island
Mailing address: PO Box 3011
Ellerslie, Prince Edward Island
C0B 1J0
Tel/Fax: (902) 831-2817
$ – $$

ABOUT THE B&B

Enjoy the quiet of the country in this renovated 1930s residence in historic Bideford — where Anne of Green Gables *author Lucy Maud Montgomery first taught school from 1894 to 1895. Relax on the second-story balcony overlooking scenic Malpeque Bay or in the large living room. Stroll about the spacious lawn, play croquet, or bike or walk around the 75-acre property. Bedrooms have a queen pillowtop bed, a double bed, or two single beds. A four-piece shared bath with a whirlpool tub is for guests only. Hilltop Acres specializes in homemade muffins and preserves served in the guest breakfast room. Just minutes from the village of Tyne Valley, Green Provincial Park, and the Shipbuilding Museum, Hilltop Acres is also a half hour from golf courses and shopping centers, and one hour from Confederation Bridge. Your hosts are non-smokers and enjoy sharing the history and culture of the area. Janice is an office clerk and Wayne is a school bus driver, carpenter, and handyman.*

SEASON

June – October
(off-season by reservation)

ACCOMMODATIONS

3 rooms with shared bath

Elgin Manor B&B

Penny and Dave Grimshaw
RR #2
Port Sandfield, Ontario P0B 1J0
Tel: (705) 765-5325
$$ – $$$$

ABOUT THE B&B

Nestled on a quiet bay of picturesque Lake Joseph is the unique and heartwarming Elgin Manor B&B, a 1920s Tudor home surrounded by English gardens and a water's edge fireplace. As you relax in a wooden Muskoka chair, you're sure to see some antique wooden launches, for which the Muskoka Lakes are famous, or perhaps the old steamship Segwun *pass by. The manor is decorated with antiques throughout and handmade quilts grace each guest room. Launch excursions and old-fashioned picnic lunches packed in wicker baskets can be arranged. Elgin Manor B&B is situated in the heart of Muskoka cottage country (two hours north of Toronto), an area that offers year-round activities — from summer nature walks, fishing, swimming, canoeing, and midnight strolls under a million glistening stars to tours of local artisans' studios, ice skating, and snowshoeing and cross-country skiing in the panoramic countryside.*

SEASON

all year

ACCOMMODATIONS

3 rooms with private baths;
1 honeymoon cabin
with private bath

Muskoka Wild Clover–Cranberry Honey

"I purchase fresh cranberries for this recipe from the local cranberry bog, and pick the clover and rose petals right from my garden. Guests enjoy this unusual honey and often like to bring a jar home with them." — Penny Grimshaw

2 cups cranberries
8 cups sugar
½ cup water
80 white wild clover flowers
40 pink wild clover flowers
4 rose petals
1 teaspoon alum (aluminum potassium sulfate)

Place the cranberries in a small saucepan, add enough hot water to cover them, and cook about 5 minutes on medium heat until the cranberries pop. Drain the cranberries, and reserve. In a heavy, non-aluminum pot, simmer the sugar and water on low heat until the sugar has dissolved. Add the clover flowers, rose petals, and alum, stir, and remove the pot from the heat. Set aside for 2 – 4 hours. Strain the sugar mixture, and discard the solids. Combine the whole cranberries with the sugar mixture. Pour into sterilized decorative jars, and store in a dry place at room temperature. ***Yield: 3 pints.***

Orange-Ginger Sauce

"A taste treat for ginger lovers to serve over pancakes, French toast, or Dutch pancakes." — Marj Wilkie

1 cup sugar
2 tablespoons grated fresh ginger
2 tablespoons light corn syrup
½ cup orange juice
½ cup water
½ teaspoon orange zest

Combine the sugar, ginger, corn syrup, orange juice, water, and orange zest in a small saucepan. Bring the sugar mixture to a boil, uncovered, over medium-high heat, and boil 5 minutes. Store in a tightly covered glass jar or plastic container for up to 2 weeks in the refrigerator.
Yield: 1½ cups.

The Lookout at Schooner Cove

Marj and Herb Wilkie
3381 Dolphin Drive
Nanoose Bay, British Columbia
V9P 9H7
Tel/Fax: (250) 468-9796
www.pixsell.bc.ca/bb/1169.htm
$$

ABOUT THE B&B

Situated halfway between Victoria and Tofino on unspoiled Vancouver Island, this West Coast contemporary cedar home stands in a woodsy setting of rocks and tall evergreens. The wrap-around deck affords a 180-degree view of the Strait of Georgia and the majestic mountains beyond. Relax and savor this "little bit of heaven" or hike, golf, kayak, sail, fish, or sightsee. Take a day trip to the wild western shore of the island and Pacific Rim National Park or head south to charming Victoria. The vacation suite will accommodate four people and, with its private entrance and deck and fully equipped kitchen, makes a popular headquarters for an island stay. Hearty breakfasts are served in the dining room overlooking the ocean. After running a store in New York's Catskill Mountains for 17 years, Marj (from Australia) and Herb (from the US) established The Lookout in 1988 and enjoy helping their guests have a memorable stay.

SEASON

May – October
(or by arrangement)

ACCOMMODATIONS

1 vacation suite with private bath;
1 room with private bath;
1 room with shared bath

Seaboard Bed & Breakfast

Sheila and Barrie Jackson
2629 Crowell Road
East Lawrencetown, Nova Scotia
B2Z 1P4
Tel: (800) SEA-6566 or
(902) 827-3747
$ – $$

ABOUT THE B&B

Seaboard Bed & Breakfast at Lawrencetown Beach is a renovated farmhouse built around 1917. Now the home of Sheila and Barrie Jackson, this large white house across the road from Porter's Lake and the Atlantic Ocean has been an area landmark for many years. Local attractions include international-caliber surfing from a sand beach; birdwatching from the shore or nearby hills, at a local marsh, or along walking trails; and fishing, canoeing, windsurfing, and — in season — skating and cross-country skiing. Seaboard is only 35 minutes from Halifax airport and 30 minutes from the cities of Halifax and Dartmouth, where you can enjoy the casino, restaurants, theaters, and special events. Sheila and Barrie are both keen Scottish country dancers and have aptly named their guest rooms after favorite dances. There are two semi-private bathrooms for the exclusive use of guests. A varied and full home-cooked breakfast is served in the sunny dining room overlooking the lake and sea, while tea and coffee are offered in the lounge or on the porch.

SEASON

all year

ACCOMMODATIONS

3 rooms with shared baths

Pear and Ginger Jam

"A simple and elegant jam that's very popular with ginger lovers. It's also a good substitute for orange marmalade at breakfast."
— Sheila Jackson

3 pounds ripe pears, peeled, cored, and chopped
3 pounds sugar
½ pound crystallized (candied) ginger or ginger in syrup (drained), finely chopped
Juice and grated peel of 1½ lemons

Place the pear, sugar, ginger, and lemon juice and peel in a heavy-bottomed saucepan. Heat the pear mixture slowly to a boil, stirring frequently. Boil 10 minutes without stirring. Stir and let cool. Place the jam in sterilized jars, and seal tightly. Store in a cool, dark, dry place.
Yield: About 6 pints.

Prize Apricot Jam

8 cups pitted quartered apricots (about 3 pounds)
4½ cups granulated sugar
¾ cup light brown sugar
1 cup crushed pineapple with juice
⅛ teaspoon salt
Juice and coarsely grated peel of 1 orange

Place the apricots, granulated sugar, brown sugar, pineapple and juice, salt, and orange juice and peel in a heavy-bottomed saucepan. Bring the apricot mixture to a boil quickly, stirring until the sugar is dissolved. Cook rapidly, stirring often, until 2 thick drops of syrup run together off the side of a cold metal spoon (about 30 – 35 minutes). Ladle the jam into sterilized jars, and seal tightly. Store in a cool, dark, dry place.
Yield: 4 pints.

Orchard Lane Bed & Breakfast

Yvonne Parker
13324 Middle Bench Road
Oyama, British Columbia V4V 2B4
Tel: (250) 548-3809
$$

ABOUT THE B&B

Smack dab between Kelowna and Vernon is Orchard Lane, a newly built Victorian B&B nestled in a private orchard. From the sprawling veranda is a panoramic view of the beautiful central Okanagan Valley, while nearby Kalamalka and Wood Lakes reflect the hills and distant mountains. Inside, a welcoming foyer and spiral staircase lead to romantic and comfortable bedrooms. Visitors lounge in the formal living room with fireplace, stroll through the flower gardens or nearby orchard, admire the terraced landscaping framed by giant trees, or take a refreshing dip in the outdoor hot tub. Your hostess, Yvonne, serves a full gourmet breakfast — made from produce grown in her garden — in the formal dining room or on the veranda. You'll quickly discover that one of her favorite hobbies is making crafts, which are displayed throughout the house. Alpine skiing, fishing, biking, hiking, and other recreational choices await you and there are golf courses and beaches aplenty to explore. This area is truly a corner of paradise.

SEASON

all year

ACCOMMODATIONS

2 rooms with shared bath;
1 room with private bath

The Inn on St. Andrews

Joan Peggs
231 St. Andrews Street
Victoria, British Columbia V8V 2N1
Tel: (800) 668-5993 or (604) 384-8613
Fax: (604) 384-6063
E-mail: joan_peggs@bc.sympatico.ca.
www.bctravel.com/andrews.html
$$

ABOUT THE B&B

The Inn on St. Andrews is as lovely today as when it was built in 1913 by Edith Carr, eldest sister of the famous Canadian artist and author Emily Carr. This Tudor-style heritage property features elegant woodwork, stained and beveled glass, and large bright bedrooms. After a wholesome breakfast in the formal dining room, you can congregate in the sunroom overlooking the east garden or on the sun deck overlooking the west garden, in the cozy TV room, or in the larger drawing room. The inn is ideally located in James Bay, close to Victoria's inner harbor with ferry and seaplane terminals, the Parliament buildings, the Royal British Columbia Museum, famed Empress Hotel, and downtown shops. A short walk brings you to Beacon Hill Park and the oceanfront. Your host Joan Peggs believes in modern comfort and old-fashioned hospitality, and provides guests with her own map highlighting walking and driving destinations and recommended restaurants.

SEASON

all year

ACCOMMODATIONS

1 room with private bath;
2 rooms with shared bath

Pumpkin Marmalade

(Recipe from Joan Peggs Eggs, *written and published by Joan Peggs)*

4 cups finely chopped pumpkin
3 cups finely chopped pear or apple
¼ teaspoon salt*
6 cups sugar
3 oranges
3 lemons

**Note: The salt, which heightens the tart flavor of the fruit, can be omitted.*

Place the pumpkin, pear, and salt in a large bowl. Sprinkle with the sugar, and let stand overnight. Grate the peel of the oranges and lemons, chop their pulp, and remove the seeds. Transfer the pumpkin mixture to a large, heavy-bottomed saucepan, and add the orange and lemon peel and pulp. Slowly bring the pumpkin mixture to a boil, stirring frequently. Cook until 2 thick drops of syrup run together off the side of a cold metal spoon (about 40 minutes). Ladle the marmalade into sterilized jars, and seal tightly. Store in a cool, dark, dry place. ***Yield: 6 half pints.***

Raspberry Syrup

"Great on pancakes, waffles, and fruit-filled omelets and crêpes."
— Sheila Derksen

2 cups thawed and drained frozen raspberries
3 tablespoons sugar
¼ cup orange- or peach-flavored liqueur
Juice of ½ lemon or 1 tablespoon lemon juice concentrate
1 teaspoon cornstarch dissolved in 1 tablespoon cold water

Place the raspberries, sugar, liqueur, and lemon juice in a blender, and purée at high speed for 10 – 15 seconds. Strain the raspberry mixture through a fine sieve to remove the seeds, and pour the strained liquid into a saucepan. Bring the liquid to a boil, and add the cornstarch mixture. Stir a few minutes until the liquid has thickened. May be served immediately or refrigerated up to 5 days. ***Yield: 1 cup.***

Fraser House

Sheila and Dennis Derksen
PO Box 211, 33 1st Street East
Letellier, Manitoba R0G 1C0
Tel: (204) 737-2284
$

ABOUT THE B&B

Memories are made at this elegant and romantic 1916 home. Hardwood floors, area rugs, and antique furniture enhance the home's Victorian decor. Spacious rooms combined with great hospitality make your stay most enjoyable. Relax with a beverage and home-baked goodies in the parlor or on the veranda or patio. Breakfast may consist of a puffy egg pancake or freshly baked croissants and muffins, along with the season's fresh fruit, served in the formal dining room. Fraser House is located just a few minutes north of the US border in the heart of Manitoba's bustling agricultural area, and is near places to golf, fish, shop, and ski. Sheila enjoys craft projects and holds painting classes during the winter months, while Dennis enjoys carpentry and is employed as a fertilizer dealer.

SEASON

all year

ACCOMMODATIONS

2 rooms with shared bath

Hawkins House Bed & Breakfast

Carla Pitzel and Garry Umbrich
303 Hawkins Street
Whitehorse, Yukon Y1A 1X5
Tel: (867) 668-7638
Fax: (867) 668-7632
$$$$

ABOUT THE B&B

To stay at the Hawkins House Bed & Breakfast is to share a once-in-a-lifetime Yukon experience with your hosts Carla, Garry, and their two sons. Each guest room in this custom-built, luxury Victorian B&B highlights a different Yukon theme and features private bath and balcony, oak floor, bar sink, refrigerator, cable TV, and VCR. Guests can take a Jacuzzi soak in the Fleur de Lys Room, watch videos about Native peoples in the First Nations Room, step back into gold rush days in the Victorian Tea Rose Room, or admire the splendid view of the SS Klondike *paddlewheeler and Canyon Mountain from the balcony of the Fireweed Room. Especially geared to the business traveler, Hawkins House provides the convenience of a private telephone line and answering machine, fax service, and a work table with a light and computer jack. Breakfast is a homemade feast of northern and international delights — from the home-smoked salmon pâté and moose sausage to jams, syrups, and sourdough pastries.*

SEASON

all year

ACCOMMODATIONS

4 rooms with private baths

Rosehip Jelly

"I love wild rosehips! Unlike berry picking, rosehip picking is even better after the first frost. Not only do rosehips become sweeter, they also become softer and easier to grind. We pick our rosehips right up to the first snowfall in October." — Carla Pitzel

Wild rosehips
Water
Sugar
Certo liquid fruit pectin

Remove the old blooms and stems from the rosehips. For each cup of rosehips, add 1½ cups water and boil until the rosehips are soft. Strain them through a jelly bag, and reserve the extract. For every 2 cups of extract, add 3 cups sugar and 1 (6-ounce) bottle (or 2 packets) Certo. Bring the mixture to a boil, and remove it from the heat. Pour it carefully into sterilized jars, and seal tightly. Store in a cool, dark, dry place. ***Tips:*** If the jelly doesn't set, use it as rosehip syrup — great on pancakes and waffles! Avoid the temptation to use rosehips from commercially grown plants; they may be bigger but they may have been grown using pesticides and fertilizers. ***Yield: 2 cups extract yields 4 half pints.***

Strawberry-Rhubarb Jam

"My guests' favorite." — June Leschied

5 cups chopped rhubarb
2¼ cups sugar
Small package strawberry Jell-O

Combine the rhubarb with 1 cup of the sugar, and let stand overnight. In the morning, add the remaining sugar, and boil gently until the rhubarb is soft. Add the Jell-O to the rhubarb mixture, and stir well. Place the jam in sterilized jars, and seal tightly. Store in a cool, dark, dry place. ***Yield: 5 half pints.***

Northgate B&B

June and Carl Leschied
106 Main Street
Lewisporte, Newfoundland
A0G 3A0
Tel: (709) 535-2258
$$

ABOUT THE B&B

Experience true Newfoundland hospitality at Northgate B&B, a large and beautifully restored country-style home overlooking Lewisporte harbor. Upon arrival, enjoy afternoon tea in one of the sitting rooms with fireplace and hardwood floors. The four charming guest rooms have either private or shared bath. A wholesome full breakfast of Northgate's own fresh brown eggs, homemade bread, cereals, and wild berry jams is served in the large dining room, a smoke-free environment. Northgate is located near craft shops, a museum, laundromat, provincial parks and swimming areas, scenic villages, strawberry "U-picks," and salmon rivers. Explore the beautiful islands of Notre Dame Bay on your hosts' 40-foot tour boat, or enjoy lunch beside an iceberg or a cook-out in a former island settlement. Trips can be arranged to Beothuk Indian haunts or to a remote island cabin for a one- or two-night stay.

SEASON

May 1 – October 31

ACCOMMODATIONS

2 rooms with private baths;
2 rooms with shared bath

Lake Crescent Inn

Evelyn and Bruce Warr
PO Box 69
Robert's Arm, Newfoundland
A0J 1R0
Tel: (709) 652-3067
Fax: (709) 652-3056
$

ABOUT THE B&B

When you think of Newfoundland, think peaceful lifestyle, clean air and rivers, and superb hospitality — all of which you'll find at Lake Crescent Inn. Walk along the quiet roads and beautiful beaches, visit fishers in the various communities along the route, or go iceberg or whale watching (in season). Boating trips can also be arranged, so why not give cod jigging or salmon fishing a try? Be sure to bring along your camera to capture the moment you reel in your first fish (you might even see "Cressie," the lake monster!). The inn offers four bedrooms and two bathrooms, one with whirlpool and shower. Breakfasts are a homemade feast of muffins, jams, jellies, and breads, and a special health-conscious menu is also available. A Jiggs dinner is served on Sundays from 5:00 pm, and a Fish Platter dinner is served on Fridays from 5:00 pm (other meals can be provided upon request).

SEASON

all year

ACCOMMODATIONS

4 rooms with shared baths

Vegetable Dip

¾ cup mayonnaise
4½ teaspoons dried minced onion
4½ teaspoons honey
4½ teaspoons ketchup
1½ teaspoons curry powder
1½ teaspoons lemon juice

Fresh raw vegetables

Combine the mayonnaise, onion, honey, ketchup, curry powder, and lemon juice, and let stand in the refrigerator for a few hours. Serve with fresh raw vegetables. ***Tip:*** This dip will keep in the refrigerator for several days. ***Yield: About 1 cup.***

Whipped Cottage Cheese

(Recipe from Joan Peggs Eggs, *written and published by Joan Peggs)*

"Excellent for pancakes and waffles." — Joan Peggs

1 cup dry or creamed cottage cheese
1 – 2 tablespoons honey
1 – 2 teaspoons lemon juice or vanilla

Place the cottage cheese, honey, and lemon juice in the small bowl of an electric mixer (a blender or food processor will also work well). Beat the cottage cheese mixture on high until it is well combined and relatively smooth. ***Yield: 1 cup.***

The Inn on St. Andrews

Joan Peggs
231 St. Andrews Street
Victoria, British Columbia V8V 2N1
Tel: (800) 668-5993 or (604) 384-8613
Fax: (604) 384-6063
E-mail: joan_peggs@bc.sympatico.ca.
www.bctravel.com/andrews.html
$$

ABOUT THE B&B

The Inn on St. Andrews is as lovely today as when it was built in 1913 by Edith Carr, eldest sister of the famous Canadian artist and author Emily Carr. This Tudor-style heritage property features elegant woodwork, stained and beveled glass, and large bright bedrooms. After a wholesome breakfast in the formal dining room, you can congregate in the sunroom overlooking the east garden or on the sun deck overlooking the west garden, in the cozy TV room, or in the larger drawing room. The inn is ideally located in James Bay, close to Victoria's inner harbor with ferry and seaplane terminals, the Parliament buildings, the Royal British Columbia Museum, famed Empress Hotel, and downtown shops. A short walk brings you to Beacon Hill Park and the oceanfront. Your host Joan Peggs believes in modern comfort and old-fashioned hospitality, and provides guests with her own map highlighting walking and driving destinations and recommended restaurants.

SEASON

all year

ACCOMMODATIONS

1 room with private bath;
2 rooms with shared bath

Gîte à la ferme MACDALE Bed and Breakfast

Anne and Gordon MacWhirter
365 Route 132, Hope, PO Box 803
Paspébiac, Québec G0C 2K0
Tel: (418) 752-5270
$

ABOUT THE B&B

For a relaxing holiday, visit the Gaspé Peninsula and MACDALE Bed and Breakfast. Situated overlooking Baie des Chaleurs on a beef farm that has been active for five generations, this spacious three-story home offers two family rooms and a variety of guest accommodations. The aroma of fresh coffee and assorted muffins and pastries will awaken you and whet your appetite for an old-fashioned home-baked breakfast that includes farm-fresh eggs. Thanks to MACDALE's central location, tourist attractions such as world-famous Percé Rock and Forillon Park are well within day-trip driving distance. A seawater therapy resort is just minutes away, as are many museums, points of historical interest, and sports facilities. Anne is a first grade teacher while Gordon has recently retired from teaching junior high school mathematics.

SEASON

all year

ACCOMMODATIONS

1 loft with private bath;
4 rooms with shared baths

Zucchini Jam

6 cups peeled, seeded, and grated zucchini
5 cups sugar
¼ cup lemon juice
19-ounce can crushed pineapple, drained
2 small packages peach Jell-O

Place the zucchini in a large saucepan. Add the sugar, and boil 6 minutes. Add the lemon juice and pineapple, and boil 6 minutes more. Remove the zucchini mixture from the heat, and add the Jell-O. Stir well. Pour the jam into sterilized jars, and seal tightly. Store in a cool, dark, dry place. ***Yield: 5 – 6 half pints.***

Index of Recipes

Metric Equivalents

Volume

1 teaspoon = 5 milliliters
1 tablespoon = 15 milliliters
¼ cup = 60 milliliters
⅓ cup = 80 milliliters
½ cup = 120 milliliters
⅔ cup = 160 milliliters
1 cup = 230 milliliters

Weight

1 ounce = 28 grams
1 pound = 454 grams

Oven Temperatures

300°F = 150°C
325°F = 165°C
350°F = 175°C
375°F = 190°C
400°F = 200°C
425°F = 220°C
450°F = 230°C
475°F = 245°C

General Formula for Metric Conversion

Ounces to grams: multiply ounce figure by 28.35

Pounds to grams: multiply pound figure by 453.59

Pounds to kilograms: multiply pound figure by 0.45

Ounces to milliliters: multiply ounce figure by 30

Cups to liters: multiply cup figure by 0.24

Fahrenheit to Celsius: subtract 32 from the Fahrenheit figure, multiply by 5, then divide by 9

Inches to centimeters: multiply inch figure by 2.54

Rise & Dine books make unique gifts!

Purchase them at a bookstore or mail this form with your payment to:

USA	*Canada*
Callawind Publications Inc.	Callawind Publications Inc.
2083 Hempstead Turnpike, Suite 355	3383 Sources Boulevard, Suite 205
East Meadow, New York 11554-1730	Dollard-des-Ormeaux, Quebec H9B 1Z8

You may return books *in original condition* at any time for a full refund on the purchase price.

Qty	Description	Total
	Rise & Dine America: Savory Secrets from America's Bed & Breakfast Inns (second edition) @ US$16.95 / C$21.95 **each**	
	Rise & Dine Canada: Savory Secrets from Canada's Bed & Breakfast Inns (second edition) @ US$16.95 / C$21.95 **each**	
	Shipping: Surface mail @ US$4.95 / C$5.95 **for 1 book** and US$0.80 / C$1.00 **for each additional book** (2 – 4 weeks delivery)	
	7% goods and services tax (GST) for Canadian orders only	
	Prices subject to change without notice.	________

Name ______________________________ Tel. ____________________

Address ____

City ____________________ State/Prov. ______________ Zip/Postal code ______________

Payment enclosed (payable to Callawind Publications): ❑ ***Check*** ❑ ***Money order***

To help us better understand our readers, kindly provide the following information:

Where did you first see this book? ______________________________

Are you buying it for yourself or as a gift? ______________________________

Comments about the book: ______________________________

Questions? Call: (514) 685-9109 / Fax: (514) 685-7055 / E-mail: info@callawind.com